CONTENTS

INTRODUCTION

A nine-to-five job really messes with your plans, doesn't it? I would much rather spend my time in the kitchen, cooking my family a delicious meal we can all enjoy around the dinner table. But, since that is not possible, I've had to look for smart ways to cut down food preparation times to prevent falling into the fast-food trap.

I must confess, before I got my Instant Pot, I caved and stopped at a drive-through after work a few times. It's fast, and it's easy—but, it's unhealthy. I always ended up chastising myself for giving my children such unwholesome food to eat. I don't have to anymore. The Instant Pot changed my life; in under an hour, I can dish-up healthy, mouth-watering meals.

This multicooker is truly an ingenious 20th-century invention. And you'll notice I didn't call it an electric pressure cooker—it is so much more than that! You can simmer, steam, braise, slow-cook, warm, and even bake a cake in an Instant Pot. It's so versatile; there's no other appliance I use as often as my multicooker.

In fact, the Instant Pot is so famous because it is one of Amazon's top-selling products on Prime Day sales events. In 2018, a whopping 300,000 units were sold in just 36 hours (Businesswire, 2018)!

In this book, I want to share the benefits of owning an Instant Pot with you. I will show you how to use it for cooking delectable meals for one, two, or a whole group of people. This book will be the only beginners' guide to Instant Pot cooking you'll ever need, and don't forget the tried and tested recipes I will share with you!

After reading, you'll be able to express yourself through your cooking without having to sacrifice any family time. Let's get started.

The Best Cooker for You

There are various makes and models on the market, and this makes it hard to know which one will fulfill your needs. Ask yourself the questions below, and you'll be able to get the right multicooker for you.

How big is your family?

If you're only cooking for two, then there's no need to buy an 8-quart cooker. Here are the breakdowns of the different sizes.

3-quart = one or two people

6-quart = three to six people

8-quart = six to nine people

Safety Tips

Furthermore, there are some safety tips you need to keep in mind:

Check that the inner pot and heating plate are both clean and dry.

Check the lid for any stuck food particles. Pay extra attention to the float valve, exhaust valve, and anti-block shield.

Check the sealing ring is secure.

Check the steam release valve is set to 'Sealing.'

Make sure not to overfill the Instant Pot. At no time should the contents in the pot surpass the three-quarter mark. If you're cooking starchy foods, the halfway mark is ideal.

Be careful when you release the steam.

Unplug the multicooker when not in use.

No part of the pot that contains electrical components should be submerged in water.

Instant Pot Cooking Timetable

Now is the time when you'll realize just how much time an Instant Pot will save you in the kitchen!

Food	Cooking Time
Vegetables	
Asparagus	1-2 min
Broccoli	1-2 min
Brussel sprouts	2-3 min
Cabbage (whole)	2-3 min
Beans	1-2 min
Butternut squash	4-6 min
Carrots	6-8 min
Corn on the cob	3-5 min
Potatoes (Large)	12-15 min
Potatoes (Small)	8-10 min
Potatoes (Cubes)	3-5 min
Sweet potatoes (Whole)	12-15 min
Sweet potatoes (Cubes)	2-4 min
Cauliflower (florets)	2-3 min
Mixed vegetables	3-4 min
Meat, Fish, & Eggs	
Beef stew	20 min (per 1lb)
Beef large	20-25 min (per 1lb)
Beef ribs	20-25 min (per 1lb)
Chicken whole	8 min (per 1lb)
Chicken breasts	6-8 min (per 1lb)
Chicken bone stock	40-45 min (per 1lb)
Lamb leg	15 min (per 1lb)
Pork roast	15 min (per 1lb)
Pork baby back ribs	15-20 min (per 1lb)
Fish whole	4-5 min

Fish fillet	2-3 min
Lobster	2-3 min
Shrimp	1-3 min
Seafood stock	7-8 min
Eggs	5 min
Rice & Grains	
Barley	20-22 min
Oatmeal	2-3 min
Oats	3-5 min
Quinoa	1 min
Porridge	5-7 min
Rice (Brown)	20-22 min
Rice (Jasmine)	4 min
Rice (Basmati)	2-3 min
Rice (White)	4 min
Rice (Wild)	20-25 min
Beans & Lentils (Dry)	
Black Beans	20-25 min
Kidney Beans (Red)	20-25 min
Kidney Beans (White)	25-30 min
Lima Beans	12-14 min
Lentils (Green)	8-10 min
Lentils (Yellow)	1-2 min
Chickpeas	30-40 min
Navy Beans	20-24 min
Pinto Beans	25-30 min
Soy Beans	35-45 min

CHAPTER 1 BASICS SAUCE AND BROTH

Béarnaise Sauce

Prep time: 6 mins, Cook Time: 3 mins, Servings: 4
- 2 tsps. freshly squeezed lemon juice
- 2 tbsps. fresh tarragon
- 4 beaten egg yolks
- ¼ tsp. onion powder
- ⅔ lb. butter

1. Press the Sauté button on the Instant Pot and melt the butter.
2. Transfer the melted butter to a mixing bowl.
3. Slowly add the egg yolks to the bowl while whisking.
4. Continue stirring so that no lumps form.
5. Add the lemon juice, onion powder, and fresh tarragon, and whisk well.
6. Béarnaise sauce is suitable for many dishes, you can serve it with roasted beef chops, grilled pork chops, or chicken tenderloin.

Chimichurri Sauce

Prep time: 6 mins, Cook Time: 3 hours, Servings: 6
- 2 garlic cloves, minced
- 1 green chili pepper, chopped
- 1 lemon, juice and zest
- 2 tbsps. olive oil
- ½ yellow bell pepper, chopped
- 1 tbsp. white wine vinegar

1. Place all ingredients in the Instant Pot and stir to combine.
2. Lock the lid. Select the Slow Cook mode, then set the timer for 3 hours at High Pressure.
3. Once the timer goes off, do a quick pressure release. Carefully open the lid.
4. Allow to cool for 30 minutes and serve with grilled meats, steaks, or sausages.

Creamy Cheese Sauce

Prep time: 6 mins, Cook Time: 4 hours, Servings: 4
- ¼ cup cream cheese
- ¼ cup heavy whipping cream
- 2 tbsps. melted butter
- Salt and pepper, to taste
- ½ cup grated Cheddar cheese

Instructions
1. Put all the ingredients in the Instant Pot and stir to combine.
2. Lock the lid. Select the Slow Cook mode, then set the timer for 4 hours at High Pressure.
3. Once the timer goes off, do a quick pressure release. Carefully open the lid.
4. You can serve this cheese sauce with French fries, Nachos, chicken nuggets, or pretzels.

Hollandaise Sauce

Prep time: 6 mins, Cook Time: 5 mins, Servings: 4
- ⅔ lb. butter
- 4 egg yolks, beaten
- 2 tbsps. lemon juice
- Salt and pepper, to taste

1. Press the Sauté button on the Instant Pot.
2. Add the butter and heat to melt.
3. Whisk vigorously while adding the yolks. Cook for 1 minute.
4. Continue stirring and add the lemon juice, salt, and pepper.
5. You can serve the hollandaise sauce with poached or grilled fish or chicken.

Satay Sauce

Prep time: 6 mins, Cook Time: 3 hours, Servings: 6
- ⅓ cup peanut butter
- 1 red chili pepper, finely chopped
- 4 tbsps. soy sauce
- 1 cup coconut milk
- 1 garlic clove, minced

1. Place all ingredients in the Instant Pot and stir until everything is well combined.
2. Lock the lid. Select the Slow Cook mode, then set the timer for 3 hours at High Pressure.
3. Once the timer goes off, do a quick pressure release. Carefully open the lid.
4. Serve the satay sauce with beef kebabs or chicken skewers, or you can serve it as dipping sauce.

Caesar Salad Dressing

Prep time: 6 mins, Cook Time: 3 hours, Servings: 6
- ½ cup olive oil
- 1 tbsp. Dijon mustard
- ½ cup grated Parmesan cheese
- ⅔ oz. chopped anchovies
- ½ freshly squeezed lemon juice
- ¼ cup water
- Salt and pepper, to taste

1. Place all the ingredients in the Instant Pot and stir to incorporate.
2. Lock the lid. Select the Slow Cook mode, then set the timer for 3 hours at High Pressure.
3. Once the timer goes off, do a quick pressure release. Carefully open the lid.
4. You can use the Caesar dressing to marinate the meat or dress the salad, or you can use it as a dipping sauce for crudités.

Spicy Thousand Island Dressing

Prep time: 10 mins, Cook Time: 2 hours, Servings: 4
- 1 tsp. tabasco
- 1 shallot, finely chopped
- 1 cup mayonnaise
- 4 tbsps. chopped dill pickles
- 1 tbsp. freshly squeezed lemon juice

- ¼ cup water
- Salt and pepper, to taste

1. Place all the ingredients in the Instant Pot and whisk to combine.
2. Lock the lid. Select the Slow Cook mode, then set the timer for 2 hours at High Pressure.
3. Once the timer goes off, do a quick pressure release. Carefully open the lid.
4. You can use this dressing to serve the burgers, sandwiches, or salads.

Chicken Bone Broth

Prep time: 12 mins, Cook time: 2 to 3 hours, Servings: 4

- 1 lb. bones of one whole chicken
- 2 tbsps. apple cider vinegar
- 2 cloves garlic, minced
- 8 cups water
- 1 tsp. sea salt

1. Add all the ingredients to the Instant Pot.
2. Lock the lid. Select the Soup mode, then set the timer for 2 to 3 hours at High Pressure.
3. Once the timer goes off, do a natural pressure release for 10 to 20 minutes, then release any remaining pressure. Carefully open the lid.
4. Strain the liquid and transfer the broth to an airtight container to store in the refrigerator for up to 5 days. Bone soup is healthy and recommended for those with a leaky gut.

Chili Aioli

Prep time: 6 mins, Cook Time: 2 mins, Servings: 6

- ½ tsp. chili flakes
- 1 tbsp. lemon juice
- 1 egg yolk
- 2 garlic cloves, minced
- ¾ cup avocado oil

1. Put all ingredients in the Instant Pot and whisk vigorously.
2. Press the Sauté button and allow to heat for 2 minutes while stirring. Do not bring to a boil.
3. You can serve the chili aioli on top of the seafood or salad.

Keto Gravy

Prep time: 6 mins, Cook Time: 10 mins, Servings: 6

- 2 tbsps. butter
- 1 white onion, chopped
- 2 cups chicken bone broth
- 1 tbsp. balsamic vinegar
- ¼ cup coconut milk

1. Press the Sauté button on the Instant Pot.
2. Melt the butter and sauté the onions for 2 minutes.
3. Add the remaining ingredients. Stir constantly for 5 minutes or until slightly thickened.
4. You can serve the gravy on top of any roasted steaks, meats, or seafoods. You can even use it as a dressing for your salad.

Ranch Dip

Prep time: 6 mins, Cook Time: 2 mins, Servings: 8

- 1 cup olive oil
- Salt and pepper, to taste
- 1 cup beaten egg whites
- 1 tsp. mustard paste
- Juice of 1 lemon

1. In the Instant Pot, add all the ingredients and mix well.
2. Press the Sauté button and heat for 2 minutes while stirring. Do not bring to a simmer.
3. You can serve the ranch dip with chicken nuggets, French fries, or green salad.

Balsamic Fresh Tomato Sauce

Prep time: 5 minutes | Cook time: 20 minutes | Makes 4 cups

2 tablespoons olive oil
2 cloves garlic, minced
2½ pounds (1.1 kg) vine-ripened tomatoes, peeled, diced and juice retained
1 tablespoon balsamic vinegar
1 teaspoon dried basil
1 teaspoon dried parsley
½ teaspoon granulated sugar
Pinch of salt
Pinch of freshly ground black pepper

1. Press the Sauté button on the Instant Pot and heat the oil. Add the garlic to the pot and sauté for 30 seconds, or until fragrant.
2. Add the tomatoes to the pot along with their juice. Add the remaining ingredients to the pot.
3. Lock the lid. Select the Manual mode and set the cooking time for 10 minutes on High Pressure. Once the timer goes off, perform a natural pressure release for 15 minutes, then release any remaining pressure. Carefully open the lid.
4. Stir the sauce. If you prefer a thicker sauce, press the Sauté button and simmer uncovered for 10 minutes, or until it reaches the desired thickness.
5. Serve immediately or refrigerate until ready to use.

Celery and Pepper Red Beans

Prep time: 10 minutes | Cook time: 43 to 45 minutes | Serves 8

3 tablespoons butter
1 cup diced white onion
1 cup diced green bell pepper
1 cup diced celery
2 cloves garlic, minced
2¼ cups dried red kidney beans
5 cups vegetable broth
1 teaspoon liquid smoke
½ teaspoon Worcestershire sauce
1 teaspoon hot sauce
½ teaspoon dried thyme
1 teaspoon cayenne pepper
2 bay leaves
2 teaspoons salt

1. Press the Sauté button on the Instant Pot and melt the butter. Add the onions, bell pepper, celery, and garlic. Stir-fry for 3 to 5 minutes, or until onions are translucent.

2.	Stir in the remaining ingredients.
3.	Lock the lid. Select the Bean/Chili mode and set the cooking time for 30 minutes on High Pressure. Once the timer goes off, perform a natural pressure release for 10 minutes, then release any remaining pressure. Carefully open the lid.
4.	If a thicker consistency is desired, press the Sauté button and simmer the bean mixture for 10 minutes to thicken.
5.	Remove the bay leaves before serving. Serve immediately.

Super Easy Caramel Sauce

Prep time: 5 minutes | Cook time: 45 minutes | Serves 4 to 6

1 (11-ounce / 312-g) can sweetened condensed coconut milk
1 cup water
1 teaspoon coarse sea salt (optional)
1.	Peel the label off the can and place the can on a trivet and into your Instant Pot. Pour in the water.
2.	Lock the lid. Select the Manual mode and set the cooking time for 45 minutes on High Pressure. Once the timer goes off, perform a natural pressure release for 20 minutes, then release any remaining pressure. Carefully open the lid.
3.	Remove the can and trivet. Set aside until cool enough to handle.
4.	Once cooled, open the can and pour the caramel sauce into a glass jar for storage. For a salted caramel, stir in the sea salt.

Celery and Carrot Broth

Prep time: 5 minutes | Cook time: 30 minutes | Makes 4 cups

3 large stalks celery, cut in half
2 large yellow onions, peeled and halved
2 medium carrots, peeled and cut into large pieces
10 whole peppercorns
1 head garlic, cloves separated and peeled
1 bay leaf
6 cups water
1.	Add all the ingredients to the Instant Pot and stir to combine.
2.	Lock the lid. Select the Manual mode and set the cooking time for 30 minutes on High Pressure. Once the timer goes off, perform a natural pressure release for 20 minutes, then release any remaining pressure. Carefully open the lid.
3.	Strain the stock through a fine-mesh strainer or through cheesecloth placed in a colander.
4.	Store in an airtight container in the refrigerator for 2 to 3 days, or in the freezer for up to 3 months.

Vanilla-Cinnamon Applesauce

Prep time: 10 minutes | Cook time: 5 minutes | Serves 6 to 8

3 pounds (1.4 kg) apples, cored and quartered
$^1/_3$ cup water
1 teaspoon ground cinnamon
1 teaspoon freshly squeezed lemon juice
1 teaspoon vanilla extract
½ teaspoon salt
1.	Add all the ingredients to the Instant Pot and stir to combine.
2.	Lock the lid. Select the Manual mode and set the cooking time for 5 minutes on High Pressure. Once the timer goes off, perform a natural pressure release for 10 minutes, then release any remaining pressure. Carefully open the lid.
3.	Using an immersion blender, blend the applesauce until smooth.
4.	Serve immediately or refrigerate until ready to use.

Fresh Garden Tomato Salsa

Prep time: 5 minutes | Cook time: 5 minutes | Makes 6 to 8 cups

8 large tomatoes, roughly chopped
6 garlic cloves, finely diced
2 jalapeño peppers, deseeded and diced
1 red bell pepper, diced
1 small red onion, diced
1 small yellow onion, diced
1 tablespoon ground cumin
3 to 4 teaspoons salt
½ teaspoon freshly ground black pepper
½ teaspoon baking soda
¼ cup tomato paste
2 tablespoons freshly squeezed lime juice
1 teaspoon chopped fresh cilantro leaves
1.	In the Instant Pot, stir together the tomatoes, garlic, jalapeños, bell pepper, red onion, yellow onion, cumin, salt, pepper, and baking soda.
2.	Lock the lid. Select the Manual mode and set the cooking time for 5 minutes on High Pressure. Once the timer goes off, perform a natural pressure release for 10 minutes, then release any remaining pressure. Carefully open the lid.
3.	Stir in the tomato paste, lime juice and cilantro.
4.	Serve chilled or at room temperature.

Baby Bella Mushroom Gravy

Prep time: 5 minutes | Cook time: 24 to 26 minutes | Serves 4 to 6

1 tablespoon olive oil
8 ounces (227 g) baby bella mushrooms, diced
½ small sweet onion, diced
2 garlic cloves, minced
2 tablespoons Worcestershire sauce
1 teaspoon Dijon mustard
1 teaspoon rubbed sage
1¼ cups vegetable stock, divided
¼ cup red wine
1 tablespoon cornstarch
1.	Press the Sauté button on the Instant Pot and heat the oil. Add the mushrooms and onion. Sauté for 2 to 3 minutes, stirring frequently. Add the garlic. Cook, stirring so it doesn't burn, for 30 seconds more.
2.	Add the Worcestershire sauce, mustard, sage, ¾ cup of the stock and the red wine.

3.   Lock the lid. Select the Manual mode and set the cooking time for 20 minutes on High Pressure. Once the timer goes off, perform a natural pressure release for 10 minutes, then release any remaining pressure.
4.   In a small bowl, whisk the remaining ½ cup of the stock and cornstarch. Carefully remove the lid and stir this slurry into the gravy.
5.   Select Sauté mode again and simmer the gravy for 2 to 3 minutes, or until thickened.

Mushroom and Carrot Broth

Prep time: 10 minutes | Cook time: 20 minutes | Makes 8 cups

4 medium carrots, peeled and cut into large pieces
2 large leeks, trimmed and cut into large pieces
2 large yellow onions, peeled and quartered
1 large stalk celery, chopped
2 cups sliced button mushrooms
5 whole cloves garlic
Pinch of dried red pepper flakes
8½ cups water
1.   Add all the ingredients to the Instant Pot and stir to combine.
2.   Lock the lid. Select the Manual mode and set the cooking time for 20 minutes on High Pressure. Once the timer goes off, perform a natural pressure release for 15 minutes, then release any remaining pressure. Carefully open the lid.
3.   Strain the broth through a fine-mesh strainer or through cheesecloth placed in a colander.
4.   Store in a covered container in the refrigerator or freezer.

Cauliflower and Cashew Sour Cream

Prep time: 5 minutes | Cook time: 3 minutes | Makes 1 cup

2 cups cauliflower florets
2 cups water
3 tablespoon cashews
1 teaspoon nutritional yeast
1 teaspoon lemon juice
½ teaspoon apple cider vinegar
Salt, to taste
1.   Add the cauliflower, water and cashews to the Instant Pot.
2.   Set the lid in place. Select the Manual mode and set the cooking time for 3 minutes on High Pressure. When the timer goes off, do a quick pressure release. Carefully open the lid.
3.   Drain, reserving the liquid for blending.
4.   In a blender, combine the cauliflower and cashews along with the nutritional yeast, lemon juice, apple cider vinegar and 1 teaspoon of the cooking liquid. Blend, scrape down the sides and add more cooking liquid if needed. Blend until smooth. Season with salt.
5.   Serve immediately or refrigerate until ready to use.

Carrot and White Bean Dip

Prep time: 10 minutes | Cook time: 3 minutes | Makes 3 cups

2 cups cooked white beans
4 or 5 carrots, scrubbed or peeled and chopped
1 cup water
1 or 2 jalapeño peppers, deseeded and chopped
2 tablespoons tahini
Grated zest and juice of 1 lime
1 teaspoon smoked paprika
1 to 2 tablespoons olive oil
½ to ¾ teaspoon salt
Freshly ground black pepper, to taste
1.   In the Instant Pot, combine the white beans, carrots, and water.
2.   Set the lid in place. Select the Manual mode and set the cooking time for 3 minutes on High Pressure. When the timer goes off, do a quick pressure release. Carefully open the lid.
3.   Drain any excess water and transfer the beans and carrots to a food processor.
4.   Add the jalapeños, tahini, lime zest and juice, and paprika. Purée, adding the olive oil, 1 tablespoon at a time, to achieve the desired texture. Taste and season with the salt and pepper.
5.   Serve immediately or refrigerate until ready to use.

Andouille-Style Sausage

Prep time: 10 minutes | Cook time: 35 minutes | Makes 8 large links

1½ cups vital wheat gluten flour
¼ cup nutritional yeast
1 teaspoon garlic powder
1 teaspoon cayenne powder
1 teaspoon dried marjoram
1 teaspoon onion powder
1 teaspoon dried thyme
1 teaspoon salt
½ teaspoon ground black pepper
¼ teaspoon ground allspice
1½ cups plus 1 cup water, divided
1.   Add all the ingredients, except for 1 cup water to a mixer and mix on low speed for about 5 minutes. Knead in a bread maker or by hand until the dough begins to smooth out.
2.   Cut into 8 equal pieces and roll into logs. Wrap in parchment paper and add to a large foil packet.
3.   Add the trivet to the Instant Pot and pour in 1 cup of the water. Place the packets on top.
4.   Lock the lid. Select the Manual mode and set the cooking time for 35 minutes on High Pressure. Once the timer goes off, perform a natural pressure release for 20 minutes, then release any remaining pressure. Carefully open the lid.
5.   Serve.

Artichoke-Spinach Dip

Prep time: 5 minutes | Cook time: 4 minutes | Makes 2½ cups

1 cup raw cashews
1 cup unsweetened coconut milk
1 tablespoon nutritional yeast
1½ tablespoons apple cider vinegar
1 teaspoon onion powder

½ teaspoon garlic powder
½ to 1 teaspoon salt
1 (14-ounce / 397-g) can artichoke hearts in water
2 cups fresh spinach
1 cup water

1. In a blender, combine the cashews, milk, nutritional yeast, vinegar, onion powder, garlic powder, and salt. Purée until smooth and creamy, about 1 minute. Add the artichoke hearts and spinach and pulse a few times to chop up a bit. Pour the mixture into a baking pan.
2. Pour the water and insert the trivet in the Instant Pot. Put the pan on the trivet.
3. Lock the lid. Select the Manual mode and set the cooking time for 4 minutes on High Pressure. Once the timer goes off, perform a natural pressure release for 10 minutes, then release any remaining pressure. Carefully open the lid.
4. Let the baking pan cool for a few minutes before carefully lifting it out of the pot with oven mitts.
5. Transfer the dip to a bowl and serve.

Instant Pot Soy Yogurt

Prep time: 5 minutes | Cook time: 8 hours | Makes 4 cups

1 (32-ounce / 907-g) container plain unsweetened soy milk
1 packet yogurt starter
1 tablespoon tapioca starch

1. Whisk together the soy milk, starter and starch in a mixing bowl. Pour the mixture into small glass jars. Sit them right on the pot bottom.
2. Set the lid in place. Select the Yogurt mode and set the cooking time for 8 hours. When the timer goes off, do a quick pressure release. Carefully open the lid.
3. Serve chilled. Store in the fridge for up to 10 days.

Simple Almond Milk

Prep time: 5 minutes | Cook time: 10 minutes | Makes 4 cups

1 cup almonds
6 cups water, divided

1. Add the almonds and 2 cups of the water to the Instant Pot.
2. Lock the lid. Select the Manual mode and set the cooking time for 10 minutes on High Pressure.
3. Once the timer goes off, perform a natural pressure release for 10 minutes, then release any remaining pressure. Carefully open the lid. Drain the almonds.
4. In a blender, combine the almonds and 4 cups of the water and blend well. Strain through a nut milk bag and store in the refrigerator.

Homemade Vegetable Bouillon

Prep time: 5 minutes | Cook time: 10 minutes | Makes 4 cups

2 large onions, quartered
½ cup water
6 medium carrots, cut into lengths to fit the Instant Pot
4 celery stalks, cut into lengths to fit the Instant Pot
8 sprigs fresh thyme
1 sprig fresh rosemary
1 cup nutritional yeast
Salt, to taste (optional)

1. Add the onions, water, carrots, celery, thyme and rosemary to the Instant Pot.
2. Lock the lid. Select the Manual mode and set the cooking time for 10 minutes on High Pressure. Once the timer goes off, perform a natural pressure release for 10 minutes, then release any remaining pressure. Carefully open the lid.
3. Scoop the cooked veggies and broth into a blender and add the nutritional yeast. Blend until smooth. Add salt and blend again.
4. Store in the refrigerator up to a week or put in ice-cube trays and freeze.

CHAPTER 2 BREAKFAST AND BRUNCH

Spinach and Bacon Quiche

Prep time: 5 minutes | Cook time: 35 minutes | Serves 3
1 cup filtered water
5 eggs, lightly beaten
½ cup spinach, chopped
½ cup full-fat coconut milk
½ cup shredded full-fat Cheddar cheese
2 slices no-sugar-added bacon, cooked and finely chopped
½ teaspoon dried parsley
½ teaspoon dried basil
½ teaspoon freshly ground black pepper
¼ teaspoon kosher salt
1.   Pour the water into the the Instant Pot, then place the trivet.
2.   Stir together the remaining ingredients in a baking dish. Cover the dish loosely with aluminum foil. Place the dish on top of the trivet.
3.   Secure the lid. Select the Manual mode and set the cooking time for 35 minutes at High Pressure.
4.   Once cooking is complete, do a natural pressure release for 10 minutes, then release any remaining pressure. Carefully open the lid.
5.   Serve warm.

Stuffed Apples with Coconut Muesli

Prep time: 10 minutes | Cook time: 3 minutes | Serves 2
$^1/_3$ cup water
2 large unpeeled organic apples, cored and tops removed
Filling:
½ cup coconut muesli
2 tablespoons butter, cubed
½ teaspoon ground cinnamon
2 teaspoons packed brown sugar
1.   Pour the water into the Instant Pot and set aside.
2.   Mix together all the ingredients for the filling in a bowl, mashing gently with a fork until incorporated.
3.   Stuff each apple evenly with the muesli mixture, then arrange them in the Instant Pot.
4.   Lock the lid. Select the Manual mode and set the cooking time for 3 minutes at Low Pressure, depending on how large the apples are.
5.   Once cooking is complete, do a natural pressure release for 10 minutes, then release any remaining pressure. Carefully open the lid.
6.   Let the apples cool for 5 minutes and serve.

Breakfast Quinoa Salad

Prep time: 15 minutes | Cook time: 1 minute | Serves 4
2 cups quinoa, rinsed well
2 cups vegetable or chicken broth
Salad:
1 (15-ounce / 425-g) can chickpeas, drained and rinsed
1 cucumber, diced
1 cup chopped flat-leaf parsley
¼ cup extra-virgin olive oil
1 red onion, diced
1 red bell pepper, diced
3 cloves garlic, minced
Juice of 2 lemons
2 tablespoons red wine vinegar
Salt and pepper, to taste
1 to 2 cups crumbled feta cheese (optional)
1.   Place the quinoa and broth into the Instant Pot and stir to incorporate.
2.   Lock the lid. Select the Manual mode and set the cooking time for 1 minute at High Pressure.
3.   Once cooking is complete, do a natural pressure release for 10 minutes, then release any remaining pressure. Carefully open the lid.
4.   Fluff the quinoa with a fork and allow to cool for 5 to 10 minutes.
5.   Remove the quinoa from the pot to a large bowl and toss together with all the salad ingredients until combined. Serve immediately.

Cheesy Breakfast Potato Casserole

Prep time: 20 minutes | Cook time: 35 minutes | Serves 6
6 large eggs
½ cup 2% milk
½ teaspoon salt
¼ teaspoon pepper
4 cups frozen shredded hash brown potatoes, thawed
2 cups shredded Cheddar cheese
1 cup cubed fully cooked ham
½ medium onion, chopped
1 cup water
1.   In a medium bowl, beat together the eggs with the milk, salt, and pepper until combined. In another bowl, thoroughly combine the potatoes, cheese, ham, and onion, then transfer to a greased baking dish. Pour the egg mixture over top. Cover the dish with foil.
2.   Pour the water into the Instant Pot and insert a trivet. Place the baking dish on top of the trivet.
3.   Secure the lid. Select the Manual mode and set the cooking time for 35 minutes at High Pressure.
4.   Once cooking is complete, do a natural pressure release for 10 minutes, then release any remaining pressure. Carefully open the lid.
5.   Allow the casserole cool for 5 to 10 minutes before serving.

Eggs and Bacon Breakfast Risotto

Prep time: 12 mins, Cook Time: 12 mins, Servings: 2
*   1½ cups chicken stock
*   2 poached eggs
*   2 tbsps. grated Parmesan cheese
*   3 chopped bacon slices
*   ¾ cup Arborio rice

1.	Set your Instant Pot to Sauté and add the bacon and cook for 5 minutes until crispy, stirring occasionally.
2.	Carefully stir in the rice and let cook for an additional 1 minute.
3.	Add the chicken stock and stir well.
4.	Lock the lid. Select the Manual mode and set the cooking time for 6 minutes at Low Pressure.
5.	Once cooking is complete, do a quick pressure release. Carefully open the lid.
6.	Add the Parmesan cheese and keep stirring until melted. Divide the risotto between two plates. Add the eggs on the side and serve immediately.

French Eggs

Prep time: 12 mins, Cook Time: 8 mins, Servings: 4

- ¼ tsp. salt
- 4 bacon slices
- 1 tbsp. olive oil
- 4 tbsps. chopped chives
- 4 eggs
- 1½ cups water

1.	Grease 4 ramekins with a drizzle of oil and crack an egg into each ramekin.
2.	Add a bacon slice on top and season with salt. Sprinkle the chives on top.
3.	Add 1½ cups water and steamer basket to your Instant Pot. Transfer the ramekins to the basket.
4.	Lock the lid. Select the Manual mode and set the cooking time for 8 minutes at High Pressure.
5.	Once cooking is complete, do a quick pressure release. Carefully open the lid.
6.	Serve your baked eggs immediately.

Ham and Spinach Frittata

Prep time: 3 mins, Cook Time: 10 mins, Servings: 8

- 1 cup diced ham
- 2 cups chopped spinach
- 8 eggs, beaten
- ½ cup coconut milk
- 1 onion, chopped
- 1 tsp. salt

1.	Put all the ingredients into the Instant Pot. Stir to mix well.
2.	Lock the lid. Set to Manual mode, then set the timer for 10 minutes at High Pressure.
3.	Once the timer goes off, perform a natural pressure release for 5 minutes. Carefully open the lid.
4.	Transfer the frittata on a plate and serve immediately.

Mini Frittata

Prep time: 12 mins, Cook Time: 5 mins, Servings: 6

- 1 chopped red bell pepper
- 1 tbsp. almond milk
- ¼ tsp. salt
- 2 tbsps. grated Cheddar cheese
- 5 whisked eggs
- 1½ cups water

1.	In a bowl, combine the salt, eggs, cheese, almond milk, and red bell pepper, and whisk well. Pour the egg mixture into 6 baking molds.
2.	Add 1½ cups water and steamer basket to your Instant Pot. Transfer the baking molds to the basket.
3.	Lock the lid. Select the Manual mode and cook for 5minutes at High Pressure.
4.	Once cooking is complete, do a quick pressure release. Carefully open the lid. Serve hot.

Eggs En Cocotte

Prep time: 10 mins, Cook Time: 20 mins, Servings: 4

- 1 cup water
- 1 tbsp. butter
- 4 tbsps. heavy whipping cream
- 4 eggs
- 1 tbsp. chives
- Salt and pepper, to taste

1.	Arrange a steamer rack in the Instant Pot, then pour in the water.
2.	Grease four ramekins with butter.
3.	Divide the heavy whipping cream in the ramekins, then break each egg in each ramekin.
4.	Sprinkle them with chives, salt, and pepper.
5.	Arrange the ramekins on the steamer rack.
6.	Lock the lid. Set to the Manual mode, then set the timer for 20 minutes at High Pressure.
7.	Once the timer goes off, perform a natural pressure release for 10 minutes, then release any remaining pressure. Carefully open the lid.
8.	Transfer them on a plate and serve immediately.

Cheesy Bacon Quiche

Prep time: 5 mins, Cook Time: 10 mins, Servings: 6

- 2 tbsps. olive oil
- 6 eggs, lightly beaten
- 1 cup milk
- Salt and pepper, to taste
- 2 cups Monterey Jack cheese, grated
- 1 cup bacon, cooked and crumbled

1.	Grease the Instant Pot with olive oil.
2.	Combine the eggs, milk, salt, and pepper in a large bowl. Stir to mix well.
3.	Put the cheese and bacon in the pot, then pour the egg mixture over. Stir to mix well.
4.	Lock the lid. Set to Manual mode, then set the timer for 10 minutes at High Pressure.
5.	Once the timer goes off, perform a natural pressure release for 5 minutes. Carefully open the lid.
6.	Transfer the quiche on a plate and serve.

Veggie Quiche

Prep time: 12 mins, Cook Time: 20 mins, Servings: 6

- ½ cup milk
- 1 red bell pepper, chopped
- 2 green onions, chopped
- Salt, to taste

- 8 whisked eggs
- 1 cup water

1. In a bowl, combine the whisked eggs with milk, bell pepper, onions and salt, and stir well. Pour the egg mixture into a pan.
2. In your Instant Pot, add the water and trivet. Place the pan on the trivet and cover with tin foil.
3. Lock the lid. Select the Manual mode and cook for 20 minutes at High Pressure.
4. Once cooking is complete, do a quick pressure release. Carefully open the lid.
5. Slice the quiche and divide between plates to serve.

Western Omelet

Prep time: 12 mins, Cook Time: 30 mins, Servings: 4

- ½ cup half-and-half
- 4 chopped spring onions
- 6 whisked eggs
- ¼ tsp. salt
- 8 oz. bacon, chopped
- 1½ cups water

1. Place the steamer basket in the Instant Pot and pour in 1½ cups water.
2. In a bowl, combine the eggs with half-and-half, bacon, spring onions and salt, and whisk well. Pour the egg mixture into a soufflé dish and transfer to the steamer basket.
3. Lock the lid. Select the Steam mode and cook for 30 minutes at High Pressure.
4. Once cooking is complete, do a quick pressure release. Carefully open the lid.
5. Allow to cool for 5 minutes before serving.

Breakfast Rice Pudding

Prep time: 12 mins, Cook Time: 12 mins, Servings: 6

- 1 cup coconut cream
- ¼ cup maple syrup
- 1¼ cups water
- 1 cup basmati rice
- 2 cups almond milk

1. In the Instant Pot, mix together the milk with water, rice, cream and maple syrup.
2. Lock the lid. Select the Manual mode and cook for 12 minutes at Low Pressure.
3. Once cooking is complete, do a natural pressure release for 5 minutes, then release any remaining pressure. Carefully open the lid.
4. Stir the pudding again and divide into bowls to serve.

Bread Pudding

Prep time: 12 mins, Cook Time: 15 mins, Servings: 8

- ½ cup maple syrup
- 1 bread loaf, cubed
- ½ cup butter
- 2 cups coconut milk
- 4 eggs
- 2 cups water

1. In a blender, blend the coconut milk with eggs, butter and maple syrup until smooth.
2. Transfer the mixture to a pudding pan and add the bread cubes. Cover the pan with tin foil.
3. Add 2 cups water and trivet to your Instant Pot. Place the pudding pan on the trivet.
4. Lock the lid. Select the Manual mode and cook for 15 minutes at High Pressure.
5. Once cooking is complete, do a quick pressure release. Carefully open the lid.
6. Allow to cool for 5 minutes before serving.

Strawberry and Orange Juice Compote

Prep time: 10 mins, Cook Time: 15 mins, Servings: 4

- 2 lbs. fresh strawberries, rinsed, trimmed, and cut in half
- 2 oz. fresh orange juice
- 1 vanilla bean, chopped
- ½ tsp. ground ginger
- ¼ cup sugar
- Toast, for serving

1. Put all the ingredients into the Instant Pot. Stir to mix well.
2. Lock the lid. Set to the Manual Mode, then set the timer for 15 minutes at High Pressure.
3. When the timer goes off, perform a natural pressure release for 10 minutes. Carefully open the lid.
4. Allow to cool and thicken before serving with the toast.

Banana Quinoa

Prep time: 5 mins, Cook Time: 12 mins, Servings: 2

- ½ cup peeled and sliced banana
- ¾ cup quinoa, soaked in water for at least 1 hour
- 1 (8 oz.) can almond milk
- 2 tbsps. honey
- 1 tsp. vanilla extract
- Pinch of salt
- ¾ cup water

1. Combine all the ingredients in the Instant Pot. Stir to mix well.
2. Lock the lid. Set to Rice mode, then set the timer for 12 minutes at Low Pressure.
3. Once the timer goes off, perform a quick pressure release. Carefully open the lid.
4. Serve immediately.

Creamy Tomatoes and Quinoa

Prep time: 12 mins, Cook Time: 12 mins, Servings: 6

- 1 tbsp. grated ginger
- 1 (28 oz) can tomatoes, chopped
- ¼ cup quinoa
- 14 oz. coconut milk
- 1 small yellow onion, chopped

1. In the Instant Pot, mix the onion with quinoa, tomatoes, milk and ginger, and stir well.

2. Lock the lid. Select the Manual mode and cook for 12 minutes at High Pressure.

3. Once cooking is complete, do a natural pressure release for 5 minutes, then release any remaining pressure. Carefully open the lid.

4. Stir the mixture one more time and divide into bowls to serve.

Strawberry Quinoa

Prep time: 12 mins, Cook Time: 2 minute, Servings: 4

- 2¼ cups water
- 2 tbsps. honey
- 2 cups chopped strawberries
- ¼ tsp. pumpkin pie spice
- 1 ½ cups quinoa

1. In the Instant Pot, mix the quinoa with honey, water, spice, and strawberries. Stir to combine.

2. Lock the lid. Select the Manual mode and set the cooking time for 2 minutes at High Pressure.

3. Once cooking is complete, do a natural pressure release for 10 minutes, then release any remaining pressure. Carefully open the lid.

4. Let the quinoa rest for 10 minutes. Give a good stir and serve immediately.

Blackberry Egg Cake

Prep time: 12 mins, Cook Time: 8 mins, Servings: 3

- Zest from ½ an orange
- ½ cup fresh blackberries
- 1 tbsp. coconut oil
- 3 tbsps. coconut flour
- 5 eggs, whisked
- 1 cup water
- Pinch salt

1. Place a steamer basket in the Instant Pot and pour in a cup of water.

2. In a mixing bowl, combine the eggs, coconut oil, and coconut flour until well combined. Season with a pinch of salt.

3. Add the blackberries and orange zest.

4. Pour into muffin cups.

5. Place the muffin cups in the steamer basket.

6. Lock the lid. Press the Steam button and set the cooking time for 8 minutes at High Pressure.

7. Once cooking is complete, do a quick pressure release. Carefully open the lid.

8. Allow to cool for 5 minutes before serving.

Special Pancake

Prep time: 12 mins, Cook Time: 30 mins, Servings: 4

- 2½ tsps. baking powder
- 2 eggs, beaten
- 2 tbsps. sugar
- 1½ cups milk
- 2 cups white flour

1. In a bowl, mix the flour with eggs, milk, sugar, and baking powder. Stir to incorporate.

2. Spread out the mixture onto the bottom of the Instant Pot.

3. Lock the lid. Select the Manual mode and cook for 30 minutes at High Pressure.

4. Once cooking is complete, do a quick pressure release. Carefully open the lid.

5. Let the pancake cool for a few minutes before slicing to serve.

Broccoli and Egg Casserole

Prep time: 5 mins, Cook Time: 15 mins, Servings: 6

- 6 eggs, beaten
- ⅓ cup all-purpose flour
- 3 cups cottage cheese
- ¼ cup butter, melted
- Salt and pepper, to taste
- 2 tbsps. chopped onions
- 3 cups broccoli florets

1. Combine the eggs, flour, cheese, butter, salt, and pepper in a large bowl. Stir to mix well.

2. Put the onions and broccoli in the Instant Pot. Pour the egg mixture over. Stir to combine well.

3. Lock the lid. Set to Manual mode, then set the timer to 15 minutes at High pressure.

4. Once the timer goes off, perform a natural pressure release for 10 minutes, then release any remaining pressure. Carefully open the lid.

5. Transfer them on a plate and serve immediately.

Cheesy Egg and Bacon Muffins

Prep time: 12 mins, Cook Time: 8 mins, Servings: 4

- 4 cooked bacon slices, crumbled
- 4 tbsps. shredded Cheddar cheese
- ¼ tsp. salt
- 1 green onion, chopped
- 4 eggs, beaten
- 1½ cups water

1. In a bowl, mix the eggs with cheese, bacon, onion and salt, and whisk well. Pour the egg mixture evenly into four muffin cups.

2. Add 1½ cups water and steamer basket to the Instant Pot. Place the muffin cups in the basket.

3. Lock the lid. Select the Manual mode and set the cooking time for 8 minutes at High Pressure.

4. Once cooking is complete, do a quick pressure release. Carefully open the lid.

5. Divide the muffins between plates and serve warm.

Pumpkin and Apple Butter

Prep time: 12 mins, Cook Time: 10 mins, Servings: 6

- 30 oz. pumpkin purée
- 4 apples, cored, peeled, and cubed
- 12 oz. apple cider
- 1 cup sugar
- 1 tbsp. pumpkin pie spice

1. In the Instant Pot, stir together the pumpkin purée with apples, apple cider, sugar, and pumpkin pie spice.
2. Lock the lid. Select the Manual mode and cook for 10 minutes at High Pressure.
3. Once cooking is complete, do a quick pressure release. Carefully open the lid.
4. Remove from the pot and serve in bowls.

Breakfast Cobbler

Prep time: 12 mins, Cook Time: 15 mins, Servings: 2

- 2 tbsps. honey
- ¼ cup shredded coconut
- 1 plum, pitted and chopped
- 3 tbsps. coconut oil, divided
- 1 apple, cored and chopped

1. In the Instant Pot, combine the plum with apple, half of the coconut oil, and honey, and blend well.
2. Lock the lid. Select the Manual mode and cook for 10 minutes at High Pressure.
3. Once cooking is complete, do a quick pressure release. Carefully open the lid.
4. Transfer the mixture to bowls and clean your Instant Pot.
5. Set your Instant Pot to Sauté and heat the remaining coconut oil. Add the coconut, stir, and toast for 5 minutes.
6. Sprinkle the coconut over fruit mixture and serve.

Simple Hard-Boiled Eggs

Prep time: 5 minutes | Cook time: 5 minutes | Serves 6

½ cup water
6 eggs

1. Place the trivet in the Instant Pot and pour in the water.
2. Crack each egg into a silicone cup. Carefully place the cups on top of the trivet.
3. Set the lid in place. Select the Manual mode and set the cooking time for 5 minutes on High Pressure. When the timer goes off, perform a quick pressure release. Carefully open the lid.
4. Carefully remove the cups from the pot. Use a spoon to pop the eggs out of the cups. Serve immediately.

Gruyère Asparagus Frittata

Prep time: 10 minutes | Cook time: 22 minutes | Serves 6

6 eggs
6 tablespoons heavy cream
½ teaspoon salt
½ teaspoon black pepper
1 tablespoon butter
2½ ounces (71 g) asparagus, chopped
1 clove garlic, minced
1¼ cup shredded Gruyère cheese, divided
Cooking spray
3 ounces (85 g) halved cherry tomatoes
½ cup water

1. In a large bowl, stir together the eggs, cream, salt, and pepper.
2. Set the Instant Pot on the Sauté mode and melt the butter. Add the asparagus and garlic to the pot and sauté for 2 minutes, or until the garlic is fragrant. The asparagus should still be crisp.
3. Transfer the asparagus and garlic to the bowl with the egg mixture. Stir in 1 cup of the cheese. Clean the pot.
4. Spritz a baking pan with cooking spray. Spread the tomatoes in a single layer in the pan. Pour the egg mixture on top of the tomatoes and sprinkle with the remaining ¼ cup of the cheese. Cover the pan tightly with aluminum foil.
5. Pour the water in the Instant Pot and insert the trivet. Place the pan on the trivet.
6. Set the lid in place. Select the Manual mode and set the cooking time for 20 minutes on High Pressure. When the timer goes off, perform a quick pressure release. Carefully open the lid.
7. Remove the pan from the pot and remove the foil. Blot off any excess moisture with a paper towel. Let the frittata cool for 5 to 10 minutes before transferring onto a plate.

Almond Pancakes

Prep time: 10 minutes | Cook time: 15 minutes per batch | Serves 6

4 eggs, beaten
2 cups almond flour
½ cup butter, melted
2 tablespoons granulated erythritol
1 tablespoon avocado oil
1 teaspoon baking powder
1 teaspoon vanilla extract
Pinch of salt
¾ cup water, divided

1. In a blender, combine all the ingredients, except for the ½ cup of the water. Pulse until fully combined and smooth. Let the batter rest for 5 minutes before cooking.
2. Fill each cup with 2 tablespoons of the batter, about two-thirds of the way full. Cover the cups with aluminum foil.
3. Pour the remaining ½ cup of the water and insert the trivet in the Instant Pot. Place the cups on the trivet.
4. Set the lid in place. Select the Manual mode and set the cooking time for 15 minutes on High Pressure. When the timer goes off, do a quick pressure release. Carefully open the lid.
5. Repeat with the remaining batter, until all the batter is used. Add more water to the pot before cooking each batch, if needed.
6. Serve warm.

Parmesan Baked Eggs

Prep time: 5 minutes | Cook time: 10 minutes | Serves 1

1 tablespoon butter, cut into small pieces
2 tablespoons keto-friendly low-carb Marinara sauce
3 eggs
2 tablespoons grated Parmesan cheese

¼ teaspoon Italian seasoning
1 cup water
1.   Place the butter pieces on the bottom of the oven-safe bowl. Spread the marinara sauce over the butter. Crack the eggs on top of the marinara sauce and top with the cheese and Italian seasoning.
2.   Cover the bowl with aluminum foil. Pour the water and insert the trivet in the Instant Pot. Put the bowl on the trivet.
3.   Set the lid in place. Select the Manual mode and set the cooking time for 10 minutes on Low Pressure. When the timer goes off, do a quick pressure release. Carefully open the lid.
4.   Let the eggs cool for 5 minutes before serving.

Cheddar Broccoli Egg Bites

Prep time: 10 minutes | Cook time: 10 minutes | Serves 7
5 eggs, beaten
3 tablespoons heavy cream
⅛ teaspoon salt
⅛ teaspoon black pepper
1 ounce (28 g) finely chopped broccoli
1 ounce (28 g) shredded Cheddar cheese
½ cup water
1.   In a blender, combine the eggs, heavy cream, salt and pepper and pulse until smooth.
2.   Divide the chopped broccoli among the egg cups equally. Pour the egg mixture on top of the broccoli, filling the cups about three-fourths of the way full. Sprinkle the Cheddar cheese on top of each cup.
3.   Cover the egg cups tightly with aluminum foil.
4.   Pour the water and insert the trivet in the Instant Pot. Put the egg cups on the trivet.
5.   Lock the lid. Select the Manual mode and set the cooking time for 10 minutes on High Pressure. Once the timer goes off, perform a natural pressure release for 5 minutes, then release any remaining pressure. Carefully open the lid.
6.   Serve immediately.

Classic Cinnamon Roll Coffee Cake

Prep time: 10 minutes | Cook time: 45 minutes | Serves 8
Cake:
2 cups almond flour
1 cup granulated erythritol
1 teaspoon baking powder
Pinch of salt
2 eggs
½ cup sour cream
4 tablespoons butter, melted
2 teaspoons vanilla extract
2 tablespoons Swerve
1½ teaspoons ground cinnamon
Cooking spray
½ cup water

Icing:
2 ounces (56 g) cream cheese, softened
1 cup powdered erythritol
1 tablespoon heavy cream
½ teaspoon vanilla extract
1.   In the bowl of a stand mixer, combine the almond flour, granulated erythritol, baking powder and salt. Mix until no lumps remain. Add the eggs, sour cream, butter and vanilla to the mixer bowl and mix until well combined.
2.   In a separate bowl, mix together the Swerve and cinnamon.
3.   Spritz the baking pan with cooking spray. Pour in the cake batter and use a knife to make sure it is level around the pan. Sprinkle the cinnamon mixture on top. Cover the pan tightly with aluminum foil.
4.   Pour the water and insert the trivet in the Instant Pot. Put the pan on the trivet.
5.   Set the lid in place. Select the Manual mode and set the cooking time for 45 minutes on High Pressure. When the timer goes off, do a quick pressure release. Carefully open the lid.
6.   Remove the cake from the pot and remove the foil. Blot off any moisture on top of the cake with a paper towel, if necessary. Let rest in the pan for 5 minutes.
7.   Meanwhile, make the icing: In a small bowl, use a mixer to whip the cream cheese until it is light and fluffy. Slowly fold in the powdered erythritol and mix until well combined. Add the heavy cream and vanilla extract and mix until thoroughly combined.
8.   When the cake is cooled, transfer it to a platter and drizzle the icing all over.

Cheddar Chicken Casserole

Prep time: 10 minutes | Cook time: 20 minutes | Serves 6
1 cup ground chicken
1 teaspoon olive oil
1 teaspoon chili flakes
1 teaspoon salt
1 cup shredded Cheddar cheese
½ cup coconut cream
1.   Press the Sauté button on the Instant Pot and heat the oil. Add the ground chicken, chili flakes and salt to the pot and sauté for 10 minutes. Stir in the remaining ingredients.
2.   Set the lid in place. Select the Manual mode and set the cooking time for 10 minutes on High Pressure. When the timer goes off, do a quick pressure release. Carefully open the lid.
3.   Let the dish cool for 10 minutes before serving.

Easy Eggs Benedict

Prep time: 5 minutes | Cook time: 1 minute | Serves 3
1 teaspoon butter
3 eggs

¼ teaspoon salt
½ teaspoon ground black pepper
1 cup water
3 turkey bacon slices, fried
1.		Grease the eggs molds with the butter and crack the eggs inside. Sprinkle with salt and ground black pepper.
2.		Pour the water and insert the trivet in the Instant Pot. Put the eggs molds on the trivet.
3.		Set the lid in place. Select the Manual mode and set the cooking time for 1 minute on High Pressure. When the timer goes off, do a quick pressure release. Carefully open the lid.
4.		Transfer the eggs onto the plate. Top the eggs with the fried bacon slices.

Lettuce Wrapped Chicken Sandwich

Prep time: 10 minutes | Cook time: 15 minutes | Serves 4
1 tablespoon butter
3 ounces (85 g) scallions, chopped
2 cups ground chicken
½ teaspoon ground nutmeg
1 tablespoon coconut flour
1 teaspoon salt
1 cup lettuce
1.		Press the Sauté button on the Instant Pot and melt the butter. Add the chopped scallions, ground chicken and ground nutmeg to the pot and sauté for 4 minutes. Add the coconut flour and salt and continue to sauté for 10 minutes.
2.		Fill the lettuce with the ground chicken and transfer it on the plate. Serve immediately.

Keto Cabbage Hash Browns

Prep time: 5 minutes | Cook time: 8 minutes | Serves 3
1 cup shredded white cabbage
3 eggs, beaten
½ teaspoon ground nutmeg
½ teaspoon salt
½ teaspoon onion powder
½ zucchini, grated
1 tablespoon coconut oil
1.		In a bowl, stir together all the ingredients, except for the coconut oil. Form the cabbage mixture into medium hash browns.
2.		Press the Sauté button on the Instant Pot and heat the coconut oil.
3.		Place the hash browns in the hot coconut oil. Cook for 4 minutes on each side, or until lightly browned.
4.		Transfer the hash browns to a plate and serve warm.

Fluffy Vanilla Pancake

Prep time: 5 minutes | Cook time: 50 minutes | Serves 6
3 eggs, beaten
½ cup coconut flour

¼ cup heavy cream
¼ cup almond flour
3 tablespoons Swerve
1 teaspoon vanilla extract
1 teaspoon baking powder
Cooking spray
1.		In a bowl, stir together the eggs, coconut flour, heavy cream, almond flour, Swerve and vanilla extract. Whisk in the baking powder until smooth.
2.		Spritz the bottom and sides of Instant Pot with cooking spray. Place the batter in the pot.
3.		Set the lid in place. Select the Manual mode and set the cooking time for 50 minutes on Low Pressure. Once the timer goes off, perform a natural pressure release for 5 minutes, then release any remaining pressure. Carefully open the lid.
4.		Let the pancake rest in the pot for 5 minutes before serving.

Pork and Quill Egg Cups

Prep time: 15 minutes | Cook time: 15 minutes | Serves 4
10 ounces (283 g) ground pork
1 jalapeño pepper, chopped
1 tablespoon butter, softened
1 teaspoon dried dill
½ teaspoon salt
1 cup water
4 quill eggs
1.		In a bowl, stir together all the ingredients, except for the quill eggs and water. Transfer the meat mixture to the silicone muffin molds and press the surface gently.
2.		Pour the water and insert the trivet in the Instant Pot. Put the meat cups on the trivet.
3.		Crack the eggs over the meat mixture.
4.		Set the lid in place. Select the Manual mode and set the cooking time for 15 minutes on High Pressure. When the timer goes off, do a quick pressure release. Carefully open the lid.
5.		Serve warm.

Bell Peppers Stuffed with Eggs

Prep time: 5 minutes | Cook time: 14 minutes | Serves 2
2 eggs, beaten
1 tablespoon coconut cream
¼ teaspoon dried oregano
¼ teaspoon salt
1 large bell pepper, cut into halves and deseeded
1 cup water
1.		In a bowl, stir together the eggs, coconut cream, oregano and salt.
2.		Pour the egg mixture in the pepper halves.
3.		Pour the water and insert the trivet in the Instant Pot. Put the stuffed pepper halves on the trivet.
4.		Set the lid in place. Select the Manual mode and set the cooking time for 14 minutes on High

Pressure. When the timer goes off, do a quick pressure release. Carefully open the lid.
5.   Serve warm.

Bacon Wrapped Avocado Bomb

Prep time: 5 minutes | Cook time: 10 minutes | Serves 4

1 avocado, peeled, pitted and halved
½ teaspoon chili flakes
½ teaspoon ground cinnamon
1 teaspoon coconut cream
4 bacon slices
1.   Sprinkle the avocado with the chili flakes and ground cinnamon.
2.   Fill the avocado with the coconut cream and wrap in the bacon slices. Secure the avocado bomb with toothpicks, if needed.
3.   Select the Sauté mode on the Instant Pot. Place the wrapped avocado bomb in the pot. Cook for 10 minutes on both sides, or until the bacon is crispy.
4.   Transfer to a platter. Slice and serve.

Tex Mex Tofu Scramble

Prep time: 5 minutes | Cook time: 10 minutes | Serves 4

1 tablespoon olive oil
3 cloves garlic, minced
1 cup chopped red bell pepper
¼ cup canned green chilies, chopped
1 teaspoon ground cumin
1 teaspoon paprika
1 teaspoon chili powder
½ teaspoon salt
½ teaspoon black pepper
1 package extra firm tofu, cubed
1 cup fresh corn kernels
1 cup diced tomatoes
¼ cup vegetable broth or water
1 avocado, sliced
¼ cup chopped fresh cilantro (optional)
1.   Set your Instant Pot to Sauté and heat the olive oil.
2.   Add the garlic, red bell pepper, green chilies, cumin, paprika, chili powder, salt, and black pepper, stirring well, and sauté for 5 minutes.
3.   Stir in the remaining ingredients, except for the avocado and cilantro.
4.   Lock the lid. Select the Manual mode and set the cooking time for 4 minutes at High Pressure.
5.   When the timer beeps, perform a quick pressure release. Carefully remove the lid and stir.
6.   Serve garnished with avocado slices and fresh cilantro (if desired).

Amaranth Banana Bread

Prep time: 5 minutes | Cook time: 4 minutes | Serves 4

1 cup amaranth
2 cups sliced bananas
2 ½ cups vanilla-flavored rice milk

2 tablespoons brown sugar
½ teaspoon nutmeg
½ teaspoon cinnamon
¼ teaspoon salt
½ cup chopped walnuts
1.   Combine all the ingredients, except for the walnuts, in the Instant Pot.
2.   Secure the lid. Select the Manual mode and set the cooking time for 4 minutes at High Pressure.
3.   Once cooking is complete, do a natural pressure release for 10 minutes, then release any remaining pressure. Carefully open the lid.
4.   Stir in the walnuts before serving.

Tropical Fruit Chutney

Prep time: 5 minutes | Cook time: 20 minutes | Serves 6

2 mangoes, chopped
1 medium-sized pear, peeled and chopped
1 papaya, chopped
1 cup apple cider vinegar
½ cup brown sugar
¼ cup golden raisins
2 tablespoons fresh grated ginger
2 teaspoons lemon zest
½ teaspoon coriander
½ teaspoon cinnamon
¼ teaspoon cardamom
1.   Stir together all the ingredients in the Instant Pot.
2.   Secure the lid. Select the Manual mode and set the cooking time for 6 minutes at High Pressure.
3.   Once cooking is complete, do a natural pressure release for 20 minutes, then release any remaining pressure. Carefully open the lid.
4.   Press the Sauté button on the Instant Pot. Cook the chutney, stirring, for approximately 12 to 15 minutes, or until thickened. Serve warm.

Coconut Strawberry Buckwheat Breakfast Pudding

Prep time: 5 minutes | Cook time: 7 minutes | Serves 4

1 cup buckwheat groats
3 cups coconut milk
1 cup chopped fresh strawberries
½ cup unsweetened shredded coconut
1 teaspoon cinnamon
½ teaspoon almond extract
½ teaspoon pure vanilla extract
½ cup sliced almonds
½ cup cold coconut cream
1.   Stir together all the ingredients, except for the almonds and coconut cream, in the Instant Pot.
2.   Secure the lid. Select the Manual mode and set the cooking time for 7 minutes at High Pressure.
3.   Once cooking is complete, do a natural pressure release for 20 minutes, then release any remaining pressure. Carefully open the lid.

4.	Spoon the buckwheat pudding into serving dishes. Garnish with coconut cream and almonds before serving.

Blueberry Baked Oatmeal with Almonds

Prep time: 5 minutes | Cook time: 25 minutes | Serves 4

1½ cups old-fashioned rolled oats
$^1/_3$ cup coconut sugar
1 tablespoon flax meal
1 teaspoon baking powder
1 teaspoon ground cinnamon
1 cup almond milk
1 teaspoon freshly grated orange zest
1 teaspoon pure vanilla extract
¼ cup applesauce
¾ cup fresh blueberries
1 cup water
$^1/_3$ cup slivered almonds, toasted
1.	Stir together the oats, coconut sugar, flax meal, baking powder, and cinnamon in a medium bowl until combined.
2.	Add the almond milk, orange zest, vanilla, and applesauce. Fold in the blueberries and stir to incorporate. Spoon the oat mixture into 4 ramekins. Cover each ramekin tightly with foil.
3.	Pour the water into the Instant Pot and insert a trivet. Place the ramekins on the trivet.
4.	Lock the lid. Select the Manual mode and set the cooking time for 25 minutes at High Pressure.
5.	When the timer beeps, perform a quick pressure release. Carefully remove the lid. Using potholders, remove the ramekins and remove the foil.
6.	Serve topped with the toasted almonds.

Nutty Raisin Oatmeal

Prep time: 10 minutes | Cook time: 5 minutes | Serves 4

¾ cup steel-cut oats
¾ cup raisins
3 cups vanilla almond milk
3 tablespoons brown sugar
4½ teaspoons butter
¾ teaspoon ground cinnamon
½ teaspoon salt
1 large apple, peeled and chopped
¼ cup chopped pecans
1.	Combine all the ingredients, except for the apple and pecans, in the Instant Pot.
2.	Lock the lid. Select the Manual mode and set the cooking time for 5 minutes at High Pressure.
3.	When the timer beeps, perform a natural pressure release for 10 minutes, then release any remaining pressure. Carefully remove the lid.
4.	Stir in the apple and let sit for 10 minutes. Spoon the oatmeal into bowls and sprinkle the pecans on top before serving.

Pear Oatmeal with Walnuts

Prep time: 5 minutes | Cook time: 7 minutes | Serves 2

1 cup old-fashioned oats
1¼ cups water
1 medium pear, peeled, cored, and cubed
¼ cup freshly squeezed orange juice
¼ cup chopped walnuts
¼ cup dried cherries
¼ teaspoon ground ginger
¼ teaspoon ground cinnamon
Pinch of salt
1.	In the Instant Pot, combine the oats, water, pear, orange juice, walnuts, cherries, ginger, cinnamon, and salt.
2.	Secure the lid. Select the Manual mode and set the cooking time for 7 minutes at High Pressure.
3.	Once cooking is complete, do a natural pressure release for 10 minutes, then release any remaining pressure. Carefully open the lid.
4.	Stir the oatmeal and spoon into two bowls. Serve warm.

Pumpkin Spice Carrot Cake Oatmeal

Prep time: 10 minutes | Cook time: 10 minutes | Serves 8

4½ cups water
2 cups shredded carrots
1 cup steel-cut oats
1 (20-ounce/ 567-g) can crushed pineapple, undrained
1 cup raisins
1 teaspoon pumpkin pie spice
2 teaspoons ground cinnamon
Brown sugar (optional)
Cooking spray
1.	Spray the bottom of the Instant Pot with cooking spray.
2.	Combine the remaining ingredients except the brown sugar in the Instant Pot.
3.	Secure the lid. Select the Manual mode and set the cooking time for 10 minutes at High Pressure.
4.	Once cooking is complete, do a natural pressure release for 10 minutes, then release any remaining pressure. Carefully open the lid.
5.	Serve sprinkled with the brown sugar, if desired.

Quick Cozy Spiced Fruit

Prep time: 5 minutes | Cook time: 1 minute | Serves 6

1 pound (454 g) frozen pineapple chunks
1 pound (454 g) sliced frozen peaches
1 cup frozen and pitted dark sweet cherries
2 ripe pears, sliced
¼ cup pure maple syrup
1 teaspoon curry powder, plus more as needed
1.	Combine all the ingredients in the Instant Pot.
2.	Secure the lid. Select the Manual mode and set the cooking time for 1 minute at High Pressure.

3.	Once cooking is complete, do a quick pressure release. Carefully open the lid.
4.	Stir the mixture well, adding more curry powder if you like it spicy. Serve warm.

Maple Cereal Bowls

Prep time: 5 minutes | Cook time: 1 minute | Serves 6
2 cups buckwheat groats, soaked for at least 20 minutes and up to overnight
3 cups water
¼ cup pure maple syrup
1 teaspoon vanilla extract
1 teaspoon ground cinnamon
¼ teaspoon fine sea salt
Almond milk, for serving
Chopped or sliced fresh fruit, for serving
1.	Drain and rinse the buckwheat. In the Instant Pot, combine the buckwheat with the water, maple syrup, cinnamon, vanilla, and salt.
2.	Lock the lid. Select the Manual mode and set the cooking time for 1 minute at High Pressure.
3.	When the timer beeps, perform a natural pressure release for 10 minutes, then release any remaining pressure. Carefully remove the lid and stir the cooked grains.
4.	Serve the buckwheat warm with almond milk and fresh fruit.

Simple Stone Fruit Compote

Prep time: 5 minutes | Cook time: 3 minutes | Makes about 2 cups
4 cups sliced stone fruit (plums, apricots, or peaches)
⅛ cup water
1 tablespoon pure maple syrup, plus additional as needed
1 tablespoon fresh lemon juice
½ teaspoon vanilla bean paste or extract
Pinch of ground cinnamon
1.	Stir together all the ingredients in the Instant Pot.
2.	Lock the lid. Select the Manual mode and set the cooking time for 1 minute at High Pressure.
3.	When the timer beeps, perform a natural pressure release for 10 minutes, then release any remaining pressure. Carefully remove the lid.
4.	Allow to simmer on Sauté for 2 minutes, stirring, or until thickened.
5.	Taste and add additional maple syrup, as needed. Serve warm.

Apple Breakfast Risotto

Prep time: 10 minutes | Cook time: 12 minutes | Serves 4 to 6
2 tablespoons butter
1½ cups Arborio rice
2 apples, cored and sliced
3 cups plant-based milk
1 cup apple juice
$^1/_3$ cup brown sugar

1½ teaspoons cinnamon powder
Salt to taste
½ cup dried cherries
1.	Set your Instant Pot to Sauté and melt the butter.
2.	Add rice, stir and cook for 5 minutes.
3.	Add the remaining ingredients, except the cherries, to the Instant Pot. Stir well.
4.	Lock the lid. Select the Manual mode and set the cooking time for 6 minutes at High Pressure.
5.	When the timer beeps, perform a natural pressure release for 6 minutes, then release any remaining pressure. Carefully remove the lid.
6.	Stir in the cherries and close the lid. Let sit for 5 minutes. Serve warm.

Breakfast Burrito with Scrambled Tofu

Prep time: 5 minutes | Cook time: 7 minutes | Serves 2
2 cups water
2 small Yukon Gold potatoes, cut into 1-in (2.5 cm) chunks
2 tablespoons extra-virgin olive oil
10 ounces (283 g) firm organic tofu, drained and crumbled
½ teaspoon ground turmeric
2 tablespoons nutritional yeast
½ teaspoon sea salt
Pinch of freshly ground black pepper
¼ cup unsweetened plant-based milk
2 flour tortillas, warmed
½ avocado, sliced
1 cup fresh baby spinach or arugula
¼ cup salsa
1.	Pour the water into the Instant Pot and insert a steamer basket. Put the potato chunks in the steamer basket.
2.	Secure the lid. Select the Manual mode and set the cooking time for 2 minutes at High Pressure.
3.	When the timer beeps, perform a quick pressure release. Carefully remove the lid and steamer basket. Pour the water out of the Instant Pot and wipe it dry.
4.	Press the Sauté button on the Instant Pot and heat the olive oil until very hot. Add the potatoes and sauté for about 3 minutes, flipping occasionally, until crisp on the outside. Remove the potatoes from the pot and set aside on a plate.
5.	Add the crumbled tofu, turmeric, nutritional yeast, salt, and pepper to the pot, and sauté for 1 to 2 minutes. For a softer scramble, you can add the milk and simmer until warm and the milk has evaporated and absorbed.
6.	Assemble the burritos: Place the potatoes and tofu scramble onto the tortillas. Top with equal portions of avocado, baby spinach, and salsa. Roll into burritos and serve immediately.

Sweet Potato and Kale Egg Bites

Prep time: 7 minutes | Cook time: 20 minutes | Makes 7 egg bites

1 (14-ounce / 397-g) package firm tofu, lightly pressed
¼ cup coconut milk
¼ cup nutritional yeast
1 tablespoon cornstarch
½ to 1 teaspoon sea salt
½ teaspoon onion powder
½ teaspoon garlic powder
½ teaspoon ground turmeric
½ cup shredded sweet potato
Handful kale leaves, chopped small
1 cup plus 1 tablespoon water, divided
Freshly ground black pepper, to taste
Nonstick cooking spray

1.　　　Lightly spray a silicone egg bites mold with nonstick cooking spray. Set aside.
2.　　　Combine the tofu, milk, yeast, cornstarch, sea salt, onion powder, garlic powder, and turmeric in a food processor. Pulse until smooth.
3.　　　Press the Sauté button to heat your Instant Pot until hot.
4.　　　Add the sweet potato, kale, and 1 tablespoon of water. Sauté for 1 to 2 minutes. Stir the veggies into the tofu mixture and spoon the mixture into the prepared mold. Cover it tightly with aluminum foil and place on a trivet.
5.　　　Pour the remaining 1 cup of water into the Instant Pot and insert the trivet.
6.　　　Lock the lid. Select the Manual mode and set the cooking time for 18 minutes at High Pressure.
7.　　　When the timer beeps, perform a natural pressure release for 10 minutes, then release any remaining pressure. Carefully remove the lid.
8.　　　Remove the silicone mold from the Instant Pot and pull off the foil. Allow to cool for 5 minutes on the trivet. The bites will continue to firm as they cool.
9.　　　Season to taste with pepper and serve warm.

Crunchy Peanut Butter Granola Bars

Prep time: 5 minutes | Cook time: 20 minutes | Serves 10

1 cup quick-cooking oats
½ cup all-natural peanut butter
$^1/_3$ cup pure maple syrup
1 tablespoon extra-virgin olive oil
¼ teaspoon fine sea salt
$^1/_3$ cup dried cranberries or raisins
½ cup raw pumpkin seeds
1 cup water

1.　　　Line a 7-inch round pan with parchment paper.
2.　　　Combine the oats, peanut butter, maple syrup, olive oil, and salt in a large bowl and stir well. Fold in the dried cranberries and pumpkin seeds, then scrape the batter into the prepared pan. Use a spatula to press the batter evenly into the bottom of the pan.
3.　　　Pour the water into the Instant Pot and insert a trivet. Place the pan on the trivet. Cover the pan with another piece of parchment to protect the granola bars from condensation.
4.　　　Secure the lid. Select the Manual mode and set the cooking time for 20 minutes at High Pressure.
5.　　　Once cooking is complete, do a natural pressure release for 10 minutes, then release any remaining pressure. Carefully open the lid.
6.　　　Remove the trivet and let the granola cool completely in the pan. Cut the cooled granola into 10 pieces and serve.

CHAPTER 3 APPETIZERS AND SNACKS

Chinese Wings

Prep time: 10 minutes | Cook time: 16 minutes | Serves 6

1 teaspoon Sriracha sauce
2 teaspoons Chinese five-spice powder
¼ cup tamari
¼ cup apple cider vinegar
3 cloves garlic, minced
1 tablespoon light brown sugar
2 tablespoons sesame oil
5 scallions, sliced and separated into whites and greens
3 pounds (1.4 kg) chicken wings, separated at the joint
1 cup water
¼ cup toasted sesame seeds

1. In a large bowl, combine the Sriracha, Chinese five-spice powder, tamari, apple cider vinegar, garlic, brown sugar, sesame oil, and whites of scallions. Stir to mix well. Transfer 2 tablespoons of the sauce mixture to a small bowl and reserve until ready to use.
2. Add wings to the remaining sauce and toss to coat well. Wrap the bowl in plastic and refrigerate for at least 1 hour or up to overnight.
3. Add the water to the Instant Pot and insert a steamer basket. Place the chicken wings in the single layer in the steamer basket. Lock the lid.
4. Press the Manual button and set the cook time for 10 minutes on High Pressure. When the timer beeps, let pressure release naturally for 5 minutes, then release any additional pressure and unlock the lid.
5. Using a slotted spoon, transfer the wings to a baking sheet. Brush with 2 tablespoons of reserved sauce. Broil the wings in the oven for 3 minutes on each side to crisp the chicken.
6. Transfer the wings to a serving dish and garnish with sesame seeds and greens of scallions. Serve immediately.

Easy Chicken in Lettuce

Prep time: 15 minutes | Cook time: 13 to 15 minutes | Serves 4

6 ounces (170 g) chicken breasts
1 cup water
1 teaspoon sesame oil
½ small onion, finely diced
1 garlic clove, minced
½ teaspoon ginger, minced
Kosher salt and ground black pepper, to taste
1 tablespoon hoisin sauce
½ tablespoon soy sauce
1 tablespoon rice vinegar
½ head butter lettuce, leaves separated

1. Add the chicken breasts and water to the Instant Pot.
2. Secure the lid. Choose the Manual mode and set the cooking time for 8 minutes at High pressure.
3. Once cooking is complete, perform a quick pressure release. Carefully open the lid. Shred the chicken with forks.
4. Press the Sauté button and heat the sesame oil.
5. Add and cook the garlic and onion for 3 to 4 minutes or until softened.
6. Add the chicken and cook for 2 to 3 minutes more.
7. Stir in the hoisin sauce, rice vinegar, soy sauce, ginger, salt, and black pepper. Cook for another minute.
8. Spoon the chicken mixture over the lettuce leaves on a large plate, wrap and serve immediately.

Eggplant and Olive Spread

Prep time: 20 minutes | Cook time: 8 minutes | Serves 6

¼ cup olive oil
2 pounds (907 g) eggplant, peeled and cut into medium chunks
4 garlic cloves, minced
½ cup water
Salt and black pepper, to taste
1 tablespoon sesame seed paste
¼ cup lemon juice
1 bunch thyme, chopped
3 olives, pitted and sliced

1. Set the Instant Pot on Sauté mode. Add the olive oil and heat until shimmering.
2. Add eggplant pieces and Sauté for 5 minutes. Add the garlic, water, salt and pepper, then stir well.
3. Close the lid, set to the Manual mode and set the cooking time for 3 minutes on High Pressure.
4. Once cooking is complete, perform a quick pressure release. Carefully open the lid.
5. Transfer to a blender, then add sesame seed paste, lemon juice and thyme, pulse to combine well.
6. Transfer to bowls, sprinkle olive slices on top and serve.

Hearty Red Pepper Hummus

Prep time: 10 minutes | Cook time: 30 minutes | Makes 1½ cups

½ cup dried chickpeas
2 cups water
1 cup jarred roasted red peppers with liquid, chopped and divided
1 tablespoon tahini paste
1 tablespoon lemon juice
1 teaspoon lemon zest
¼ teaspoon ground cumin
2 cloves garlic, minced
¼ teaspoon smoked paprika
⅛ teaspoon cayenne pepper
¼ teaspoon salt
1 teaspoon sesame oil
1 tablespoon olive oil

1. Add chickpeas and water to the Instant Pot. Drain liquid from the roasted peppers into the pot. Set aside the drained peppers.
2. Lock the lid. Press the Beans / Chili button and set the time to 30 minutes on High Pressure. When the timer beeps, let pressure release naturally for 5 minutes, then release any remaining pressure. Unlock the lid.
3. Drain pot, reserving the liquid in a small bowl.
4. Make the hummus: Transfer the chickpeas into a food processor. Add ¼ cup of chopped red peppers, tahini paste, lemon juice and zest, cumin, garlic, smoked paprika, cayenne pepper, salt, sesame oil, and olive oil. If consistency is too thick, slowly add reserved liquid, 1 tablespoon at a time until it has a loose paste consistency.
5. Transfer the hummus to a serving dish. Garnish with remaining chopped roasted red peppers and serve.

Hungarian Cornmeal Squares

Prep time: 15 minutes | Cook time: 55 minutes | Serves 4

1¼ cup water, divided
1 cup yellow cornmeal
1 cup yogurt
1 egg, beaten
½ cups sour cream
1 teaspoon baking soda
2 tablespoons safflower oil
¼ teaspoon salt
4 tablespoons plum jam

1. Pour 1 cup of water in the Instant Pot. Set a trivet in the pot. Spritz a baking pan with cooking spray.
2. Combine the cornmeal, yogurt, egg, sour cream, baking soda, ¼ cup of water, safflower oil, and salt in a large bowl. Stir to mix well.
3. Pour the mixture into the prepared baking pan. Spread the plum jam over. Cover with aluminum foil. Lower the pan onto the trivet.
4. Secure the lid. Choose the Manual mode and set the cooking time for 55 minutes at High pressure. Once cooking is complete, perform a quick pressure release, carefully open the lid.
5. Transfer the corn meal chunk onto a cooling rack and allow to cool for 10 minutes. Slice into squares and serve.

Herbed Polenta Squares

Prep time: 1 hour 15 minutes | Cook time: 15 minutes | Serves 4

½ cup cornmeal
½ cup milk
1½ cups water
½ teaspoon kosher salt
½ tablespoon butter
$^1/_3$ cup cream cheese
1 tablespoon chives, finely chopped
1 tablespoon cilantro, finely chopped
½ teaspoon basil
½ tablespoon thyme
½ teaspoon rosemary
$^1/_3$ cup bread crumbs
1 tablespoon olive oil

1. Make the polenta: Add the cornmeal, milk, water, and salt to the Instant Pot. Stir to mix well.
2. Press the Sauté button and bring the mixture to a simmer.
3. Secure the lid. Choose the Manual mode and set the cooking time for 8 minutes at High pressure.
4. Once cooking is complete, perform a quick pressure release. Carefully open the lid.
5. Grease a baking pan with butter. Add the cream cheese and herbs to the polenta.
6. Scoop the polenta into the prepared baking pan and refrigerate for an hour or until firm. Cut into small squares. Spread the breadcrumbs on a large plate, coat the polenta squares with breadcrumbs.
7. Heat the olive oil in a skillet over medium heat.
8. Cook the polenta squares in the skillet for about 3 minutes per side or until golden brown. Serve immediately.

Honey Carrots with Raisins

Prep time: 5 minutes | Cook time: 5 minutes | Serves 3

1 pound (454 g) carrots, peeled and cut into chunks
2 tablespoons golden raisins
½ cup water
½ tablespoon honey
$^2/_3$ teaspoon crushed red pepper flakes
½ tablespoon melted butter
Salt, to taste

1. Add the carrots, raisins, and water to the Instant Pot
2. Secure the lid and select the Manual function. Set the cooking time for 5 minutes on Low Pressure.
3. When the timer beeps, do a quick release, then open the lid.
4. Strain the carrots and transfer them to a large bowl.
5. Put the remaining ingredients into the bowl and toss well.
6. Serve warm.

Herbed Button Mushrooms

Prep time: 10 minutes | Cook time: 4 minutes | Serves 4

6 ounces (170 g) button mushrooms, rinsed and drained
1 clove garlic, minced
½ cup vegetable broth
½ teaspoon dried basil
½ teaspoon onion powder
½ teaspoon dried oregano
$^1/_3$ teaspoon dried rosemary
½ teaspoon smoked paprika
Coarse sea salt and ground black pepper, to taste
1 tablespoon tomato paste
1 tablespoon butter

1.   Put all the ingredients, except for the tomato paste and butter, in the Instant Pot. Stir to mix well.
2.   Secure the lid. Choose the Manual mode and set the cooking time for 4 minutes at High pressure.
3.   Once cooking is complete, perform a quick pressure release. Carefully open the lid.
4.   Stir in the tomato paste and butter. Serve immediately.

Jalapeño Peanuts

Prep time: 3 hours 20 minutes | Cook time: 45 minutes | Serves 4

4 ounces (113 g) raw peanuts in the shell
1 jalapeño, sliced
1 tablespoon Creole seasoning
½ tablespoon cayenne pepper
½ tablespoon garlic powder
1 tablespoon salt
1.   Add all ingredients to the Instant Pot. Pour in enough water to cover. Stir to mix well. Use a steamer to gently press down the peanuts.
2.   Secure the lid. Choose the Manual mode and set the cooking time for 45 minutes at High pressure.
3.   Once cooking is complete, perform a natural pressure release for 15 minutes, then release any remaining pressure. Carefully open the lid.
4.   Transfer the peanut and the liquid in a bowl, then refrigerate for 3 hours before serving.

Lentil and Beef Slider Patties

Prep time: 25 minutes | Cook time: 25 minutes | Makes 15 patties

1 cup dried yellow lentils
2 cups beef broth
½ pound (227 g) 80/20 ground beef
½ cup chopped old-fashioned oats
2 large eggs, beaten
2 teaspoons Sriracha sauce
2 tablespoons diced yellow onion
½ teaspoon salt
1.   Add the lentils and broth to the Instant Pot. Lock the lid.
2.   Press the Manual button and set the cook time for 15 minutes on High Pressure. When the timer beeps, let pressure release naturally for 10 minutes, then release any remaining pressure. Unlock the lid.
3.   Transfer the lentils to a medium bowl with a slotted spoon. Smash most of the lentils with the back of a spoon until chunky.
4.   Add beef, oats, eggs, Sriracha, onion, and salt. Whisk to combine them well. Form the mixture into 15 patties.
5.   Cook in a skillet on stovetop over medium-high heat in batches for 10 minutes. Flip the patties halfway through.
6.   Transfer patties to serving dish and serve warm.

Lemony Potato Cubes

Prep time: 5 minutes | Cook time: 10 minutes | Serves 2

2½ medium potatoes, scrubbed and cubed
1 tablespoon chopped fresh rosemary
½ tablespoon olive oil
Freshly ground black pepper, to taste
1 tablespoon fresh lemon juice
½ cup vegetable broth
1.   Put the potatoes, rosemary, oil, and pepper to the Instant Pot. Stir to mix well.
2.   Set to the Sauté mode and sauté for 4 minutes.
3.   Fold in the remaining ingredients.
4.   Secure the lid and select the Manual function. Set the cooking time for 6 minutes at High Pressure.
5.   Once cooking is complete, do a quick release, then open the lid.
6.   Serve warm.

Little Smokies with Grape Jelly

Prep time: 10 minutes | Cook time: 2 minutes | Serves 4

3 ounces (85 g) little smokies
2 ounces (57 g) grape jelly
¼ teaspoon jalapeño, minced
¼ cup light beer
¼ cup chili sauce
1 tablespoon white vinegar
½ cup roasted vegetable broth
2 tablespoons brown sugar
1.   Place all ingredients in the Instant Pot. Stir to mix.
2.   Secure the lid. Choose the Manual mode and set the cooking time for 2 minutes at High pressure.
3.   Once cooking is complete, perform a quick pressure release. Carefully open the lid.
4.   Serve hot.

Pinto Bean Dip

Prep time: 12 mins, Cook Time: 8 mins, Servings: 4

•   2 tbsps. chopped tomatoes
•   1 (8 oz) can pinto beans, drained
•   3 tbsps. lemon juice
•   1¼ cup chopped parsley
•   4 rosemary sprigs, chopped
1.   In the Instant Pot, mix pinto beans with rosemary and tomatoes.
2.   Lock the lid. Select the Manual mode, then set the timer for 8 minutes at High Pressure.
3.   Once the timer goes off, do a quick pressure release. Carefully open the lid.
4.   Blend the mixture with an immersion blender. Add the parsley and lemon juice, and pulse until well combined.
5.   Store in an airtight container in the fridge until ready to serve.

Steamed Asparagus with Mustard Dip

Prep time: 7 mins, Cook Time: 8 mins, Servings: 4

•   1 tsp. Dijon mustard
•   2 tbsps. mayonnaise
•   Salt and black pepper, to taste
•   1 cup water

- 12 asparagus stems
- 3 tbsps. lemon juice

1. Mix the Dijon mustard, mayonnaise, salt and black pepper in a bowl. Set aside.
2. Set trivet to the Instant Pot and add the water.
3. Place asparagus stems on the trivet and drizzle with lemon juice.
4. Lock the lid. Select the Manual mode, then set the timer for 8 minutes at High Pressure.
5. Once the timer goes off, do a quick pressure release. Carefully open the lid.
6. Dip the asparagus into mustard mixture.

Brussels Sprouts and Apples Appetizer

Prep time: 12 mins, Cook Time: 6 mins, Servings: 4

- 1½ cups water
- 1 lb. halved Brussels sprouts
- 1 cup dried cranberries
- 2 tbsps. canola oil
- 1 green apple, cored and roughly chopped
- 2 tbsps. lemon juice

1. Pour the water into the Instant Pot and arrange the steamer basket in the pot, then add Brussels sprouts.
2. Lock the lid. Select the Manual mode, then set the timer for 4 minutes at High Pressure.
3. Once the timer goes off, do a quick pressure release. Carefully open the lid.
4. Drain the Brussels sprouts and transfer to a bowl.
5. Clean the pot and set it to Sauté. Heat the oil and add Brussels sprouts, stir and cook for 1 minute.
6. Stir in apple, cranberries and lemon juice, and cook for 1 minute. Serve warm.

Creamy Broccoli Appetizer

Prep time: 12 mins, Cook Time: 3 mins, Servings: 4

- 1 cup water
- 2 tbsps. mayonnaise
- 1 tbsp. honey
- ½ cup Greek yogurt
- 1 head broccoli, cut into florets
- 1 apple, cored and sliced

1. In the Instant Pot, add the water. Arrange the steamer basket in the pot, then add the broccoli inside.
2. Lock the lid. Select the Manual mode, then set the timer for 3 minutes at Low Pressure.
3. Once the timer goes off, do a quick pressure release. Carefully open the lid.
4. Drain the broccoli florets and transfer to a bowl. Add the apple, mayo, yogurt and honey, and toss well. Serve immediately.

Lemony Endives Appetizer

Prep time: 12 mins, Cook Time: 13 mins, Servings: 4

- 3 tbsps. olive oil
- ½ cup chicken stock
- Juice of ½ lemon
- 2 tbsps. chopped parsley
- 8 endives, trimmed

1. Set the Instant Pot to Sauté and heat the olive oil. Add the endives and cook them for 3 minutes.
2. Add lemon juice and stock, and whisk well.
3. Lock the lid. Select the Manual mode, then set the timer for 10 minutes at High Pressure.
4. Once the timer goes off, do a quick pressure release. Carefully open the lid.
5. Transfer the endives to a large bowl. Drizzle some cooking juices all over and sprinkle with the chopped parsley before serving.

Carrot and Beet Spread

Prep time: 12 mins, Cook Time: 12 mins, Servings: 6

- 1 bunch basil, chopped
- 8 carrots, chopped
- ¼ cup lemon juice
- 4 beets, peeled and chopped
- 1 cup vegetable stock

1. In the Instant Pot, combine the beets with stock and carrots.
2. Lock the lid. Select the Manual mode and set the cooking time for 12 minutes at High Pressure.
3. Once cooking is complete, do a quick pressure release. Carefully open the lid.
4. Blend the ingredients with an immersion blender, and add the lemon juice and basil, and whisk well. Serve immediately.

Cashew Spread

Prep time: 12 mins, Cook Time: 6 mins, Servings: 8

- ¼ cup nutritional yeast
- ¼ tsp. garlic powder
- ½ cup soaked and drained cashews
- 10 oz. hummus
- ½ cup water

1. In the Instant Pot, combine the cashews and water.
2. Lock the lid. Select the Manual mode, then set the timer for 6 minutes at High Pressure.
3. Once the timer goes off, do a quick pressure release. Carefully open the lid.
4. Transfer the cashews to the blender, and add hummus, yeast and garlic powder, and pulse until well combined. Serve immediately.

Crab Spread

Prep time: 12 mins, Cook Time: 15 mins, Servings: 4

- 1 tsp. Worcestershire sauce
- ½ bunch scallions, chopped
- ½ cup sour cream
- ¼ cup half-and-half
- 8 oz. crab meat

1. In the Instant Pot, mix the crabmeat with sour cream, half-and-half, scallions and Worcestershire sauce, and stir to combine well.

2.   Lock the lid. Select the Manual mode, then set the timer for 15 minutes at Low Pressure.
3.   Once the timer goes off, do a quick pressure release. Carefully open the lid.
4.   Allow the spread cool for a few minutes and serve.

Creamy Avocado Spread

Prep time: 12 mins, Cook Time: 2 mins, Servings: 4

- 1 cup coconut milk
- 2 pitted, peeled and halved avocados
- Juice of 2 limes
- ½ cup chopped cilantro
- ¼ tsp. stevia
- 1 cup water

1.   In the Instant Pot, add the water and steamer basket. Place the avocados in the basket.
2.   Lock the lid. Select the Manual mode and set the cooking time for 2 minutes at High Pressure.
3.   Once cooking is complete, do a quick pressure release. Carefully open the lid.
4.   Transfer the avocados to your blender, and add the cilantro, stevia, lime juice, and coconut milk, and blend, or until it reaches your desired consistency. Serve immediately or refrigerate to chill until ready to use.

Scallion and Mayo Spread

Prep time: 12 mins, Cook Time: 3 mins, Servings: 6

- 3 tbsps. chopped dill
- 1 cup sour cream
- 1 tbsp. grated lemon zest
- ½ cup chopped scallions
- ¼ cup mayonnaise

1.   Set the Instant Pot to Sauté and add the scallions. Stir and cook for 1 minute.
2.   Add the sour cream and stir to combine well.
3.   Lock the lid. Select the Manual mode, then set the timer for 2 minutes at High Pressure.
4.   Once the timer goes off, do a quick pressure release. Carefully open the lid.
5.   Leave this mixture to rest until cooled completely. Add the mayo, dill, and lemon zest, and stir well. You can serve this with tortilla chips on the side.

Simple Egg Spread

Prep time: 12 mins, Cook Time: 5 mins, Servings: 4

- 1 tbsp. olive oil
- 4 eggs
- 1 cup water
- Salt, to taste
- ½ cup mayonnaise
- 2 green onions, chopped

1.   Grease a baking dish with olive oil and crack the eggs in it.
2.   Add the water and trivet to the Instant Pot. Place the baking dish on the trivet.
3.   Lock the lid. Select the Manual mode, then set the timer for 5 minutes at High Pressure.
4.   Once the timer goes off, do a natural pressure release for 3 to 5 minutes. Carefully open the lid.
5.   Cool eggs down and mash them with a fork. Sprinkle with salt, mayo, and green onions. Stir well and serve immediately.

Special Ranch Spread

Prep time: 12 mins, Cook Time: 10 mins, Servings: 12

- 4 green onions, chopped
- 1 cup sour cream
- 1 lb. bacon, chopped
- 1 cup shredded Monterey Jack cheese
- 1 cup mayonnaise

1.   Set the Instant Pot to Sauté and cook the bacon for about 4 minutes on each side until it is crispy.
2.   Add the sour cream and green onions, and stir to mix well.
3.   Lock the lid. Select the Manual mode, then set the timer for 6 minutes at High Pressure.
4.   Once the timer goes off, do a natural pressure release for 5 minutes. Carefully open the lid.
5.   Add the cheese and mayo and stir. Allow to cool for a few minutes and serve.

Zucchini Spread

Prep time: 12 mins, Cook Time: 9 mins, Servings: 6

- ½ cup water
- 1 tbsp. olive oil
- 1 bunch basil, chopped
- 1½ lbs. zucchinis, chopped
- 2 garlic cloves, minced

1.   Set the Instant Pot to Sauté and heat the olive oil. Cook the garlic cloves for 3 minutes, stirring occasionally.
2.   Add zucchinis and water, and mix well.
3.   Lock the lid. Select the Manual mode, then set the timer for 3 minutes at High Pressure.
4.   Once the timer goes off, do a quick pressure release. Carefully open the lid.
5.   Add the basil and blend the mixture with an immersion blender until smooth.
6.   Select the Simmer mode and cook for 2 minutes more.
7.   Transfer to a bowl and serve warm.

Cheesy Shrimp and Tomatoes

Prep time: 12 mins, Cook Time: 4 mins, Servings: 6

- 1 lb. shrimp, shelled and deveined
- 2 tbsps. butter
- 1 cup crumbled feta cheese
- 1½ cups chopped onion
- 15 oz. chopped canned tomatoes

1.   Set the Instant Pot to Sauté and melt the butter.
2.   Add the onion, stir, and cook for 2 minutes.

3. Add the shrimp and tomatoes and mix well.
4. Lock the lid. Select the Manual mode, then set the timer for 2 minutes at Low Pressure.
5. Once the timer goes off, do a quick pressure release. Carefully open the lid.
6. Divide shrimp and tomatoes mixture into small bowls. Top with feta cheese and serve.

Chicken Meatballs in Barbecue Sauce

Prep time: 6 mins, Cook Time: 15 mins, Servings: 8

- 24 oz. frozen chicken meatballs
- ½ tsp. crushed red pepper
- 12 oz. barbecue sauce
- ¼ cup water
- 12 oz. apricot preserves

1. Add all the ingredients to the Instant Pot. Stir to mix well.
2. Lock the lid. Select the Manual mode, then set the timer for 5 minutes at High Pressure.
3. Once the timer goes off, do a quick pressure release. Carefully open the lid.
4. Serve the meatballs on a platter.

Chili Endives Platter

Prep time: 12 mins, Cook Time: 7 mins, Servings: 4

- ¼ tsp. chili powder
- 1 tbsp. butter
- 4 trimmed and halved endives
- 1 tbsp. lemon juice
- Salt, to taste

1. Set the Instant Pot to Sauté and melt the butter. Add the endives, salt, chili powder and lemon juice to the pot.
2. Lock the lid. Select the Manual mode, then set the timer for 7 minutes at High Pressure.
3. Once the timer goes off, do a quick pressure release. Carefully open the lid.
4. Divide the endives into bowls. Drizzle some cooking juice over them and serve.

Fish and Carrot Balls

Prep time: 12 mins, Cook Time: 10 mins, Servings: 16

- ¼ cup cornstarch
- 1 carrot, grated
- 1½ cups fish stock
- 3 egg whites
- 1½ lbs. skinless, boneless and ground pike fillets

1. In a bowl, mix the fillets with egg whites, cornstarch and carrot. Form the mixture into equal-sized balls with your hands.
2. Put the stock and fish balls into the Instant pot.
3. Lock the lid. Select the Manual function and cook for 10 minutes at Low Pressure.
4. Once cooking is complete, do a quick pressure release. Carefully open the lid.
5. Drain the fish balls and arrange them on a platter and serve.

Greek Meatballs

Prep time: 12 mins, Cook Time: 12 mins, Servings: 10

- 1 egg, whisked
- ¼ cup chopped mint
- 1 lb. ground beef
- 3 tbsps. olive oil
- ¼ cup white vinegar

1. In a bowl, mix the beef with mint and egg, and whisk well. Shape the beef mixture into 10 meatballs with your hands.
2. Set the Instant Pot to Sauté and heat the olive oil.
3. Add the beef meatballs and brown them for about 4 minutes on each side.
4. Add the vinegar and stir to mix well.
5. Lock the lid. Select the Manual mode, then set the timer for 4 minutes at High Pressure.
6. Once the timer goes off, do a quick pressure release. Carefully open the lid.
7. Divide the meatballs among plates and serve them with a yogurt dip on the side.

Green Olive Pâté

Prep time: 12 mins, Cook Time: 2 mins, Servings: 4

- ½ cup olive oil
- 2 anchovy fillets
- 1 tbsp. chopped capers
- 2 cups pitted green olives
- 2 garlic cloves, minced

1. In a food processor, process the olives with anchovy fillets, garlic, capers and olive oil, then transfer to the Instant Pot.
2. Lock the lid. Select the Manual mode, then set the timer for 2 minutes at Low Pressure.
3. Once the timer goes off, do a quick pressure release. Carefully open the lid.
4. Remove from the pot and serve warm.

Broccoli and Bacon Appetizer Salad

Prep time: 12 mins, Cook Time: 12 mins, Servings: 4

- 1½ cups water
- ½ tbsp. apple cider vinegar
- ¼ cup chopped cilantro
- 2 tbsps. olive oil
- 1 head broccoli, cut into florets
- 4 bacon slices, chopped

1. Add the water and steamer basket to the Instant Pot. Arrange the broccoli florets in the basket.
2. Lock the lid. Select the Manual mode, then set the timer for 3 minutes at High Pressure.
3. Once the timer goes off, do a quick pressure release. Carefully open the lid.
4. Drain the broccoli and transfer to a bowl.
5. Clean the pot and set it to Sauté. Add the bacon, stir and cook for 4 minutes per side until it's crispy.
6. Roughly chop broccoli and return it to the Instant Pot. Stir and cook for 1 minute more.

7. Add the oil, cilantro and vinegar, and mix well. Remove from the heat to a plate and serve.

Brussels Sprouts and Broccoli Appetizer Salad

Prep time: 12 mins, Cook Time: 6 mins, Servings: 6

- 1½ cups water
- 2 tsps. mustard
- 1 head broccoli, cut into florets
- ½ cup walnut oil
- 1 lb. halved Brussels sprouts
- ¼ cup balsamic vinegar

1. Put the water in the Instant Pot and arrange the steamer basket in the pot, then add broccoli and Brussels sprouts.
2. Lock the lid. Select the Manual mode, then set the timer for 4 minutes at High Pressure.
3. Once the timer goes off, do a quick pressure release. Carefully open the lid.
4. Drain the vegetables and transfer to a bowl.
5. Clean the pot and set it to Sauté. Heat the oil and add broccoli and Brussels sprouts. Stir and cook for 1 minute.
6. Drizzle with the vinegar and cook for 1 minute more, then transfer to a bowl.
7. Add the mustard and toss well. Serve immediately or refrigerate to chill.

Cheesy Broccoli Appetizer Salad

Prep time: 12 mins, Cook Time: 4 mins, Servings: 4

- 1½ cups water
- 2 tbsps. balsamic vinegar
- 4 oz. cubed Cheddar cheese
- 1 cup mayonnaise
- 1 head broccoli, cut into florets
- ⅛ cup pumpkin seeds

1. Put the water into the Instant Pot and arrange the steamer basket in the pot, then add the broccoli.
2. Lock the lid. Select the Manual mode, then set the timer for 3 minutes at High Pressure.
3. Once the timer goes off, do a quick pressure release. Carefully open the lid.
4. Drain the broccoli and chop, then transfer to a bowl.
5. Add the cheese, pumpkin seeds, mayo and vinegar, and toss to combine. Serve immediately.

Grated Carrot Appetizer Salad

Prep time: 12 mins, Cook Time: 3 mins, Servings: 4

- 1 lb. carrots, grated
- ¼ cup water
- Salt, to taste
- 1 tbsp. lemon juice
- 1 tsp. red pepper flakes
- 1 tbsp. chopped parsley

1. In the Instant Pot, mix the carrots with water and salt.

2. Lock the lid. Select the Manual mode, then set the timer for 3 minutes at High Pressure.
3. Once the timer goes off, do a quick pressure release. Carefully open the lid.
4. Drain the carrots and cool them in a bowl.
5. Add the lemon juice, pepper flakes and parsley to the bowl, and toss well. Serve immediately.

Creamy Endives Appetizer Salad

Prep time: 12 mins, Cook Time: 18 mins, Servings: 3

- 1 cup vegetable soup
- 3 big endives, roughly chopped
- 3 tbsps. heavy cream
- 2 tbsps. extra virgin olive oil
- ½ yellow onion, chopped

1. Set the Instant Pot to Sauté and heat the olive oil. Add the onion, stir and cook for 4 minutes until tender.
2. Add the endives, stir and cook for 4 minutes more. Pour in the stock and whisk to combine.
3. Lock the lid. Select the Manual mode, then set the timer for 10 minutes at High Pressure.
4. Once the timer goes off, do a quick pressure release. Carefully open the lid.
5. Stir in the heavy cream and cook for 1 minute. Remove from the pot and serve in bowls.

Green Beans Appetizer Salad

Prep time: 12 mins, Cook Time: 2 mins, Servings: 4

- 1 tbsp. red wine vinegar
- 1 lb. green beans
- ½ cup water
- 2 sliced red onions
- 1 tbsp. olive oil
- 1 tbsp. Creole mustard

1. In the Instant Pot, mix green beans with water.
2. Lock the lid. Select the Manual mode, then set the timer for 2 minutes at High Pressure.
3. Once the timer goes off, do a quick pressure release. Carefully open the lid.
4. Drain the green beans and transfer to a bowl. Add the onion slices, mustard, vinegar, and oil, and gently toss to combine. Serve immediately.

Crunchy Brussels Sprouts Salad

Prep time: 12 mins, Cook Time: 6 mins, Servings: 4

- 2 tbsps. apple cider vinegar
- 1 lb. halved Brussels sprouts
- 1 tbsp. olive oil
- ½ cup chopped pecans
- 1 tbsp. brown sugar
- 1½ cups water

1. Place the water in the Instant Pot and arrange the steamer basket in the pot, then add Brussels sprouts.
2. Lock the lid. Select the Manual mode, then set the timer for 4 minutes at High Pressure.

3. Once the timer goes off, do a quick pressure release. Carefully open the lid.
4. Drain the Brussels sprouts and transfer to a bowl.
5. Clean the pot and set it to Sauté. Heat the olive oil and add Brussels sprouts and vinegar, stir and cook for 1 minute.
6. Add the sugar and pecans, stir, and cook for 30 seconds more. Remove from the pot to a plate and serve.

Kale and Carrots Salad

Prep time: 12 mins, Cook Time: 7 mins, Servings: 4
- 1 tbsp. olive oil
- 3 carrots, sliced
- 1 red onion, chopped
- 10 oz. kale, roughly chopped
- ½ cup chicken stock
1. Set the Instant Pot to Sauté and heat the olive oil.
2. Add the onion and carrots, stir, and cook for 1 to 2 minutes.
3. Stir in stock and kale.
4. Lock the lid. Select the Manual mode, then set the timer for 5 minutes at High Pressure.
5. Once the timer goes off, do a quick pressure release. Carefully open the lid.
6. Divide the vegetables among four bowls and serve.

Kale and Wild Rice Appetizer Salad

Prep time: 12 mins, Cook Time: 25 mins, Servings: 4
- 1 tsp. olive oil
- 1 avocado, peeled, pitted and chopped
- 3 oz. goat cheese, crumbled
- 1 cup cooked wild rice
- 1 bunch kale, roughly chopped
1. Set the Instant Pot to Sauté and heat the olive oil.
2. Add the rice and toast for 2 to 3 minutes, stirring often.
3. Add kale and stir well.
4. Lock the lid. Select the Manual mode, then set the timer for 20 minutes at Low Pressure.
5. Once the timer goes off, do a natural pressure release for 10 minutes, then release any remaining pressure. Carefully open the lid.
6. Add avocado and toss well. Sprinkle the cheese on top and serve.

Minty Kale Salad with Pineapple

Prep time: 12 mins, Cook Time: 3 mins, Servings: 4
- 2 tbsps. lemon juice
- 2 tbsps. chopped mint
- 1 bunch kale, roughly chopped
- 1 tsp. sesame oil
- 1 cup chopped pineapple
1. Set the Instant Pot to Sauté and heat the oil.
2. Add kale, stir, and cook for 1 minute.

3. Add pineapple, lemon juice and mint, and stir well. Divide the salad among plates and serve.

Watercress Appetizer Salad

Prep time: 12 mins, Cook Time: 2 mins, Servings: 4
- 1 bunch watercress, roughly torn
- ½ cup water
- 1 tbsp. lemon juice
- 1 cubed watermelon
- 1 tbsp. olive oil
- 2 peaches, pitted and sliced
1. In the Instant Pot, mix watercress with water.
2. Lock the lid. Select the Manual mode, then set the timer for 2 minutes at High Pressure.
3. Once the timer goes off, do a quick pressure release. Carefully open the lid.
4. Drain the watercress and transfer to a bowl. Add peaches, watermelon, oil, and lemon juice, and toss well. Divide the salad into salad bowls and serve.

Saucy Mushroom Lettuce Cups

Prep time: 5 minutes | Cook time: 9 minutes | Serves 4
1 tablespoon vegetable oil
¼ cup minced shallots
2 tablespoons cooking sherry
4 cups cremini mushrooms, quartered
½ cup chopped water chestnuts
¼ cup low-sodium soy sauce
¼ cup vegetable broth
¼ cup fresh basil
8 butter lettuce leaves
1. Press the Sauté button on the Instant Pot and heat the oil. Add the scallions to the pot and sauté for 3 minutes, or until tender. Add the cooking sherry and continue to cook for 2 minutes. Stir in the remaining ingredients, except for the lettuce leaves.
2. Set the lid in place. Select the Manual mode and set the cooking time for 4 minutes on High Pressure. When the timer goes off, do a quick pressure release. Carefully open the lid.
3. Select the Sauté mode and cook the mushroom mixture, stirring frequently, until the sauce thickens. Let cool for 5 minutes.
4. Spoon equal amounts of the mushroom mixture into lettuce leaves and serve.

Citrus Barley and Buckwheat Salad

Prep time: 10 minutes | Cook time: 35 minutes | Serves 4
1 cup wheat berries
1 cup pearl barley
3 cups vegetable broth
¼ cup minced shallots
¼ cup olive oil
¼ cup lemon juice
2 cloves garlic, crushed and minced
¼ cup pine nuts
1 cup finely chopped kale
1 cup chopped tomatoes
½ teaspoon salt

½ teaspoon black pepper
1.	In the Instant Pot, combine the wheat berries, pearl barley, vegetable broth and shallots. Mix well.
2.	Lock the lid. Select the Manual mode and set the cooking time for 35 minutes on High Pressure. Once the timer goes off, perform a natural pressure release for 20 minutes, then release any remaining pressure. Carefully open the lid.
3.	Meanwhile, combine the olive oil, lemon juice and garlic in a bowl. Whisk until well combined.
4.	Remove the grains from the cooker and transfer them to a large bowl. Allow them to sit out long enough to cool slightly.
5.	Add the dressing, pine nuts, kale and tomatoes to the grains and stir.
6.	Season with salt and black pepper, as desired.
7.	Serve warm or cover and chill until ready to serve.

Vanilla Rice Pudding

Prep time: 5 minutes | Cook time: 20 minutes | Serves 4
2 cups whole milk
1¼ cups water
1 teaspoon cinnamon
½ teaspoon grated nutmeg
Pinch of salt
1 cup long-grain rice, rinsed and drained
1 teaspoon vanilla extract
1 can (14-ounce / 397-g) condensed milk
1.	Add the whole milk, water, cinnamon, nutmeg and salt into the Instant Pot.
2.	Add rice and stir to combine.
3.	Lock the lid. Select the Porridge mode and set the cooking time for 20 minutes on High Pressure. Once the timer goes off, perform a natural pressure release for 10 minutes, then release any remaining pressure. Carefully open the lid.
4.	Add the vanilla extract and condensed milk. Stir well until creamy and serve.

Red Wine Poached Pears

Prep time: 5 minutes | Cook time: 8 minutes | Serves 3
3 firm pears
½ teaspoon grated ginger
½ bottle red wine
½ grated cinnamon
1 cup granulated sugar
1 bay laurel leaf
1.	Add all the ingredients to the Instant Pot and stir to combine.
2.	Lock the lid. Select the Manual mode and set the cooking time for 8 minutes on High Pressure. Once the timer goes off, perform a natural pressure release for 10 minutes, then release any remaining pressure.
3.	Carefully open the lid and transfer the pears to a bowl.

4.	Select the Sauté mode and let the mixture simmer for 10 more minutes to reduce its consistency and drizzle the red wine sauce on pears.
5.	Serve immediately.

Rhubarb Strawberry Tarts

Prep time: 5 minutes | Cook time: 5 minutes | Serves 12
1 pound (454 g) rhubarb, cut into small pieces
½ pound (227 g) strawberries
¼ cup minced crystallized ginger
½ cup honey
1 cup water
12 tart shells, short crust
½ cup whipped cream
1.	Add all the ingredients, except for the tart shells and whipped cream, to the Instant Pot and stir to combine.
2.	Lock the lid. Select the Manual mode and set the cooking time for 5 minutes on High Pressure. Once the timer goes off, perform a natural pressure release for 10 minutes, then release any remaining pressure. Carefully open the lid.
3.	Place the mixture in the tart shells. Top with whipped cream and serve.

Pear and Apple Crisp

Prep time: 5 minutes | Cook time: 5 minutes | Serves 4
3 tablespoons butter, melted
1 teaspoon ground cinnamon
½ cup packed brown sugar
½ cup all-purpose flour
½ cup old-fashioned rolled oats
½ teaspoon freshly grated nutmeg
2 apples, peeled and sliced
2 pears, peeled and sliced
½ cup water
1.	Take a bowl and mix together the brown sugar, butter, oats, flour, cinnamon, and nutmeg.
2.	Evenly layer the apples and pears in the inner pot. Then evenly spread the oat mixture on top of the fruit and pour the water on top of the oat mixture.
3.	Set the lid in place. Select the Manual mode and set the cooking time for 5 minutes on High Pressure. When the timer goes off, do a quick pressure release. Carefully open the lid.
4.	Stir the crisp. Select the Sauté mode and cook until it bubbles.
5.	Serve warm.

Stuffed Eggs

Prep time: 5 minutes | Cook time: 6 minutes | Serves 4
4 eggs
1½ tablespoons Greek yogurt
1½ tablespoons mayonnaise
½ teaspoon chopped jalapeño
¼ teaspoon onion powder
¼ teaspoon paprika
¼ teaspoon lemon zests
Salt and black pepper, to taste

1 cup water, for the pot
1. Pour the water and insert the trivet in the Instant Pot. Place the eggs on the trivet.
2. Set the lid in place. Select the Manual mode and set the cooking time for 6 minutes on High Pressure. When the timer goes off, do a quick pressure release. Carefully open the lid.
3. Place the eggs into ice-cold water. Peel the eggs, and cut in half, lengthwise. Scoop out the egg yolks and mix them with the remaining ingredients. Fill the hollow eggs with the mixture and serve.

Egg-Crusted Zucchini

Prep time: 5 minutes | Cook time: 5 minutes | Serves 2

1 zucchini, cut into ½-inch round slices
½ teaspoon dried dill
½ teaspoon paprika
1 egg
1½ tablespoons coconut flour
1 tablespoon milk
Salt and black pepper, to taste
1 tablespoon coconut oil
1. Whisk egg and milk in a bowl. Mix the salt, black pepper, paprika, dried dill, and flour in another bowl. Dip the zucchini slices in the egg mixture, then in the dry mixture.
2. Press the Sauté button on the Instant Pot and heat the oil. Add the zucchini slices to the pot and sauté for 5 minutes.
3. Serve immediately.

Egg and Veggie Mix

Prep time: 5 minutes | Cook time: 8 minutes | Serves 8

16 eggs, beaten
2 sweet potatoes, peeled and shredded
2 red bell peppers, deseeded and chopped
2 onions, chopped
2 garlic cloves, minced
4 teaspoons chopped fresh basil
Salt and black pepper, to taste
2 tablespoons oil
1. Add all the ingredients to the Instant Pot and stir to combine.
2. Set the lid in place. Select the Manual mode and set the cooking time for 8 minutes on High Pressure. When the timer goes off, do a quick pressure release. Carefully open the lid.
3. Serve immediately.

Ginger-Garlic Egg Potatoes

Prep time: 5 minutes | Cook time: 10 minutes | Serves 3

2 eggs, whisked
1 teaspoon ground turmeric
1 teaspoon cumin seeds
2 tablespoons olive oil
2 potatoes, peeled and diced
1 onion, finely chopped
2 teaspoons ginger-garlic paste
½ teaspoon red chili powder
Salt and black pepper, to taste

1. Press the Sauté button on the Instant Pot and heat the oil. Add the cumin seed, ginger-garlic paste, and onions to the pot and sauté for 4 minutes. Stir in the remaining ingredients.
2. Set the lid in place. Select the Manual mode and set the cooking time for 6 minutes on High Pressure. When the timer goes off, do a quick pressure release. Carefully open the lid.
3. Serve immediately.

Honey Carrots with Soy Sauce

Prep time: 5 minutes | Cook time: 6 minutes | Serves 4

8 medium carrots
1 cup water
1 clove garlic, finely chopped
1 tablespoon honey
2 tablespoons soy sauce
½ tablespoon sesame seeds
Salt, to taste
Chopped green onions, for garnish
1. Add the carrots and water to the Instant Pot.
2. Set the lid in place. Select the Manual mode and set the cooking time for 3 minutes on High Pressure. When the timer goes off, do a quick pressure release. Carefully open the lid.
3. Remove the carrots. Drain the water.
4. Select the Sauté mode and add the remaining ingredients, except for the green onions and sesame seeds. Cook for 3 minutes, or until sticky.
5. Put the carrots back into the pot and coat well. Sprinkle with the green onions and seeds and serve.

Thyme Carrots

Prep time: 5 minutes | Cook time: 2 minutes | Serves 2

4 carrots, peeled and cut into sticks
1½ teaspoon fresh thyme
2 tablespoons butter
½ cup water
Salt, to taste
1. Press the Sauté button on the Instant Pot and melt the butter. Add the carrots, thyme, salt, and water to the pot.
2. Set the lid in place. Select the Manual mode and set the cooking time for 2 minutes on High Pressure. When the timer goes off, do a quick pressure release. Carefully open the lid.
3. Serve hot.

Vinegary Pearl Onion

Prep time: 5 minutes | Cook time: 5 minutes | Serves 4

1 pound (454 g) pearl onions, peeled
Pinch of salt and black pepper
½ cup water
1 bay leaf
4 tablespoons balsamic vinegar
1 tablespoon coconut flour
1 tablespoon stevia
1. In the pot, mix the pearl onions with salt, pepper, water, and bay leaf.

2.	Set the lid in place. Select the Manual mode and set the cooking time for 5 minutes on Low Pressure. When the timer goes off, do a quick pressure release. Carefully open the lid.
3.	Meanwhile, in a pan, add the vinegar, stevia, and flour. Mix and bring to a simmer. Remove from the heat. Pour over the pearl onions. Mix and serve.

Mustard Flavored Artichokes

Prep time: 5 minutes | Cook time: 12 minutes | Serves 3

3 artichokes
3 tablespoons mayonnaise
1 cup water, for the pot
2 pinches paprika
2 lemons, sliced in half
2 teaspoons Dijon mustard
1.	Mix mayonnaise, paprika, and mustard.
2.	Pour the water and insert the trivet in the Instant Pot. Place the artichokes upwards and arrange the lemon slices on it.
3.	Set the lid in place. Select the Manual mode and set the cooking time for 12 minutes on High Pressure. When the timer goes off, do a quick pressure release. Carefully open the lid.
4.	Put the artichokes in the mayonnaise mixture. Serve.

Spinach Mushroom Treat

Prep time: 5 minutes | Cook time: 11 minutes | Serves 3

½ cup spinach
½ pound (227 g) fresh mushrooms, sliced
2 garlic cloves, minced
2 tablespoons chopped fresh thyme
1 onion, chopped
1 tablespoon olive oil
1 tablespoon chopped fresh cilantro, for garnish
Salt and black pepper, to taste
1.	Press the Sauté button on the Instant Pot and heat the oil. Add the garlic and onions to the pot and sauté for 4 minutes. Stir in the remaining ingredients.
2.	Set the lid in place. Select the Manual mode and set the cooking time for 7 minutes on High Pressure. When the timer goes off, do a quick pressure release. Carefully open the lid.
3.	Serve garnished with the cilantro.

Cooked Guacamole

Prep time: 5 minutes | Cook time: 9 minutes | Serves 4

1 large onion, finely diced
4 tablespoons lemon juice
¼ cup cilantro, chopped
4 avocados, peeled and diced
3 tablespoons olive oil
3 jalapeños, finely diced
Salt and black pepper, to taste
1.	Press the Sauté button on the Instant Pot and heat the oil. Add the onions to the pot and sauté for 3 minutes, or until tender. Stir in the remaining ingredients.

2.	Set the lid in place. Select the Manual mode and set the cooking time for 6 minutes on High Pressure. When the timer goes off, do a quick pressure release. Carefully open the lid.
3.	Serve immediately.

Sweet Roasted Cashews

Prep time: 5 minutes | Cook time: 20 minutes | Serves 2

¾ cup cashews
¼ teaspoon salt
¼ teaspoon ginger powder
1 teaspoon minced orange zest
4 tablespoons honey
1 cup water, for the pot
1.	Stir together the honey, orange zest, ginger powder, and salt in a bowl. Add the cashews to the mixture and place it in a ramekin.
2.	Pour the water and insert the trivet in the Instant Pot. Place the ramekin on the trivet.
3.	Set the lid in place. Select the Manual mode and set the cooking time for 20 minutes on High Pressure. When the timer goes off, do a quick pressure release. Carefully open the lid.
4.	Serve immediately.

Celery Wheat Berry Salad

Prep time: 15 minutes | Cook time: 40 minutes | Serves 12

1½ tablespoons vegetable oil
6¾ cups water
1½ cups wheat berries
1½ teaspoons Dijon mustard
1 teaspoon granulated sugar
1 teaspoon sea salt
½ teaspoon freshly ground black pepper
¼ cup white wine vinegar
½ cup extra-virgin olive oil
½ small red onion, peeled and diced
2 medium stalks celery, finely diced
1 medium zucchini, peeled, grated and drained
1 medium red bell pepper, deseeded and diced
4 green onions, diced
1$^1/_3$ cups frozen corn, thawed
¼ cup diced sun-dried tomatoes
¼ cup chopped fresh Italian flat-leaf parsley
1.	Add the vegetable oil, water, and wheat berries to the Instant Pot.
2.	Set the lid in place. Select the Multigrain mode and set the cooking time for 40 minutes on High Pressure. When the timer goes off, do a quick pressure release. Carefully open the lid.
3.	Fluff the wheat berries with a fork. Drain and transfer to a large bowl.
4.	Make the dressing by processing the mustard, sugar, salt, pepper, vinegar, olive oil, and red onion in a food processor until smooth.
5.	Stir ½ cup of the dressing into the cooled wheat berries. Toss the seasoned wheat berries with the remaining ingredients.
6.	Serve immediately. Cover and refrigerate any leftover dressing up to 3 days.

Three Bean Salad with Parsley

Prep time: 10 minutes | Cook time: 30 minutes | Serves 8

$^1/_3$ cup apple cider vinegar
¼ cup granulated sugar
2½ teaspoons salt, divided
½ teaspoon freshly ground black pepper
¼ cup olive oil
½ cup dried chickpeas
½ cup dried kidney beans
1 cup frozen green beans pieces
4 cups water
1 tablespoon vegetable oil
1 cup chopped fresh Italian flat-leaf parsley
½ cup peeled and diced cucumber
½ cup diced red onion

1. For the dressing: In a small bowl, whisk together the vinegar, sugar, 1½ teaspoons of the salt and pepper. While whisking continuously, slowly add the olive oil. Once well combined, cover in plastic and refrigerate.
2. Add the chickpeas, kidney beans, green beans, water, vegetable oil, and the remaining 1 teaspoon of the salt to the Instant Pot. Stir to combine.
3. Lock the lid. Select the Manual mode and set the cooking time for 30 minutes on High Pressure. Once the timer goes off, perform a natural pressure release for 10 minutes, then release any remaining pressure. Carefully open the lid.
4. Transfer the cooked beans to a large mixing bowl. Stir in all the remaining ingredients along with the dressing. Toss to combine thoroughly. Cover and refrigerate for 2 hours before serving.

Tomato and Parsley Quinoa Salad

Prep time: 5 minutes | Cook time: 21 minutes | Serves 4

2 tablespoons olive oil
2 cloves garlic, minced
1 cup diced tomatoes
¼ cup chopped fresh Italian flat-leaf parsley
1 tablespoon fresh lemon juice
1 cup quinoa
2 cups water
1 teaspoon salt

1. Press the Sauté button on the Instant Pot and heat the olive oil. Add the garlic and sauté for 30 seconds. Add the tomatoes, parsley and lemon juice. Sauté for an additional minute. Transfer the tomato mixture to a small bowl.
2. Add the quinoa and water to the Instant Pot.
3. Lock the lid. Select the Manual mode and set the cooking time for 20 minutes on High Pressure. Once the timer goes off, perform a natural pressure release for 10 minutes, then release any remaining pressure. Carefully open the lid.
4. Fluff the cooked quinoa with a fork. Stir in the tomato mixture and salt.
5. Serve immediately.

CHAPTER 4 SIDE DISHES

Steamed Broccoli with Lemon

Prep time: 5 minutes | Cook time: 0 minutes | Serves 4

1 cup water
1 medium head broccoli, chopped
2 teaspoons ghee
1 teaspoon lemon juice
½ teaspoon sea salt
1.   Add the water to the Instant Pot. Place a steamer basket and layer the broccoli on top. Secure the lid.
2.   Select the Steam mode and set the cooking time for 0 minutes on High Pressure.
3.   When the timer goes off, do a quick pressure release. Carefully open the lid.
4.   Remove the broccoli from the steamer basket to a serving dish. Mix in the ghee, lemon juice, and salt and toss to combine.
5.   Serve warm.

Healthy Strawberry Applesauce

Prep time: 10 minutes | Cook time: 5 minutes | Serves 6

4 cups frozen strawberries
6 cups roughly chopped Gala apples
½ cup water
½ cup granulated sugar
¼ teaspoon salt
1.   Place the strawberries and apples in your Instant Pot.
2.   Mix in the water, sugar, and salt and stir well. Lock the lid.
3.   Press the Manual button on your Instant Pot and cook for 5 minutes at High Pressure.
4.   Once cooking is complete, perform a natural pressure release for 15 minutes and then release any remaining pressure. Carefully open the lid.
5.   Blend the mixture with an immersion blender until smooth.
6.   Place in the refrigerator for 2 hours.
7.   Serve chilled.

Carrots with Honey Glaze

Prep time: 10 minutes | Cook time: 16 minutes | Serves 4

$^1/_3$ cup olive oil
1 pound (454 g) carrots, cut into ½-inch slices
1 teaspoon cumin
½ teaspoon salt
¼ teaspoon black pepper
¼ cup honey
1.   Press the Sauté button on your Instant Pot. Add the oil and let heat for 1 minute.
2.   Add the carrots, cumin, salt, and pepper. Lock the lid and sauté for 10 minutes.
3.   Stir in the honey and secure the lid. Sauté for another 5 minutes, or until the carrots are evenly glazed.
4.   Transfer to a serving dish and serve hot.

Maple-Glazed Carrots

Prep time: 10 minutes | Cook time: 5 minutes | Serves 6

1 pound (454 g) carrots, peeled and diced large
1 tablespoon pure maple syrup
1 tablespoon ghee
1 tablespoon minced fresh dill
1 cup water
½ teaspoon sea salt
1.   Place all the ingredients in the Instant Pot. Secure the lid.
2.   Select the Manual mode and set the cooking time for 5 minutes on High Pressure.
3.   Once cooking is complete, perform a natural pressure release for 10 minutes and then release any remaining pressure. Carefully open the lid.
4.   Transfer to a serving dish and serve immediately.

Spiced Orange Carrots

Prep time: 5 minutes | Cook time: 4 to 5 minutes | Serves 6

2 pounds (907 g) medium carrots or baby carrots, cut into ¾-inch pieces
½ cup orange juice
½ cup packed brown sugar
2 tablespoons butter
¾ teaspoon ground cinnamon
¼ teaspoon ground nutmeg
½ teaspoon salt
¼ cup cold water
1 tablespoon cornstarch
1.   Mix together all the ingredients except the water and cornstarch in your Instant Pot.
2.   Secure the lid. Press the Manual button on your Instant Pot and cook for 3 minutes on Low Pressure.
3.   When the timer goes off, use a quick pressure release. Carefully remove the lid.
4.   Press the sauté button on your Instant Pot and bring the liquid to a boil. Fold in the water and cornstarch and stir until smooth.
5.   Continue to cook for 1 to 2 minutes and stir until the sauce is thickened.
6.   Transfer to a serving dish and serve immediately.

Garlic Mashed Root Vegetables

Prep time: 15 minutes | Cook time: 5 minutes | Serves 4

2 medium parsnips, peeled and diced
2 medium turnips, peeled and diced
3 cloves garlic, peeled and halved
1 large Yukon gold potato, peeled and diced
1 medium shallot, peeled and quartered
½ cup chicken broth, plus more as needed
1 cup water
2 tablespoons ghee
¼ cup unsweetened almond milk
½ teaspoon sea salt

½ teaspoon ground black pepper
1. Place the parsnips, turnips, garlic, potato, shallot, broth, and water in the Instant Pot. Secure the lid.
2. Select the Manual mode and set the cooking time for 5 minutes on High Pressure.
3. Once the timer goes off, use a natural pressure release for 10 minutes and then release any remaining pressure. Carefully open the lid.
4. Remove the vegetables from the pot to a medium bowl.
5. Stir in the ghee, milk, salt, and pepper. Blitz the mixture with an immersion blender until smooth. Add more broth, 1 tablespoon at a time, from the Instant Pot if a thinner consistency is desired.
6. Transfer to a serving plate and serve warm.

Brussels Sprouts with Maple Glaze

Prep time: 10 minutes | Cook time: 3 minutes | Serves 10

2 pounds (907 g) fresh Brussels sprouts, sliced
$^1/_3$ cup dried cranberries
2 large apples (Fuji or Braeburn), chopped
8 bacon strips, cooked and crumbled, divided
¼ cup maple syrup
2 tablespoons olive oil
$^1/_3$ cup cider vinegar
1 teaspoon salt
½ teaspoon coarsely ground pepper
¾ cup chopped hazelnuts or pecans, toasted
1. In a large bowl, mix together the Brussels sprouts, cranberries, apples, and 4 slices of bacon.
2. In a small bowl, stir together the syrup, oil, vinegar, salt, and pepper. Pour this mixture over the Brussels sprouts mixture and toss until well coated.
3. Transfer to the Instant Pot. Secure the lid.
4. Press the Manual on the Instant Pot and set the cooking time for 3 minutes on High Pressure.
5. Once cooking is complete, use a quick pressure release. Carefully remove the lid.
6. Serve sprinkled with the remaining 4 slices of bacon and hazelnuts.

Bacon and Red Cabbage with Apple

Prep time: 10 minutes | Cook time: 18 minutes | Serves 4

1 tablespoon olive oil
1 small onion, peeled and diced
3 slices bacon, diced
5 cups chopped red cabbage
1 small apple, peeled, cored, and diced
½ cup apple cider vinegar
1 cup chicken broth
½ teaspoon sea salt
¼ cup crumbled goat cheese
1. Set your Instant Pot to Sauté and heat the oil.
2. Add the onion and sauté until translucent, 3 to 5 minutes. Add the bacon and sauté for 3 minutes more, stirring occasionally, or until the bacon begins to crisp. Stir in the cabbage, apple, chicken broth, and vinegar.

3. Secure the lid. Select the Manual mode and set the cooking time for 10 minutes at High Pressure.
4. Once cooking is complete, do a quick pressure release. Carefully open the lid.
5. Remove from the Instant Pot to a plate and season with salt. Sprinkle the goat cheese on top for garnish before serving.

Sriracha Collard Greens

Prep time: 10 minutes | Cook time: 10 minutes | Serves 6

2 pounds (907 g) collard greens, washed, spines removed, and chopped
1 cup chicken broth
1 small onion, peeled and diced
¼ cup apple cider vinegar
1 slice bacon
1 teaspoon sriracha
½ teaspoon sea salt
¼ teaspoon ground black pepper
1. Combine all the ingredients in Instant Pot.
2. Secure the lid. Select the Manual mode and set the cooking time for 10 minutes at High Pressure.
3. Once cooking is complete, do a natural pressure release for 10 minutes, then release any remaining pressure. Carefully open the lid.
4. Discard the bacon and transfer the collard greens to a bowl. Serve immediately.

Chow-Chow Relish

Prep time: 15 minutes | Cook time: 20 minutes | Serves 8

2 large green bell peppers, deseeded and diced small
1 large red bell pepper, deseeded and diced small
2 cups finely diced cabbage
2 large green tomatoes, diced small
1 large sweet onion, peeled and diced small
1 cup water
1 cup apple cider vinegar
½ cup granulated sugar
½ cup packed dark brown sugar
1 tablespoon ground mustard
1 tablespoon sea salt
2 teaspoons celery seed
2 teaspoons red pepper flakes
2 teaspoons ground ginger
1 teaspoon ground turmeric
1. Combine all the ingredients in the Instant Pot.
2. Secure the lid. Select the Manual mode and set the cooking time for 20 minutes at High Pressure.
3. Once cooking is complete, do a natural pressure release for 10 minutes, then release any remaining pressure. Carefully open the lid.
4. Give the mixture a good stir and transfer to a bowl. Serve warm.

Summer Squash and Tomatoes

Prep time: 20 minutes | Cook time: 1 minute | Serves 8

1 pound (454 g) medium yellow summer squash, cut into ¼-inch-thick slices
2 medium tomatoes, chopped

¼ cup thinly sliced green onions
1 cup vegetable broth
¼ teaspoon pepper
½ teaspoon salt
1½ cups coarsely crushed Caesar salad croutons, for serving
4 bacon strips, cooked and crumbled, for serving
½ cup shredded Cheddar cheese, for serving

1. Combine all the ingredients except the croutons, bacon, and cheese in the Instant Pot.
2. Secure the lid. Select the Manual mode and set the cooking time for 1 minute at High Pressure.
3. Once cooking is complete, do a quick pressure release. Carefully open the lid.
4. Remove the squash from the Instant Pot to a plate. Serve topped with the croutons, bacon, and cheese.

Spaghetti Squash With Olives and Tomatoes

Prep time: 15 minutes | Cook time: 10 minutes | Serves 10

1 cup water
1 medium spaghetti squash, halved lengthwise and seeds removed
¼ cup sliced green olives with pimientos
1 can (14-ounce / 397-g) diced tomatoes, drained
1 teaspoon dried oregano
½ teaspoon salt
½ teaspoon pepper
½ cup shredded Cheddar cheese, for serving
¼ cup minced fresh basil, for serving

1. Pour the water into the Instant Pot and insert a trivet. Place the spaghetti squash on top of the trivet.
2. Secure the lid. Select the Manual mode and set the cooking time for 7 minutes at High Pressure.
3. Once cooking is complete, do a quick pressure release. Carefully open the lid.
4. Remove the spaghetti squash and trivet from the Instant Pot. Drain the cooking liquid from the pot.
5. Separate the squash into strands resembling spaghetti with a fork and discard the skin.
6. Return the squash to the Instant Pot. Add the olives, tomatoes, oregano, salt, and pepper and stir to combine.
7. Press the Sauté button on the Instant Pot and cook for about 3 minutes until heated through.
8. Serve topped with the cheese and basil.

Steamed Leeks with Tomato and Orange

Prep time: 10 minutes | Cook time: 2 minutes | Serves 6

1 large tomato, chopped
1 small navel orange, peeled, sectioned, and chopped
2 tablespoons sliced Greek olives
2 tablespoons minced fresh parsley
1 teaspoon red wine vinegar
1 teaspoon capers, drained
1 teaspoon olive oil
½ teaspoon pepper
½ teaspoon grated orange zest
1 cup water
6 medium leeks (white part only), halved lengthwise, cleaned
Crumbled feta cheese, for serving

1. Stir together the tomato, orange, olives, parsley, vinegar, capers, olive oil, pepper, and orange zest in a large bowl and set aside.
2. Pour the water into the Instant Pot and insert a trivet. Place the leeks on top of the trivet.
3. Secure the lid. Select the Steam mode and set the cooking time for 2 minutes at High Pressure.
4. Once cooking is complete, do a quick pressure release. Carefully open the lid.
5. Transfer the leeks to a serving plate and spoon the tomato mixture over top. Scatter with the feta cheese and serve immediately.

Easy Mushroom Rice Pilaf

Prep time: 20 minutes | Cook time: 10 minutes | Serves 6

¼ cup butter
1 cup medium grain rice
1 cup water
4 teaspoon beef base
2 garlic cloves, minced
6 green onions, chopped
½ pound (227 g) baby portobello mushrooms, sliced

1. Set your Instant Pot to Sauté and melt the butter.
2. Add the rice and cook for 3 to 5 minutes, stirring frequently, or until lightly browned.
3. Meanwhile, whisk together the water and beef base in a small bowl.
4. Add the garlic, green onions, and mushrooms to the Instant Pot and stir well. Pour the sauce over the top of the rice mixture.
5. Secure the lid. Select the Manual mode and set the cooking time for 4 minutes at High Pressure.
6. Once cooking is complete, do a natural pressure release for 10 minutes, then release any remaining pressure. Carefully open the lid.
7. Allow to cool for 5 minutes before serving.

Instant Pot Black-Eyed Peas With Ham

Prep time: 10 minutes | Cook time: 18 minutes | Serves 10

4 cups water
1 package (16-ounce / 454-g) dried black-eyed peas, rinsed
1 cup cubed fully cooked ham
3 garlic cloves, minced
1 medium onion, finely chopped
2 teaspoons seasoned salt
1 teaspoon pepper
Thinly sliced green onions, for garnish (optional)

1. Combine all the ingredients except the green onions in the Instant Pot.
2. Lock the lid. Select the Manual mode and set the cooking time for 18 minutes at High Pressure.
3. Once cooking is complete, do a natural pressure release for 10 minutes, then release any remaining pressure. Carefully open the lid.

4.	Serve garnished with the sliced green onions, if desired.

Zucchini and Chickpea Tagine

Prep time: 30 minutes | Cook time: 5 minutes | Serves 12
2 tablespoons olive oil
2 garlic cloves, minced
2 teaspoons paprika
1 teaspoon ground cumin
1 teaspoon ground ginger
½ teaspoon salt
¼ teaspoon ground cinnamon
¼ teaspoon pepper
2 medium zucchini, cut into ½-inch pieces
1 small butternut squash, peeled and cut into ½-inch cubes
1 can (15-ounce / 425-g) chickpeas or garbanzo beans, rinsed and drained
12 dried apricots, halved
½ cup water
1 medium sweet red pepper, coarsely chopped
1 medium onion, coarsely chopped
2 teaspoon honey
2 to 3 teaspoon harissa chili paste
1 can (14.5-ounce / 411-g) crushed tomatoes, undrained
¼ cup chopped fresh mint leaves
1.	Press the Sauté button on the Instant Pot and heat the olive oil until it shimmers.
2.	Add the garlic, paprika, cumin, ginger, salt, cinnamon, and pepper and cook for about 1 minute until fragrant. Add the remaining ingredients except the tomatoes and mint to the Instant Pot and stir to combine.
3.	Secure the lid. Select the Manual mode and set the cooking time for 3 minutes at High Pressure.
4.	Once cooking is complete, do a quick pressure release. Carefully open the lid.
5.	Stir in the tomatoes and mint until heated though. Serve warm.

Sweet and Sour Beet Salad

Prep time: 15 minutes | Cook time: 20 minutes | Serves 8
1½ cups water
6 medium fresh beets (about 2 pounds / 907 g), scrubbed and tops trimmed
2 small red onions, halved and thinly sliced
2 large ruby red grapefruit, peeled and sectioned
Sauce:
¼ cup extra virgin olive oil
3 tablespoons lemon juice
2 tablespoons honey
2 tablespoons cider vinegar
¼ teaspoon pepper
¼ teaspoon salt
1.	Pour the water into the Instant Pot and insert a trivet. Place the beets on top of the trivet.
2.	Secure the lid. Select the Manual mode and set the cooking time for 20 minutes at High Pressure.
3.	Once cooking is complete, do a natural pressure release for 10 minutes, then release any remaining pressure. Carefully open the lid.
4.	Remove the beets from the Instant Pot and let cool to room temperature before peeling, halving and thinly slicing them. Transfer the beets to a salad bowl.
5.	Whisk together all the ingredients for the sauce in a small bowl until smooth. Pour the sauce over the beets and add the red onions and grapefruit. Toss gently to coat and serve immediately.

Citrus Bacon Brussels Sprouts

Prep time: 5 minutes | Cook time: 7 to 9 minutes | Serves 4
1 tablespoon avocado oil
2 slices bacon, diced
½ cup water
½ cup freshly squeezed orange juice
1 pound (454 g) Brussels sprouts, trimmed and halved
2 teaspoons orange zest
1.	Press the Sauté button on your Instant Pot. Add the avocado oil and let heat for 1 minute.
2.	Add the bacon. Sauté for 3 to 5 minutes, or until the bacon is almost crisp and the fat is rendered. Pour in the water and orange juice and deglaze the Instant Pot by scraping the bits from the pot.
3.	Fold in the Brussels sprouts. Secure the lid.
4.	Press the Manual button on your Instant Pot and set the cooking time for 3 minutes at High Pressure.
5.	Once the timer goes off, use a quick pressure release and then release any remaining pressure. Carefully open the lid.
6.	Remove the Brussels sprouts from the Instant Pot to a serving dish with a slotted spoon.
7.	Serve warm garnished with the orange zest.

Balsamic Brussels Sprouts

Prep time: 5 minutes | Cook time: 5 minutes | Serves 4 to 6
2 tablespoons (¼ stick) salted butter
2 shallots, diced
2 to 3 pounds (907 g to 1.4 kg) Brussels sprouts, stems trimmed and halved
¼ cup maple syrup
$^1/_3$ cup balsamic vinegar
10 to 20 almonds, crushed
1 cup dried cranberries
Balsamic glaze, for topping (optional)
1.	Set your Instant Pot to Sauté and melt the butter.
2.	Add the shallots and sauté until slightly softened, about 3 minutes.
3.	Add the Brussels sprouts, maple syrup, vinegar, almonds, and cranberries and stir until the Brussels sprouts are fully coated in the sauce.
4.	Lock the lid. Select the Manual mode and set the cooking time for 1 minute at High Pressure.
5.	Once cooking is complete, do a quick pressure release. Carefully open the lid.

6. Transfer the Brussels sprouts to a platter, along with their sauce. Serve with a drizzle of balsamic glaze, if desired.

Spicy Green Beans

Prep time: 5 minutes | Cook time: 3 minutes | Serves 4 to 6

1½ pounds (680 g) green beans, ends trimmed
¼ cup low-sodium soy sauce
¼ cup vegetable or garlic broth
3 cloves garlic, minced
2 tablespoons sriracha
2 tablespoons sesame oil
1 tablespoon paprika
1 tablespoon rice vinegar
2 teaspoons garlic powder
1 teaspoon onion powder
2 tablespoons chopped almonds (optional)
¼ teaspoon crushed red pepper flakes (optional)
¼ teaspoon cayenne pepper (optional)
1. Stir together all the ingredients in the Instant Pot.
2. Lock the lid. Select the Manual mode and set the cooking time for 3 minutes at High Pressure.
3. Once cooking is complete, do a quick pressure release. Carefully open the lid.
4. Serve warm.

Black-Eyed Peas with Greens

Prep time: 10 minutes | Cook time: 15 minutes | Serves 2

1 tablespoon oil
½ yellow onion, diced
2 garlic cloves, minced
½ pound (227 g) dried black-eyed peas
2 cups chopped Swiss chard or kale
1 cup chicken stock
1½ teaspoons red pepper flakes
½ teaspoon dried thyme or 2 fresh thyme sprigs
½ tablespoon kosher salt
¼ teaspoon freshly ground black pepper
1 tablespoon apple cider vinegar
1 to 2 teaspoons hot sauce (optional)
1. Press the Sauté button on the Instant Pot and heat the oil until shimmering.
2. Add the onion and cook for 2 minutes until tender, stirring frequently.
3. Stir in the garlic and cook for about 1 minute until fragrant.
4. Add the peas, Swiss chard, chicken stock, red pepper flakes, thyme, salt, and pepper. Using a wooden spoon, scrape the bottom of the pot, then mix well.
5. Lock the lid. Select the Manual mode and set the cooking time for 10 minutes at High Pressure.
6. Once cooking is complete, do a natural pressure release for 10 minutes, then release any remaining pressure. Carefully open the lid.
7. Whisk in the vinegar and hot sauce, if desired. Taste and adjust the seasoning, if needed. Serve warm.

Creamy Macaroni and Cheese

Prep time: 5 minutes | Cook time: 7 minutes | Serves 2

6 ounces (170 g) elbow macaroni
¾ cup vegetable stock, plus more as needed
½ teaspoon kosher salt
1 tablespoon unsalted butter
2 ounces (57 g) cream cheese
$1/_3$ cup whole milk
½ tablespoon Dijon mustard
½ tablespoon hot sauce (optional)
$1/_3$ cup shredded Gruyère cheese
$1/_3$ cup shredded fontina cheese
$1/_3$ cup shredded Cheddar cheese
Salt and freshly ground black pepper, to taste
1. Combine the macaroni, vegetable stock, and kosher salt in the Instant Pot.
2. Lock the lid. Select the Manual mode and set the cooking time for 5 minutes at High Pressure.
3. Once cooking is complete, do a quick pressure release. Carefully open the lid.
4. Set your Instant Pot to Sauté and stir in the butter until melted.
5. Add the cream cheese, milk, mustard, and hot sauce (if desired) and stir well.
6. Add the shredded cheeses, about $1/_3$ cup at a time, mixing well after each addition.
7. Sprinkle with the salt and pepper and serve.

Instant Pot Pinto Beans

Prep time: 10 minutes | Cook time: 20 minutes | Serves 4

3 cups water
1 cup dried pinto beans, soaked for 8 hours and drained
2 cloves garlic, minced
½ yellow onion, chopped
1 teaspoon chili powder
1 teaspoon ground cumin
¼ teaspoon freshly ground black pepper
½ fine sea salt, or more to taste
Pinch of cayenne pepper (optional)
Chopped fresh cilantro, for garnish
Lime wedges, for garnish
1. In the Instant Pot, combine the water, beans, garlic, and onion.
2. Lock the lid. Select the Manual mode and set the cooking time for 20 minutes at High Pressure.
3. Once cooking is complete, do a natural pressure release for 10 minutes, then release any remaining pressure. Carefully open the lid.
4. Drain the beans and reserve the liquid.
5. Return the cooked beans to the pot and stir in ½ cup of the reserved liquid. Add the chili powder, cumin, black pepper, salt, and cayenne pepper (if desired) and stir well. Using a potato masher, mash the beans until smooth, leaving some texture if you like. If you prefer a more smooth texture, you can purée the beans with an immersion blender.
6. Taste and add more salt, if desired. Garnish with the cilantro and lime wedges and serve warm.

Spicy Ratatouille

Prep time: 15 minutes | Cook time: 8 minutes | Serves 6
1 (1-pound / 454-g) globe eggplant, cut into 1-inch pieces
3 zucchinis, cut into 1-inch pieces
1 teaspoon fine sea salt
2 tablespoons extra-virgin olive oil, plus more for serving
1 large yellow onion, cut into 1-inch pieces
2 cloves garlic, minced
1 teaspoon dried basil
½ teaspoon freshly ground black pepper
½ teaspoon dried thyme
½ teaspoon red pepper flakes
1 bay leaf
3 red bell peppers, stemmed, deseeded and cut into 1-inch pieces
1 (14½-ounce / 411-g) can diced tomatoes
¼ cup dry white wine
Fresh basil leaves, for serving
Crusty bread, for serving
1.   In a large bowl, toss together the eggplant and zucchini with the salt. Let stand for 15 minutes.
2.   Select the Sauté setting on the Instant Pot, add the oil, and heat for 1 minute. Add the onion and garlic and sauté for about 4 minutes, or until the onion softens. Add the basil, black pepper, thyme, red pepper flakes, and bay leaf and sauté for about 1 minute. Add the eggplant-zucchini mixture and any liquid that has pooled in the bottom of the bowl, along with the bell peppers, tomatoes and their liquid, and wine. Stir to combine.
3.   Set the lid in place. Select the Manual mode and set the cooking time for 2 minutes on Low Pressure. When the timer goes off, do a quick pressure release. Carefully open the lid.
4.   Discard the bay leaf. Spoon the ratatouille into a serving bowl.
5.   Drizzle the ratatouille with oil and sprinkle with fresh basil. Serve warm, with crusty bread.

Smoky Carrots and Collard Greens

Prep time: 10 minutes | Cook time: 12 minutes | Serves 4 to 6
1 tablespoon extra-virgin olive oil
1 yellow onion, diced
8 ounces (227 g) carrots, peeled and diced
2 bunches collard greens, stems discarded and leaves sliced into 1-inch ribbons
½ teaspoon smoked paprika
½ teaspoon fine sea salt, plus more as needed
¼ teaspoon freshly ground black pepper
½ cup water
1 tablespoon tomato paste
1.   Select the Sauté setting on the Instant Pot, add the oil, and heat for 1 minute. Add the onion and carrots and sauté for about 4 minutes, or until the onion begins to soften. Stir in the collards and sauté for about 2 minutes, or until wilted. Stir in the smoked paprika, salt, pepper, and water. Dollop the tomato paste on top, but do not stir it in.
2.   Set the lid in place. Select the Manual mode and set the cooking time for 5 minutes on High

Pressure. When the timer goes off, do a quick pressure release. Carefully open the lid.
3.   Stir to incorporate the tomato paste. Taste and adjust the seasoning with salt, if needed.
4.   Spoon the collards into a serving bowl or onto serving plates. Serve warm.

Classic Succotash

Prep time: 5 minutes | Cook time: 10 minutes | Serves 6 to 8
2 tablespoons extra-virgin olive oil
1 clove garlic, minced
1 yellow onion, diced
1 (16-ounce / 454-g) bag frozen baby lima beans
1 (12-ounce / 340-g) bag frozen corn kernels
1 (14½-ounce / 411-g) can diced tomatoes
½ cup low-sodium vegetable broth
½ teaspoon dried thyme
½ teaspoon fine sea salt
¼ teaspoon freshly ground black pepper
1.   Select the Sauté setting on the Instant Pot, add the oil and garlic, and heat for 2 minutes, or until the garlic is bubbling but not browned. Add the onion and sauté for about 5 minutes, or until the onion softens. Add the lima beans, corn, tomatoes and their liquid, broth, thyme, salt, and pepper, and vegetable broth. Stir to combine.
2.   Set the lid in place. Select the Manual mode and set the cooking time for 3 minutes on High Pressure. When the timer goes off, do a quick pressure release. Carefully open the lid.
3.   Stir the succotash, then transfer to a serving bowl. Serve warm.

Artichoke-Spinach Dip

Prep time: 10 minutes | Cook time: 10 to 11 minutes | Serves 8
2 teaspoons corn oil
¼ cup chopped onion
2 garlic cloves, finely chopped
8 ounces (227 g) fresh spinach, roughly chopped
½ teaspoon kosher salt
1 teaspoon freshly ground black pepper
5 ounces (142 g) cream cheese
1 (8½-ounce / 241-g) can water-packed artichoke hearts, drained and quartered
$^1/_3$ cup heavy cream
$^1/_3$ cup water
Chips or sliced veggies, for serving
1.   Press the Sauté button on the Instant Pot and heat the oil. Add the onion and garlic and sauté for 1 minute. Add the spinach, salt, and pepper. Continue to sauté for 2 to 3 minutes, or until the spinach is wilted. Add the cream cheese, artichokes, cream, and water and mix thoroughly.
2.   Set the lid in place. Select the Manual mode and set the cooking time for 7 minutes on High Pressure. When the timer goes off, do a quick pressure release. Carefully open the lid.
3.   Stir the dip, then let cool for 5 minutes. Transfer to a serving bowl and serve with chips or sliced veggies.

Deviled Potatoes

Prep time: 10 minutes | Cook time: 10 minutes | Serves 6

6 medium Yukon Gold potatoes, halved
1 cup water
5 tablespoons mayonnaise
1 teaspoon Dijon mustard
1 tablespoon sweet pickle relish
1 teaspoon sugar
½ teaspoon freshly squeezed lemon juice
½ teaspoon kosher salt
½ teaspoon freshly ground black pepper
1 tablespoon finely chopped fresh cilantro
1 teaspoon paprika

1. Place the halved potatoes in the steamer rack. Pour the water and insert the trivet in the Instant Pot. Place the steamer rack on the trivet.
2. Set the lid in place. Select the Manual mode and set the cooking time for 10 minutes on High Pressure. When the timer goes off, do a quick pressure release. Carefully open the lid.
3. Using tongs, carefully transfer the potatoes to a platter. Set aside to cool for 15 minutes.
4. In a medium bowl, stir together the mayonnaise, mustard, relish, sugar, lemon juice, salt and pepper.
5. Using a melon scooper or spoon, remove the middle part of the potatoes, creating a well. Spoon 1 to 1½ teaspoons of the mayonnaise mixture into each potato. Garnish each deviled potato with the cilantro and paprika before serving.

Citrus Corn and Beet Salad

Prep time: 10 minutes | Cook time: 8 minutes | Serves 6

2 medium red beets, peeled
1 corn on the cob, husks removed, washed
1½ cups water
¼ cup finely chopped onion
¼ cup finely chopped fresh cilantro
3 tablespoons mayonnaise
1 tablespoon extra-virgin olive oil
2 teaspoons freshly squeezed lemon juice
1 teaspoon grated lemon zest
1 teaspoon sugar
1 teaspoon kosher salt
1 teaspoon freshly ground black pepper

1. Place the whole beets and corn in the steamer rack. Pour the water and insert the trivet in the Instant Pot. Place the steamer rack on the trivet.
2. Set the lid in place. Select the Manual mode and set the cooking time for 4 minutes on High Pressure. When the timer goes off, do a quick pressure release. Carefully open the lid.
3. Using tongs, transfer the corn to a plate and set aside to cool.
4. Set the lid in place again. Select the Manual mode and set the cooking time for 4 minutes on High Pressure. When the timer goes off, do a quick pressure release. Carefully open the lid.
5. Using tongs, transfer the beets to the plate with the corn and set aside to cool.
6. Using a knife, carefully remove the corn kernels from the cob. Cut the beets into ½-inch cubes.
7. In a large bowl, combine the beets, corn, onion, cilantro, mayonnaise, olive oil, lemon juice and zest, sugar, salt, and pepper. Mix thoroughly and chill in the refrigerator for 1 hour.
8. Serve chilled.

Green Bean Stir-Fry

Prep time: 5 minutes | Cook time: 4 minutes | Serves 4

12 ounces (340 g) green beans, trimmed
1 cup water
2 tablespoons corn oil
2 garlic cloves, finely chopped
3 tablespoons crushed peanuts
2 tablespoons soy sauce
¼ teaspoon kosher salt
½ teaspoon cane sugar
2 teaspoons chili flakes

1. Place the beans in the steamer basket. Pour the water and insert the trivet in the Instant Pot. Place the basket on the trivet.
2. Set the lid in place. Select the Manual mode and set the cooking time for 1 minute on High Pressure. When the timer goes off, do a quick pressure release. Carefully open the lid.
3. Drain the beans and wipe the inner pot dry.
4. Press the Sauté button on the Instant Pot and heat the oil. Add the garlic and sauté for 1 minute. Add the peanuts and soy sauce and sauté for 2 more minutes.
5. In a large bowl, combine the green beans, garlic, peanuts, salt, and sugar. Mix until the sugar and salt are dissolved. Sprinkle with the chili flakes and serve hot.

Brussels Sprouts with Sesame Seeds

Prep time: 5 minutes | Cook time: 4 minutes | Serves 4

25 Brussels sprouts, halved lengthwise
1 cup water
1 tablespoon extra-virgin olive oil
2 garlic cloves, finely chopped
1 tablespoon balsamic vinegar
1 teaspoon kosher salt
½ teaspoon freshly ground black pepper
1 tablespoon roasted sesame seeds

1. Place the Brussels sprouts in the steamer basket. Pour the water and insert the trivet in the Instant Pot. Place the basket on the trivet.
2. Set the lid in place. Select the Manual mode and set the cooking time for 1 minute on High Pressure. When the timer goes off, do a quick pressure release. Carefully open the lid.
3. Using tongs, carefully transfer the Brussels sprouts to a serving plate. Discard the water and wipe the inner pot dry.
4. Press the Sauté button on the Instant Pot and heat the oil. Add the garlic and sauté for 1 minute. Add the Brussels sprouts, vinegar, salt, and pepper, and sauté for 2 minutes. Sprinkle with the roasted sesame seeds and serve hot.

Szechuan Honey-Glazed Asparagus

Prep time: 5 minutes | Cook time: 1 minute | Serves 4

2 bunches asparagus, woody ends removed
1 tablespoon extra-virgin olive oil
½ teaspoon kosher salt
½ teaspoon freshly ground black pepper
1 cup water
2 tablespoons honey
1 tablespoon Szechuan sauce

1. Place the asparagus in a large bowl. Drizzle with the olive oil, salt, and pepper, and toss to combine.
2. Place the asparagus in the steaming rack. Pour the water and insert the trivet in the Instant Pot. Place the steamer rack on the trivet. Lock the lid into place.
3. Set the lid in place. Select the Manual mode and set the cooking time for 1 minute on High Pressure. When the timer goes off, do a quick pressure release. Carefully open the lid.
4. Using tongs, transfer the asparagus to a serving bowl.
5. In a small bowl, combine the honey and Szechuan sauce. Drizzle over the asparagus and serve hot.

Sweet Potato Gratin

Prep time: 20 minutes | Cook time: 30 minutes | Serves 8

2 medium sweet potatoes, peeled and thinly sliced
2 tablespoons extra-virgin olive oil
1 teaspoon kosher salt
1 teaspoon freshly ground black pepper
1 tablespoon dried basil
1 tablespoon dried thyme
1 tablespoon butter, melted
½ cup heavy cream
1 cup Mexican-blend shredded cheese
2 tablespoons panko bread crumbs
1 cup water

1. In a large bowl, drizzle the olive oil over the sweet potato slices. Season with the salt, pepper, basil, and thyme. Mix thoroughly to coat the sweet potatoes. Set aside.
2. In a small bowl, mix the butter and cream.
3. In a springform pan, arrange a single layer of sweet potatoes. Spread about 2 tablespoons of the cream-butter mixture on top and sprinkle with 4 to 5 tablespoons of the cheese. Repeat these steps until all the sweet potato slices have been used, about three layers. After the last layer, sprinkle the bread crumbs on top. Cover the pan with aluminum foil.
4. Pour the water and insert the trivet in the Instant Pot. Place the springform pan on the trivet.
5. Lock the lid. Select the Manual mode and set the cooking time for 30 minutes on High Pressure. Once the timer goes off, perform a natural pressure release for 15 minutes, then release any remaining pressure. Carefully open the lid.
6. Carefully remove the pan. Let the sweet potatoes cool for at least 1 hour before serving so the cheese sets.

Spaghetti Squash with Pesto

Prep time: 5 minutes | Cook time: 12 minutes | Serves 6

1½ cups plus 3 tablespoons water, divided
1 (3-pound / 1.4-kg) spaghetti squash, pierced with a knife about 10 times
¼ cup pesto

1. Pour 1½ cups of the water and insert the trivet in the Instant Pot. Put the pan on the trivet. Place the squash on the trivet.
2. Lock the lid. Select the Manual mode and set the cooking time for 12 minutes on High Pressure. Once the timer goes off, perform a natural pressure release for 10 minutes, then release any remaining pressure. Carefully open the lid.
3. Using tongs, carefully transfer the squash to a cutting board to cool for about 10 minutes.
4. Halve the spaghetti squash lengthwise. Using a spoon, scoop out and discard the seeds. Using a fork, scrape the flesh of the squash and shred into long "noodles". Place the noodles in a medium serving bowl.
5. In a small bowl, mix the pesto with the remaining 3 tablespoons of the water. Drizzle over the squash, toss to combine, and serve warm.

Asparagus with Gribiche

Prep time: 10 minutes | Cook time: 5 minutes | Serves 4

2 large eggs
1½ cups water
1 pound (454 g) asparagus, trimmed and cut into 1-inch pieces
1 tablespoon Dijon mustard
¼ cup vegetable oil
1 tablespoon apple cider vinegar
2 to 3 tablespoons chopped dill pickle
1 tablespoon chopped fresh parsley
1 teaspoon granulated sugar
½ teaspoon kosher salt
½ teaspoon black pepper

1. Pour the water and insert the trivet in the Instant Pot. Place the eggs on one side of the trivet.
2. Tightly wrap the asparagus in foil and place on the trivet next to the eggs.
3. Set the lid in place. Select the Manual mode and set the cooking time for 5 minutes on High Pressure. When the timer goes off, do a quick pressure release. Carefully open the lid.
4. Meanwhile, fill a medium bowl with ice cubes and water.
5. Remove the eggs and place them in the ice water bath for 5 minutes. Peel and finely dice the eggs.
6. In a small bowl, combine the mustard, oil, vinegar, pickle, parsley, sugar, salt, and pepper. Stir in the chopped eggs.
7. Place the asparagus on a serving platter and spoon the gribiche on top. Serve.

Beet Salad with Orange and Avocado

Prep time: 10 minutes | Cook time: 20 minutes | Serves 4

Salad:
1 pound (454 g) beets, each about 2½ inches in diameter
2 navel oranges, peeled and cut into segments
1 large avocados, pitted, peeled and sliced
1 (5- to 6-ounce / 142- to 170-g) bag baby spinach
4 sprigs fresh mint, leaves removed and torn if large
¾ cup Feta cheese
1 cup water
Vinaigrette:
¼ cup extra-virgin olive oil
2 tablespoons fresh lemon juice
½ teaspoon dried oregano
¼ teaspoon fine sea salt
¼ teaspoon freshly ground black pepper
1 clove garlic, minced
1.	Pour the water into the Instant Pot and place the wire metal steam rack in the pot. Arrange the beets in a single layer on the steam rack.
2.	Set the lid in place. Select the Manual mode and set the cooking time for 20 minutes on High Pressure.
3.	While the beets are cooking, prepare an ice bath.
4.	To make the vinaigrette: In a widemouthed 1-pint jar, combine the oil, lemon juice, oregano, salt, pepper, and garlic. Using an immersion blender, blend until an emulsified vinaigrette forms. Set aside.
5.	When the timer goes off, do a quick pressure release. Carefully open the lid. Using tongs, transfer the beets to the ice bath and let cool for 10 minutes.
6.	Using a paring knife, remove the skins from the beets; they should peel off very easily. Trim and discard the ends of the beets, then slice them into wedges.
7.	In a large bowl, toss the spinach with half of the vinaigrette. Arrange the spinach on a large serving plate or on individual salad plates, then top with the beets, oranges, avocado, and mint.
8.	Using a pair of spoons, scoop bite-sized pieces of the feta out of its container and dollop it onto the salad. Spoon the rest of the vinaigrette over the salad and serve immediately.

Adobo-Style Eggplant

Prep time: 10 minutes | Cook time: 6 minutes | Serves 4
1 (1-pound / 454-g) eggplant, cut into 1-inch pieces
1 teaspoon fine sea salt
¼ cup low-sodium soy sauce
2 tablespoons palm vinegar
2 tablespoons avocado oil
4 cloves garlic, minced
1 large shallot, diced
1 red bell pepper, deseeded and cut into 1-inch squares
½ teaspoon freshly ground black pepper
2 tablespoons water
Hot steamed rice, for serving
1 green onion, tender green part only, thinly sliced
1.	In a colander, toss the eggplant with the salt. Let sit in the sink or on top of a dish for 30 minutes (some liquid will release from the eggplant as it sits),
then rinse the eggplant well under running water. Pat the pieces dry with paper towels.
2.	In a small bowl, combine the soy sauce and vinegar. Set aside.
3.	Press the Sauté button on the Instant Pot and heat the oil for 1 minute. Add the garlic and shallot and sauté for 3 minutes, or until the shallot softens and the garlic begins to color.
4.	Add the eggplant, bell pepper, and black pepper, and stir to coat the vegetables with the oil. Pour in the vinegar mixture and water.
5.	Set the lid in place. Select the Manual mode and set the cooking time for 2 minutes on Low Pressure. When the timer goes off, do a quick pressure release. Carefully open the lid.
6.	Give the vegetables a gentle stir to coat with the sauce, then let sit for a minute or two.
7.	Spoon over bowls of steamed rice and sprinkle green onions on top. Serve hot.

Maple Mashed Sweet Potato Casserole

Prep time: 5 minutes | Cook time: 30 to 35 minutes | Serves 6 to 8
3 pounds (1.4 kg) sweet potatoes, peeled and cut into 1-inch pieces
¼ cup coconut oil
¼ cup dark maple syrup
1 teaspoon fine sea salt
½ teaspoon ground cinnamon
10 marshmallows, cut in half lengthwise
1 cup water
1.	Pour the water into the Instant Pot and place a steamer basket in the pot. Add the sweet potatoes to the basket.
2.	Set the lid in place. Select the Manual mode and set the cooking time for 5 minutes on High Pressure.
3.	While the sweet potatoes are steaming, preheat the oven to 325ºF (163ºC). Grease a baking dish with coconut oil and line a baking sheet with aluminum foil.
4.	When the timer goes off, do a quick pressure release. Carefully open the lid. Wearing heat-resistant mitts, lift out the steamer basket. Lift out the inner pot and discard the water.
5.	Return the sweet potatoes to the still-warm inner pot. Add the coconut oil, maple syrup, salt, and cinnamon, then use a potato masher to mash the sweet potatoes until smooth.
6.	Spoon the mashed potatoes into the baking dish. Top with a single layer of the marshmallows, cut side down. Place the dish on the prepared baking sheet. Bake for 25 to 30 minutes, until the marshmallows are puffed and golden brown on top. Serve warm.

Spiced Carrots

Prep time: 5 minutes | Cook time: 5 minutes | Serves 6
2 pounds (907 g) baby carrots, chopped
½ cup packed brown sugar
½ cup orange juice
2 tablespoons butter

¾ teaspoon ground cinnamon
½ teaspoon salt
¼ teaspoon ground nutmeg
1 tablespoon cornstarch
¼ cup cold water
1.	Add all the ingredients, except for the cornstarch and water, to the Instant Pot and stir to combine.
2.	Set the lid in place. Select the Manual mode and set the cooking time for 3 minutes on Low Pressure. When the timer goes off, do a quick pressure release. Carefully open the lid.
3.	Select the Sauté mode and bring it to a boil. Mix water and cornstarch in a bowl and add to the carrot mixture. Cook for 2 minutes.
4.	Serve hot.

Sweet Turnip Greens

Prep time: 5 minutes | Cook time: 5 minutes | Serves 10

2 pounds (907 g) turnips, peeled and chopped
12 ounces (340 g) fresh turnip greens
1 medium onion, chopped
2 tablespoons sugar
Salt and pepper, to taste
5 cups vegetable broth
1.	Add all the ingredients to the Instant Pot and stir to combine.
2.	Set the lid in place. Select the Manual mode and set the cooking time for 5 minutes on High Pressure. When the timer goes off, do a quick pressure release. Carefully open the lid.
3.	Serve hot.

Grapefruit and Beet Salad

Prep time: 5 minutes | Cook time: 20 minutes | Serves 8

6 medium fresh beets
1½ cups water
¼ cup extra-virgin olive oil
3 tablespoons lemon juice
2 tablespoons cider vinegar
2 tablespoons honey
¼ teaspoon salt
¼ teaspoon black pepper
2 large grapefruits, peeled and sectioned
2 small red onions, halved and sliced
1.	Scrub the beets, trimming the tops to 1 inch.
2.	Pour the water and insert the trivet in the Instant Pot. Place the beets on the trivet.
3.	Set the lid in place. Select the Manual mode and set the cooking time for 20 minutes on High Pressure. When the timer goes off, do a quick pressure release. Carefully open the lid.
4.	Whisk together the remaining ingredients, except for the grapefruits and onion. Pour over beets. Stir in the grapefruits and onion and serve.

BBQ Baked Beans

Prep time: 5 minutes | Cook time: 33 minutes | Serves 8

16 ounces (454 g) dried great northern beans, soaked overnight and drained

2 cups water
1 medium onion, chopped
2 teaspoons garlic powder, divided
2 teaspoons onion powder, divided
1 cup barbecue sauce
¾ cup packed brown sugar
½ teaspoon ground nutmeg
¼ teaspoon ground cloves
2 teaspoons hot pepper sauce
1.	In the pot, combine the beans, water, onion, 1 teaspoon of the garlic powder and 1 teaspoon of the onion powder.
2.	Set the lid in place. Select the Manual mode and set the cooking time for 30 minutes on High Pressure. When the timer goes off, do a quick pressure release. Carefully open the lid.
3.	Stir in the barbecue sauce, sugar, nutmeg, cloves, hot pepper sauce, and the remaining garlic and onion powder.
4.	Set the lid in place. Select the Manual mode and set the cooking time for 3 minutes on High Pressure. When the timer goes off, do a quick pressure release. Carefully open the lid.
5.	Serve hot.

Steamed Leeks with Tomato Sauce

Prep time: 10 minutes | Cook time: 2 minutes | Serves 6

1 large tomato, chopped
1 small navel orange, chopped
2 tablespoons minced fresh parsley
2 tablespoons sliced olives
1 teaspoon capers, drained
1 teaspoon red wine vinegar
1 teaspoon olive oil
½ teaspoon grated orange zest
½ teaspoon pepper
6 medium leeks, white portion only, halved lengthwise and cleaned
Crumbled Feta cheese, for serving
1 cup water, for the pot
1.	In a bowl, stir together all the ingredients, except for the leeks, cheese and water. Set aside.
2.	Pour the water and insert the trivet in the Instant Pot. Place the leeks on the trivet.
3.	Set the lid in place. Select the Manual mode and set the cooking time for 2 minutes on High Pressure. When the timer goes off, do a quick pressure release. Carefully open the lid.
4.	Transfer the leeks to a platter. Spoon the tomato mixture on top. Sprinkle with the cheese and serve.

Mushroom Rice Pilaf

Prep time: 5 minutes | Cook time: 9 minutes | Serves 6

¼ cup butter
1 cup medium-grain rice
2 garlic cloves, minced
6 green onions, chopped
½ pound (227 g) baby portobello mushrooms, sliced
1 cup water
4 teaspoons Better Than Bouillon

1.   Press the Sauté button on the Instant Pot and melt the butter. Add the rice and cook for 5 minutes. Add the garlic, green onions, and mushrooms.
2.   In a bowl, whisk together the water and bouillon. Pour over the rice mixture.
3.   Set the lid in place. Select the Manual mode and set the cooking time for 4 minutes on High Pressure. When the timer goes off, do a quick pressure release. Carefully open the lid.
4.   Serve hot.

Instant Pot Spanish Risotto

Prep time: 5 minutes | Cook time: 10 minutes | Serves 6
3 tablespoons olive oil
1 cup chopped yellow onion
2 garlic cloves, minced
2 cups white rice
2½ cups vegetable stock
¾ cup crushed tomatoes
½ teaspoon chili powder
¼ cup chopped cilantro
Salt and black pepper, to taste
1.   Press the Sauté button on the Instant Pot and heat the oil. Add the onion and garlic and cook for 4 minutes. Add the rice and cook for 2 minutes. Stir in the stock, tomatoes, and chili powder.
2.   Set the lid in place. Select the Manual mode and set the cooking time for 4 minutes on High Pressure. When the timer goes off, do a quick pressure release. Carefully open the lid.
3.   Sprinkle with the cilantro and season with salt and pepper. Stir and serve.

Caramelized Sweet Potatoes

Prep time: 5 minutes | Cook time: 19 minutes | Serves 2
2 sweet potatoes, scrubbed
1 cup water
2 tablespoons coconut oil
Pinch of salt and black pepper
Pinch of chili powder
1.   Pour the water and insert the trivet in the Instant Pot. Put the pan on the trivet.
2.   Pour the water to the Instant Pot and place the steamer basket at the bottom. Add the sweet potatoes to the basket.
3.   Set the lid in place. Select the Manual mode and set the cooking time for 15 minutes on High Pressure. When the timer goes off, do a quick pressure release. Carefully open the lid.
4.   Remove and slice the potatoes. Clean the pot.
5.   Press the Sauté button on the Instant Pot and heat the oil. Add the sliced sweet potatoes. Season with salt, pepper and chili powder and brown for 2 minutes on each side.
6.   Serve hot.

Braised Kale with Garlic

Prep time: 5 minutes | Cook time: 5 minutes | Serves 4

1 large bunch kale
2 tablespoons extra-virgin olive oil
6 cloves garlic, thinly sliced crosswise
½ cup vegetable broth
¼ teaspoon sea salt
Freshly ground black pepper, to taste
1.   Remove and discard the middle stems from the kale and roughly chop the leafy parts. Rinse and drain the kale.
2.   Press the Sauté button on the Instant Pot and heat the oil. Add the garlic and sauté for about 2 minutes until tender and golden. Transfer the garlic and oil to a small bowl and set aside.
3.   Add the broth to the inner pot. Place the kale on top and sprinkle with salt and pepper.
4.   Set the lid in place. Select the Manual mode and set the cooking time for 3 minutes on Low Pressure. When the timer goes off, do a quick pressure release. Carefully open the lid.
5.   Return the garlic and oil to the pot, and toss to combine.
6.   Serve immediately.

Balsamic Glazed Brussels Sprouts

Prep time: 5 minutes | Cook time: 9 to 14 minutes | Serves 4
14 ounces (397 g) whole medium-sized Brussels sprouts
1 cup water
1 tablespoon extra-virgin olive oil
Sea salt, to taste
Freshly ground black pepper, to taste
½ cup balsamic vinegar
1.   Trim a thin slice off the bottom of the Brussels sprouts and remove a few outer leaves from each. Fit the pot with a steamer basket and add 1 cup water. Add the Brussels sprouts to the steamer basket.
2.   Set the lid in place. Select the Manual mode and set the cooking time for 1 minute on High Pressure. When the timer goes off, do a quick pressure release. Carefully open the lid.
3.   Remove the steamer basket. Discard the water in the pot.
4.   Press the Sauté button on the Instant Pot and heat the oil. Add the steamed Brussels sprouts and season with salt and pepper. Turn occasionally with tongs or a spatula, until seared, about 3 minutes.
5.   Meanwhile, make the balsamic glaze. Pour the balsamic vinegar into a small saucepan over medium-low heat. Simmer until the vinegar is reduced and syrupy and coats the back of a spoon, 5 to 10 minutes.
6.   Serve the Brussels sprouts hot with a small bowl of the balsamic glaze on the side for drizzling.

Sweet Potato Mash with Sage

Prep time: 5 minutes | Cook time: 5 minutes | Serves 4
4 cups peeled sweet potato chunks
1 cup water
3 tablespoon butter
4 sage leaves, thinly sliced

Sea salt, to taste
Freshly ground black pepper, to taste
1. Fit the inner pot with a steamer basket and add 1 cup water. Place the sweet potato chunks into the basket.
2. Set the lid in place. Select the Manual mode and set the cooking time for 3 minutes on High Pressure. When the timer goes off, do a quick pressure release. Carefully open the lid.
3. Use tongs to carefully remove the steamer basket and potatoes. Discard the water and return the inner pot to the Instant Pot.
4. Press the Sauté button on the Instant Pot and melt the butter. Sauté the sage leaves until fragrant, about 2 minutes. Add the sweet potatoes to the pot and mash with a potato masher to the desired consistency. Season to taste with salt and pepper.
5. Serve immediately.

Steamed Artichoke with Aioli

Prep time: 10 minutes | Cook time: 15 minutes | Serves 2
1 large artichoke
1 cup water
Juice of ½ lemon
The Aioli Dipping Sauce:
½ cup raw cashews, soaked overnight or 2 hours in hot water
1½ tablespoons Dijon mustard
1 tablespoon apple cider vinegar
Juice of ½ lemon
2 cloves garlic
Pinch of ground turmeric
½ teaspoon sea salt
$^1/_3$ cup water
1. Fit the inner pot with the trivet and add 1 cup water. Trim the artichoke stem so that it is 1 to 2 inches long, and trim about 1 inch off the top. Squeeze the lemon juice over the top of the artichoke and add the lemon rind to the water. Place the artichoke, top-side down, on the trivet.
2. Set the lid in place. Select the Steam mode and set the cooking time for 15 minutes on High Pressure. When the timer goes off, do a quick pressure release. Carefully open the lid.
3. Check for doneness. Leaves should be easy to remove and the "meat" at the base of each leaf should be tender.
4. Meanwhile, make the aioli dipping sauce. Drain the cashews and place them in a blender. Add the Dijon, vinegar, lemon juice, garlic, turmeric, and sea salt. Add half the water and blend. Continue adding water as you blend until the sauce is smooth and creamy. Transfer the sauce to a small bowl or jar. Refrigerate until ready to use.
5. Use tongs to remove the hot artichoke and place on a serving dish. Serve the artichoke warm with the aioli.

Smokey Garbanzo Mash

Prep time: 5 minutes | Cook time: 20 minutes | Serves 6
2 cups dried garbanzo beans

1 tablespoon liquid smoke
½ teaspoon salt
1 teaspoon black pepper
1 teaspoon smoked paprika
½ teaspoon cayenne powder
¼ cup fresh parsley
¼ cup coconut milk
1. Place the garbanzo beans in the Instant Pot and add enough water just to cover. Sprinkle in the liquid smoke and stir.
2. Lock the lid. Select the Bean/Chili mode and set the cooking time for 20 minutes on High Pressure. Once the timer goes off, perform a natural pressure release for 10 minutes, then release any remaining pressure. Carefully open the lid. Drain off any excess liquid.
3. Add the salt, black pepper, smoked paprika, cayenne powder, fresh parsley and coconut milk to the garbanzo beans.
4. Use an immersion blender or a potato masher to mash the garbanzo beans to a desired consistency.
5. Serve immediately.

Sour and Sweet Beets and Kale

Prep time: 10 minutes | Cook time: 10 minutes | Serves 6
4 cups quartered beets
3 cups roughly chopped kale
1 cup sliced onion
1½ cups water
¼ cup walnut oil
¼ cup apple cider vinegar
1 tablespoon brown sugar
½ teaspoon salt
1 teaspoon black pepper
1. Combine the beets and the water in the Instant Pot.
2. Set the lid in place. Select the Manual mode and set the cooking time for 5 minutes on High Pressure. When the timer goes off, do a quick pressure release. Carefully open the lid.
3. Add in the kale and the onion.
4. Lock the lid again. Select the Manual mode and set the cooking time for 5 minutes on High Pressure. Once the timer goes off, perform a natural pressure release for 5 minutes, then release any remaining pressure.
5. While the steam is releasing, combine the walnut oil, apple cider vinegar, brown sugar, salt and black pepper. Whisk together until well blended.
6. Carefully open the lid. Remove the vegetables from the pot and thoroughly drain them.
7. Transfer the vegetables to a bowl and add in the dressing. Toss to coat.
8. Serve warm, or cover and refrigerate for several hours for a chilled side dish.

Maple Brussels Sprouts with Walnuts

Prep time: 10 minutes | Cook time: 10 to 12 minutes | Serves 4
1 tablespoon olive oil
¼ cup minced shallots

4 cups halved Brussels sprouts
1 cup orange juice
¼ cup cranberry juice
2 tablespoons maple syrup
¼ cup chopped dried cranberries
¼ cup chopped walnuts
1.	Combine the orange juice, cranberry juice and maple syrup in a small bowl. Whisk together until well blended.
2.	Press the Sauté button on the Instant Pot and heat the oil. Add in the shallots and sauté them for 3 minutes. Add the sauce and the Brussels sprouts to the pot.
3.	Set the lid in place. Select the Manual mode and set the cooking time for 4 minutes on High Pressure. When the timer goes off, do a quick pressure release. Carefully open the lid.
4.	Use a slotted spoon to remove the Brussels sprouts from the pot and transfer them to a serving plate or bowl.
5.	Press the Sauté button on the Instant Pot and cook the remaining sauce for 3 to 5 minutes, or until it thickens slightly and reduces.
6.	Pour the sauce over the Brussels sprouts and toss to coat.
7.	Garnish the Brussels sprouts with the dried cranberries and walnuts before serving.

Fresh Lemony Peas with Mint

Prep time: 5 minutes | Cook time: 2 minutes | Serves 4

4 cups fresh peas, not in pods
1 cup vegetable broth
1 tablespoon coconut oil, melted
¼ cup chopped fresh mint
¼ cup chopped fresh parsley
1 teaspoon lemon zest
1.	Combine the peas and vegetable broth in the Instant Pot.
2.	Set the lid in place. Select the Manual mode and set the cooking time for 2 minutes on High Pressure. When the timer goes off, do a quick pressure release. Carefully open the lid.
3.	Drain off the excess liquid from the peas and place them in a bowl.
4.	Drizzle the peas with the melted coconut oil and toss to coat.
5.	Add the mint, parsley and lemon zest to the bowl and stir.
6.	Serve immediately.

Easy Braised Savoy Cabbage

Prep time: 5 minutes | Cook time: 7 to 8 minutes | Serves 4

1 tablespoon olive oil
¼ cup minced shallots
¼ cup white wine
4 cups savoy cabbage
1 cup vegetable broth
1.	Press the Sauté button on the Instant Pot and heat the oil. Add in the shallots and sauté for 3 minutes. Add the white wine and cook for 1 to 2

minutes, or until the wine reduces. Add the savoy cabbage and the vegetable broth to the pot.
2.	Lock the lid. Select the Manual mode and set the cooking time for 3 minutes on High Pressure. Once the timer goes off, perform a natural pressure release for 5 minutes, then release any remaining pressure. Carefully open the lid.
3.	Serve immediately.

Simple Mexican Corn

Prep time: 5 minutes | Cook time: 3 minutes | Serves 4

4 cups fresh corn kernels
1 cup water
½ teaspoon salt
1 tablespoon olive oil
1 teaspoon cumin
1 teaspoon smoked paprika
¼ cup fresh cilantro
1 tablespoon lime juice
1.	Place the corn kernels, water and salt in the Instant Pot.
2.	Lock the lid. Select the Manual mode and set the cooking time for 3 minutes on High Pressure.
3.	While the corn is in the pot, combine the olive oil, cumin and paprika in a small saucepan or microwave-safe bowl. Heat just until warmed through and the oil is infused with the spices.
4.	Once the timer goes off, perform a natural pressure release for 5 minutes, then release any remaining pressure. Carefully open the lid. Remove the corn from the pot and drain off any excess liquid.
5.	Pour the spice-infused oil over the corn and toss to coat.
6.	Add in the cilantro and lime juice and stir.
7.	Serve immediately.

Spicy Ginger-Garlic Kale

Prep time: 5 minutes | Cook time: 6 minutes | Serves 4

1 tablespoon olive oil
5 cloves garlic
1 tablespoon fresh grated ginger
1 tablespoon crushed red pepper flakes
8 cups kale, stems removed and chopped
1½ cups vegetable broth
1 tablespoon garlic chili paste
1.	Press the Sauté button on the Instant Pot and heat the oil. Add in the garlic, ginger and crushed red pepper flakes. Sauté the mixture for 2 minutes or until highly fragrant.
2.	Add in the vegetable broth and garlic chili paste. Whisk until well blended. Add in the kale and stir.
3.	Lock the lid. Select the Manual mode and set the cooking time for 4 minutes on High Pressure. Once the timer goes off, perform a natural pressure release for 5 minutes, then release any remaining pressure. Carefully open the lid.
4.	Stir before serving.

Creamy Spinach with Mushrooms

Prep time: 10 minutes | Cook time: 10 minutes | Serves 4

1 tablespoon olive oil
1 cup sliced fennel
2 cloves garlic, crushed and minced
¼ cup white wine
10 cups fresh spinach
2 cups sliced portabella mushrooms,
1 cup coconut milk
½ cup vegetable broth
½ teaspoon salt
1 teaspoon coarse ground black pepper
1 teaspoon nutmeg
½ teaspoon thyme

1. Press the Sauté button on the Instant Pot and heat the oil. Add the fennel and garlic. Sauté the mixture for 3 minutes.
2. Add the white wine and sauté an additional 2 minutes, or until the wine reduces. Add the remaining ingredients and stir.
3. Lock the lid. Select the Manual mode and set the cooking time for 5 minutes on High Pressure. Once the timer goes off, perform a natural pressure release for 10 minutes, then release any remaining pressure. Carefully open the lid.
4. Stir before serving.

CHAPTER 5 PASTA AND RICE

Basic Tomato Rice

Prep time: 6 mins, Cook Time:5 mins, Servings: 4

- 1 tbsp. extra virgin olive oil
- 2 cups white rice, rinsed and drained
- 4½ cups water
- 1 large, ripe tomato
- Salt and pepper, to taste

1. Add olive oil, rice, and water to Instant Pot. Gently stir.
2. Place whole tomato, bottom-side up, in the middle.
3. Lock the lid. Select the Rice mode, then set the timer for 5 minutes at Low Pressure.
4. Once the timer goes off, do a natural pressure release for 3 to 5 minutes, then release any remaining pressure. Carefully open the lid.
5. Using a rice paddle, break up tomato while fluffing up rice. Season with salt and pepper.
6. Serve immediately.

Black Olives in Tomato Rice

Prep time: 12 mins, Cook Time:5 mins, Servings: 4

- ¼ tsp. balsamic vinegar
- 4½ cups water
- ¼ cup black olives in brine rings
- 1 cup ripe tomato, deseeded and minced
- 2 cups Basmati rice, rinsed and drained
- Salt and pepper, to taste

1. Pour all the ingredients into Instant Pot. Gently stir.
2. Lock the lid. Select the Rice mode, then set the timer for 5 minutes at Low Pressure.
3. Once the timer goes off, do a natural pressure release for 3 to 5 minutes, then release any remaining pressure. Carefully open the lid.
4. Using a rice paddle, fluff up rice.
5. Serve warm.

Cauliflower and Pineapple Rice

Prep time: 20 mins, Cook Time: 20 mins, Servings: 4

- 2 tsps. extra virgin olive oil
- 2 cups jasmine rice
- 1 cauliflower, florets separated and chopped
- ½ pineapple, peeled and chopped
- 4 cups water
- Salt and ground black pepper, to taste

1. Mix all the ingredients in your Instant Pot and stir to incorporate.
2. Lock the lid. Select the Manual mode and cook for 20 minutes at Low Pressure.
3. Once cooking is complete, do a natural pressure release for 10 minutes, then release any remaining pressure. Carefully open the lid.
4. Using a fork to fluff the rice and serve in bowls.

Chickpea and Tomato Rice

Prep time: 12 mins, Cook Time:25 mins, Servings: 4

- ½ cup canned chickpeas
- 4½ cups water
- 1 cup deseeded and minced ripe tomato
- Salt and pepper, to taste
- 2 cups rinsed and drained white rice

1. Pour all the ingredients into Instant Pot. Gently stir.
2. Lock the lid. Select the Rice mode, then set the timer for 5 minutes at Low Pressure.
3. Once the timer goes off, do a quick pressure release. Carefully open the lid.
4. Using a rice paddle, fluff up rice.
5. Serve immediately.

Chipotle-Style Cilantro Rice

Prep time: 20 mins, Cook Time: 20 mins, Servings: 4

- 2 cups brown rice, rinsed
- 4 small bay leaves
- 2¾ cups water
- 1½ tbsps. olive oil
- ½ cup chopped cilantro
- 1 lime, juiced
- 1 tsp. salt

1. Place the brown rice, bay leaves, and water in the Instant Pot.
2. Lock the lid. Select the Rice mode and cook for 20 minutes at High Pressure.
3. Once cooking is complete, do a natural pressure release for 10 minutes, then release any remaining pressure. Carefully open the lid.
4. Add the olive oil, cilantro, lime juice, and salt to the pot and stir until well combined. Serve warm.

Copycat Cilantro Lime Rice

Prep time: 3 minutes; Cook Time: 10 mins, Servings: 2

- 1¼ cups water
- 1 cup white rice
- Salt, to taste
- 3 tbsps. fresh chopped cilantro
- 1 tbsp. fresh lime juice
- 2 tbsps. vegetable oil

1. Mix the rice and water together in the Instant Pot and stir to combine. Season with salt.
2. Lock the lid. Select the Rice mode, then set the timer for 5 minutes at Low Pressure.
3. Once the timer goes off, do a natural pressure release for 3 to 5 minutes. Carefully open the lid.
4. Use a quick release to get rid of the remaining pressure. Use a fork to fluff up the rice.
5. Mix the lime juice, cilantro, and oil in a bowl.
6. Whisk well and mix into the rice. Serve immediately.

Wild Rice and Basmati Pilaf

Prep time: 5 minutes | Cook time: 35 minutes | Serves 6

2 tablespoon olive oil
2 brown onions, minced
2 cloves garlic, minced
12 ounces (340 g) mushrooms, sliced
½ teaspoon salt
6 sprigs fresh thyme
2 cups broth
2 cups wild rice and basmati rice mixture
½ cup pine nuts
½ cup minced parsley
1.	Set your Instant Pot to Sauté. Add the olive oil and onions and cook for 6 minutes.
2.	Add minced garlic and cook for 1 minute more. Place the remaining ingredients, except for nuts and parsley, into the Instant Pot and stir well.
3.	Lock the lid. Select the Manual mode and set the cooking time for 28 minutes at High Pressure.
4.	When the timer beeps, perform a natural pressure release for 15 minutes, then release any remaining pressure. Carefully remove the lid.
5.	Sprinkle with the pine nuts and parsley, then serve.

Jollof Rice

Prep time: 10 minutes | Cook time: 22 minutes | Serves 4

1 tablespoon corn oil
2 dried bay leaves
1 onion, finely chopped
2 garlic cloves, finely chopped
1 teaspoon finely chopped fresh ginger
1 jalapeño, seeded and finely chopped
2 tomatoes, coarsely chopped
2 tablespoons tomato paste
1½ teaspoons kosher salt
1 teaspoon paprika
½ teaspoon curry powder
1 cup chopped carrots
1 cup cauliflower florets (7 or 8 florets)
1 cup short-grain white rice, rinsed
2 cups water
1.	Press the Sauté button on the Instant Pot and heat the oil.
2.	Once hot, add the bay leaves, onion, garlic, ginger, and jalapeños, and sauté for 5 minutes, or until the onion is translucent.
3.	Stir in the tomatoes, tomato paste, and salt. Loosely place the lid on top, and cook for 3 minutes, or until the tomatoes are softened. Mix in the paprika and curry powder, then stir in the carrots and cauliflower. Add the rice and water and stir well.
4.	Secure the lid. Select the Rice mode and set the cooking time for 12 minutes at Low Pressure.
5.	Once cooking is complete, do a natural pressure release for 10 minutes, then release any remaining pressure. Carefully open the lid.
6.	Let the rice cool for 15 minutes. Remove the bay leaves. Using a fork, gently fluff the rice and serve hot.

Confetti Rice

Prep time: 5 minutes | Cook time: 12 minutes | Serves 4

3 tablespoons butter
1 small onion, chopped
1 cup long-grain white rice
3 cups frozen peas, thawed
1 cup vegetable broth
¼ cup lemon juice
2 cloves garlic, minced
1 tablespoon cumin powder
½ teaspoon salt
½ teaspoon black pepper
1.	Set your Instant Pot to Sauté and melt the butter.
2.	Add the onion and sauté for 3 minutes until soft. Add the remaining ingredients to the Instant Pot, stirring well.
3.	Secure the lid. Select the Manual mode and set the cooking time for 8 minutes at High Pressure.
4.	Once cooking is complete, do a quick pressure release. Carefully open the lid.
5.	Fluff the rice and serve hot.

Vegetarian Thai Pineapple Fried Rice

Prep time: 10 minutes | Cook time: 10 minutes | Serves 4

1 tablespoon corn oil
3 tablespoons cashews
¼ cup finely chopped onion
¼ cup finely chopped scallions, white parts only
2 green Thai chiles, finely chopped
1 cup canned pineapple chunks
2 tablespoons roughly chopped fresh basil leaves
½ teaspoon curry powder
¼ teaspoon ground turmeric
2 teaspoons soy sauce
1 teaspoon kosher salt
1 cup steamed short-grain white rice
1¼ cups water
1.	Press the Sauté button on the Instant Pot and heat the oil.
2.	Once hot, add the cashews and stir for 1 minute. Add the onion, scallions, and chiles, and sauté for 3 to 4 minutes, until the onion is translucent.
3.	Mix in the pineapple, basil, curry powder, turmeric, soy sauce, and salt. Add the rice and water and stir to combine.
4.	Secure the lid. Select the Manual mode and set the cooking time for 3 minutes at High Pressure.
5.	Once cooking is complete, do a natural pressure release for 3 minutes, then release any remaining pressure. Carefully open the lid.
6.	Let the rice rest for 15 minutes. Remove the bay leaves. Using a fork, fluff the rice and serve hot.

Cinnamon Brown Rice

Prep time: 5 minutes | Cook time: 25 minutes | Serves 4

1 tablespoon olive oil
3 cloves garlic, crushed and minced
½ cup chopped sweet yellow onion

½ teaspoon cumin
½ teaspoon nutmeg
½ teaspoon cinnamon
½ teaspoon sweet paprika
½ teaspoon sea salt
1½ cups brown rice
2½ cups vegetable broth
½ cup chopped fresh parsley
1. Set your Instant Pot to Sauté and heat the olive oil.
2. Add the garlic, onion, cumin, nutmeg, cinnamon, sweet paprika, and sea salt and sauté for 2 to 3 minutes, stirring frequently, or until the onions are softened.
3. Add the rice and vegetable broth to the Instant Pot.
4. Secure the lid. Select the Manual mode and set the cooking time for 20 minutes at High Pressure.
5. Once cooking is complete, do a quick pressure release. Carefully open the lid.
6. Fluff the rice with a fork and stir in the fresh parsley before serving.

Creamy Mushroom Alfredo Rice

Prep time: 5 minutes | Cook time: 25 minutes | Serves 4

2 tablespoons olive oil
¾ cup finely chopped onion
2 garlic cloves, minced
1 cup rice
2¾ cups vegetable broth
1½ tablespoons fresh lemon juice
Salt and black pepper, to taste
2 ounces (57 g) creamy mushroom Alfredo sauce
¼ cup coarsely chopped walnuts
1. Set your Instant Pot to Sauté. Add the oil, onion, and garlic to the pot and sauté for 3 minutes. Stir in the rice and broth.
2. Secure the lid. Select the Manual mode and set the cooking time for 22 minutes at High Pressure.
3. Once cooking is complete, do a natural pressure release for 10 minutes, then release any remaining pressure. Carefully open the lid.
4. Add lemon juice, salt, pepper, and sauce and stir to combine. Garnish with the chopped walnuts and serve.

Spaghetti with Veggie Bolognese

Prep time: 10 minutes | Cook time: 10 minutes | Serves 6

Pasta:
1 teaspoon extra-virgin olive oil
1 teaspoon kosher salt
8 ounces (227 g) spaghetti pasta
5 cups water
Sauce:
1 tablespoon extra-virgin olive oil
1 onion, minced
5 garlic cloves, minced
5 mushrooms, roughly minced
2 cups canned crushed tomatoes
1 cup vegetable broth
½ cup dried green lentils

¼ cup finely minced basil leaves
1 teaspoon kosher salt
2 teaspoons freshly ground black pepper
½ cup shredded Parmesan cheese
1. Add all the ingredients for the pasta to the Instant Pot and stir to combine.
2. Lock the lid. Select the Manual mode and set the cooking time for 2 minutes on High Pressure. Once the timer goes off, perform a natural pressure release for 5 minutes, then release any remaining pressure. Carefully open the lid.
3. Drain the pasta and transfer to a bowl..
4. Press the Sauté button on the Instant Pot and heat the oil. Add the onion and garlic to the pot and sauté for 3 minutes. Stir in the remaining ingredients, except for the cheese.
5. Lock the lid. Select the Manual mode and set the cooking time for 5 minutes on High Pressure. Once the timer goes off, perform a natural pressure release for 10 minutes, then release any remaining pressure. Carefully open the lid.
6. Using a potato masher, mash the lentils and tomatoes until it reaches a chunky texture.
7. Stir in the spaghetti, sprinkle with the cheese and serve hot.

Penne Pasta with Tomato-Vodka Sauce

Prep time: 5 minutes | Cook time: 4 minutes | Serves 2

½ cup uncooked penne pasta
½ cup crushed tomatoes
1 cup water
⅛ cup coconut oil
1 tablespoon vodka
1 teaspoon garlic powder
½ teaspoon salt
¼ teaspoon paprika
½ cup coconut cream
⅛ cup minced cilantro
1. Add all the ingredients, except for the coconut cream and cilantro, to the Instant Pot and stir to combine.
2. Set the lid in place. Select the Manual mode and set the cooking time for 4 minutes on High Pressure. When the timer goes off, do a quick pressure release. Carefully open the lid.
3. Stir in the coconut cream and fresh cilantro and serve hot.

Creamy Broccoli Fettucine Pasta

Prep time: 10 minutes | Cook time: 8 to 9 minutes | Serves 8

1 teaspoon olive oil
3 garlic cloves, minced
2 cups minced broccoli
4¼ cups water, divided
1 pound (454 g) fettucine pasta
1 tablespoon butter
Salt, to taste
1 cup heavy cream
½ cup shredded Parmesan cheese
Ground black pepper, to taste
2 tablespoons minced parsley

1.   Press the Sauté button on the Instant Pot and heat the oil. Add the garlic to the pot and sauté for 1 minute, or until fragrant. Stir in the broccoli and ¼ cup of the water.
2.   Set the lid in place. Select the Manual mode and set the cooking time for 3 minutes on High Pressure. When the timer goes off, do a quick pressure release. Carefully open the lid.
3.   Drain the broccoli and transfer to a bowl.
4.   Add the remaining 4 cups of the water, pasta, butter and salt to the Instant Pot and stir to combine.
5.   Set the lid in place. Select the Manual mode and set the cooking time for 3 minutes on High Pressure. When the timer goes off, do a quick pressure release. Carefully open the lid. Drain any excess liquid from the pot.
6.   Select the Sauté mode and stir in the cooked broccoli, heavy cream, Parmesan, salt and black pepper. Cook for 1 to 2 minutes.
7.   Serve garnished with the parsley.

Cabbage and Mushroom Pasta

Prep time: 10 minutes | Cook time: 5 minutes | Serves 4
4 cups chopped green cabbage
2 cups dried bowtie pasta
1½ cups water
1 cup diced onion
1 cup sliced button mushrooms
2 tablespoons butter, melted
1 teaspoon ground marjoram
1 teaspoon kosher salt
1 teaspoon black pepper
1 cup frozen peas and carrots
1.   Add all the ingredients, except for the frozen peas and carrots, to the Instant Pot and stir to combine.
2.   Scatter the peas and carrots on top of the mixture. Do not stir.
3.   Lock the lid. Select the Manual mode and set the cooking time for 5 minutes on High Pressure. Once the timer goes off, perform a natural pressure release for 10 minutes, then release any remaining pressure. Carefully open the lid.
4.   Spoon into individual bowls and serve.

Baked Eggplant Parmesan Pasta

Prep time: 10 minutes | Cook time: 9 to 10 minutes | Serves 6 to 8
1 (14-ounce / 397-g) can diced tomatoes
3 cloves garlic, minced
4 cups peeled, chopped eggplant
1½ cups water
1 cup diced onion
3 tablespoons unsalted butter, divided
1 tablespoon dried Italian seasoning
1 tablespoon tomato paste
1½ teaspoons kosher salt
1 teaspoon red pepper flakes
9 ounces (255 g) penne pasta
½ cup bread crumbs
$^1/_3$ cup shredded Parmesan cheese

1½ cups bocconcini
1.   In the Instant Pot, stir together the tomatoes, garlic, eggplant, water, onion, 2 tablespoons of the butter, Italian seasoning, tomato paste, salt and red pepper flakes. Stir in the pasta.
2.   Lock the lid. Select the Manual mode and set the cooking time for 7 minutes on High Pressure. Once the timer goes off, perform a natural pressure release for 10 minutes, then release any remaining pressure. Carefully open the lid.
3.   Meanwhile, in a small skillet, melt the remaining 1 tablespoon of the butter over medium heat. Add the bread crumbs and mix well. Remove from the heat and let cool. Mix with the Parmesan cheese and set aside.
4.   Preheat the broiler to 500ºF (260ºC).
5.   Add the bocconcini to the pasta and transfer the pasta to a casserole dish. Sprinkle with the bread crumb mixture and broil for 2 to 3 minutes.
6.   Serve hot.

Mascarpone-Mushroom Pasta

Prep time: 10 minutes | Cook time: 5 minutes | Serves 4
2 tablespoons butter
3 cloves garlic, minced
1 teaspoon dried thyme
½ teaspoon red pepper flakes
8 ounces (227 g) cremini mushrooms, trimmed and sliced
1 cup chopped onion
1¾ cups water
1 teaspoon kosher salt
1 teaspoon black pepper
8 ounces (227 g) fettuccine, broken in half
8 ounces (227 g) Mascarpone cheese
1 cup shredded Parmesan cheese
2 teaspoons fresh thyme leaves, for garnish
1.   Press the Sauté button on the Instant Pot and melt the butter. Add the garlic, thyme, and red pepper flakes to the pot and sauté for 30 seconds. Stir in the mushrooms, onion, water, salt and pepper.
2.   Add the fettuccine, pushing it down into the liquid. Add the Mascarpone on top of the pasta. Do not stir.
3.   Lock the lid. Select the Manual mode and set the cooking time for 5 minutes on High Pressure. Once the timer goes off, perform a natural pressure release for 5 minutes, then release any remaining pressure. Carefully open the lid.
4.   Stir in the Parmesan cheese.
5.   Divide the pasta among four dishes, garnish with the thyme and serve.

Vinegary Brown Rice Noodles

Prep time: 5 minutes | Cook time: 3 minutes | Serves 6
8 ounces (227 g) uncooked brown rice noodles
2 cups water
½ cup soy sauce
2 tablespoons brown sugar
2 tablespoons white vinegar
2 tablespoons butter

1 tablespoon chili garlic paste
2 red bell peppers, thinly sliced
Topping:
Green onions
Peanuts
Sesame seeds
1.   Add all the ingredients, except for the red bell peppers, to the Instant Pot and stir to combine.
2.   Set the lid in place. Select the Manual mode and set the cooking time for 3 minutes on High Pressure. When the timer goes off, do a quick pressure release. Carefully open the lid.
3.   Stir in the red bell peppers. Sprinkle with the green onions, peanuts and sesame seeds. Serve immediately.

Penne Pasta with Zucchini

Prep time: 10 minutes | Cook time: 10 minutes | Serves 5

1 tablespoon butter
1 yellow onion, thinly sliced
1 shallot, finely chopped
Salt and black pepper, to taste
2 garlic cloves, minced
12 mushrooms, thinly sliced
1 zucchini, thinly sliced
Pinch of dried oregano
Pinch of dried basil
2 cups water
1 cup vegetable stock
2 tablespoons soy sauce
Splash of sherry wine
15 ounces (425 g) penne pasta
5 ounces (142 g) tomato paste
1.   Press the Sauté button on the Instant Pot and melt the butter. Add the onion, shallot, salt and pepper to the pot and sauté for 3 minutes. Add the garlic and continue to sauté for 1 minute.
2.   Stir in the mushrooms, zucchini, oregano and basil. Cook for 1 minute more. Pour in the water, stock, soy sauce and wine. Add the penne, tomato paste, salt and pepper.
3.   Set the lid in place. Select the Manual mode and set the cooking time for 5 minutes on High Pressure. When the timer goes off, do a quick pressure release. Carefully open the lid.
4.   Serve hot.

Fusilli Pasta with Spinach and Pine Nuts

Prep time: 5 minutes | Cook time: 12 minutes | Serves 4

1 tablespoon butter
2 garlic cloves, crushed
1 pound (454 g) spinach
1 pound (454 g) fusilli pasta
Salt and black pepper, to taste
Water, as needed
2 garlic cloves, chopped
¼ cup chopped pine nuts
Grated cheese, for serving
1.   Press the Sauté button on the Instant Pot and melt the butter. Add the crushed garlic and spinach to the pot and sauté for 6 minutes. Add the

pasta, salt and pepper. Pour in the water to cover the pasta and mix.
2.   Set the lid in place. Select the Manual mode and set the cooking time for 6 minutes on Low Pressure. When the timer goes off, do a quick pressure release. Carefully open the lid.
3.   Stir in the chopped garlic and nuts. Garnish with the cheese and serve.

Creamy Marsala Tofu Pasta

Prep time: 5 minutes | Cook time: 15 minutes | Serves 2

1 tablespoon butter
2 cups sliced mushrooms
1 small onion, diced
½ cup sun-dried tomatoes
½ cup tofu, diced into chunks
½ teaspoon garlic powder
1 cup white Marsala wine
1½ cups vegetable broth
1 cup Pennette pasta
½ cup grated goat cheese
¼ cup cream
1.   Press the Sauté button on the Instant Pot and melt the butter. Add the mushrooms and onion to the pot and cook for 4 minutes. Add the tomatoes and tofu and cook for 3 minutes.
2.   Add the garlic powder and cook for 1 minute. Pour in the white wine and cook for 1 minute. Stir in the broth. Add the pasta and don't stir.
3.   Set the lid in place. Select the Manual mode and set the cooking time for 6 minutes on High Pressure. When the timer goes off, do a quick pressure release. Carefully open the lid.
4.   Add the cheese and cream and let sit for 5 minutes. Serve hot.

Parmesan Mushroom-Spinach Pasta

Prep time: 5 minutes | Cook time: 10 minutes | Serves 4

1 tablespoon oil
8 ounces (227 g) mushrooms, minced
½ teaspoon kosher salt
½ teaspoon black ground pepper
8 ounces (227 g) uncooked spaghetti pasta
1¾ cups water
5 ounces (142 g) spinach
½ cup pesto
$^1/_3$ cup grated Parmesan cheese
1.   Press the Sauté button on the Instant Pot and heat the oil. Add the mushrooms, salt and pepper to the pot and sauté for 5 minutes. Add the pasta and water.
2.   Set the lid in place. Select the Manual mode and set the cooking time for 5 minutes on High Pressure. When the timer goes off, do a quick pressure release. Carefully open the lid.
3.   Stir in the spinach, pesto, and cheese. Serve immediately.

Lemony Spinach Pasta

Prep time: 5 minutes | Cook time: 4 minutes | Serves 6

1 pound (454 g) fusilli pasta
4 cups chopped fresh spinach
4 cups vegetable broth
2 cloves garlic, crushed and minced
1 cup plain coconut milk
1 teaspoon lemon zest
1 teaspoon lemon juice
¼ cup chopped fresh parsley
1 tablespoon chopped fresh mint
½ teaspoon sea salt
½ teaspoon coarse ground black pepper
1.   Stir together the fusilli pasta, spinach, vegetable broth and garlic in the Instant Pot.
2.   Set the lid in place. Select the Manual mode and set the cooking time for 4 minutes on High Pressure.
3.   Meanwhile, whisk together the coconut milk, lemon zest and lemon juice in a bowl.
4.   When the timer goes off, do a quick pressure release. Carefully open the lid. Drain off any excess liquid that might remain.
5.   Add the coconut milk mixture to the pasta, along with the parsley and mint. Season with salt and pepper.
6.   Stir gently and let sit for 5 minutes before serving.

Sumptuous One-Pot Garden Pasta

Prep time: 10 minutes | Cook time: 11 minutes | Serves 6
1 tablespoon olive oil
1 cup leeks, sliced thin
3 cloves garlic, crushed and minced
2 cups sliced portabella mushrooms
¼ cup dry red wine
2 cups sliced summer squash
1 teaspoon oregano
1 teaspoon rosemary
1 teaspoon sea salt
1 teaspoon coarse ground black pepper
1 pound (454 g) small pasta of choice
2 cups chopped tomatoes
2 cups vegetable broth
1 cup water
1 tablespoon tomato paste
½ cup chopped fresh basil
1.   Press the Sauté button on the Instant Pot and heat the oil. Add the leeks and garlic to the pot and sauté for 3 minutes. Add the mushrooms and red wine and continue to sauté for 3 minutes, or until the wine reduces.
2.   Add the summer squash and season with the oregano, rosemary, sea salt and black pepper. Stir in the remaining ingredients, except for the fresh basil.
3.   Set the lid in place. Select the Manual mode and set the cooking time for 5 minutes on High Pressure. When the timer goes off, do a quick pressure release. Carefully open the lid.
4.   Serve garnished with the fresh basil.

Simple Tomato Pasta

Prep time: 5 minutes | Cook time: 8 to 10 minutes | Serves 6
1 tablespoon olive oil
¼ cup minced shallots
¼ cup dry red wine
1 pound (454 g) spaghetti pasta, broken in half
4 cups vegetable broth
3 cups chopped tomatoes
½ cup chopped fresh basil
½ teaspoon salt
1 teaspoon black pepper
1.   Press the Sauté button on the Instant Pot and heat the oil. Add the scallions to the pot and sauté for 1 to 2 minutes, or until tender. Pour in the red wine and continue to cook for 2 to 3 minutes, or until the wine reduces. Stir in the remaining ingredients.
2.   Set the lid in place. Select the Manual mode and set the cooking time for 5 minutes on High Pressure. When the timer goes off, do a quick pressure release. Carefully open the lid.
3.   Stir before serving.

Creamy Kimchi Pasta

Prep time: 5 minutes | Cook time: 4 to 5 minutes | Serves 4 to 6
8 ounces (227 g) dried small pasta
$2^{1}/_{3}$ cups vegetable stock
2 garlic cloves, minced
½ red onion, sliced
½ to 1 teaspoon salt
1¼ cups kimchi, with any larger pieces chopped
½ cup coconut cream
1.   In the Instant Pot, combine the pasta, stock, garlic, red onion and salt.
2.   Set the lid in place. Select the Manual mode and set the cooking time for 1 minute on High Pressure. When the timer goes off, do a quick pressure release. Carefully open the lid.
3.   Select Sauté mode. Stir in the kimchi. Simmer for 3 to 4 minutes. Stir in the coconut cream and serve.

Tomato Basil Campanelle Pasta

Prep time: 5 minutes | Cook time: 2 minutes | Serves 2
2 cups dried campanelle pasta
1¾ cups vegetable stock
½ teaspoon salt
2 tomatoes, cut into large dices
1 or 2 pinches red pepper flakes
½ teaspoon dried oregano
½ teaspoon garlic powder
10 to 12 fresh sweet basil leaves, finely chopped
Freshly ground black pepper, to taste
1.   In the Instant Pot, stir together the pasta, stock, and salt. Spread the tomatoes on top.
2.   Set the lid in place. Select the Manual mode and set the cooking time for 2 minutes on High Pressure. When the timer goes off, do a quick pressure release. Carefully open the lid.
3.   Stir in the red pepper flakes, oregano and garlic powder.

4.   Sprinkle the basil and pepper. Serve immediately.

Lemony Bow Tie Pasta

Prep time: 5 minutes | Cook time: 11 to 12 minutes | Serves 4 to 5
1 Vidalia onion, diced
2 garlic cloves, minced
1 tablespoon olive oil
3½ cups water
10 ounces (284 g) bow tie pasta
Grated zest and juice of 1 lemon
¼ cup black olives, pitted and chopped
Salt and freshly ground black pepper, to taste
1.   Press the Sauté button on the Instant Pot and heat the oil. Add the onion and garlic to the pot. Cook for 7 to 8 minutes, stirring occasionally, or until the onion is lightly browned.
2.   Add the water and pasta.
3.   Set the lid in place. Select the Manual mode and set the cooking time for 4 minutes on High Pressure. When the timer goes off, do a quick pressure release. Carefully open the lid.
4.   Stir the pasta and drain any excess water. Stir in the lemon zest and juice and the olives. Season with salt and pepper.
5.   Serve immediately.

Tomato and Black Bean Rotini

Prep time: 5 minutes | Cook time: 9 to 10 minutes | Serves 4
1 red onion, diced
1 to 2 teaspoons olive oil
1 to 2 teaspoons ground chipotle pepper
1 (28-ounce / 794-g) can crushed tomatoes
8 ounces (227 g) rotini
1 cup water
1½ cups fresh corn
1½ cups cooked black beans
Salt and freshly ground black pepper, to taste
1.   Press the Sauté button on the Instant Pot and heat the oil. Add the red onion and cook for 5 to 6 minutes, stirring occasionally, or until the onion is lightly browned.
2.   Stir in the chipotle pepper, tomatoes, rotini and water.
3.   Lock the lid. Select the Manual mode and set the cooking time for 4 minutes on High Pressure. Once the timer goes off, perform a natural pressure release for 4 minutes, then release any remaining pressure. Carefully open the lid.
4.   Stir in the corn and black beans. Taste and season with salt and pepper.
5.   Serve immediately.

Basil Tomato Pasta

Prep time: 10 minutes | Cook time: 10 minutes | Serves 4
1 teaspoon olive oil, plus more for drizzling
1 large Vidalia onion, diced
10 ounces (284 g) penne, rotini, or fusilli
2 cups water
¼ cup sun-dried tomatoes, chopped
½ teaspoon salt, plus more as needed
1 cup cherry tomatoes, halved or quartered
2 tablespoons finely chopped fresh basil
½ teaspoon garlic powder (optional)
Freshly ground black pepper, to taste
1.   Set your Instant Pot to Sauté and heat 1 teaspoon of olive oil.
2.   Add the onion and sauté for 4 to 5 minutes, stirring occasionally, until the onion is tender.
3.   Add the pasta, water, tomatoes, and a pinch of salt. Stir well.
4.   Secure the lid. Select the Manual mode and set the cooking time for 4 minutes at High Pressure.
5.   Once cooking is complete, do a natural pressure release for 5 minutes, then release any remaining pressure. Carefully open the lid.
6.   Set your Instant Pot to Sauté again and stir in the cherry tomatoes, basil, garlic powder (if desired), and another drizzle of olive oil.
7.   Taste and season with more salt and pepper, as needed. Serve warm.

Creamy Tomato Pasta

Prep time: 5 minutes | Cook time: 9 minutes | Serves 4
1 (28-ounce / 794-g) can crushed tomatoes
10 ounces (284 g) penne, rotini, or fusilli (about 3 cups)
1 tablespoon dried basil
½ teaspoon garlic powder
½ teaspoon salt, plus more as needed
1½ cups water
1 cup unsweetened coconut milk
2 cups chopped fresh spinach (optional)
Freshly ground black pepper, to taste
1.   Combine the tomatoes, pasta, basil, garlic powder, salt, and water in the Instant Pot.
2.   Secure the lid. Select the Manual mode and set the cooking time for 4 minutes at High Pressure.
3.   Once cooking is complete, do a natural pressure release for 5 minutes, then release any remaining pressure. Carefully open the lid.
4.   Stir in the milk and spinach (if desired). Taste and season with more salt and pepper, as needed.
5.   Set your Instant Pot to Sauté and let cook for 4 to 5 minutes, or until the sauce is thickened and the greens are wilt. Serve warm.

CHAPTER 6 GRAINS AND BEANS

Almond Arborio Risotto

Prep time: 10 mins, Cook Time: 5 mins, Servings: 2

- ½ cup Arborio rice
- 2 cups vanilla almond milk
- 1 tsp. vanilla extract
- 2 tbsps. agave syrup
- ¼ cup toasted almond flakes, for garnish

1. Add all the ingredients, except for the almond flakes, to the Instant Pot. Stir to mix well.
2. Lock the lid. Set to the Manual mode, then set the timer for 5 minutes at Low Pressure.
3. Once the timer goes off, perform a natural pressure release. Carefully open the lid.
4. Serve the risotto with almond flakes immediately.

Butternut Squash Arborio Risotto

Prep time: 10 mins, Cook Time: 12 mins, Servings: 4

- 1 tbsp. olive oil
- 2 garlic cloves, whole
- 1 sprig sage, leaves removed
- ½ butternut squash, diced
- 1 cup Arborio rice
- ½ tsp. freshly ground nutmeg
- 2 tbsps. white wine
- 1 tsp. sea salt
- 2 cups water

1. Grease the Instant Pot with olive oil.
2. Set the pot to Sauté mode, then add the garlic and sage. Sauté for 2 minutes or until fragrant.
3. Add the butternut squash and sauté for 5 minutes.
4. Add the remaining ingredients. Stir to mix well.
5. Lock the lid. Set to the Manual mode, then set the timer for 5 minutes at Low Pressure.
6. Once the timer goes off, perform a natural pressure release. Carefully open the lid.
7. Serve immediately.

Quinoa Risotto

Prep time: 6 mins, Cook Time: 3 hours, Servings: 4

- ¾ cup diced onion
- 1 garlic clove, minced
- 1 tbsp. butter
- Salt and pepper, to taste
- 2½ cups chicken broth
- 1 cup rinsed quinoa
- ¼ cup shredded Parmesan cheese

1. Combine the onion, garlic, and butter in a microwave-safe bowl.
2. Microwave for 5 minutes, stirring every 90 seconds.
3. Put the mixture in the Instant Pot.
4. Add the salt, pepper, broth, and quinoa and stir to combine.
5. Lock the lid. Select the Slow Cook mode, then set the timer for 3 hours at High Pressure.
6. Once the timer goes off, perform a natural release for 10 minutes, then release any remaining pressure. Carefully open the lid.
7. Mix the Parmesan into the mixture. Taste and adjust the seasoning, if needed.

Parmesan Risotto

Prep time: 6 mins, Cook Time: 20 mins, Servings: 4

- 4 cups chicken broth, divided
- 4 tbsps. butter
- 1 small onion, diced
- 2 garlic cloves, minced
- 1½ cups Arborio rice
- Salt and pepper, to taste
- ¼ cup shredded Parmesan cheese

1. Set the Instant Pot to sauté and melt the butter.
2. Mix the onions in and let them cook for 2 minutes until they have become soft.
3. Add the garlic and rice and stir. Cook for 1 more minute.
4. Add 1 cup of broth and cook about 3 minutes, or until the broth is absorbed.
5. Add 3 cups of broth, salt, and pepper.
6. Sprinkle with Parmesan cheese.
7. Lock the lid. Select the Manual mode, then set the timer for 10 minutes at Low Pressure.
8. Once the timer goes off, perform a natural release for 5 minutes, then release any remaining pressure. Carefully open the lid.
9. Ladle the rice into bowls and serve.

Khichdi Dal

Prep time: 4 minutes; Cook Time: 12 mins, Servings: 4

- 1 tbsp. butter
- 2 cups water
- ¼ tsp. salt
- 1 tsp. Balti seasoning
- 1 cup khichdi mix

1. Set the Instant Pot to Sauté. Add the butter and heat to melt.
2. Mix in the Balti seasoning and cook for 1 minute.
3. Add the Khichdi mix, water, and salt to the pot.
4. Lock the lid. Select the Porridge mode, then set the timer for 10 minutes at High Pressure.
5. Once the timer goes off, do a natural pressure release for 3 to 5 minutes. Carefully open the lid.
6. Fluff the khichdi with a fork and serve warm.

Couscous with Spinach and Tomato

Prep time: 12 mins, Cook Time: 6 mins, Servings: 4

- 1 tbsp. butter
- 1 cup couscous
- 1¼ cups vegetable broth
- ½ cup chopped spinach, blanched
- 1½ tomatoes, chopped

1. Set the Instant Pot to Sauté mode, then add and melt the butter.
2. Add the couscous and sauté for 1 minute.
3. Pour in the vegetable broth. Stir to mix well.
4. Lock the lid. Set to the Manual mode, then set the timer for 5 minutes at High Pressure.
5. Once the timer goes off, perform a quick pressure release. Carefully open the lid.
6. Mix in the spinach and tomatoes, then serve warm.

Chili Polenta

Prep time: 2 minutes | Cook time: 9 minutes | Serves 6

10 cups water
3 cups polenta
3 teaspoons salt
3 tablespoons red paprika flakes

1. Combine the water, polenta, salt, and red paprika flakes in the Instant Pot.
2. Lock the lid. Select the Manual mode and set the cooking time for 9 minutes at High Pressure.
3. When the timer beeps, perform a natural pressure release for 15 minutes, then release any remaining pressure. Carefully remove the lid.
4. Cool for 5 minutes and serve.

Pea and Mint Risotto

Prep time: 5 minutes | Cook time: 20 minutes | Serves 2

2 tablespoons coconut oil
1 onion, peeled and diced
½ teaspoon garlic powder
½ cup barley
1 cup vegetable broth, divided
Salt and pepper, to taste
½ cup fresh peas
¼ teaspoon lime zest
¼ cup chopped fresh mint leaves

1. Press the Sauté button on the Instant Pot and heat the oil.
2. Add the onion and stir-fry for 5 minutes.
3. Add garlic powder and barley and cook for 1 minute more.
4. Pour in ½ cup of vegetable broth and stir for 3 minutes until it is absorbed by barley.
5. Add the remaining ½ cup of broth, salt, and pepper.
6. Secure the lid. Select the Manual mode and set the cooking time for 10 minutes at High Pressure.
7. Once cooking is complete, do a natural pressure release for 10 minutes, then release any remaining pressure. Carefully open the lid.
8. Stir in peas, lime zest, and mint and let sit for 3 minutes until heated through. Serve immediately.

Easy Vegetable Biryani

Prep time: 10 minutes | Cook time: 15 minutes | Serves 6

2 tablespoons butter
3 cardamom seeds
3 whole cloves
2 dried bay leaves
1 (2-inch) cinnamon stick
1 onion, finely chopped
2 garlic cloves, finely chopped
2 teaspoons finely chopped fresh ginger
1½ cups roughly chopped fresh mint leaves
2 tomatoes, finely chopped
1½ teaspoons kosher salt
2 teaspoons ground coriander
1 teaspoon red chili powder
2 tablespoons plain Greek yogurt, plus more for serving
2 cups mixed vegetables
4 tablespoons finely chopped fresh cilantro, divided
1½ cups basmati rice
2¼ cups water

1. Set your Instant Pot to Sauté and melt the butter.
2. Add the cardamom, cloves, bay leaves, and cinnamon stick. Stir-fry for 30 seconds, then add the onion, garlic, ginger, and mint leaves. Sauté for 3 to 4 minutes until the onion is translucent.
3. Stir in the tomatoes and salt. Loosely place the lid on top and cook for 3 minutes, or until the tomatoes are softened.
4. Add the coriander, chili powder, and yogurt. Mix well and cook for 2 minutes more. Add the mixed vegetables and 2 tablespoons of cilantro, and mix well. Stir in the rice and water.
5. Secure the lid. Select the Manual mode and set the cooking time for 4 minutes at High Pressure.
6. Once cooking is complete, do a natural pressure release for 3 minutes, then release any remaining pressure. Carefully open the lid.
7. Let the rice cool for 15 minutes and remove the bay leaves. Using a fork, fluff the rice and stir in the remaining 2 tablespoons of cilantro. Serve hot with additional yogurt.

Mushroom Barley Risotto

Prep time: 10 minutes | Cook time: 40 minutes | Serves 6

3 tablespoons butter
1 onion, finely chopped
1 cup coarsely chopped shiitake mushrooms
1 cup coarsely chopped cremini mushrooms
1 cup coarsely chopped brown bella mushrooms
1 teaspoon kosher salt
1 teaspoon freshly ground black pepper
1 teaspoon Italian dried herb seasoning
1 cup pearl barley
1 (32-ounce / 907-g) container vegetable broth
½ cup shredded Parmesan cheese

1. Set your Instant Pot to Sauté and melt the butter.
2. Add the onion and cook for about 3 minutes, or until the onion is translucent. Mix in the mushrooms, salt, pepper, and Italian seasoning. Cook

for 5 to 6 minutes or until the mushrooms shrink. Stir in the barley and broth.
3.   Secure the lid. Select the Manual mode and set the cooking time for 30 minutes at High Pressure.
4.   Once cooking is complete, do a natural pressure release for 10 minutes, then release any remaining pressure. Carefully open the lid.
5.   Stir in the Parmesan cheese. Serve hot.

Mediterranean Couscous Salad

Prep time: 20 minutes | Cook time: 2 minutes | Serves 6
Couscous:
1 cup couscous
2¾ cups water, divided
Salad:
½ cup salad greens (such as a mix of spinach, arugula, and red and green lettuce leaves)
4 tablespoons finely chopped carrot
4 tablespoons finely chopped black olives
4 tablespoons finely chopped cucumber
½ cup thinly sliced red onion, marinated in 2 tablespoons each of lemon juice and water for 20 minutes, then drained
½ cup shredded red cabbage, marinated in 2 tablespoons each of lemon juice and water for 20 minutes, then drained
1 teaspoon kosher salt
1 teaspoon freshly ground black pepper
2 tablespoons extra-virgin olive oil
1.   Combine the couscous and 1¼ of cups water in a heatproof bowl.
2.   Pour the remaining 1½ cups of water into the Instant Pot and insert a trivet. Place the bowl on the trivet.
3.   Secure the lid. Select the Manual mode and set the cooking time for 2 minutes at High Pressure.
4.   Once cooking is complete, do a natural pressure release for 5 minutes, then release any remaining pressure. Carefully open the lid.
5.   Let the couscous cool for 15 minutes before fluffing with a fork.
6.   Assemble the salad: Add the salad greens, carrot, olives, cucumber, onion, cabbage, salt, pepper, and olive oil to the couscous. Mix gently and serve immediately.

Polenta and Mushrooms

Prep time: 5 minutes | Cook time: 23 minutes | Serves 4
1 cup yellow cornmeal
4 cups vegetable broth
1 tablespoon butter
2 portobello mushrooms caps, finely chopped
1 teaspoon onion powder
1 teaspoon kosher salt
1 teaspoon freshly ground black pepper
1.   In a large bowl, whisk together the cornmeal and broth until there are no lumps. Set aside.
2.   Set your Instant Pot to Sauté and melt the butter.

3.   Add the mushrooms, onion powder, salt, and pepper, and sauté for 2 minutes. Add the cornmeal mix to the Instant Pot, stirring well.
4.   Lock the lid. Select the Porridge mode and set the cooking time for 20 minutes at High Pressure.
5.   When the timer beeps, perform a natural pressure release for 10 minutes, then release any remaining pressure. Carefully remove the lid.
6.   Stir the polenta and serve hot.

Za'atar-Spiced Bulgur Wheat Salad

Prep time: 10 minutes | Cook time: 2 minutes | Serves 6
Bulgur Wheat:
1 cup bulgur wheat
2¼ cups water, divided
Salad:
¼ cup finely chopped cucumber
¼ cup finely chopped fresh parsley
2 tablespoons finely chopped fresh mint
2 tablespoons extra-virgin olive oil
2 tablespoons freshly squeezed lemon juice
5 cherry tomatoes, finely chopped
1 teaspoon kosher salt
½ teaspoon freshly ground black pepper
1 teaspoon za'atar spice blend
1.   Combine the bulgur wheat and 1¼ cups of water in a heatproof bowl.
2.   Pour the remaining 1 cup of water into the Instant Pot and insert a trivet. Place the bowl on the trivet.
3.   Secure the lid. Select the Manual mode and set the cooking time for 2 minutes at High Pressure.
4.   Once cooking is complete, do a natural pressure release for 5 minutes, then release any remaining pressure. Carefully open the lid.
5.   Let the bulgur wheat cool for 20 minutes before fluffing it with a fork.
6.   Assemble the salad: Add the cucumber, parsley, mint, olive oil, lemon juice, tomatoes, salt, pepper, and za'atar seasoning to the bulgur wheat. Mix gently and serve immediately.

Vegetable Fried Millet

Prep time: 10 minutes | Cook time: 25 minutes | Serves 4
1 teaspoon vegetable oil
½ cup thinly sliced oyster mushrooms
1 cup finely chopped leeks
2 garlic cloves, minced
½ cup green lentils, rinsed
1 cup millet, soaked and drained
½ cup sliced bok choy
1 cup chopped asparagus
1 cup chopped snow peas
2¼ cups vegetable stock
Salt and black pepper, to taste
A drizzle of lemon juice
¼ cup mixed chives and parsley, finely chopped
1.   Press the Sauté button on the Instant Pot and heat the oil.

2.	Cook the mushrooms, leeks, and garlic for 3 minutes. Add lentils and millet, stir, and cook for 4 minutes.
3.	Stir in the bok choy, asparagus, snow peas, and vegetable stock.
4.	Secure the lid. Select the Manual mode and set the cooking time for 10 minutes at High Pressure.
5.	Once cooking is complete, do a quick pressure release. Carefully open the lid.
6.	Season to taste with salt and pepper. Serve sprinkled with the lemon juice, chives, and parsley.

Mushrooms Farro Risotto

Prep time: 10 minutes | Cook time: 30 minutes | Serves 3
½ cup farro
2 tablespoons barley
3 cups chopped mushrooms
1 tablespoon red curry paste
1 jalapeño pepper, seeded and chopped
1 tablespoon shallot powder
2 tablespoons onion powder
Salt and pepper, to taste
4 garlic cloves, minced
1½ cups water
2 tomatoes, diced
Chopped cilantro, for serving
Chopped scallions, for serving
1.	Combine all the ingredients, except for the tomatoes, cilantro, and scallion, in the Instant Pot.
2.	Secure the lid. Select the Manual mode and set the cooking time for 30 minutes at High Pressure.
3.	Once cooking is complete, do a quick pressure release. Carefully open the lid.
4.	Stir in the tomatoes and let sit for 2 to 3 minutes until warmed through. Sprinkle with the cilantro and scallions and serve.

Curried Sorghum

Prep time: 10 minutes | Cook time: 20 minutes | Serves 4
1 cup sorghum
3 cups water
Salt, to taste
1 cup milk
2 teaspoons sugar
3 tablespoons rice wine vinegar
1 tablespoon curry powder
½ teaspoon chili powder
2 cups carrots
¼ cup finely chopped green onion
½ cup golden raisins
1.	Combine the sorghum, water, and salt in the Instant Pot.
2.	Secure the lid. Select the Manual mode and set the cooking time for 20 minutes at High Pressure.
3.	Once cooking is complete, do a quick pressure release. Carefully open the lid.
4.	In a medium bowl, add the milk, sugar, vinegar, salt, curry powder, and chili powder and whisk well.

5.	Drain the sorghum and transfer to a large bowl. Add the milk mixture, carrots, green onion, and raisins. Stir to combine and serve.

Mujadara (Lebanese Lentils and Rice)

Prep time: 5 minutes | Cook time: 15 minutes | Serves 6
$^1/_3$ cup dried brown lentils
2 tablespoons vegetable oil
1 large yellow onion, sliced
1 teaspoon kosher salt, or more to taste
1 cup basmati rice, rinsed and drained
½ teaspoon ground cumin
½ teaspoon ground coriander
2 cups water
1.	Place the lentils in a small bowl. Cover with hot water and soak for 15 to 20 minutes, then drain.
2.	Press the Sauté button on the Instant Pot and heat the oil.
3.	Add the onion and season with a little salt and cook, stirring, until the onions begin to crisp around the edges but are not burned, 5 to 10 minutes. Remove half the onions from the pot and reserve as a garnish.
4.	Add the soaked lentils, rice, cumin, coriander, salt, and water, stirring well.
5.	Lock the lid. Select the Manual mode and set the cooking time for 6 minutes at High Pressure.
6.	When the timer beeps, perform a natural pressure release for 10 minutes, then release any remaining pressure. Carefully remove the lid.
7.	Transfer to a serving dish. Sprinkle with the reserved cooked onions and serve.

Cilantro and Lime Millet Pilaf

Prep time: 5 minutes | Cook time: 10 minutes | Serves 4
1 cup chopped green onions
1 cup millet
1 teaspoon kosher salt
1 tablespoon olive oil
1 cup water
1 cup chopped fresh cilantro or parsley
Zest and juice of 1 lime
1.	In the Instant Pot, combine the green onions, millet, salt, olive oil, and water.
2.	Lock the lid. Select the Manual mode and set the cooking time for 10 minutes at High Pressure.
3.	When the timer beeps, perform a natural pressure release for 10 minutes, then release any remaining pressure. Carefully remove the lid.
4.	Stir in the cilantro and lime zest and juice and serve.

Cinnamon Bulgur and Lentil Pilaf

Prep time: 5 minutes | Cook time: 10 minutes | Serves 6
2 tablespoons vegetable oil
1 large onion, thinly sliced
1½ teaspoons kosher salt
½ teaspoon ground cinnamon
½ teaspoon ground allspice
1¾ cups water, divided

1 cup whole-grain red wheat bulgur
½ cup dried red lentils
¼ cup chopped fresh parsley
Toasted pine nuts (optional)
1.	Press the Sauté button on the Instant Pot and heat the oil.
2.	Once the oil is hot, add the onion and salt. Cook, stirring occasionally, until the onion is browned, about 5 minutes.
3.	Stir in the cinnamon and allspice and cook for 30 seconds.
4.	Add ¼ cup of water to deglaze the pot, scraping up the browned bits. Add the bulgur, lentils, and remaining 1½ cups of water.
5.	Lock the lid. Select the Manual mode and set the cooking time for 5 minutes at High Pressure.
6.	When the timer beeps, perform a natural pressure release for 10 minutes, then release any remaining pressure. Carefully remove the lid.
7.	Stir gently to fluff up the bulgur. Stir in the parsley and pine nuts (if desired), then serve.

Red Onion-Feta Couscous Pilaf

Prep time: 5 minutes | Cook time: 5 minutes | Serves 4
2 tablespoons vegetable oil
1 teaspoon cumin seeds
1 teaspoon ground turmeric
1 cup frozen peas and carrots
1 cup Israeli couscous
½ cup diced yellow onion
1 teaspoon kosher salt
1 teaspoon garam masala
1 cup water
½ cup chopped red onion
½ cup crumbled feta cheese
Black pepper, to taste
1.	Press the Sauté button on the Instant Pot and heat the oil.
2.	Once the oil is hot, stir in the cumin seeds and turmeric, allowing them to sizzle for 10 seconds. Turn off the Instant Pot.
3.	Add the peas and carrots, couscous, yellow onion, salt, garam masala, and water. Stir to combine.
4.	Lock the lid. Select the Manual mode and set the cooking time for 3 minutes at High Pressure.
5.	When the timer beeps, perform a natural pressure release for 5 minutes, then release any remaining pressure. Carefully remove the lid.
6.	Stir in the red onion and feta cheese. Season to taste with black pepper and serve.

White Beans with Poblano and Tomatillos

Prep time: 15 minutes | Cook time: 39 minutes | Serves 6
1 cup chopped poblano, deseeded and stem removed
2 cups chopped tomatillos
1 cup chopped onion
½ jalapeño, deseeded
1½ teaspoons ground cumin
1½ cups dried white beans, soaked for 8 hours, drained
2 teaspoons dried oregano

1½ cups water
Salt and ground black pepper, to taste
1.	Add the poblano, tomatillos, onion and jalapeño to a food processor. Pulse to break them into tiny pieces.
2.	Set the Sauté setting of the Instant Pot and pour in the blended mixture.
3.	Fold in the cumin. Sauté for 4 minutes or until the onion is translucent.
4.	Stir in the beans, oregano, and water. Put the lid on.
5.	Select the Manual setting and set cooking time for 35 minutes at High Pressure.
6.	When timer beeps, allow the pressure to release naturally for 15 minutes, then release any remaining pressure. Open the lid.
7.	Sprinkle with salt and pepper before serving.

Kidney Beans with Ajwain Sauce

Prep time: 15 minutes | Cook time: 40 minutes | Serves 6
Bean:
2 cups dried kidney beans, soaked for at least 8 hours and drained
6 cups water
1 tablespoon grated ginger
1 teaspoon salt
Sauce:
1 onion, minced
½ teaspoon ajwain seeds
1 teaspoon minced garlic
2 cups finely diced tomatoes
¼ cup yogurt
1 teaspoon ground fenugreek
1 teaspoon garam masala
¾ teaspoon turmeric
2 tablespoons ground coriander
⅛ teaspoon ground red chile pepper
1.	Pour the water in the Instant Pot and sprinkle with ginger and salt. Add soak the beans in the water.
2.	Set the Manual mode of the pot and set the cooking time for 10 minutes on High Pressure.
3.	When timer beeps, allow the pressure to release naturally for 5 minutes, then release any remaining pressure. Open the lid.
4.	Carefully pour the beans into a bowl. Let them sit. Clean the Instant Pot.
5.	Set the Sauté setting of the pot. Sauté the onion for 4 minutes or until lightly browned.
6.	Add the ajwain and garlic and sauté for 1 minute or until fragrant.
7.	Mix in the tomatoes and cook until their liquid has evaporated, 5 minutes. Stir in the yogurt, fenugreek, garam masala, turmeric, coriander, and red chile pepper.
8.	Drain 2 cups of liquid from the beans and stir 1 cup into the sauce. Add the beans to the sauce and mix well.
9.	Simmer on the Sauté setting for 20 minutes or until thickened, stirring occasionally.
10.	Transfer to a serving dish and serve.

Black Chickpea Curry

Prep time: 15 minutes | Cook time: 15 minutes | Serves 6

1 tablespoon olive oil
2 cups minced onion
2 teaspoons garam masala
½ teaspoon ground coriander
2 teaspoons cumin seeds
3 teaspoons minced garlic
½ teaspoon ground turmeric
½ teaspoon ground chile
1 cup black chickpeas, soaked in water for at least 8 hours, drained
1½ cups diced tomatoes
1½ cups water
2 tablespoons grated ginger
2 teaspoons crushed curry leaves
Salt, to taste

1.	Select the Sauté setting on the Instant Pot, and heat the oil until shimmering.
2.	Add the onion and sauté for 5 minutes or until transparent.
3.	Add the garam masala, coriander, cumin seeds, garlic, turmeric and chile and sauté for 2 minutes.
4.	Add the chickpeas, tomatoes, water, ginger and curry leaves, and stir to combine.
5.	Put the lid on. Select the Manual setting and set the timer for 8 minutes on High Pressure.
6.	When timer beeps, allow the pressure to release naturally for 5 minutes, then release any remaining pressure. Open the lid.
7.	Sprinkle with salt and serve.

Kidney Bean Vegetarian Étouffée

Prep time: 20 minutes | Cook time: 28 minutes | Serves 4

1 tablespoon olive oil
1 cup minced onion
2 cups minced bell pepper
2 teaspoons minced garlic
1 cup dried kidney beans, soaked in water for 8 hours, drained
1½ teaspoons dried thyme
3 bay leaves
2 teaspoons smoked paprika
1 cup water
2 teaspoons dried marjoram
½ teaspoon ground cayenne pepper
1 (14.5-ounce / 411-g) can crushed tomatoes
1 teaspoon dried oregano
Salt and ground black pepper, to taste

1.	Select the Sauté setting of the Instant Pot and heat the oil until shimmering.
2.	Add the onion and sauté for 5 minutes or until transparent.
3.	Add the bell pepper and garlic. Sauté for 5 more minutes or until the bell peppers are tender.
4.	Add the beans, thyme, bay leaves, smoked paprika, water, marjoram and cayenne to the pot. Stir to combine.
5.	Put the lid on. Select the Manual setting and set the timer for 15 minutes at High Pressure.

6.	When timer beeps, use a natural pressure release for 5 minutes, then release any remaining pressure. Open the lid. Remove the bay leaves.
7.	Mix in the crushed tomatoes and oregano. Sprinkle with salt and pepper. Set the cooking time for 3 minutes on High Pressure.
8.	When timer beeps, release the pressure naturally for 5 minutes, then release any remaining pressure. Open the lid.
9.	Serve immediately.

Black-Eyed Peas with Swiss Chard

Prep time: 15 minutes | Cook time: 10 minutes | Serves 6

1 teaspoon olive oil
1 medium large onion, thinly sliced
1 small jalapeño, minced
1 cup diced red bell pepper
3 cloves garlic, minced
1½ cups dried black-eyed peas, soaked overnight, drained
1 teaspoon chili powder
2 teaspoons smoked paprika
4 dates, finely chopped
1½ cups water
1 (15-ounce / 425-g) can fire-roasted tomatoes with green chiles
2 cups chopped Swiss chard
Salt, to taste

1.	Select the Sauté setting of the Instant Pot and heat the oil until shimmering.
2.	Add the onion and sauté for 5 minutes or until transparent.
3.	Add the peppers and garlic. Sauté for a minute more or until fragrant.
4.	Add the black-eyed peas, chili powder, and smoked paprika, and stir. Add the dates and water.
5.	Put the lid on. Set to Manual mode and set cooking time for 3 minutes at High Pressure.
6.	When timer beeps, let the pressure release naturally for 5 minutes, then release any remaining pressure. Open the lid.
7.	Add the tomatoes and Swiss chard. Set cooking time for 1 minute on High Pressure.
8.	When cooking is complete, quick release the pressure and open the lid.
9.	Sprinkle with salt and serve.

Super Bean and Grain Burgers

Prep time: 25 minutes | Cook time: 1 hour 15 minutes | Makes 12 patties

1 tablespoon olive oil
½ cup chopped onion
8 cloves garlic, minced
1 cup dried black beans
½ cup quinoa, rinsed
½ cup brown rice
4 cups water
Patties:
½ cup ground flaxseed
1 tablespoon dried marjoram
2 teaspoons smoked paprika
2 teaspoons salt

1 teaspoon ground black pepper
1 teaspoon dried thyme
1.	Select the Sauté setting of the Instant Pot and heat the oil until shimmering.
2.	Add the onion and sauté for 5 minutes or until transparent.
3.	Add the garlic and sauté a minute more or until fragrant.
4.	Add the black beans, quinoa, rice and water to the onion mixture and stir to combine.
5.	Put the lid on. Set to Manual mode. Set cooking time for 34 minutes on High Pressure.
6.	When timer beeps, release the pressure naturally for 15 minutes, then release any remaining pressure. Open the lid.
7.	Preheat the oven to 350°F (180°C) and line 2 baking sheets with parchment paper.
8.	Mash the beans in the pot, then mix in the ground flaxseed, marjoram, paprika, salt, pepper and thyme.
9.	Divide and shape the mixture into 12 patties and put on the baking sheet.
10.	Cook in the preheated oven for 35 minutes or until firmed up. Flip the patties halfway through the cooking time.
11.	Serve immediately.

One Pot Black-Eyed Peas with Rice

Prep time: 15 minutes | Cook time: 14 minutes | Serves 4

1 teaspoon extra-virgin olive oil
1 large onion, diced
2 carrots, diced
3 celery stalks, diced
3 cloves garlic, minced
1 cup dried black-eyed peas
½ cup white rice
1 medium tomato, diced
1 teaspoon dried oregano
1 teaspoon dried parsley
¼ teaspoon ground cumin
1 teaspoon crushed red pepper
¼ teaspoon ground black pepper
¼ cup tomato paste
2½ cups vegetable broth
2 tablespoons lemon juice
Salt, to taste
1.	Select the Sauté setting of the Instant Pot and heat the oil until shimmering.
2.	Add the onion, carrots, celery and garlic and sauté for 6 minutes or until tender.
3.	Add the black-eyed peas, rice, tomato, oregano, parsley, cumin red and black peppers, tomato paste and broth to the onion mixture and stir to combine.
4.	Put the lid on. Select the Manual setting and set the timer for 8 minutes at High Pressure.
5.	When timer beeps, let the pressure release naturally for 5 minutes, then release any remaining pressure. Open the lid.
6.	Mix in the lemon juice and salt before serving.

Green Pea and Asparagus Risotto

Prep time: 10 minutes | Cook time: 10 minutes | Serves 4

1½ cups Arborio rice
4 cups water, divided
1 tablespoon vegetable bouillon
1 cup fresh sweet green peas
1½ cups chopped asparagus
2 tablespoons nutritional yeast
1 tablespoon lemon juice
Fresh chopped thyme, for garnish
Salt and ground black pepper, to taste
1.	Add the rice, 3½ cups of water, and vegetable bouillon to the Instant Pot. Put the lid on.
2.	Select Manual setting and set a timer for 5 minutes on High Pressure.
3.	When timer beeps, perform a natural pressure release for 5 minutes, then release any remaining pressure. Open the lid.
4.	Stir in the peas, asparagus, nutritional yeast, remaining water, and lemon juice.
5.	Set to Sauté function. Sauté for 5 minutes or until the asparagus and peas are soft.
6.	Spread the thyme on top and sprinkle with salt and pepper before serving.

Lentils with Rutabaga and Rice

Prep time: 15 minutes | Cook time: 30 minutes | Serves 4

1 tablespoon olive oil
½ cup chopped onion
2 cloves garlic, minced
3½ cups water
1 cup brown lentils
1 cup peeled and diced rutabaga
1½ cups brown rice
2-inch sprig fresh rosemary
1 tablespoon dried marjoram
Salt and ground black pepper, to taste
1.	Select the Sauté setting of the Instant Pot and heat the oil until shimmering.
2.	Add the onion and sauté for 5 minutes or until transparent.
3.	Add the garlic and sauté a minute more or until fragrant.
4.	Add the lentils, rutabaga, brown rice, rosemary, water, and marjoram to the pot and stir to combine.
5.	Put the lid on. Set the Manual mode and set cooking time for 23 minutes at High Pressure.
6.	When timer beeps, let the pressure release naturally for 10 minutes, then release any remaining pressure. Open the lid.
7.	Sprinkle with salt and pepper before serving.

Lentils with Spinach

Prep time: 15 minutes | Cook time: 15 minutes | Serves 2

1 tablespoon olive oil
½ teaspoon cumin seeds
¼ teaspoon mustard seeds
3 cloves garlic, finely chopped

1 green chili, finely chopped
1 large tomato, chopped
1½ cups spinach, finely chopped
¼ teaspoon turmeric powder
½ teaspoon salt
¼ cup split pigeon peas, rinsed
¼ cup split red lentil, rinsed
1½ cups water
¼ teaspoon garam masala
2 teaspoons lemon juice
Cilantro, for garnish
1.	Press the Sauté button on the Instant Pot. Add the oil and then the cumin seeds and mustard seeds.
2.	Let the seeds sizzle for a few seconds and then add the garlic and green chili. Sauté for 1 minute or until fragrant.
3.	Add the tomato and cook for 1 minute. Add the chopped spinach, turmeric powder and salt, and cook for 2 minutes.
4.	Add the rinsed peas and lentils and stir. Pour in the water and put the lid on.
5.	Press the Manual button and set the cooking time for 10 minutes on High Pressure.
6.	When timer beeps, let the pressure release naturally for 5 minutes, then release any remaining pressure.
7.	Open the pot and add the garam masala, lemon juice and cilantro. Serve immediately.

Black-Eyed Pea and Kale Curry

Prep time: 15 minutes | Cook time: 30 minutes | Serves 4
1 tablespoon olive oil
½ teaspoon cumin seeds
1 medium red onion, chopped
4 cloves garlic, finely chopped
1-inch piece ginger, finely chopped
1 green chili, finely chopped
2 large tomatoes, chopped
½ teaspoon turmeric powder
1 teaspoon coriander powder
¼ teaspoon garam masala
1 teaspoon salt
1 cup dried black-eyed peas, soaked in water for 3 hours, drained
2 cups water
3 cups kale, chopped
2 teaspoons lime juice
1.	Press the Sauté button on the Instant Pot. Add the oil and the cumin seeds and let them sizzle for a few seconds.
2.	Add the onion and sauté for 2 minutes or until soft.
3.	Add the garlic, ginger and green chili and sauté for 1 minute or until golden brown.
4.	Add the tomatoes and cook for 3 minutes, or until soft.
5.	Add the turmeric powder, coriander powder, garam masala and salt. Cook for 1 minute.
6.	Fold in the black-eyed peas and water. Lock the lid.
7.	Press the Manual button and set the timer for 20 minutes on High Pressure.

8.	When timer beeps, let the pressure release naturally for 10 minutes, then release any remaining pressure.
9.	Open the pot and press the Sauté button. Add the kale and simmer for 3 minutes.
10.	Stir in the lime juice and serve.

Chickpeas with Jackfruit

Prep time: 20 minutes | Cook time: 15 minutes | Serves 2 to 3
2 teaspoons olive oil
½ teaspoon cumin seeds
½-inch piece cinnamon stick
2 bay leaves
4 cloves, crushed
2 black cardamoms, crushed
4 green cardamoms, crushed
8 black peppercorns, crushed
2 dried red chilies
4 cloves garlic, chopped
2 medium tomatoes, chopped
½ cup split chickpeas, soaked in water for 40 minutes, drained
1 (20-ounce / 567-g) can jackfruit, drained, rinsed and diced
1 teaspoon coriander powder
¾ teaspoon salt
¾ cup water
2 teaspoons lemon juice
Cilantro, for garnish
1.	Press the Sauté button on the Instant Pot. Add the oil and then add the cumin seeds, cinnamon stick, bay leaves, crushed spices, and dried red chilies. Sauté for a few seconds until fragrant.
2.	Add the chopped garlic and cook for 1 minute or until golden brown and then add the tomato.
3.	Cook the tomato for 2 minutes and then add the chickpeas, jackfruit, coriander powder, and salt and mix to combine. Cook for 1 minute and then pour in the water.
4.	Lock the lid. Press the Manual button and set the timer for 10 minutes on High Pressure.
5.	When timer beeps, let the pressure release naturally for 5 minutes, then release any remaining pressure.
6.	Open the pot and press the Sauté button. Stir in the lemon juice, garnish with cilantro and serve.

Moong Bean with Cabbage

Prep time: 10 minutes | Cook time: 8 minutes | Serves 2
2 teaspoons olive oil
½ teaspoon mustard seeds
1 small red onion, chopped
2 green chilies, sliced
5 cups cabbage, shredded
½ cup split moong bean, rinsed
½ teaspoon turmeric powder
½ teaspoon salt
$^1/_3$ cup water
¼ cup fresh dill, chopped

Garam masala, for topping

1. Press the Sauté button on the Instant Pot. Add the oil and the mustard seeds. Heat for a few seconds until the mustard seeds pop.
2. Add the onion and sliced green chilies. Sauté for 2 minutes or until softened.
3. Add the shredded cabbage and sauté for 1 minute.
4. Add the moong bean, turmeric powder, and salt and mix well.
5. Pour in the water and close the pot. Press the Manual button and set the timer for 5 minutes on High Pressure.
6. When timer beeps, let the pressure release naturally for 5 minutes, then release any remaining pressure.
7. Open the pot, add the chopped dill, and sprinkle with garam masala. Stir to mix well. Serve hot.

Ritzy Bean, Pea, and Lentils Mix

Prep time: 20 minutes | Cook time: 11 minutes | Serves 4

1 tablespoon plus 1 teaspoon butter, divided
4 green cardamoms
1 bay leaf
3 cloves
1 teaspoon cumin seeds
2 dried red chilies
¼ teaspoon asafetida
2-inch piece ginger, finely chopped
1 green chili, chopped
1 large tomato, chopped
¼ cup split pigeon peas, rinsed and soaked for 30 minutes, drained
¼ cup split chickpeas, rinsed and soaked for 30 minutes, drained
¼ cup split black beans, rinsed and soaked for 30 minutes, drained
¼ cup split mung beans, rinsed and soaked for 30 minutes, drained
¼ cup split red lentils, rinsed and soaked for 30 minutes, drained
½ teaspoon turmeric powder
1 teaspoon salt
3 cups water
2 tablespoons cilantro, chopped
2 teaspoons lemon juice

1. Press the Sauté button on the Instant Pot. Add 1 tablespoon of butter to the pot and then add the green cardamoms, bay leaf, cloves and cumin seeds. Sauté for a few seconds, until fragrant.
2. Add the dried red chilies and asafetida and sauté for a few seconds.
3. Add the chopped ginger and green chili and cook for a minute.
4. Stir in the tomato and cook for 2 minutes, or until tender.
5. Add the soaked peas, beans, and lentils. Sprinkle with turmeric powder and salt. Mix well.
6. Pour in the water and close the lid. Press the Manual button and set the timer for 7 minutes on High Pressure.

7. When timer beeps, let the pressure release naturally for 10 minutes, then release any remaining pressure.
8. Open the pot, stir and add the remaining 1 teaspoon of butter, cilantro and lemon juice. Serve hot.

Red Lentils with Butternut Squash

Prep time: 15 minutes | Cook time: 12 minutes | Serves 4

2 teaspoons olive oil
½ teaspoon mustard seeds
½ teaspoon cumin seeds
⅛ teaspoon asafetida
1 green chili, sliced
2 dried red chilies, broken
1½ teaspoons ginger, finely chopped
12 curry leaves
2 medium tomatoes, chopped
2 cups butternut squash, diced into 1-inch pieces
¾ cup split red lentils
2½ cups water, divided
½ teaspoon turmeric powder
1 teaspoon salt
1 tablespoon cilantro, chopped
1½ teaspoons lemon juice

1. Press the Sauté button of the Instant Pot. Add the oil, mustard seeds and cumin seeds. Let the mustard seeds pop for a few seconds.
2. Add the asafetida, green chili and broken dried red chilies. Sauté for a few seconds.
3. Add the ginger and curry leaves and cook for a minute or until the ginger is golden brown.
4. Stir in the tomatoes and squash. Cook for 2 minutes. Add the lentils and mix well. Pour in 1 cup of the water, turmeric powder and salt and mix well.
5. Secure the lid, press the Manual button. Set cooking time for 6 minutes on High Pressure.
6. When timer beeps, naturally release the pressure for 5 minutes, then release any remaining pressure.
7. Open the pot, press the Sauté button and add the remaining 1½ cups of water, cilantro and lemon juice. Simmer for 2 minutes.
8. Serve warm.

Green Beans with Beetroot

Prep time: 15 minutes | Cook time: 5 minutes | Serves 2 to 3

1 cup water
1 cup green beans, cut into ½-inch pieces
1 large beetroot, diced small, around ½-inch pieces
1½ tablespoons olive oil
½ teaspoon mustard seeds
2 teaspoons split and dehusked black gram lentils
2 teaspoons chickpeas
2 dried red chilies, broken
⅛ teaspoon asafetida
12 curry leaves
⅛ teaspoon turmeric powder
½ teaspoon salt
$^1/_3$ cup fresh grated coconut

1. Pour the water in the Instant Pot. Put the chopped green beans and beetroot in a steamer basket and then put the steamer basket in the pot.
2. Close the lid. Press the Steam button and set the time to 2 minutes on High Pressure.
3. When timer beeps, do a quick pressure release. Open the lid. Remove the steamer basket from the pot and transfer the steamed vegetables to a bowl. Set aside.
4. Press the Sauté button, add the oil and mustard seeds. Heat for a few seconds until pop.
5. Add the lentils and chickpeas and cook for 2 minutes, or until golden.
6. Add the dried red chilies and asafetida and sauté for a few seconds.
7. Add the curry leaves, stir, then add the steamed vegetables, turmeric powder and salt.
8. Toss to combine well, then fold in the fresh grated coconut. Transfer to a serving dish and serve.

Lemony Black Bean Curry

Prep time: 15 minutes | Cook time: 35 minutes | Serves 6

1 tablespoon butter
1 teaspoon cumin seeds
1 onion, minced
1 tablespoon ginger paste
1 tablespoon garlic paste
1 teaspoon chili powder
½ teaspoon garam masala
½ teaspoon ground turmeric
2 teaspoons ground coriander
1 cup black beans, rinsed, soaked in water overnight, drained
2 cups water
1 teaspoon fresh lemon juice
Salt, to taste
1. Add the butter to the Instant Pot and select Sauté mode. Add the cumin seeds and cook for 30 seconds or until pops.
2. Add the onion, ginger paste, garlic paste, chili powder, garam masala, turmeric, and coriander, and cook for 4 minutes.
3. Stir in the chickpeas and water. Secure the lid. Select the Bean/Chili mode and set the timer for 30 minutes on High Pressure.
4. When timer beeps, use a natural pressure release for 15 minutes, then release any remaining pressure.
5. Remove the lid and stir in the lemon juice. Sprinkle with salt and serve.

Sumptuous Navy Beans

Prep time: 20 minutes | Cook time: 50 minutes | Serves 10

2 tablespoons extra-virgin olive oil
1 green bell pepper, deseeded and chopped
1 onion, minced
1 jalapeño pepper, minced
3 garlic cloves, minced
6 ounces (170 g) tomato paste
¼ cup molasses
1 teaspoon balsamic vinegar

2 cups vegetable broth
1 tablespoon mustard
¼ teaspoon smoked paprika
¼ cup sugar
¼ teaspoon ground black pepper
1 pound (454 g) navy beans, soaked in water for at least 4 hours, drained
2 cups water
Salt, to taste
1. Add the butter to the Instant Pot and select Sauté setting.
2. Add the bell pepper and onion and cook for 4 minutes or until the onion is translucent.
3. Add the jalapeño and garlic and cook for 1 minute or until fragrant.
4. Meanwhile, combine remaining ingredients in a bowl, except the beans and water, and beat until smooth to make the sauce.
5. Stir the beans, water and sauce mixture in the pot. Secure the lid.
6. Set on Manual mode and set cooking time for 45 minutes on High Pressure.
7. When timer beeps, allow a natural pressure release for 15 minutes, then release any remaining pressure.
8. Remove the lid and stir in the salt before serving.

Beluga Lentils with Lacinato Kale

Prep time: 15 minutes | Cook time: 40 minutes | Serves 6

¼ cup olive oil, plus more for serving
2 shallots, diced
5 cloves garlic, minced
½ teaspoon red pepper flakes
½ teaspoon ground nutmeg
1 teaspoon fine sea salt
2 bunches (about 1 pound / 454 g) lacinato kale, stems discarded and leaves chopped into 1-inch pieces
2 large carrots, peeled and diced
2½ cups water
1 cup beluga lentils, rinsed
1. Select the Sauté setting on the Instant Pot, add the oil, and heat for 1 minute.
2. Add the shallots and garlic and sauté for about 4 minutes until the shallots soften.
3. Add the red pepper flakes, nutmeg, and salt and sauté for 1 minute more.
4. Stir in the kale and carrots and sauté for about 3 minutes, until the kale fully wilts. Stir in the water and lentils.
5. Secure the lid. Select Bean/Chili setting and set the cooking time for 30 minutes at High Pressure.
6. When timer beeps, let the pressure release naturally for 10 minutes, then release any remaining pressure.
7. Open the pot and give the mixture a stir.
8. Ladle the lentils into serving dishes and drizzle with oil. Serve warm.

Bean Tagine with Ras el Hanout

Prep time: 20 minutes | Cook time: 37 minutes | Serves 8
2½ cups (about 1 pound / 454 g) dried Northern beans, soaked in salted water overnight, rinsed and drained
¼ cup olive oil, plus more for serving
4 cloves garlic, minced
1 yellow onion, sliced
3 cups vegetable broth
8 medium carrots (about 1 pound / 454 g in total), peeled and cut into ½-inch rounds
1 tablespoon tomato paste
1 tablespoon fresh lemon juice
Salt, to taste
2 tablespoons chopped fresh mint
Ras el Hanout:
2 teaspoons paprika
½ teaspoon ground cinnamon
½ teaspoon ground coriander
½ teaspoon ground cumin
¼ teaspoon cayenne pepper.
1.	Select the Sauté setting on the Instant Pot, add the oil and garlic, and heat for 2 minutes, until the garlic is bubbling but not browned.
2.	Add the onion and sauté for 5 minutes until the onion is softened and the garlic is toasty and brown.
3.	Stir in the broth and use a wooden spoon to nudge loose any browned bits from the bottom of the pot.
4.	Stir in the carrots, ingredients for the ras el hanout, and salt. Stir in the beans, making sure all of the beans are submerged in the cooking liquid.
5.	Secure the lid. Select Bean/Chili setting and set the cooking time for 30 minutes at High Pressure.
6.	When timer beeps, let the pressure release naturally for 20 minutes, then release any remaining pressure.
7.	Open the pot and stir in the tomato paste and lemon juice.
8.	Ladle the tagine into bowls. Drizzle with oil and sprinkle with mint. Serve hot.

Quinoa Salad with Apples and Pecans

Prep time: 7 minutes | Cook time: 8 minutes | Serves 4 to 6
1 cup quinoa, rinsed
1 cup water
¼ teaspoon salt, plus more as needed
2 apples, unpeeled and cut into large dices
2 tablespoons freshly squeezed lemon juice
1 tablespoon white rice vinegar
2 celery stalks, halved lengthwise and chopped
½ bunch scallions, green and light green parts, sliced
¾ to 1 cup dried cranberries, white raisins, and regular raisins
2 tablespoons avocado oil
½ to 1 teaspoon chili powder, plus more as needed
Pinch freshly ground black pepper
½ to 1 cup chopped pecans
½ cup chopped fresh cilantro
1.	Combine the quinoa, water, and salt in the Instant Pot.

2.	Secure the lid. Select the Manual mode and set the cooking time for 8 minutes at High Pressure.
3.	Once cooking is complete, do a natural pressure release for 10 minutes, then release any remaining pressure. Carefully open the lid.
4.	Transfer the quinoa to a large salad bowl. Refrigerate for 5 minutes to cool.
5.	Mix the apples, lemon juice, and vinegar in a small resealable container. Cover and shake lightly to coat the apples, then refrigerate.
6.	Remove the cooled quinoa and stir in the celery, scallions, cranberry-raisin mix, oil, and chili powder. Taste and season with more salt and pepper, as needed. Add the apples and lemon-vinegar juice into the salad and stir well.
7.	Serve topped with the pecans and cilantro.

Greek-Style Quinoa

Prep time: 10 minutes | Cook time: 13 minutes | Serves 4
1 tablespoon olive oil
3 cloves garlic, minced
1 cup chopped red onion
½ cup quinoa
2 cups chopped tomatoes
2 cups spinach, torn
2 cups chopped zucchini
2 cups vegetable broth
½ cup chopped black olives
½ cup pine nuts
1.	Set your Instant Pot to Sauté and heat the olive oil.
2.	Add the garlic and onion and sauté for approximately 5 minutes, stirring frequently.
3.	Add the remaining ingredients, except for the pine nuts, to the Instant Pot and stir to combine.
4.	Secure the lid. Select the Manual mode and set the cooking time for 8 minutes at High Pressure.
5.	Once cooking is complete, do a natural pressure release for 10 minutes, then release any remaining pressure. Carefully open the lid.
6.	Fluff the quinoa and stir in the pine nuts, then serve.

Quinoa and Spinach

Prep time: 5 minutes | Cook time: 2 minutes | Serves 4
1½ cups quinoa, rinsed
1½ cups water
4 cups spinach
1 bell pepper, chopped
3 stalks of celery, chopped
¼ teaspoon salt
1.	Combine all ingredients in the Instant Pot.
2.	Secure the lid. Select the Manual mode and set the cooking time for 2 minutes at High Pressure.
3.	Once cooking is complete, do a natural pressure release for 10 minutes, then release any remaining pressure. Carefully open the lid.
4.	Fluff the quinoa and serve.

Leek and Mushroom Risotto

Prep time: 7 minutes | Cook time: 13 minutes | Serves 4 to 6
4 tablespoons butter, divided
1 leek, white and lightest green parts only, halved and sliced, rinsed well
12 ounces (340 g) baby bella mushrooms, sliced
2 garlic cloves, minced
1 cup Arborio rice, rinsed and drained
2¾ cups vegetable stock
½ teaspoon salt, plus more as needed
1 teaspoon dried thyme
Juice of ½ lemon
Freshly ground black pepper, to taste
Chopped fresh parsley, for garnish
1.   Set your Instant Pot to Sauté and heat 2 tablespoons of butter until melted.
2.   Add the leek and mushrooms and sauté for about 2 minutes, stirring frequently. Add the garlic and cook for about 30 seconds.
3.   Add the rice and toast it for 1 minute. Turn off the Instant Pot.
4.   Stir in the stock, thyme, and salt.
5.   Secure the lid. Select the Manual mode and set the cooking time for 8 minutes at High Pressure.
6.   Once cooking is complete, do a quick pressure release. Carefully open the lid.
7.   Stir in the remaining 2 tablespoons of butter and lemon juice. Taste and season with more salt and pepper, as needed. Serve garnished with fresh parsley.

Quinoa Pilaf with Cranberries and Almonds

Prep time: 2 minutes | Cook time: 10 minutes | Serves 2 to 4
1 cup quinoa, rinsed
2 cups water
1 cup dried cranberries
½ cup slivered almonds
¼ cup salted sunflower seeds
1.   Combine the water and quinoa in the Instant Pot.
2.   Lock the lid. Select the Manual mode and set the cooking time for 10 minutes at High Pressure.
3.   Once cooking is complete, do a quick pressure release. Carefully open the lid.
4.   Add the cranberries, almonds, and sunflower seeds and gently mix until well incorporated. Serve warm.

Israeli Couscous with Veggies

Prep time: 15 minutes | Cook time: 5 minutes | Serves 4 to 6
1 tablespoon olive oil
½ large onion, chopped
2 bay leaves
1 large red bell pepper, chopped
1 cup grated carrot
1¾ cups Israeli couscous
1¾ cups water
½ teaspoon garam masala
2 teaspoons salt, or more to taste
1 tablespoon lemon juice
Chopped cilantro, for garnish
1.   Set your Instant Pot to Sauté and heat the olive oil.
2.   Add the onion and bay leaves and sauté for 2 minutes.
3.   Stir in the bell pepper and carrot and sauté for another 1 minute.
4.   Add the couscous, water, garam masala, and salt. Stir to combine well.
5.   Lock the lid. Select the Manual mode and set the cooking time for 2 minutes at High Pressure.
6.   When the timer beeps, perform a natural pressure release for 10 minutes, then release any remaining pressure. Carefully remove the lid.
7.   Fluff the couscous and stir in the lemon juice. Taste and season with more salt, if needed. Garnish with the chopped cilantro and serve hot.

Spinach and Tomato Couscous

Prep time: 10 minutes | Cook time: 8 minutes | Serves 4
2 tablespoons butter
1 cup couscous
1¼ cups water
½ cup chopped spinach
1½ tomatoes, chopped
1.   Set your Instant Pot to Sauté and melt the butter.
2.   Add the couscous and cook for 1 minute.
3.   Pour in the water and stir well.
4.   Lock the lid. Select the Manual mode and set the cooking time for 5 minutes at High Pressure.
5.   When the timer beeps, perform a quick pressure release. Carefully remove the lid.
6.   Transfer the couscous to a large bowl. Add the spinach and tomatoes, stir, and serve.

Farro Salad with Cherries

Prep time: 5 minutes | Cook time: 40 minutes | Serves 4 to 6
3 cups water
1 cup whole grain farro, rinsed
1 tablespoon extra-virgin olive oil
1 tablespoon apple cider vinegar
2 cups cherries, cut into halves
¼ cup chopped green onions
1 teaspoon lemon juice
Salt, to taste
10 mint leaves, chopped
1.   Combine the water and farro in the Instant Pot.
2.   Lock the lid. Select the Manual mode and set the cooking time for 40 minutes at High Pressure.
3.   When the timer beeps, perform a quick pressure release. Carefully remove the lid.
4.   Drain the farro and transfer to a bowl. Stir in the olive oil, vinegar, cherries, green onions, lemon juice, salt, and mint. Serve immediately.

Easy Pearl Barley

Prep time: 2 minutes | Cook time: 25 minutes | Serves 4
3 cups water

1½ cups pearl barley, rinsed
Salt, to taste
Peanut butter, to taste (optional)
1.   Combine the water, barley, and salt in the Instant Pot.
2.   Lock the lid. Select the Manual mode and set the cooking time for 25 minutes at High Pressure.
3.   Once cooking is complete, do a natural pressure release for 15 minutes, then release any remaining pressure. Carefully open the lid.
4.   Add the peanut butter to taste, if desired. Serve hot.

Apple and Celery Barley Salad

Prep time: 10 minutes | Cook time: 20 minutes | Serves 2 to 4

2½ cups water
1 cup pearl barley, rinsed
Salt and white pepper, to taste
1 green apple, chopped
¼ cup chopped celery
¾ cup jarred spinach pesto
1.   Combine the water, barley, salt, and white pepper in the Instant Pot.
2.   Lock the lid. Select the Manual mode and set the cooking time for 20 minutes at High Pressure.
3.   When the timer beeps, perform a quick pressure release. Carefully remove the lid.
4.   Drain the barley and transfer to a bowl. Add the chopped apple, celery, and spinach pesto, tossing to coat, and serve.

Sautéed Beluga Lentil and Zucchinis

Prep time: 15 minutes | Cook time: 10 minutes | Serves 4

2 tablespoons olive oil
2 large zucchinis, chopped
4 garlic cloves, minced
½ tablespoon dried oregano
½ tablespoon curry powder
Salt and ground black pepper, to taste
2 cups canned beluga lentils, drained
¼ cup chopped parsley, divided
½ cup chopped basil
1 small red onion, diced
2 tablespoons balsamic vinegar
1 teaspoon Dijon mustard
1.   Set the Instant Pot to Sauté mode. Heat the oil and sauté the zucchinis until tender.
2.   Mix in the garlic and cook until fragrant, 30 seconds. Top with oregano, curry, salt, and pepper. Allow to combine for 1 minute, stirring frequently.
3.   Pour in lentils, cook for 3 minutes, and stir in half of parsley, basil, and onion. Sauté until onion softens, about 5 minutes.
4.   Meanwhile, in a bowl, combine vinegar with mustard and pour mixture over lentils. Plate and garnish with remaining parsley.

Scarlet Runner Bean and Potato Hash

Prep time: 5 minutes | Cook time: 20 minutes | Serves 4

1 tablespoon avocado oil

3 cups diced potatoes
2 cups diced red and yellow pepper
4 cloves garlic, minced
1 cup diced celery
1 cup Scarlet Runner beans, soaked in water overnight, rinsed and drained
2 vegetable broth
1 tablespoon dried oregano
1 teaspoon chili powder
Salt, to taste
1.   Heat the oil in the Instant Pot on the Sauté function.
2.   Add the potatoes, peppers, garlic, and celery, and sauté for 4 minutes.
3.   Add the beans. Begin adding broth until cover the beans. Stir in the dried oregano and chili powder.
4.   Cover the pot. Select Manual mode and set cooking time for 12 minutes on High Pressure.
5.   When timer beeps, use a natural pressure release for 5 minutes, then release any remaining pressure.
6.   Remove the cover. Sprinkle with salt and serve.

Adzuki Beans and Vegetable Bowl

Prep time: 5 minutes | Cook time: 25 minutes | Serves 4

1 teaspoon sesame oil
2 cloves garlic, minced
1 teaspoon grated ginger
1 cup dried adzuki beans
½ cup brown rice
½ cup sliced shiitake mushrooms
2 cups shredded collard greens
1-inch strip kombu
3 cups water
3 umeboshi plums, mashed
1 tablespoon lemon juice
1 tablespoon tamari
1.   In the Instant Pot, heat the oil on Sauté mode.
2.   Add the garlic and ginger and sauté for 2 minutes until the garlic is softened
3.   Stir in the adzuki beans, brown rice, mushrooms, greens, kombu, and water.
4.   Secure the lid. Select Manual mode and set cooking time for 22 minutes on High Pressure.
5.   When timer beeps, use a natural pressure release for 15 minutes, then release any remaining pressure.
6.   Remove the cover and stir. Return to the pot, and simmer while stirring in the mashed umeboshi plums, lemon juice, and tamari on Sauté mode for 3 minutes.
7.   Serve immediately.

Balsamic Black Beans with Parsnip

Prep time: 5 minutes | Cook time: 11 minutes | Serves 6

1 cup dried black beans, soaked in water overnight, rinsed and drained
1 teaspoon olive oil

2 cloves garlic, minced
1 cup diced parsnip
½ teaspoon ground coriander
½ teaspoon ground cardamom
2 cups water
2 tablespoons balsamic vinegar
1. In the Instant Pot, heat the oil on Sauté mode. Add the garlic and sauté for a minute or until soft, but not brown.
2. Add the parsnip, coriander, and cardamom and sauté for 5 minutes.
3. Add the black beans and water. Stir to combine.
4. Secure the lid. Select Manual mode and set cooking time for 5 minutes on High Pressure.
5. When timer beeps, use a natural pressure release for 5 minutes, then release any remaining pressure.
6. Remove the lid and stir in 2 tablespoons of the balsamic vinegar. Serve immediately.

Barbecue Northern Bean Bake

Prep time: 20 minutes | Cook time: 54 minutes | Serves 8
2½ cups (about 1 pound / 454 g) dried great Northern beans, soaked in water for at least 8 hours, rinsed and drained
1 cup barbecue sauce
¼ cup yellow mustard
2 tablespoons maple syrup
1¾ cups water
1½ teaspoons freshly ground black pepper
1½ teaspoons smoked paprika
3 tablespoons avocado oil
1 large yellow onion, diced
2 cloves garlic, minced
1 bay leaf
1. In a small bowl, stir together the barbecue sauce, mustard, maple syrup, water, pepper, and smoked paprika.
2. Select the Sauté setting on the Instant Pot, add the oil, and heat for 2 minutes.
3. Add the onion and sauté for about 10 minutes, stirring often, until it begins to caramelize.
4. Add the garlic and sauté for about 2 minutes more until the garlic is no longer raw.
5. Add the barbecue sauce mixture, beans, and bay leaf. Stir to combine, using a wooden spoon to nudge loose any browned bits from the bottom of the pot.
6. Secure the lid. Select Bean/Chili setting and set the cooking time for 40 minutes at High Pressure.
7. When timer beeps, let the pressure release naturally for 20 minutes, then release any remaining pressure. Open the pot, stir the beans, and discard the bay leaf.
8. Ladle the beans into bowls and serve hot.

Black Bean and Pepper Tacos

Prep time: 10 minutes | Cook time: 23 minutes | Serves 2
1 tablespoon sesame oil
½ onion, chopped

1 teaspoon garlic, minced
1 sweet pepper, deseeded and sliced
1 jalapeño pepper, deseeded and minced
1 teaspoon ground cumin
½ teaspoon ground coriander
8 ounces (227 g) black beans, rinsed
2 (8-inch) whole wheat tortillas, warmed
½ cup cherry tomatoes, halved
$^1/_3$ cup coconut cream
1. Press the Sauté button and heat the oil. Cook the onion, garlic, and peppers for 3 minutes or until tender and fragrant.
2. Add the ground cumin, coriander, and beans to the Instant Pot.
3. Secure the lid. Choose the Manual mode and cook for 20 minutes at High Pressure.
4. Once cooking is complete, use a natural pressure release for 10 minutes, then release any remaining pressure. Carefully remove the lid.
5. Serve the bean mixture in the tortillas, then garnish with the cherry tomatoes and coconut cream.

Black Beans with Crumbled Tofu

Prep time: 15 minutes | Cook time: 23 minutes | Serves 2
1 cup canned black beans
2 cups vegetable broth
1 tablespoon avocado oil
1 small red onion, finely chopped
3 garlic cloves, minced
3 tomatoes, chopped
1 (14-ounce / 397-g) extra-firm tofu, crumbled
1 teaspoon turmeric powder
1 teaspoon cumin powder
1 teaspoon smoked paprika
Salt and ground black pepper, to taste
1. Pour the beans and broth in Instant Pot. Seal the lid, select Manual mode, and set cooking time for 10 minutes on High Pressure.
2. When timer beeps, do a quick pressure release. Transfer the beans to a medium bowl. Drain excess liquid and wipe Instant Pot clean.
3. Select Sauté mode. Heat the avocado oil and sauté onion, garlic, and tomatoes until softened, 4 minutes.
4. Crumble the tofu into the pan and cook for 5 minutes.
5. Season with turmeric, cumin, paprika, salt, and black pepper. Cook for 1 minute. Add black beans, stir, and allow heating for 3 minutes.
6. Serve immediately.

Chickpea Tagine with Pickled Raisins

Prep time: 30 minutes | Cook time: 25 minutes | Serves 4
1 cup dried chickpeas, soaked in salted water for 8 hours, rinsed and drained
2 teaspoons kosher salt
Spicy Pickled Raisins:
$^1/_3$ cup golden raisins
$^1/_3$ cup apple cider vinegar
2½ tablespoons organic cane sugar
¼ teaspoon crushed red pepper flakes, to taste

Tagine:
2 tablespoons olive oil
1 large yellow onion, diced
2 medium carrots, diced
5 garlic cloves, minced
2 teaspoons ground cinnamon
2 teaspoons ground coriander
1 teaspoon cumin seeds or ground cumin
1 teaspoon sweet paprika
2 bay leaves
1½ teaspoons kosher salt, plus more to taste
1¼ cups vegetable broth or water
3 cups peeled and finely diced peeled butternut squash (from one 1½-pound / 680-g butternut squash)
¼ cup finely diced dried apricots (about 8 apricots)
1 (14.5-ounce / 411-g) can crushed tomatoes
4 ounces (113 g) Tuscan kale, stems and midribs removed, roughly chopped
¼ cup roughly chopped fresh cilantro
Zest and juice of 1 small lemon
1.	Place the raisins in a bowl. In a small saucepan, combine the vinegar, sugar, and pepper flakes and bring to a boil over medium-high heat, whisking until the sugar is dissolved.
2.	Remove the vinegar mixture from the heat and carefully pour the hot vinegar mixture over the raisins. Leave the bowl uncovered and allow the mixture to come to room temperature. Set aside.
3.	Select the Sauté setting on the Instant Pot and let the pot heat for a few minutes before adding the olive oil.
4.	Once the oil is hot, add the onion and carrots. Cook until the vegetables have softened, 4 to 5 minutes.
5.	Add the garlic and cook for 1 minute, stirring frequently.
6.	Add the cinnamon, coriander, cumin seeds, paprika, bay leaves, and salt. Stir the spices into the vegetables for 30 seconds until the mixture is fragrant.
7.	Pour in the broth, drained chickpeas, butternut squash, and dried apricots. Stir to combine all the ingredients. Pour the crushed tomatoes on top, but do not stir, allowing the tomatoes to sit on top.
8.	Secure the lid. Select the Manual mode and set the cook time for 12 minutes on High Pressure.
9.	When timer beeps, use a natural pressure release for 5 minutes, then release any remaining pressure.
10.	Open the pot, discard the bay leaves, and stir in the kale. Select the Sauté setting and cook for 2 to 3 minutes to wilt the kale.
11.	Add the cilantro and lemon zest and half of the lemon juice.
12.	Transfer the tagine to bowls and add a few spoons of the spicy pickled raisins to each bowl. Serve immediately.

Cinnamon Chickpeas Curry

Prep time: 15 minutes | Cook time: 35 minutes | Serves 4
1 cup dried chickpeas
1 tablespoon baking soda
4 cups water, divided
1 teaspoon olive oil
1 clove garlic, minced
¼ cup diced onion
½ teaspoon hot curry powder
¼ teaspoon ground cinnamon
1 bay leaf
½ teaspoon sea salt
1.	Add the chickpeas, baking soda, and 2 cups of the water to a large bowl and soak for 1 hour. Rinse the chickpeas and drain.
2.	In the Instant Pot, heat the oil on Sauté mode. Add the garlic and onion and sauté for 3 minutes.
3.	Add the curry, cinnamon, and bay leaf and stir well. Stir in the chickpeas and 2 cups of the water.
4.	Cover the lid. Select Manual mode and set cooking time for 32 minutes on High Pressure.
5.	When timer beeps, use a natural pressure release for 15 minutes, then release any remaining pressure.
6.	Remove the lid and stir in the sea salt. Remove the bay leaf before serving.

Hearty Black-Eyed Peas with Collard

Prep time: 5 minutes | Cook time: 3 to 4 minutes | Serves 4 to 6
1 yellow onion, diced
1 tablespoon olive oil
1 cup dried black-eyed peas
¼ cup chopped sun-dried tomatoes
¼ cup tomato paste
1 teaspoon smoked paprika
2 cups water
4 large collard green leaves
Salt and freshly ground black pepper, to taste
1.	In the Instant Pot, select Sauté mode. Add the onion and olive oil and cook for 3 to 4 minutes, stirring occasionally, until the onion is softened.
2.	Add the black-eyed peas, tomatoes, tomato paste, paprika, water, and stir to combine.
3.	Close the lid, then select Manual mode and set cooking time for 30 minutes on High Pressure.
4.	Once the cook time is complete, let the pressure release naturally for about 15 minutes, then release any remaining pressure.
5.	Trim off the thick parts of the collard green stems, then slice the leaves lengthwise in half or quarters. Roll them up together, then finely slice into ribbons.
6.	Sprinkle the sliced collard greens with salt and massage it into them with hands to soften.
7.	Open the lid. Add the collard greens and ½ teaspoon of salt to the pot, stirring to combine and letting the greens wilt in the heat.
8.	Serve immediately.

CHAPTER 7 VEGETABLES

Mushroom and Cabbage Dumplings

Prep time: 20 minutes | Cook time: 15 to 16 minutes | Makes 12 dumplings

1 tablespoon olive oil
1 cup minced shiitake mushrooms
1½ cups minced cabbage
½ cup shredded carrot
2 tablespoons soy sauce
1 tablespoon rice wine vinegar
1 teaspoon grated fresh ginger
12 round dumpling wrappers
1½ cups water

1. Select the Sauté setting of the Instant Pot. Heat the oil until shimmering.
2. Add the mushrooms and sauté for 3 or 4 minutes until the mushrooms release the juices.
3. Add the cabbage, carrot, soy sauce and rice wine vinegar and sauté for 5 minutes or until the mixture is dry. Mix in the ginger.
4. Line a steamer with parchment paper. Prepare a small bowl of water.
5. Put a wrapper on the clean work surface and rub the water around the edge of the wrapper. Add 1 tablespoon of the vegetable filling to the middle of the wrapper and fold in half. Press to make a dumpling. Then put the dumpling in the steamer. Repeat with remaining wrappers and fillings.
6. Arrange the trivet in the pot. Put the steamer on the trivet and pour the water in the pot.
7. Put the lid on. Select the Steam setting and set the timer for 7 minutes on High Pressure.
8. When timer beeps, use a natural pressure release for 5 minutes, then release any remaining pressure. Open the lid.
9. Serve hot.

Jackfruit and Tomatillos Tinga

Prep time: 15 minutes | Cook time: 21 minutes | Serves 4

1 tablespoon olive oil
1½ cups minced onion
6 cloves garlic, minced
2 tablespoons minced jalapeño
1 (20-ounce / 565-g) can jackfruit in brine, rinsed, shredded
1 (14.5-ounce / 411-g) can diced tomatoes
1 cup diced tomatillos
1½ teaspoons dried thyme
1 teaspoon dried oregano
¼ cup water
½ teaspoon ground cumin
Salt, to taste

1. Select the Sauté setting of the Instant Pot and heat the oil until shimmering.
2. Add the onion and sauté for 5 minutes or until transparent. Then add the garlic and jalapeño and sauté for 1 minute more.
3. Add the jackfruit, tomatoes, tomatillos, thyme, oregano, water, and cumin to the pot and stir to combine.

4. Put the lid on. Select the Manual setting and set the timer for 15 minutes on High Pressure.
5. When timer beeps, allow the pressure to release naturally for 5 minutes, then release any remaining pressure. Open the lid.
6. Sprinkle with salt and serve.

Mini Tofu and Vegetable Frittatas

Prep time: 15 minutes | Cook time: 25 to 26 minutes | Serves 4

1 tablespoon olive oil
½ cup minced onion
½ cup minced mushrooms
$^{1}/_{3}$ cup minced bell pepper
$^{1}/_{3}$ cup grated carrot
$^{1}/_{3}$ cup minced kale, collards or spinach
1 (14-ounce / 397-g) package firm tofu, quickly pressed to remove most of the liquid
2 tablespoons nutritional yeast
2 teaspoons Italian herb seasoning
1½ teaspoons salt
½ teaspoon ground turmeric
Salt and ground black pepper, to taste
1½ cups water

1. Select the Sauté setting of the Instant Pot. Heat the oil until shimmering, add the onion and sauté until translucent, 5 minutes.
2. Add the mushrooms and cook for 3 minutes or until they release juices, then add the bell pepper and carrot, and sauté for 2 or 3 minutes or until the mixture is dry. Stir in the kale and set aside to cool.
3. Add the tofu, nutritional yeast, Italian herb seasoning, salt, and turmeric to the blender. Blend until smooth.
4. Combine the cooled vegetables and tofu mixture in a bowl. Sprinkle with salt and pepper.
5. Grease 4 ramekins and divide the mixture among them. Cover with foil. Put the trivet in the Instant Pot and pour in the water. Arrange the ramekins on the trivet.
6. Put the lid on. Set to Manual mode and set cooking time for 15 minutes at High Pressure.
7. When timer beeps, allow a natural pressure release for 5 minutes, then release any remaining pressure. Open the lid.
8. Serve hot.

Potatoes and Cauliflower Masala

Prep time: 15 minutes | Cook time: 13 to 14 minutes | Serves 4

1 tablespoon vegetable oil
½ teaspoon cumin seeds
1 large red onion, finely chopped
1½ teaspoons ginger garlic paste
2 medium tomatoes, chopped
½ teaspoon dried mango powder
¼ teaspoon garam masala
¼ teaspoon red chili powder
1 teaspoon coriander powder
½ teaspoon turmeric powder
¾ teaspoon salt

6 tablespoons water, divided
2 medium potatoes, diced into 1-inch pieces
1 (1-pound / 454-g) medium head cauliflower, cut into medium to large florets
2 tablespoons cilantro, chopped, plus more for garnish
1.　　Press the Sauté button on the Instant Pot. Add the oil and the cumin seeds and let them sizzle for a few seconds.
2.　　Add the chopped onion and cook for 3 minutes until soft and translucent.
3.　　Add the ginger garlic paste and cook for another minute or until fragrant.
4.　　Add the tomatoes and cook for 2 minutes or until the tomatoes are soft.
5.　　Add the dried mango powder, garam masala, red chili powder, coriander powder, turmeric powder, and salt and mix to combine.
6.　　Cook the spices for 30 seconds, and then add 2 tablespoons of water and diced potatoes.
7.　　Toss to coat well. Cover the pot and let the potatoes cook for 3 to 4 minutes, stirring once halfway through.
8.　　Remove the lid, add 4 tablespoons of water and mix well to deglaze the pot.
9.　　Put the cauliflower florets on top. Sprinkle 2 tablespoons of cilantro on top of the cauliflower.
10.　　Close the pot. Press the Manual button and set the timer for 3 minutes on Low Pressure. When timer beeps, do a quick pressure release.
11.　　Open the pot and gently mix the cauliflower with the potatoes and the masala. Transfer them to a serving bowl, garnish with more cilantro and serve.

Kashmiri Tofu

Prep time: 20 minutes | Cook time: 20 minutes | Serves 4

8 small dried red chilies
5 cloves
3 tablespoons coriander seeds
5 green cardamoms
2 tablespoons unsalted butter
½ tablespoon olive oil
½ tablespoon grated garlic
½ tablespoon grated ginger
2 small red onions, cubed
4 large tomatoes
½ teaspoon kashmiri red chili powder
¾ cup water, divided
1 small green bell pepper, diced, divided
1 small red bell pepper, diced, divided
1 pound (454 g) extra-firm tofu, cubed
1½ teaspoons fenugreek leaves, crushed
3 tablespoons heavy cream
1 teaspoon sugar
2 tablespoons cilantro, chopped
1.　　In a pan over medium heat, roast the red chilies, cloves, coriander seeds, and green cardamoms for 6 minutes or until fragrant.
2.　　Turn off the heat. Transfer them to a spice grinder and grind to a fine powder. Set aside.

3.　　Press the Sauté button on the Instant Pot. Add the butter and oil to the pot and then add the garlic and ginger and sauté for a few seconds.
4.　　Add the onion and sauté for 2 minutes until softened. Add the tomatoes and sauté for 3 minutes.
5.　　Add the kashmiri red chili powder, salt, and the prepared spice mix. Mix until well combined and then add ½ cup of water and half of the bell peppers.
6.　　Close the pot, and then press the Manual button. Set cooking time for 4 minutes on High Pressure.
7.　　When timer beeps, do a quick pressure release.
8.　　Open the pot and press the Sauté button. Add the remaining water and then stir in the cubed tofu and the remaining half of the bell peppers.
9.　　Fold in the fenugreek leaves, heavy cream, sugar, and cilantro and simmer for 4 minutes.
10.　　Serve hot.

Soya Granules and Green Pea Tacos

Prep time: 20 minutes | Cook time: 8 minutes | Serves 8

2 cups soya granules, soaked in water for at least 20 minutes, drained
½ cup frozen green peas, soaked in water for at least 5 minutes, drained
1 tablespoon olive oil
1 medium red onion, chopped
2 teaspoons ginger garlic paste
3 jalapeños, deseeded, sliced, plus more for garnish
1 tablespoon tomato paste
¾ teaspoon taco seasoning
½ teaspoon garam masala
½ teaspoon coriander powder
1 teaspoon salt
1 cup plus 2 tablespoons water
2 tablespoons cilantro, chopped, plus more for garnish
2 teaspoons lime juice
8 small corn tortillas
Sliced onions, for garnish
Salsa, for garnish
Diced avocados, for garnish
1.　　Press the Sauté button on the Instant Pot. Add the oil and then add the chopped onion. Cook the onion for 2 minutes until softened.
2.　　Add the ginger garlic paste and cook for another minute
3.　　Add the sliced jalapeños and cook for 30 seconds. Add the soya granules to the pot along with the green peas.
4.　　In a small bowl, mix the tomato paste with 2 tablespoons of water, then add it to the pot, along with the taco seasoning, garam masala, coriander powder and salt, and mix until well combined. Add the remaining water and close the lid.
5.　　Press the Manual button and set the timer for 4 minutes at High Pressure.
6.　　When timer beeps, let the pressure release naturally for 5 minutes, then release any remaining pressure.
7.　　Remove the lid, add the cilantro and lime juice and mix.

8.	Warm the tortillas and fill with the prepared keema filling. Top with sliced onions, jalapeños, cilantro, salsa and diced avocados and serve.

Ritzy Green Pea and Cauliflower Curry

Prep time: 20 minutes | Cook time: 8 minutes | Serves 4

3 large tomatoes
4 large cloves garlic
1-inch piece ginger
1 green chili
12 raw cashews
1½ tablespoons olive oil
1 bay leaf
3 green cardamoms
6 peppercorns
3 cloves
1 large red onion, chopped
1½ teaspoons coriander powder
1 teaspoon garam masala
½ teaspoon red chili powder
½ teaspoon turmeric powder
1 teaspoon salt
¼ cup plain yogurt, at room temperature
½ cup plus 2 tablespoons coconut milk
¼ cup water
1 large head cauliflower, cut into florets
½ cup frozen green peas Cilantro, for garnish
1.	Using a blender, purée the tomatoes, garlic, ginger, green chili and cashews to a smooth paste. Set aside.
2.	Press the Sauté button on the Instant Pot. Add the oil and then add the bay leaf, green cardamoms, peppercorns and cloves. Sauté for a few seconds until the spices are fragrant and then add the onion. Cook the onion until soft, around 2 minutes.
3.	Add the puréed tomato mixture. Cook for 2 minutes and then add the coriander powder, garam masala, red chili powder, turmeric powder and salt. Stir to combine the spices and cook them for 30 seconds.
4.	Add the yogurt, whisking continuously until well combined.
5.	Add the coconut milk and the water and mix to combine.
6.	Add the cauliflower florets and peas and toss to combine them with the masala.
7.	Close the lid and press the Manual button. Set the timer for 3 minutes on Low Pressure.
8.	When timer beeps, do a quick pressure release.
9.	Open the pot, give them a stir. Garnish with cilantro and serve.

Baby Eggplants with Coconut

Prep time: 20 minutes | Cook time: 10 minutes | Serves 4

¼ cup dried coconut powder
1 tablespoon coriander powder
1 teaspoon cumin powder
½ teaspoon red chili powder
½ teaspoon garam masala
¼ teaspoon turmeric powder
1 teaspoon salt, divided
12 baby eggplants (1 pound / 454 g in total), each eggplant is 2 inches, rinsed and patted dry
1 tablespoon olive oil
½ teaspoon mustard seeds
1 medium red onion, chopped
1 teaspoon ginger garlic paste
2 medium tomatoes, chopped
¾ cup water, divided
Cilantro, for garnish
1.	In a bowl, mix the coconut powder, coriander powder, cumin powder, red chili powder, garam masala, turmeric powder and ½ teaspoon salt.
2.	Make crosswise and lengthwise slits through the flesh of each eggplant, but without cutting all the way through. Carefully open the eggplants up and divide half of the coconut mixture in each baby eggplant. Reserve remaining half of the coconut stuffing for the curry. Set the stuffed eggplants and reserved stuffing mixture aside.
3.	Press the Sauté button on the Instant Pot. Add the oil and the mustard seeds and let them heat until they pop.
4.	Add the onion and cook for 2 minutes until soft and translucent.
5.	Add the ginger garlic paste and cook for 1 minute, then add the tomatoes and ¼ cup of water. Cook the tomatoes for 2 minutes until they turn soft, and then add the reserved coconut stuffing. Cook for 1 minute and then add ½ cup of water and ½ teaspoon of salt and mix well.
6.	Put the stuffed eggplants on top of the masala and close the lid.
7.	Press the Manual button. Set cooking time for 4 minutes on High Pressure.
8.	When timer beeps, do a quick pressure release.
9.	Open the pot, garnish with cilantro and serve.

Tofu and Greens with Fenugreek Sauce

Prep time: 25 minutes | Cook time: 15 to 18 minutes | Serves 3

1 yellow onion, quartered
15 cashews
3 cloves garlic
1-inch piece ginger
1 green chili
4 green cardamoms
1½ cups water, divided
1½ tablespoons olive oil
1 bay leaf
1 teaspoon coriander powder
¼ teaspoon garam masala
¼ teaspoon turmeric powder
¼ teaspoon red chili powder
1 teaspoon salt
1½ cups fenugreek leaves, stems removed, chopped
6 ounces (170 g) extra-firm tofu, cubed
1 teaspoon fenugreek leaves, crushed
¼ cup heavy cream
½ teaspoon sugar
1 cup broccoli florets

10 thin asparagus stalks, hard end removed and then cut into 1-inch pieces

1. Put the onion and cashews into the steamer basket. Pour 1 cup of water in the Instant Pot and then put the steamer basket inside it.
2. Close the lid and then press the Steam button. Set cooking time for 2 minutes on High Pressure.
3. When timer beeps, do a quick pressure release. Open the lid.
4. Transfer the steamed onion and cashews to a blender and add the garlic, ginger, green chili, green cardamoms and ½ cup of water and purée to a smooth paste.
5. Press the Sauté button on the Instant Pot. Add the oil and then add the bay leaf along with the prepared onion paste. Cook the onion paste for 4 to 5 minutes, until there's no smell of raw onion, and then stir in the coriander powder, garam masala, turmeric powder, red chili powder and salt. Cook for 1 minute, then add the chopped fenugreek leaves and cook for another 1 to 2 minutes.
6. Add 1 cup of water and the tofu, mix well and then close the lid. Press the Manual button and set the timer for 3 minutes on High Pressure.
7. When timer beeps, do a quick pressure release.
8. Open the lid and press the Sauté button. Add the fenugreek leaves, heavy cream, sugar, broccoli florets and asparagus.
9. Cover the pot and let it simmer for 4 to 5 minutes. Serve warm.

Minty Paneer Cubes with Cashews

Prep time: 20 minutes | Cook time: 10 to 11 minutes | Serves 4

1½ cups cilantro, roughly chopped
¾ cup mint leaves
1 small red onion
2 green chilies
15 cashews
1-inch piece ginger
2 cloves garlic
¼ teaspoon ground black pepper
1¼ cups water, divided
1 tablespoon olive oil or unsalted butter
1 bay leaf
¾ teaspoon cumin seeds
½ cup yogurt, whisked with ¼ teaspoon cornstarch
½ teaspoon cumin powder
½ teaspoon coriander powder
¼ teaspoon crushed red pepper, optional
½ teaspoon salt
2 teaspoons heavy cream
Garam masala, to sprinkle
½ teaspoon sugar
1 cup paneer, cut into cubes
Sliced onions, for serving

1. In a blender, grind together the cilantro, mint leaves, onion, green chilies, cashews, ginger, garlic, black pepper and ¼ cup of water to form a smooth paste. Set it aside.
2. Press the Sauté button on the Instant Pot. Add the oil, bay leaf and cumin seeds and let the cumin seeds sizzle for a few seconds.
3. Then add the prepared cilantro mint paste to the pot and cook for 2 to 3 minutes, or until the raw smell of the onion in the paste goes away.
4. Whisk the yogurt with the cornstarch and then fold into the pot. Cook for 2 minutes.
5. Add cumin powder, coriander powder, crushed red pepper and ¾ cup of water and cook for a few seconds.
6. Close the lid, and then press the Soup button and set the cooking time for 3 minutes on High Pressure.
7. When timer beeps, do a quick pressure release.
8. Open the pot, stir the curry and press the Sauté button. Add ¼ cup of water along with the salt, heavy cream, garam masala and sugar. Mix well and then add the paneer cubes.
9. Let the curry simmer for 2 minutes. Serve with sliced onions on the side.

Simple Spiced Russet Potatoes

Prep time: 15 minutes | Cook time: 12 minutes | Serves 3 to 4

2 large russet potatoes, cut in half and skin left on
1 tablespoon olive oil
1¼ teaspoon cumin seeds
2 teaspoons coriander seeds, roughly crushed
2 green chilies, sliced
1-inch piece ginger, chopped
½ teaspoon turmeric powder
⅛ teaspoon red chili powder
½ teaspoon salt
2 teaspoons lemon juice
Cilantro, to garnish

1. Add 1 cup of water to the Instant Pot. Put the trivet inside the pot, then put the potatoes, cut side up, on top of the trivet.
2. Secure the lid. Press the Manual button and set the timer for 10 minutes on High Pressure.
3. When timer beeps, let the pressure release naturally for 5 minutes, then release any remaining pressure. Open the lid.
4. Carefully remove the potatoes from the trivet. When they have cooled down a bit, peel the potatoes and dice them into small pieces.
5. Drain the water from the pot, wipe it dry and then put it back into the Instant Pot.
6. Press the Sauté button, add the oil and then the cumin seeds. Let the seeds sizzle for a few seconds, then add the coriander seeds and green chilies. Sauté for a few seconds and then add the ginger. Sauté for a minute until the ginger is golden.
7. Add the potatoes, turmeric powder, red chili powder and salt and mix, until all the potato pieces are well coated with the spices. Mix gently.
8. Add the lemon juice and toss to combine. Garnish with cilantro and serve.

Tofu and Mango Curry

Prep time: 15 minutes | Cook time: 9 minutes | Serves 2

8 ounces (227 g) extra-firm tofu, pressed to remove the moisture, cubed
¼ teaspoon smoked paprika
¼ teaspoon crushed red pepper
1¼ teaspoon salt, divided
⅛ teaspoon ground black pepper
2 tablespoons olive oil, divided
½ teaspoon mustard seeds
2 dried red chilies
½ medium white onion, diced
1½-inch piece ginger, grated
¾ cup gresh mango purée
½ cup coconut milk
1 teaspoon curry powder
½ cup water
Juice of ½ lemon
Cilantro, to garnish
1.   Toss the tofu cubes with smoked paprika, crushed red pepper, ¼ teaspoon salt and ground black pepper.
2.   Press the Sauté button on the Instant Pot. Add 1 tablespoon of oil to the pot, then add the spiced tofu cubes and cook for 4 minutes, or until lightly browned on all sides. Remove the tofu cubes to a bowl and set aside.
3.   Add another tablespoon of oil to the pot, then add the mustard seeds. Let the mustard seeds pop and then add the dried red chilies. Sauté for a few seconds, then add the onion and ginger. Cook the onion and ginger for a minute until the onion turns a little soft.
4.   Add the mango purée, coconut milk, and curry powder, then add 1 teaspoon of salt and let it all cook for a minute.
5.   Add the water along with the sautéed tofu cubes and close the lid. Press the Manual button and set the timer for 3 minutes on High Pressure.
6.   When timer beeps, do a quick pressure release. Open the lid.
7.   Stir in the lemon juice, then transfer the curry to a serving bowl. Garnish with cilantro and serve.

Creamy Mushrooms and Green Beans

Prep time: 15 minutes | Cook time: 5 minutes | Serves 8

2 cups finely chopped mushrooms
1 cup chopped onion
3 cloves garlic, minced
1 teaspoon kosher salt
½ teaspoon black pepper
¼ cup water
1 pound (454 g) trimmed fresh green beans
2 tablespoons diced cream cheese, at room temperature
¼ cup half-and-half
Sliced toasted almonds (optional)
Fried onions (optional)
1.   In the Instant Pot, combine the mushrooms, onion, garlic, salt, pepper, and water. Put the green beans on top. Set the cream cheese on top of the beans.
2.   Lock the lid. Select Manual mode and set the timer for 3 minutes on High Pressure.
3.   When timer beeps, use a quick pressure release. Open the lid.
4.   Select Sauté mode. Stir in the half-and-half. Cook, stirring frequently, until the sauce has thickened, about 2 minutes.
5.   Transfer them to a serving bowl. Top with almonds and fried onions, and serve.

Green Beans with Coconut

Prep time: 10 minutes | Cook time: 3 minutes | Serves 4

2 tablespoons vegetable oil
1 teaspoon mustard seeds
1 teaspoon cumin seeds
1 cup diced onion
1 teaspoon ground turmeric
1 teaspoon kosher salt
½ teaspoon cayenne pepper
1 (12-ounce / 340-g) package frozen green beans
¼ cup unsweetened shredded coconut
½ cup water
¼ cup chopped fresh cilantro
1.   Select Sauté mode on the Instant Pot. When the pot is hot, add the oil. Once the oil is hot, add the mustard seeds and cumin seeds, and allow to sizzle for 15 to 20 seconds.
2.   Stir in the onion. Add the turmeric, salt, and cayenne and stir to coat. Add the green beans, coconut, and water; stir to combine.
3.   Lock the lid. Select Manual mode and set the timer for 2 minutes at High Pressure.
4.   When timer beeps, use a quick pressure release. Open the lid.
5.   Transfer to a serving dish and garnish with the cilantro. Serve warm.

Grape Leaves with Rice and Nuts

Prep time: 15 minutes | Cook time: 4 minutes | Serves 4

1 cup chopped onion
1 cup chopped tomato
1 cup basmati rice, rinsed and drained
1 cup pine nuts
8 ounces (227 g) brined grape leaves, drained and chopped
2 tablespoons olive oil
3 cloves garlic, minced
1 tablespoon dried parsley
1½ teaspoons ground allspice
1 teaspoon kosher salt
1 teaspoon black pepper
1 cup water
$^{1}/_{3}$ cup fresh lemon juice
¼ cup chopped fresh mint
1.   In the Instant Pot, combine the onion, tomato, rice, pine nuts, grape leaves, olive oil, garlic, parsley, allspice, salt, pepper, and water. Stir to combine.
2.   Lock the lid. Select Manual mode and set the timer for 4 minutes on High Pressure.

3. When timer beeps, perform a natural pressure release for 10 minutes, then release any remaining pressure. Open the lid.
4. Stir in the lemon juice and mint and serve.

Cheesy Spaghetti Squash and Spinach

Prep time: 10 minutes | Cook time: 8 minutes | Serves 4

1 large spaghetti squash, cut into 8 pieces
1½ cups water
3 tablespoons olive oil
8 cloves garlic, thinly sliced
½ cup slivered almonds
1 teaspoon red pepper flakes
4 cups chopped fresh spinach
1 teaspoon kosher salt
1 cup shredded Parmesan cheese

1. Pour the water into the Instant Pot. Put a trivet in the pot. Set the squash on the trivet.
2. Lock the lid. Select Manual mode and set the timer for 7 minutes on High Pressure.
3. When timer beeps, perform a natural pressure release for 10 minutes, then release any remaining pressure.
4. Remove the squash, and cut it in half lengthwise. Use a fork to scrape the strands of one half into a large bowl. Measure out 4 cups. Reserve the other half for other use.
5. Set the squash shell aside to use as a serving vessel. Clean the pot.
6. Select Sauté mode. When the pot is hot, add the olive oil. Once the oil is hot, add the garlic, almonds, and pepper flakes. Cook, stirring constantly and being careful not to burn the garlic for 1 minute.
7. Add the spinach, salt, and spaghetti squash. Stir well to thoroughly combine ingredients until the spinach wilts.
8. Transfer the mixture to the reserved squash shell. Sprinkle with the Parmesan cheese before serving.

Sumptuous Vegetable and Tofu Curry

Prep time: 5 minutes | Cook time: 6 minutes | Serves 4

2 cups diced peeled butternut squash
2 cups chopped bok choy
1 cup button or cremini mushrooms, trimmed and quartered
1 cup stemmed, deseeded, and roughly chopped yellow bell pepper
1 block Japanese curry paste, diced
2 cups water
1 (14-ounce / 397-g) package firm tofu, diced

1. In the Instant Pot, combine the butternut squash, bok choy, mushrooms, bell pepper, curry paste, and water. Stir to mix well.
2. Lock the lid. Select Manual mode and set the timer for 4 minutes at High Pressure.
3. When timer beeps, perform a natural pressure release for 10 minutes, then release any remaining pressure.
4. Open the lid. Stir in the tofu. Set the pot to Sauté mode and sauté for 2 minutes or until the tofu is lightly browned.
5. Serve immediately.

Jamaican Pumpkin and Potato Curry

Prep time: 15 minutes | Cook time: 6 minutes | Serves 6

2 tablespoons vegetable oil
3 cloves garlic, minced
1 tablespoon minced fresh ginger
1 cup chopped onion
1 tablespoon plus 1½ teaspoons Jamaican curry powder
1 stemmed, deseeded, and sliced Scotch bonnet pepper
3 sprigs fresh thyme
1 teaspoon kosher salt
½ teaspoon ground allspice
4 cups (1-inch cubes) peeled pumpkin
1½ cups (1-inch cubes) peeled potatoes
2 cups stemmed, deseeded, and diced red, yellow bell peppers
1 cup water

1. Select Sauté on the Instant Pot. Heat the vegetable oil.
2. Add the garlic and ginger. Sauté for a minute or until fragrant.
3. Add the onion and sauté for 2 minutes or until translucent.
4. Fold in the curry powder, Scotch bonnet pepper, thyme, salt, and allspice. Stir to coat well. Add the pumpkin, potatoes, bell peppers, and water.
5. Lock the lid. Select Manual mode and set the timer for 3 minutes at High Pressure.
6. When timer beeps, perform a natural pressure release for 10 minutes, then release any remaining pressure. Open the lid.
7. Serve immediately.

Lemony Peas with Bell Pepper

Prep time: 5 minutes | Cook time: 1 minutes | Serves 4

2 cups frozen peas
1 cup stemmed, deseeded, and diced red bell pepper
1 cup thinly sliced onion
1 tablespoon butter, melted
2 tablespoons water
1 teaspoon kosher salt
½ teaspoon black pepper
2 tablespoons chopped fresh mint
Zest of 1 lemon
1 tablespoon fresh lemon juice

1. In the Instant Pot, combine the peas, bell pepper, onion, butter, water, salt, and pepper. Stir to mix well.
2. Lock the lid. Select Manual mode and set the timer for 1 minute on High Pressure.
3. When timer beeps, use a quick pressure release. Open the lid.
4. Stir in the mint along with the lemon zest and juice and serve.

Glazed Brussels Sprouts and Cranberries

Prep time: 10 minutes | Cook time: 3 minutes | Serves 6

1½ cups
2 pounds (907 g) small Brussels sprouts, rinsed and trimmed
1 cup dried cranberries
½ cup orange marmalade
2 tablespoons butter, melted
1 teaspoon kosher salt
½ teaspoon cayenne pepper

1. Pour the water into the Instant Pot. Put a steamer basket in the pot. Put the Brussels sprouts and cranberries in the steamer basket.
2. Lock the lid. Select Manual mode and set the timer for 3 minutes on High Pressure.
3. When timer beeps, use a quick pressure release. Open the lid.
4. Transfer the Brussels sprouts and cranberries to a serving bowl. Add the orange marmalade, butter, salt, and cayenne. Toss to combine well. Serve hot.

Lemony Broccoli

Prep time: 5 minutes | Cook time: 4 minutes | Serves 4

2 cups broccoli florets
1 tablespoon ground paprika
1 tablespoon lemon juice
1 teaspoon grated lemon zest
1 teaspoon olive oil
½ teaspoon chili powder
1 cup water

1. Pour the water in the Instant Pot and insert the trivet.
2. In the Instant Pot pan, stir together the remaining ingredients.
3. Place the pan on the trivet.
4. Set the lid in place. Select the Manual mode and set the cooking time for 4 minutes on High Pressure. When the timer goes off, do a quick pressure release. Carefully open the lid.
5. Serve immediately.

Simple Cauliflower Gnocchi

Prep time: 5 minutes | Cook time: 2 minutes | Serves 4

2 cups cauliflower, boiled
½ cup almond flour
1 tablespoon sesame oil
1 teaspoon salt
1 cup water

1. In a bowl, mash the cauliflower until puréed. Mix it up with the almond flour, sesame oil and salt.
2. Make the log from the cauliflower dough and cut it into small pieces.
3. Pour the water in the Instant Pot and add the gnocchi.
4. Lock the lid. Select the Manual mode and set the cooking time for 2 minutes on High Pressure. Once the timer goes off, perform a natural pressure release for 5 minutes, then release any remaining pressure. Carefully open the lid.

5. Remove the cooked gnocchi from the water and serve.

Zucchini and Daikon Fritters

Prep time: 10 minutes | Cook time: 8 minutes | Serves 4

2 large zucchinis, grated
1 daikon, diced
1 egg, beaten
1 teaspoon ground flax meal
1 teaspoon salt
1 tablespoon coconut oil

1. In the mixing bowl, combine all the ingredients, except for the coconut oil. Form the zucchini mixture into fritters.
2. Press the Sauté button on the Instant Pot and melt the coconut oil.
3. Place the zucchini fritters in the hot oil and cook for 4 minutes on each side, or until golden brown.
4. Transfer to a plate and serve.

Sesame Zoodles with Scallions

Prep time: 10 minutes | Cook time: 3 minutes | Serves 6

2 large zucchinis, trimmed and spiralized
¼ cup chicken broth
1 tablespoon chopped scallions
1 tablespoon coconut aminos
1 teaspoon sesame oil
1 teaspoon sesame seeds
¼ teaspoon chili flakes

1. Set the Instant Pot on the Sauté mode. Add the zucchini spirals to the pot and pour in the chicken broth. Sauté for 3 minutes and transfer to the serving bowls.
2. Sprinkle with the scallions, coconut aminos, sesame oil, sesame seeds and chili flakes. Gently stir the zoodles.
3. Serve immediately.

Falafel and Lettuce Salad

Prep time: 10 minutes | Cook time: 6 to 8 minutes | Serves 4

1 cup shredded cauliflower
$^1/_3$ cup coconut flour
1 teaspoon grated lemon zest
1 egg, beaten
2 tablespoons coconut oil
2 cups chopped lettuce
1 cucumber, chopped
1 tablespoon olive oil
1 teaspoon lemon juice
½ teaspoon cayenne pepper

1. In a bowl, combine the cauliflower, coconut flour, grated lemon zest and egg. Form the mixture into small balls.
2. Set the Instant Pot to the Sauté mode and melt the coconut oil. Place the balls in the pot in a single layer. Cook for 3 to 4 minutes per side, or until they are golden brown.
3. In a separate bowl, stir together the remaining ingredients.

4.   Place the cooked balls on top and serve.

Instant Pot Zucchini Sticks

Prep time: 5 minutes | Cook time: 8 minutes | Serves 2

2 zucchinis, trimmed and cut into sticks
2 teaspoons olive oil
½ teaspoon white pepper
½ teaspoon salt
1 cup water
1.   Place the zucchini sticks in the Instant Pot pan and sprinkle with the olive oil, white pepper and salt.
2.   Pour the water and put the trivet in the pot. Place the pan on the trivet.
3.   Lock the lid. Select the Manual setting and set the cooking time for 8 minutes at High Pressure. Once the timer goes off, use a quick pressure release. Carefully open the lid.
4.   Remove the zucchinis from the pot and serve.

Curried Cauliflower and Tomatoes

Prep time: 10 minutes | Cook time: 2 minutes | Serves 4 to 6

1 medium head cauliflower, cut into bite-size pieces
1 (14-ounce / 397-g) can sugar-free diced tomatoes, undrained
1 bell pepper, thinly sliced
1 (14-ounce / 397-g) can full-fat coconut milk
½ to 1 cup water
2 tablespoons red curry paste
1 teaspoon salt
1 teaspoon garlic powder
½ teaspoon onion powder
½ teaspoon ground ginger
¼ teaspoon chili powder
Freshly ground black pepper, to taste
1.   Add all the ingredients, except for the black pepper, to the Instant Pot and stir to combine.
2.   Lock the lid. Select the Manual setting and set the cooking time for 2 minutes at High Pressure. Once the timer goes off, use a quick pressure release. Carefully open the lid.
3.   Sprinkle the black pepper and stir well. Serve immediately.

Gobi Masala

Prep time: 5 minutes | Cook time: 4 to 5 minutes | Serves 4 to 6

1 tablespoon olive oil
1 teaspoon cumin seeds
1 white onion, diced
1 garlic clove, minced
1 head cauliflower, chopped
1 tablespoon ground coriander
1 teaspoon ground cumin
½ teaspoon garam masala
½ teaspoon salt
1 cup water
1.   Set the Instant Pot to the Sauté mode and heat the olive oil. Add the cumin seeds to the pot and sauté for 30 seconds, stirring constantly. Add the onion and sauté for 2 to 3 minutes, stirring constantly. Add the garlic and sauté for 30 seconds, stirring frequently.
2.   Stir in the remaining ingredients.
3.   Lock the lid. Select the Manual mode and set the cooking time for 1 minute on High Pressure. When the timer goes off, perform a quick pressure release. Carefully open the lid.
4.   Serve immediately.

Spaghetti Squash Noodles with Tomatoes

Prep time: 15 minutes | Cook time: 14 to 16 minutes | Serves 4

1 medium spaghetti squash
1 cup water
2 tablespoons olive oil
1 small yellow onion, diced
6 garlic cloves, minced
2 teaspoons crushed red pepper flakes
2 teaspoons dried oregano
1 cup sliced cherry tomatoes
1 teaspoon kosher salt
½ teaspoon freshly ground black pepper
1 (14.5-ounce / 411-g) can sugar-free crushed tomatoes
¼ cup capers
1 tablespoon caper brine
½ cup sliced olives
1.   With a sharp knife, halve the spaghetti squash crosswise. Using a spoon, scoop out the seeds and sticky gunk in the middle of each half.
2.   Pour the water into the Instant Pot and place the trivet in the pot with the handles facing up. Arrange the squash halves, cut side facing up, on the trivet.
3.   Lock the lid. Select the Manual mode and set the cooking time for 7 minutes on High Pressure. When the timer goes off, use a quick pressure release. Carefully open the lid.
4.   Remove the trivet and pour out the water that has collected in the squash cavities. Using the tines of a fork, separate the cooked strands into spaghetti-like pieces and set aside in a bowl.
5.   Pour the water out of the pot. Select the Sauté mode and heat the oil.
6.   Add the onion to the pot and sauté for 3 minutes. Add the garlic, pepper flakes and oregano to the pot and sauté for 1 minute.
7.   Stir in the cherry tomatoes, salt and black pepper and cook for 2 minutes, or until the tomatoes are tender.
8.   Pour in the crushed tomatoes, capers, caper brine and olives and bring the mixture to a boil. Continue to cook for 2 to 3 minutes to allow the flavors to meld.
9.   Stir in the spaghetti squash noodles and cook for 1 to 2 minutes to warm everything through.
10.   Transfer the dish to a serving platter and serve.

Lemony Asparagus with Gremolata

Prep time: 15 minutes | Cook time: 2 minutes | Serves 2 to 4

Gremolata:
1 cup finely chopped fresh Italian flat-leaf parsley leaves
3 garlic cloves, peeled and grated
Zest of 2 small lemons
Asparagus:
1½ pounds (680 g) asparagus, trimmed
1 cup water
Lemony Vinaigrette:
1½ tablespoons fresh lemon juice
1 teaspoon Swerve
1 teaspoon Dijon mustard
2 tablespoons extra-virgin olive oil
Kosher salt and freshly ground black pepper, to taste
Garnish:
3 tablespoons slivered almonds
1.	In a small bowl, stir together all the ingredients for the gremolata.
2.	Pour the water into the Instant Pot. Arrange the asparagus in a steamer basket. Lower the steamer basket into the pot.
3.	Lock the lid. Select the Steam mode and set the cooking time for 2 minutes on Low Pressure.
4.	Meanwhile, prepare the lemony vinaigrette: In a bowl, combine the lemon juice, swerve and mustard and whisk to combine. Slowly drizzle in the olive oil and continue to whisk. Season generously with salt and pepper.
5.	When the timer goes off, perform a quick pressure release. Carefully open the lid. Remove the steamer basket from the Instant Pot.
6.	Transfer the asparagus to a serving platter. Drizzle with the vinaigrette and sprinkle with the gremolata. Serve the asparagus topped with the slivered almonds.

Garlicky Broccoli with Roasted Almonds

Prep time: 10 minutes | Cook time: 4 minutes | Serves 4 to 6
6 cups broccoli florets
1 cup water
1½ tablespoons olive oil
8 garlic cloves, thinly sliced
2 shallots, thinly sliced
½ teaspoon crushed red pepper flakes
Grated zest and juice of 1 medium lemon
½ teaspoon kosher salt
Freshly ground black pepper, to taste
¼ cup chopped roasted almonds
¼ cup finely slivered fresh basil
1.	Pour the water into the Instant Pot. Place the broccoli florets in a steamer basket and lower into the pot.
2.	Close and secure the lid. Select the Steam setting and set the cooking time for 2 minutes at Low Pressure. Once the timer goes off, use a quick pressure release. Carefully open the lid.
3.	Transfer the broccoli to a large bowl filled with cold water and ice. Once cooled, drain the broccoli and pat dry.
4.	Select the Sauté mode on the Instant Pot and heat the olive oil. Add the garlic to the pot and sauté for 30 seconds, tossing constantly. Add the shallots and pepper flakes to the pot and sauté for 1 minute.
5.	Stir in the cooked broccoli, lemon juice, salt and black pepper. Toss the ingredients together and cook for 1 minute.
6.	Transfer the broccoli to a serving platter and sprinkle with the chopped almonds, lemon zest and basil. Serve immediately.

Vinegary Broccoli with Cheese

Prep time: 5 minutes | Cook time: 5 minutes | Serves 4
1 pound (454 g) broccoli, cut into florets
1 cup water
2 garlic cloves, minced
1 cup crumbled Cottage cheese
2 tablespoons balsamic vinegar
1 teaspoon cumin seeds
1 teaspoon mustard seeds
Salt and pepper, to taste
1.	Pour the water into the Instant Pot and put the steamer basket in the pot. Place the broccoli in the steamer basket.
2.	Close and secure the lid. Select the Manual setting and set the cooking time for 5 minutes at High Pressure. Once the timer goes off, do a quick pressure release. Carefully open the lid.
3.	Stir in the remaining ingredients.
4.	Serve immediately.

Asparagus with Copoundy Cheese

Prep time: 5 minutes | Cook time: 1 minute | Serves 4
10 minutes
1½ pounds (680 g) fresh asparagus
1 cup water
2 tablespoons olive oil
4 garlic cloves, minced
Sea salt, to taste
¼ teaspoon ground black pepper
½ cup shredded Copoundy cheese
1.	Pour the water into the Instant Pot and put the steamer basket in the pot.
2.	Place the asparagus in the steamer basket. Drizzle the asparagus with the olive oil and sprinkle with the garlic on top. Season with salt and black pepper.
3.	Close and secure the lid. Select the Manual mode and set the cooking time for 1 minute at High Pressure. Once cooking is complete, do a quick pressure release. Carefully open the lid.
4.	Transfer the asparagus to a platter and served topped with the shredded cheese.

Chanterelle Mushrooms with Cheddar Cheese

Prep time: 10 minutes | Cook time: 5 minutes | Serves 4
1 tablespoon olive oil
2 cloves garlic, minced
1 (1-inch) ginger root, grated
16 ounces (454 g) Chanterelle mushrooms, brushed clean and sliced

½ cup unsweetened tomato purée
½ cup water
2 tablespoons dry white wine
1 teaspoon dried basil
½ teaspoon dried thyme
½ teaspoon dried dill weed
$^1/_3$ teaspoon freshly ground black pepper
Kosher salt, to taste
1 cup shredded Cheddar cheese
1.	Press the Sauté button on the Instant Pot and heat the olive oil. Add the garlic and grated ginger to the pot and sauté for 1 minute, or until fragrant. Stir in the remaining ingredients, except for the cheese.
2.	Lock the lid. Select the Manual mode and set the cooking time for 5 minutes on Low Pressure. When the timer goes off, perform a quick pressure release. Carefully open the lid..
3.	Serve topped with the shredded cheese.

Satarash with Eggs

Prep time: 10 minutes | Cook time: 5 minutes | Serves 4
2 tablespoons olive oil
1 white onion, chopped
2 cloves garlic
2 ripe tomatoes, puréed
1 green bell pepper, deseeded and sliced
1 red bell pepper, deseeded and sliced
1 teaspoon paprika
½ teaspoon dried oregano
½ teaspoon turmeric
Kosher salt and ground black pepper, to taste
1 cup water
4 large eggs, lightly whisked
1.	Press the Sauté button on the Instant Pot and heat the olive oil. Add the onion and garlic to the pot and sauté for 2 minutes, or until fragrant. Stir in the remaining ingredients, except for the eggs.
2.	Lock the lid. Select the Manual mode and set the cooking time for 3 minutes on High Pressure. When the timer goes off, perform a quick pressure release. Carefully open the lid.
3.	Fold in the eggs and stir to combine. Lock the lid and let it sit in the residual heat for 5 minutes. Serve warm.

Chinese-Style Pe-Tsai with Onion

Prep time: 5 minutes | Cook time: 8 minutes | Serves 4
2 tablespoons sesame oil
1 yellow onion, chopped
1 pound (454 g) pe-tsai cabbage, shredded
¼ cup rice wine vinegar
1 tablespoon coconut aminos
1 teaspoon finely minced garlic
½ teaspoon salt
¼ teaspoon Szechuan pepper
1.	Set the Instant Pot on the Sauté mode and heat the sesame oil. Add the onion to the pot and sauté for 5 minutes, or until tender. Stir in the remaining ingredients.

2.	Lock the lid. Select the Manual mode and set the cooking time for 3 minutes on High Pressure. When the timer goes off, perform a quick pressure release. Carefully open the lid.
3.	Transfer the cabbage mixture to a bowl and serve immediately.

Steamed Tomato with Halloumi Cheese

Prep time: 5 minutes | Cook time: 3 minutes | Serves 4
8 tomatoes, sliced
1 cup water
½ cup crumbled Halloumi cheese
2 tablespoons extra-virgin olive oil
2 tablespoons snipped fresh basil
2 garlic cloves, smashed
1.	Pour the water into the Instant Pot and put the trivet in the pot. Place the tomatoes in the trivet.
2.	Lock the lid. Select the Manual mode and set the cooking time for 3 minutes on High Pressure. When the timer goes off, perform a quick pressure release. Carefully open the lid.
3.	Toss the tomatoes with the remaining ingredients and serve.

Aromatic Spicy Zucchini

Prep time: 5 minutes | Cook time: 4 minutes | Serves 4
1½ tablespoons olive oil
2 garlic cloves, minced
1½ pounds (680 g) zucchinis, sliced
½ cup vegetable broth
1 teaspoon dried basil
½ teaspoon smoked paprika
½ teaspoon dried rosemary
Salt and pepper, to taste
1.	Set the Instant Pot to the Sauté mode and heat the olive oil. Add the garlic to the pot and sauté for 1 minute, or until fragrant. Stir in the remaining ingredients.
2.	Lock the lid. Select the Manual mode and set the cooking time for 3 minutes on Low Pressure. When the timer goes off, perform a quick pressure release. Carefully open the lid.
3.	Serve immediately.

Braised Collards with Red Wine

Prep time: 5 minutes | Cook time: 2 minutes | Serves 4
1 pound (454 g) Collards, torn into pieces
¾ cup water
¼ cup dry red wine
1½ tablespoons sesame oil
1 teaspoon ginger-garlic paste
½ teaspoon fennel seeds
½ teaspoon mustard seeds
Sea salt and ground black pepper, to taste
1.	Add all the ingredients to the Instant Pot and stir to combine.
2.	Lock the lid. Select the Manual mode and set the cooking time for 2 minutes on High Pressure. When the timer goes off, perform a quick pressure release. Carefully open the lid.

3.   Ladle into individual bowls and serve warm.

Spinach with Almonds and Olives

Prep time: 15 minutes | Cook time: 2 to 3 minutes | Serves 4

1 tablespoon olive oil
3 cloves garlic, smashed
Bunch scallions, chopped
2 pounds (907 g) spinach, washed
1 cup vegetable broth
1 tablespoon champagne vinegar
½ teaspoon dried dill weed
¼ teaspoon cayenne pepper
Seasoned salt and ground black pepper, to taste
½ cup almonds, soaked overnight and drained
2 tablespoons green olives, pitted and halved
2 tablespoons water
1 tablespoon extra-virgin olive oil
2 teaspoons lemon juice
1 teaspoon garlic powder
1 teaspoon onion powder
1.   Press the Sauté button on the Instant Pot and heat the olive oil. Add the garlic and scallions to the pot and sauté for 1 to 2 minutes, or until fragrant.
2.   Stir in the spinach, vegetable broth, vinegar, dill, cayenne pepper, salt and black pepper.
3.   Lock the lid. Select the Manual mode and set the cooking time for 1 minute on High Pressure. When the timer goes off, perform a quick pressure release. Carefully open the lid.
4.   Stir in the remaining ingredients.
5.   Transfer to serving plates and serve immediately.

Zoodles with Mediterranean Sauce

Prep time: 10 minutes | Cook time: 5 minutes | Serves 2

1 tablespoon olive oil
2 tomatoes, chopped
½ cup water
½ cup roughly chopped fresh parsley
3 tablespoons ground almonds
1 tablespoon fresh rosemary, chopped
1 tablespoon apple cider vinegar
1 teaspoon garlic, smashed
2 zucchinis, spiralized and cooked
½ avocado, pitted and sliced
Salt and ground black pepper, to taste
1.   Add the olive oil, tomatoes, water, parsley, ground almonds, rosemary, apple cider vinegar and garlic to the Instant Pot.
2.   Lock the lid. Select the Manual mode and set the cooking time for 5 minutes on High Pressure. When the timer beeps, perform a natural pressure release for 10 minutes, then release any remaining pressure. Carefully open the lid.
3.   Divide the cooked zucchini spirals between two serving plates. Spoon the sauce over each serving. Top with the avocado slices and season with salt and black pepper.
4.   Serve immediately.

Cauliflower Spinach Medley

Prep time: 10 minutes | Cook time: 3 minutes | Serves 4

1 pound (454 g) cauliflower, cut into florets
1 yellow onion, peeled and chopped
1 red bell pepper, deseeded and chopped
1 celery stalk, chopped
2 garlic cloves, crushed
2 tablespoons olive oil
1 tablespoon grated lemon zest
1 teaspoon Hungarian paprika
Sea salt and ground black pepper, to taste
2 cups spinach, torn into pieces
1.   Add all the ingredients, except for the spinach, to the Instant Pot.
2.   Close and secure the lid. Select the Manual setting and set the cooking time for 3 minutes at High Pressure. Once the timer goes off, use a quick pressure release. Carefully open the lid.
3.   Stir in the spinach and lock the lid. Let it sit in the residual heat for 5 minutes, or until wilted.
4.   Serve warm.

Green Beans with Onion

Prep time: 5 minutes | Cook time: 6 to 7 minutes | Serves 6

6 slices bacon, diced
1 cup diced onion
4 cups halved green beans
¼ cup water
1 teaspoon salt
1 teaspoon freshly ground black pepper
1.   Press the Sauté button on the Instant Pot and add the bacon and onion to the pot and sauté for 2 to 3 minutes. Stir in the remaining ingredients.
2.   Close and secure the lid. Select the Manual setting and set the cooking time for 4 minutes at High Pressure. Once the timer goes off, use a quick pressure release. Carefully open the lid.
3.   Serve immediately.

Spaghetti Squash Noodles

Prep time: 5 minutes | Cook time: 18 minutes | Serves 4

2 pounds (907 g) spaghetti squash
1 cup water
3 garlic cloves
1 cup fresh basil leaves
½ cup olive oil
$^1/_3$ cup unsalted toasted almonds
¼ cup flat-leaf parsley
3 tablespoons grated Parmesan cheese
½ teaspoon fine grind sea salt
½ teaspoon ground black pepper
1.   Using a knife, pierce all sides of the squash to allow the steam to penetrate during cooking.
2.   Pour the water into the Instant Pot and put the trivet in the pot. Place the squash on the trivet.
3.   Lock the lid. Select the Manual mode and set the cooking time for 18 minutes at High Pressure. When the timer goes off, use a natural pressure release for 10 minutes, then release any remaining pressure. Carefully open the lid.

4. Remove the trivet and squash from the pot. Set aside to cool for 15 minutes, or until the squash is cool enough to handle.
5. Make the pesto sauce by placing the remaining ingredients in a food processor. Pulse until the ingredients are well combined and form a thick paste. Set aside.
6. Cut the cooled spaghetti squash in half lengthwise. Using a spoon, scoop out and discard the seeds.
7. Using a fork, scrape the flesh of the squash to create the noodles. Transfer the noodles to a large bowl.
8. Divide the squash noodles among 4 serving bowls. Top each serving with the pesto sauce. Serve hot.

Cabbage in Cream Sauce

Prep time: 10 minutes | Cook time: 13 minutes | Serves 4

1 tablespoon unsalted butter
½ cup diced pancetta
¼ cup diced yellow onion
1 cup chicken broth
1 pound (454 g) green cabbage, finely chopped
1 bay leaf
$^1/_3$ cup heavy cream
1 tablespoon dried parsley
1 teaspoon fine grind sea salt
¼ teaspoon ground nutmeg
¼ teaspoon ground black pepper
1. Press the Sauté button on the Instant Pot and melt the butter. Add the pancetta and onion to the pot and sauté for about 4 minutes, or until the onion is tender and begins to brown.
2. Pour in the chicken broth. Using a wooden spoon, stir and loosen any browned bits from the bottom of the pot. Stir in the cabbage and bay leaf.
3. Lock the lid. Select the Manual mode and set the cooking time for 4 minutes on High Pressure. When the timer goes off, perform a quick pressure release. Carefully open the lid.
4. Select Sauté mode and bring the ingredients to a boil. Stir in the remaining ingredients and simmer for 5 additional minutes.
5. Remove and discard the bay leaf. Spoon into serving bowls. Serve warm.

Garlic Baby Potatoes

Prep time: 30 mins, Cook Time: 11 mins, Servings: 4

- 1 tbsp. olive oil
- 3 garlic cloves
- 2 lbs. baby potatoes
- 1 sprig rosemary
- 1 cup vegetable stock
- Salt and pepper, to taste
1. Hit the Sauté button in the Instant Pot.
2. Add the olive oil.
3. Add the garlic, baby potatoes and rosemary.
4. Brown the outside of the potatoes.
5. Pierce each potato with a fork.
6. Add the vegetable stock.

7. Lock the lid. Set the Instant Pot to Manual mode, then set the timer for 11 minutes at High Pressure.
8. Once cooking is complete, do a quick pressure release. Carefully open the lid.
9. Season with salt and pepper and serve.

Stuffed Sweet Potatoes

Prep time: 42 mins, Cook Time: 17 mins, Servings: 2

- 1 cup cooked couscous
- 2 sweet potatoes
- 1 tbsp. olive oil
- 1 tsp. paprika
- Salt and pepper, to taste
- 1 cup cooked chickpeas
- 2 spring onions, chopped
1. Use a fork to pierce sweet potatoes.
2. To the Instant Pot, add enough water to cover.
3. Add the steamer rack inside and set the potatoes on top.
4. Lock the lid. Set the Instant Pot to Manual mode, then set the timer for 8 minutes on High Pressure.
5. Once cooking is complete, do a natural pressure release for 5 minutes. Carefully open the lid.
6. Set the sweet potato aside on a plate. Drain the pot.
7. While the Instant Pot is on Sauté mode, heat the olive oil. Set in chickpeas and paprika with salt and pepper.
8. Half the potatoes and mash the inside.
9. Add the chickpeas and couscous.
10. Top with the chopped spring onion and serve.

Italian Vegetable Medley

Prep time: 50 mins, Cook Time: 8 mins, Servings: 4

- 1 cup water
- 1 tbsp. raisins
- 1 zucchini, sliced
- 1 eggplant, cubed
- 3 tbsps. olive oil
- 10 halved cherry tomatoes
- 2 potatoes, cubed
- 2 tbsps. raisins
1. In the Instant Pot, add the water. Add the potatoes and zucchini.
2. Lock the lid. Set the Instant Pot to Manual mode, then set the timer for 8 minutes on High Pressure.
3. Once cooking is complete, do a quick pressure release. Carefully open the lid.
4. Drain water and add olive oil.
5. Mix in the tomatoes and eggplant. Let cook for 2 minutes.
6. Top with the raisins before serving.

Instant Ratatouille

Prep time: 20 mins, Cook Time: 10 mins, Servings: 4

- 2 cups water
- 2 medium zucchini, sliced
- 3 tomatoes, sliced
- 2 eggplants, sliced
- 1 tbsp. olive oil
- Salt and pepper, to taste

1. Pour the water into the Instant Pot.
2. In a baking dish, arrange a layer of the zucchini.
3. Top with a layer of the tomatoes.
4. Place a layer of eggplant slices on top.
5. Continue layering until you use all the ingredients.
6. Drizzle with olive oil.
7. Place the baking dish on the trivet and lower it.
8. Lock the lid. Set the Instant Pot to Manual mode, then set the timer for 10 minutes at High Pressure.
9. Once cooking is complete, do a quick pressure release. Carefully open the lid.
10. Sprinkle with salt and pepper and serve warm!

Kale and Sweet Potatoes with Tofu

Prep time: 45 mins, Cook time: 6 mins, Servings: 4

- 1 tbsp. tamari sauce
- ⅔ cup vegetable broth
- 1 sweet potato, cubed
- 2 cups chopped kale
- 8 oz. cubed tofu
- Salt and pepper, to taste

1. Add tofu in the Instant Pot.
2. Drizzle with half of the tamari and the broth.
3. Cook for about 3 minutes on Sauté function.
4. Add the rest of the ingredients.
5. Lock the lid. Set the Instant Pot to Manual mode, then set the timer for about 3 minutes at High Pressure.
6. Once cooking is complete, do a quick pressure release. Carefully open the lid.
7. Serve immediately!

Broccoli and Mushrooms

Prep time: 15 mins, Cook Time: 8 mins, Servings: 4

- 2 tbsps. coconut oil
- 1 cup sliced mushrooms
- 2 cups broccoli florets
- 1 tbsp. soy sauce
- 1 cup vegetable broth
- Salt and pepper, to taste

1. Set the Instant Pot to Sauté mode and add the coconut oil to melt.
2. Add the mushrooms and sauté for 4 to 5 minutes.
3. Add broccoli and soy sauce and sauté for 1 more minute.

4. Pour the broth over. Sprinkle with salt and pepper.
5. Lock the lid. Set the Instant Pot to Manual mode, then set the timer for 2 minutes at High Pressure.
6. Once cooking is complete, do a quick pressure release. Carefully open the lid.
7. Serve the veggies drizzled with the cooking liquid.
8. Serve immediately!

Instant Pot Mushrooms

Prep time: 12 mins, Cook Time: 10 mins, Servings: 1

- ½ cup water
- 4 oz. mushrooms, sliced
- 2 garlic cloves, minced
- 1 tbsp. olive oil
- Salt and pepper, to taste

1. Pour water along with mushrooms in an Instant Pot.
2. Lock the lid. Set the Instant Pot to Manual mode, then set the timer for 5 minutes at High Pressure.
3. Once cooking is complete, do a quick pressure release. Carefully open the lid.
4. Drain the mushroom and then return back to the Instant Pot.
5. Now add olive oil to the pot and mix.
6. Press the Sauté function of the pot and let it cook for 3 minutes.
7. Sauté every 30 seconds.
8. Add the garlic and sauté for 2 minutes or until fragrant. Sprinkle with salt and pepper, then serve the dish.

Instant Pot Steamed Asparagus

Prep time: 5mins, Cook time: 5 mins, Servings: 1

- 7 asparagus spears, washed and trimmed
- ¼ tsp. pepper
- 1 tbsp. extra virgin olive oil
- Juice from freshly squeezed ¼ lemon
- ¼ tsp. salt
- 1 cup water

1. Place a trivet or the steamer rack in the Instant Pot and pour in the water.
2. In a mixing bowl, combine the asparagus spears, salt, pepper, and lemon juice.
3. Place on top of the trivet.
4. Lock the lid. Set the Instant Pot to Steam mode, then set the timer for 5 minutes at High Pressure.
5. Once cooking is complete, do a quick pressure release. Carefully open the lid.
6. Drizzle the asparagus with olive oil.

Steamed Paprika Broccoli

Prep time: 6 mins, Cook time: 6 mins, Servings: 2

- ¼ tsp. ground black pepper
- 1 tbsp. freshly squeezed lemon juice
- ¼ tsp. salt
- 1 head broccoli, cut into florets

- 1 tbsp. paprika
- 1 cup water

1. Place a trivet or the steamer rack in the Instant Pot and pour in the water.
2. Place the broccoli florets on the trivet and sprinkle salt, pepper, paprika, and lemon juice.
3. Lock the lid. Set the Instant Pot to Steam mode, then set the timer for 6 minutes at High Pressure.
4. Once cooking is complete, do a quick pressure release. Carefully open the lid.
5. Serve immediately.

Sautéed Brussels Sprouts And Pecans

Prep time: 4 mins, Cook time: 6 mins, Servings: 4

- ¼ cup chopped pecans
- 2 garlic cloves, minced
- Salt and pepper, to taste
- 2 tbsps. water
- 2 cups baby Brussels sprouts
- 1 tbsp. coconut oil

1. Press the Sauté button on the Instant Pot and heat the oil.
2. Sauté the garlic for 1 minute or until fragrant.
3. Add the Brussels sprouts. Sprinkle salt and pepper for seasoning.
4. Add the water.
5. Lock the lid. Set the Instant Pot to Manual mode, then set the timer for 3 minutes at High Pressure.
6. Once cooking is complete, do a quick pressure release. Carefully open the lid.
7. Add the pecans and set to the Sauté mode and sauté for 3 minutes or until the pecans are roasted.
8. Serve immediately.

Coconut Cabbage

Prep time: 6 mins, Cook time: 20 mins, Servings: 4

- 2 cups freshly squeezed coconut milk
- 1 halved onion
- 1 thumb-size ginger, sliced
- 1 garlic bulb, crushed
- 1 cabbage head, shredded
- Salt and pepper, to taste

1. In the Instant Pot, add all the ingredients. Stir to mix well.
2. Lock the lid. Set the Instant Pot to Manual mode, then set the timer for 20 minutes at High Pressure.
3. Once cooking is complete, do a quick pressure release. Carefully open the lid.
4. Serve warm.

Cauliflower Mushroom Risotto

Prep time: 7 mins, Cook time: 10 mins, Servings: 3

- 1 cup freshly squeezed coconut milk
- 1 tbsp. coconut oil
- 1 cauliflower head, cut into florets

- 1 onion, chopped
- 1 lb. shiitake mushrooms, sliced
- Salt and pepper, to taste

1. Press the Sauté button and heat the coconut oil.
2. Sauté the onions for 3 minutes or until fragrant. Add the cauliflower and shiitake mushrooms.
3. Sprinkle salt and pepper for seasoning.
4. Add the coconut milk in three batches.
5. Allow to simmer for 10 minutes.
6. Garnish with chopped parsley if desired.

Vegetarian Smothered Cajun Greens

Prep time: 6 mins, Cook time: 3 mins, Servings: 4

- 2 tsps. crushed garlic
- Salt and pepper, to taste
- 1 onion, chopped
- 6 cups raw greens
- 1 tbsp. coconut oil
- 1 cup water

1. Press the Sauté button on the Instant Pot and heat the coconut oil.
2. Sauté the onion and garlic for 2 minutes or until fragrant.
3. Add the greens and Sprinkle salt and pepper for seasoning.
4. Add the water.
5. Lock the lid. Set the Instant Pot to Manual mode, then set the timer for 3 minutes at High Pressure.
6. Once cooking is complete, do a quick pressure release. Carefully open the lid.
7. Sprinkle with red chili flakes, then serve.

Caramelized Onions

Prep time: 6 mins, Cook time: 35 mins, Servings: 2

- 1 tbsp. freshly squeezed lemon juice
- 3 tbsps. coconut oil
- Salt and pepper, to taste
- 3 white onions, sliced
- 1 cup water

1. Press the Sauté button on the Instant Pot and heat the coconut oil.
2. Sauté the onions for 5 minutes and add the remaining ingredients.
3. Add the water and stir.
4. Lock the lid. Set the Instant Pot to Manual mode, then set the timer for 20 minutes at High Pressure.
5. Once cooking is complete, do a quick pressure release. Carefully open the lid.
6. Press the Sauté button and continue cooking for another 10 minutes.
7. Serve warm.

Zucchini and Tomato Melange

Prep time: 13 mins, Cook time: 10 mins, Servings: 4

- 5 garlic cloves, minced
- 3 medium zucchinis, chopped

- 1 lb. puréed tomatoes
- 1 onion, chopped
- 1 tbsp. coconut oil
- Salt and pepper, to taste
- 1 cup water

1. Place the tomatoes in a food processor and blend until smooth.
2. Press the Sauté button on the Instant Pot and heat the oil.
3. Sauté the garlic and onions for 2 minutes or until fragrant.
4. Add the zucchini and tomato purée.
5. Sprinkle salt and pepper for seasoning.
6. Add the water to add more moisture.
7. Lock the lid. Set the Instant Pot to Manual mode, then set the timer for 10 minutes at High Pressure.
8. Once cooking is complete, do a quick pressure release. Carefully open the lid.
9. Serve warm.

Instant Pot Veggie Stew

Prep time: 6 mins, Cook time: 10 mins, Servings: 5

- ½ cup chopped tomatoes
- 1 stalk celery, minced
- 2 zucchinis, chopped
- 1 lb. mushrooms, sliced
- 1 onion, chopped
- Salt and pepper, to taste

1. Place all ingredients in the Instant Pot.
2. Pour in enough water until half of the vegetables are submerged.
3. Lock the lid. Set the Instant Pot to Manual mode, then set the timer for 10 minutes at High Pressure.
4. Once cooking is complete, do a quick pressure release. Carefully open the lid.
5. Serve warm.

Zucchini and Bell Pepper Stir Fry

Prep time: 6 mins, Cook time: 5 mins, Servings: 6

- 2 large zucchinis, sliced
- 1 tbsp. coconut oil
- 4 garlic cloves, minced
- 2 red sweet bell peppers, julienned
- 1 onion, chopped
- Salt and pepper, to taste
- ¼ cup water

1. Press the Sauté button on the Instant Pot.
2. Heat the coconut oil and sauté the onion and garlic for 2 minutes or until fragrant.
3. Add the zucchini and red bell peppers.
4. Sprinkle salt and pepper for seasoning.
5. Pour in the water.
6. Lock the lid. Set the Instant Pot to Manual mode, then set the timer for 5 minutes at High Pressure.
7. Once cooking is complete, do a quick pressure release. Carefully open the lid.
8. Serve warm.

Eggplant, Zucchini, And Tomatoes

Prep time: 6 mins, Cook time: 8 mins, Servings: 6

- 3 zucchinis, sliced
- 1 eggplant, chopped
- 3 tbsps. olive oil
- 3 tomatoes, sliced
- 1 onion, diced
- Salt and pepper, to taste
- ¼ cup water

1. Press the Sauté button on the Instant Pot and heat the olive oil.
2. Sauté the onions for 3 minutes or until translucent, then add the eggplants. Sauté for another 2 minutes.
3. Add the tomatoes and zucchini.
4. Sprinkle salt and pepper for seasoning.
5. Add the water.
6. Lock the lid. Set the Instant Pot to Manual mode, then set the timer for 6 minutes at High Pressure.
7. Once cooking is complete, do a quick pressure release. Carefully open the lid.
8. Serve warm.

Instant Pot Baby Bok Choy

Prep time: 9 mins, Cook time: 4 mins, Servings: 6

- 1 tsp. peanut oil
- 1 lb. baby Bok choy, trimmed and washed
- Salt and pepper, to taste
- 4 garlic cloves, minced
- 1 tsp. red pepper flakes
- 1 cup water

1. Press the Sauté button on the Instant Pot.
2. Heat the oil and sauté the garlic for 1 minute until fragrant.
3. Add the Bok choy and sprinkle salt and pepper for seasoning.
4. Pour in the water.
5. Lock the lid. Set the Instant Pot to Manual mode, then set the timer for 4 minutes at High Pressure.
6. Once cooking is complete, do a quick pressure release. Carefully open the lid.
7. Sprinkle with red pepper flakes, then serve.

Sesame Bok Choy

Prep time: 6 mins, Cook Time: 4 mins, Servings: 4

- 1 tsp. soy sauce
- ½ tsp. sesame oil
- 1½ cups water
- 1 medium Bok choy
- 2 tsps. sesame seeds

1. Pour the water into the Instant Pot.
2. Place the Bok choy inside the steamer basket.
3. Lower the basket
4. Lock the lid. Set the Instant Pot to Manual mode, then set the timer for 4 minutes at High Pressure.
5. Once cooking is complete, do a quick pressure release. Carefully open the lid.

6.	In a serving bowl, set in the Bok choy. Toss with the remaining ingredients to coat.
7.	Serve immediately!

Instant Pot Artichokes

Prep time: 6 mins, Cook time: 30 mins, Servings: 8

- ½ cup organic chicken broth
- Salt and pepper, to taste
- 4 large artichokes, trimmed and cleaned
- 1 onion, chopped
- 1 garlic clove, crushed

1.	Place all ingredients in the Instant Pot.
2.	Lock the lid. Set the Instant Pot to Manual mode, then set the timer for 30 minutes at High Pressure.
3.	Once cooking is complete, do a quick pressure release. Carefully open the lid.
4.	Serve the artichokes with lemon juice.

Cauliflower Mash

Prep time: 12 mins, Cook time: 10 mins, Servings: 4

- 1 cup water
- 1 cauliflower head, cut into florets
- ¼ tsp. salt
- ¼ tsp. ground black pepper
- ¼ tsp. garlic powder
- 1 handful chopped chives

1.	Set a trivet in the Instant Pot and pour in the water.
2.	Place the cauliflower.
3.	Lock the lid. Set the Instant Pot to Steam mode, then set the timer for 10 minutes at High Pressure.
4.	Once cooking is complete, do a quick pressure release. Carefully open the lid.
5.	Using a food processor, pulse the cauliflower.
6.	Add the garlic powder, salt, and pepper.
7.	Garnish with chives, then serve.

Vegetarian Mac and Cheese

Prep time: 30 mins, Cook time: 4 mins, Servings: 10

- 4 cups water
- 1 tsp. garlic powder
- 16 oz. elbow macaroni pasta
- Salt and pepper, to taste
- 2 cups frozen mixed vegetables
- 1 cup shredded Cheddar
- 1 cup milk
- Fresh parsley, for garnish

1.	To the Instant Pot, add the water, garlic powder and pasta. Sprinkle with salt and pepper.
2.	Lock the lid. Set the Instant Pot to Manual mode, then set the timer for 4 minutes at High Pressure.
3.	Once cooking is complete, do a quick pressure release. Carefully open the lid.
4.	Add the vegetables, Cheddar and milk, then cover the pot and press Sauté.
5.	Simmer until the vegetables have softened.
6.	Garnish with fresh parsley and serve.

Couscous with Vegetables

Prep time: 30 mins, Cook time: 10 mins, Servings: 3

- 2 tsps. olive oil
- 1 onion, chopped
- 1 red bell pepper, chopped
- 1 cup grated carrot
- 2 cups couscous
- 2 cups water
- Salt, to taste
- ½ tbsp. lemon juice

1.	Grese the Instant Pot with olive oil. Add the onion.
2.	Set to the Sauté mode and sauté the onion for 2 minutes.
3.	Add the red bell pepper and carrot.
4.	Cook for 3 minutes.
5.	Add the couscous and water.
6.	Season with salt.
7.	Lock the lid. Set the Instant Pot to Manual mode, then set the timer for 2 minutes at High Pressure.
8.	Once cooking is complete, do a natural pressure release. Carefully open the lid.
9.	Fluff the couscous with a fork.
10.	Drizzle with the lemon juice before serving.

Quinoa and Veggies

Prep time: 15 mins, Cook Time: 5 mins, Servings: 4

- 1½ cups water
- 1 cup rinsed and drained uncooked quinoa
- ¼ cup crumbled feta cheese
- Greek seasoning and olive oil mixture
- ¼ cup sliced cucumber
- ¼ cup diced black olives

1.	Pour the water into the Instant Pot.
2.	Add the quinoa.
3.	Lock the lid. Set the Instant Pot to Manual mode, then set the timer for 1 minute at High Pressure.
4.	Once cooking is complete, do a natural pressure release. Carefully open the lid.
5.	In a bowl, mix cucumber and black olives.
6.	Top with the quinoa and feta cheese.
7.	Drizzle with the dressing, then serve.

CHAPTER 8 FISH AND SEAFOOD

Steamed Cod and Veggies

Prep time: 5 minutes | Cook time: 2 to 4 minutes | Serves 2

½ cup water
Kosher salt and freshly ground black pepper, to taste
2 tablespoons freshly squeezed lemon juice, divided
2 tablespoons melted butter
1 garlic clove, minced
1 zucchini or yellow summer squash, cut into thick slices
1 cup cherry tomatoes
1 cup whole Brussels sprouts
2 (6-ounce / 170-g) cod fillets
2 thyme sprigs or ½ teaspoon dried thyme
Hot cooked rice, for serving

1. Pour the water into your Instant Pot and insert a steamer basket.
2. Sprinkle the fish with the salt and pepper. Mix together 1 tablespoon of the lemon juice, the butter, and garlic in a small bowl. Set aside.
3. Add the zucchini, tomatoes, and Brussels sprouts to the basket. Sprinkle with the salt and pepper and drizzle the remaining 1 tablespoon of lemon juice over the top.
4. Place the fish fillets on top of the veggies. Brush with the mixture and then turn the fish and repeat on the other side. Drizzle any remaining mixture all over the veggies. Place the thyme sprigs on top.
5. Lock the lid. Select the Steam mode and set the cooking time for 2 to 4 minutes on High Pressure, depending on the thickness of the fish.
6. Once cooking is complete, use a quick pressure release. Carefully open the lid.
7. Serve the cod and veggies over the cooked rice.

Cod Fillets with Lemon and Dill

Prep time: 5 minutes | Cook time: 5 minutes | Serves 2

1 cup water
2 cod fillets
¼ teaspoon garlic powder
Salt and ground black pepper, to taste
2 sprigs fresh dill
4 slices lemon
2 tablespoons butter

1. Add the water to the Instant Pot and put the trivet in the bottom of the pot.
2. Arrange the cod fillets on the trivet. Sprinkle with the garlic powder, salt, and pepper.
3. Layer 1 sprig of dill, 2 lemon slices, and 1 tablespoon of butter on each fillet.
4. Secure the lid. Select the Manual mode and set the cooking time for 5 minutes on High Pressure.
5. Once the timer beeps, use quick pressure release. Carefully remove the lid.
6. Serve.

Wild Alaskan Cod with Cherry Tomatoes

Prep time: 5 minutes | Cook time: 8 minutes | Serves 2

1 large fillet wild Alaskan Cod
1 cup cherry tomatoes, chopped
Salt and ground black pepper, to taste
2 tablespoons butter

1. Add the tomatoes to your Instant Pot. Top with the cod fillet. Sprinkle with the salt and pepper.
2. Secure the lid. Press the Manual button on your Instant Pot and set the cooking time for 8 minutes on High Pressure.
3. Once the timer goes off, perform a quick pressure release. Carefully remove the lid.
4. Add the butter to the cod fillet. Secure the lid and let stand for 1 minute.
5. Transfer to a serving plate and serve.

Garlic and Lemon Cod

Prep time: 10 minutes | Cook time: 5 minutes | Serves 4

1 pound (454 g) cod fillets
4 cloves garlic, smashed
1 medium lemon, cut into wedges
½ teaspoon salt
¼ teaspoon black pepper
1 tablespoon olive oil
1 cup water

1. Place the cod, garlic, and lemon in the center of aluminum foil. Sprinkle with the salt and pepper. Drizzle the oil over the top. Fold the foil up on all sides and crimp the edges tightly.
2. Place the trivet in the bottom of your Instant Pot. Pour in the water. Carefully lower the foil packet into the pot.
3. Secure the lid. Select the Manual mode and cook for 5 minutes on Low Pressure.
4. Once the timer goes off, do a quick release pressure. Carefully open the lid.
5. Lift the foil packet out of your Instant Pot. Carefully open the foil packet.
6. Squeeze fresh lemon juice over the cod and serve.

Cod with Orange Sauce

Prep time: 10 minutes | Cook time: 7 minutes | Serves 4

4 cod fillets, boneless
1 cup white wine
Juice from 1 orange
A small grated ginger piece
Salt and ground black pepper, to taste
4 spring onions, chopped

1. Combine the wine, orange juice, and ginger in your Instant Pot and stir well.
2. Insert a steamer basket. Arrange the cod fillets on the basket. Sprinkle with the salt and pepper.
3. Secure the lid. Press the Manual button on your Instant Pot and set the cooking time for 7 minutes on High Pressure.

4. Once the timer beeps, do a quick pressure release. Carefully remove the lid.
5. Drizzle the sauce all over the fish and sprinkle with the green onions.
6. Transfer to a serving plate and serve immediately.

Lemony Salmon

Prep time: 6 mins, Cook Time: 3 mins, Servings: 2
- ¼ cup lemon juice
- Cooking spray
- Salt and pepper, to taste
- 2 salmon fillets, frozen
- 1 cup water

1. Add the water and steamer rack to the Instant Pot. Spray the rack with cooking spray.
2. Place the salmon fillets in the steamer rack. Season with salt and pepper.
3. Drizzle with lemon juice.
4. Lock the lid. Select the Steam mode and cook for 3 minutes at Low Pressure.
5. Once cooking is complete, do a quick pressure release. Carefully open the lid.
6. Remove from the pot and serve on a plate.

Savory Salmon with Dill

Prep time: 12 mins, Cook Time: 10 mins, Servings: 2
- 2 tbsps. dill
- ⅓ cup olive oil
- 1 tbsp. fresh lemon juice
- 2 tbsps. butter
- 2 salmon fillets
- 1 cup water
- Salt and pepper, to taste

1. Add the water and steam rack to the Instant Pot.
2. Put the remaining ingredients in a heatproof dish and stir well.
3. Place the dish on the steam rack.
4. Lock the lid. Select the Steam mode and cook for 10 minutes at Low Pressure.
5. Once cooking is complete, do a quick pressure release. Carefully open the lid.
6. Divide the salmon fillets among two serving plates and serve.

Salmon with Basil Pesto

Prep time: 6 mins, Cook Time: 6 mins, Servings: 6
- 3 garlic cloves, minced
- 1½ lbs. salmon fillets
- 2 cups basil leaves
- 2 tbsps. freshly squeezed lemon juice
- ½ cup olive oil
- Salt and pepper, to taste

1. Make the pesto sauce: Put the basil leaves, olive oil, lemon juice, and garlic in a food processor, and pulse until smooth.
2. Season with salt and pepper.
3. Place the salmon fillets in the Instant Pot and add the pesto sauce.

4. Lock the lid. Select the Manual mode and set the cooking time for 6 minutes at Low Pressure.
5. Once cooking is complete, do a quick pressure release. Carefully open the lid.
6. Divide the salmon among six plates and serve.

Salmon Tandoori

Prep time: 2 hours, Cook Time: 6 mins, Servings: 4
- 1½ lbs. salmon fillets
- 3 tbsps. coconut oil
- Salt and pepper, to taste
- 1 tbsp. tandoori spice mix

1. In a bowl, add all the ingredients. Toss well until the fish is fully coated. Allow the fish to marinate for 2 hours in the fridge.
2. Place the marinated salmon in the Instant Pot.
3. Lock the lid. Select the Manual mode and cook for 6 minutes at Low Pressure. Flip the fish halfway through the cooking time.
4. Once cooking is complete, do a quick pressure release. Carefully open the lid.
5. Remove from the pot and serve on a plate.

Simple Steamed Salmon Fillets

Prep time: 6 mins, Cook time: 10 mins, Servings: 3
- 1 cup water
- 2 tbsps. freshly squeezed lemon juice
- 2 tbsps. soy sauce
- 10 oz. salmon fillets
- Salt and pepper, to taste
- 1 tsp. toasted sesame seeds

1. Set a trivet in the Instant Pot and pour the water into the pot.
2. Using a heat-proof dish, combine all ingredients.
3. Place the heat-proof dish on the trivet.
4. Lock the lid. Select the Manual mode and cook for 10 minutes at Low Pressure.
5. Once cooking is complete, do a quick pressure release. Carefully open the lid.
6. Garnish with toasted sesame seeds and serve.

Instant Pot Curried Salmon

Prep time: 6 mins, Cook Time: 8 mins, Servings: 4
- 2 cups coconut milk
- 2 tbsps. coconut oil
- 1 onion, chopped
- 1 lb. raw salmon, diced
- 1½ tbsps. minced garlic

1. Press the Sauté button on the Instant Pot and heat the oil.
2. Sauté the garlic and onions until fragrant, about 2 minutes.
3. Add the diced salmon and stir for 1 minute.
4. Pour in the coconut milk.
5. Lock the lid. Select the Manual mode and cook for 4 minutes at Low Pressure.

6.	Once cooking is complete, do a quick pressure release. Carefully open the lid.
7.	Let the salmon cool for 5 minutes before serving.

Lemon Pepper Salmon

Prep time: 15 mins, Cook time: 5 mins, Servings: 4

- 1 cup water
- 1 tsp. ground dill
- 1 tsp. ground tarragon
- 1 tsp. ground basil
- 4 salmon fillets
- 2 tbsps. olive oil
- Salt, to taste
- 4 lemon slices
- 1 carrot, sliced
- 1 zucchini, sliced

1.	In the Instant Pot, add the water, dill, tarragon, and basil.
2.	Place the steamer basket inside.
3.	Set in the salmon. Drizzle with a tablespoon of olive oil, pepper and salt. Top with lemon slices.
4.	Lock the lid. Select the Steam mode and cook for 3 minutes at Low Pressure.
5.	Once cooking is complete, do a quick pressure release. Carefully open the lid.
6.	Transfer the fish to a plate and discard the lemon slices.
7.	Drizzle the Instant Pot with remaining olive oil. Add the carrot and zucchini to the Instant Pot. Set to Sauté mode, then sauté for 2minutes or until the vegetables are tender.
8.	Serve the salmon with the veggies.
9.	Garnish with fresh lemon wedges.

Chili-Garlic Salmon

Prep time: 3 mins, Cook time: 7 mins, Servings: 4

- ¼ cup soy sauce
- 4 salmon fillets
- 5 tbsps. organic sugar-free chili sauce
- Salt and pepper, to taste
- ¼ cup water
- 3 tbsps. chopped green onions

1.	In the Instant Pot, add all the ingredients except for the green onions.
2.	Lock the lid. Select the Manual mode and cook for 7 minutes at Low Pressure.
3.	Once cooking is complete, do a quick pressure release. Carefully open the lid.
4.	Garnish with green onions and serve.

Steamed Herbed Red Snapper

Prep time: 3 mins, Cook time: 12 mins, Servings: 4

- 1 cup water
- 4 red snapper fillets
- 1½ tsps. chopped fresh herbs
- ¼ tsp. paprika
- 3 tbsps. freshly squeezed lemon juice
- Salt and pepper, to taste

1.	Set a trivet in the Instant Pot and pour the water into the pot.
2.	Mix all ingredients in a heat-proof dish that will fit in the Instant Pot. Combine to coat the fish with all ingredients.
3.	Place the heat-proof dish on the trivet.
4.	Lock the lid. Select the Manual mode and cook for 12 minutes at Low Pressure.
5.	Once cooking is complete, do a quick pressure release. Carefully open the lid.
6.	Serve warm.

Steamed Greek Snapper

Prep time: 6 mins, Cook time: 10 mins, Servings: 4

- 1 cup water
- 12 snapper fillets
- 3 tbsps. olive oil
- 2 tbsps. Greek yogurt
- 1 garlic clove, minced
- Salt and pepper, to taste

1.	Set a trivet in the Instant Pot and pour the water into the pot.
2.	In a mixing bowl, combine the olive oil, garlic, and Greek yogurt. Sprinkle salt and pepper for seasoning.
3.	Apply Greek yogurt mixture to the fish fillets. Place the fillets on the trivet.
4.	Lock the lid. Select the Steam mode and cook for 10 minutes at Low Pressure.
5.	Once cooking is complete, do a quick pressure release. Carefully open the lid.
6.	Serve warm.

Cod with Orange Sauce

Prep time: 12 mins, Cook Time: 7 mins, Servings: 4

- 1 cup white wine
- 1 small ginger piece, grated
- 4 spring onions, finely chopped
- Juice of 1 orange
- 4 boneless cod fillets

1.	In the Instant Pot, combine the wine with ginger, spring onions and orange juice, stir, add steamer basket, add cod fillets inside.
2.	Lock the lid. Select the Manual mode, then set the timer for 7 minutes at Low Pressure.
3.	Once the timer goes off, do a quick pressure release. Carefully open the lid.
4.	Divide fish on plates, drizzle orange juice all over and serve.

Steamed Lemon Mustard Salmon

Prep time: 8 mins, Cook time: 10 mins, Servings: 4

- 1 cup water
- 1 garlic clove, minced
- 4 skinless salmon fillets
- 2 tbsps. Dijon mustard
- Salt and pepper, to taste
- 2 tbsps. freshly squeezed lemon juice

1. Set a trivet in the Instant Pot and pour the water into the pot.
2. In a bowl, mix lemon juice, mustard, and garlic. Sprinkle salt and pepper for seasoning.
3. Top the salmon fillets with the mustard mixture. Place the fish fillets on the trivet.
4. Lock the lid. Select the Steam mode and cook for 10 minutes at Low Pressure.
5. Once cooking is complete, do a quick pressure release. Carefully open the lid.
6. Serve warm.

Quick Salmon

Prep time: 12 mins, Cook Time: 5 mins, Servings: 4

- 1 cup water
- ¼ cup lemon juice
- 1 tbsp. butter
- ¼ tsp. salt
- 4 boneless salmon fillets
- 1 bunch dill, chopped

1. Place the water in the Instant Pot, add lemon juice, add steamer basket, add salmon inside, season with some salt, sprinkle dill and drizzle melted butter.
2. Lock the lid. Select the Manual mode and cook for 5 minutes at Low Pressure.
3. Once cooking is complete, do a quick pressure release. Carefully open the lid.
4. Divide salmon between plates and serve with a side dish.

Lemon Pepper Salmon

Prep time: 12 mins, Cook Time: 10 mins, Servings: 4

- 1 cup water
- 1 lemon, sliced
- 1 red bell pepper, julienned
- 1 lb. boneless salmon fillets
- Black pepper, to taste
- 3 tsps. melted butter

1. Set the water in the Instant Pot, add steamer basket, add salmon fillets, season them with black pepper, drizzle melted butter all over, divide bell pepper and lemon slices on top.
2. Lock the lid. Select the Manual mode and cook for 7 minutes at Low Pressure.
3. Once cooking is complete, do a quick pressure release. Carefully open the lid.
4. Divide salmon and bell pepper on plates, top with lemon slices and serve.

Flounder with Dill and Capers

Prep time: 3 mins, Cook time: 10 mins, Servings: 4

- 1 cup water
- 1 tbsp. chopped fresh dill
- 4 lemon wedges
- 2 tbsps. chopped capers
- 4 flounder fillets
- Salt and pepper, to taste

1. In the Instant Pot, set in a steamer basket and pour the water into the pot.
2. Sprinkle salt and pepper to the flounder fillets. Sprinkle with dill and chopped capers on top. Add lemon wedges on top for garnish.
3. Place the fillets on the trivet.
4. Lock the lid. Select the Steam mode and cook for 10 minutes at Low Pressure.
5. Once cooking is complete, do a quick pressure release. Carefully open the lid.
6. Serve warm.

Italian Salmon with Lemon Juice

Prep time: 6 mins, Cook Time: 8 mins, Servings: 5

- 1½ lbs. salmon fillets
- 2 tbsps. butter
- 3 tbsps. olive oil
- 1 tbsp. Italian herb seasoning mix
- 3 tbsps. freshly squeezed lemon juice
- Salt and pepper, to taste
- ⅓ cup water

1. Place all ingredients in the Instant Pot and stir well.
2. Lock the lid. Select the Manual mode and set the cooking time for 8 minutes at Low Pressure. Flip the fish halfway through the cooking time.
3. Once cooking is complete, do a quick pressure release. Carefully open the lid.
4. Divide the salmon among plates and serve.

Thai Fish Curry

Prep time: 6 mins, Cook Time: 6 mins, Servings: 6

- 1½ lbs. salmon fillets
- 2 cups fresh coconut milk
- ¼ cup chopped cilantro
- ⅓ cup olive oil
- 2 tbsps. curry powder
- Salt and pepper, to taste

1. In the Instant Pot, add all the ingredients. Give a good stir.
2. Lock the lid. Select the Manual mode and set the cooking time for 6 minutes at Low Pressure.
3. Once cooking is complete, do a quick pressure release. Carefully open the lid. Set warm.

Coconut Curry Cod

Prep time: 4 mins, Cook time: 8 mins, Servings: 4

- 2 tsps. curry powder
- 2 tsps. grated ginger
- 4 cod fillets
- 1½ cups coconut milk
- 1 cilantro sprig, chopped
- Salt and pepper, to taste

1. In the Instant Pot, set in all ingredients excluding the cilantro. Give a good stir to combine.
2. Lock the lid. Select the Steam mode and cook for 8 minutes at Low Pressure.
3. Once cooking is complete, do a quick pressure release. Carefully open the lid.
4. Garnish with chopped cilantro before serving.

Cod Meal

Prep time: 6 mins, Cook Time: 5 mins, Servings: 2

- 1 cup water
- 2 tbsps. ghee
- 1 fresh large fillet cod
- Salt and pepper, to taste

1. Cut fillet into 3 pieces. Coat with the ghee and season with salt and pepper.
2. Pour the water into the pot and place steamer basket/trivet inside.
3. Arrange the fish pieces over the basket/trivet.
4. Lock the lid. Select the Manual mode and cook for 5 minutes at Low Pressure.
5. Once cooking is complete, do a quick pressure release. Carefully open the lid.
6. Serve warm.

Tuna Salad with Lettuce

Prep time: 12 mins, Cook Time: 10 mins, Servings: 4

- 2 tbsps. olive oil
- ½ lb. tuna, sliced
- 1 tbsp. fresh lemon juice
- 2 eggs
- 1 head lettuce
- Salt and pepper, to taste
- 1 cup water

1. In a large bowl, season the tuna with lemon juice, salt and pepper. Transfer the tuna to a baking dish.
2. Add the eggs, water, and steamer rack to the Instant Pot. Place the baking dish on the steamer rack.
3. Lock the lid. Select the Steam mode and set the cooking time for 10 minutes at Low Pressure.
4. Once cooking is complete, do a quick pressure release. Carefully open the lid.
5. Allow the eggs and tuna to cool. Peel the eggs and slice into wedges. Set aside.
6. Assemble the salad by shredding the lettuce in a salad bowl. Toss in the cooled tuna and eggs.
7. Sprinkle with olive oil, then serve.

Steamed Chili-Rubbed Tilapia

Prep time: 6 mins, Cook time: 10 mins, Servings: 4

- 1 cup water
- ½ tsp. garlic powder
- 1 lb. skinless tilapia fillet
- 2 tbsps. extra virgin olive oil
- Salt and pepper, to taste
- 2 tbsps. chili powder

1. Set a trivet in the Instant Pot and pour the water into the pot.
2. Season the tilapia fillets with salt, pepper, chili powder, and garlic powder. Drizzle with olive oil on top.
3. Place in the steamer basket.
4. Lock the lid. Select the Steam mode and cook for 10 minutes at Low Pressure.

5. Once cooking is complete, do a quick pressure release. Carefully open the lid.
6. Serve warm.

Halibut and Broccoli Casserole

Prep time: 6 mins, Cook Time: 6 mins, Servings: 6

- 1 tbsp. Dijon mustard
- 1¼ cup full-fat coconut cream
- 2 tbsps. olive oil
- 1½ lbs. halibut fillets, sliced
- 1 cup broccoli florets
- Salt and pepper, to taste

1. In the Instant Pot, add all the ingredients. Give a good stir.
2. Lock the lid. Select the Manual mode and set the cooking time for 8 minutes at Low Pressure.
3. Once cooking is complete, do a quick pressure release. Carefully open the lid.
4. Let the fish and broccoli cool for 5 minutes before serving.

Halibut with Pesto

Prep time: 12 mins, Cook time: 8 mins, Servings: 4

- 2 tbsps. extra virgin olive oil
- 1 tbsp. freshly squeezed lemon juice
- 1 cup basil leaves
- 2 garlic cloves, minced
- 4 halibut fillets
- ¼ cup water
- Salt and pepper, to taste

1. Place the halibut fish in the Instant Pot. Set aside.
2. In a food processor, pulse the basil, olive oil, garlic, and lemon juice until coarse. Sprinkle salt and pepper for seasoning.
3. Spread pesto sauce over halibut fillets. Add the water.
4. Lock the lid. Select the Manual mode and cook for 8 minutes at Low Pressure.
5. Once cooking is complete, do a quick pressure release. Carefully open the lid.
6. Serve warm.

Halibut En Papillote

Prep time: 12 mins, Cook time: 10 mins, Servings: 4

- 1 cup water
- 1 cup chopped tomatoes
- 1 thinly sliced shallot
- 4 halibut fillets
- ½ tbsp. grated ginger
- Salt and pepper, to taste

1. In the Instant Pot, set in a steamer basket and pour the water into the pot.
2. Get a large parchment paper and place the fillet in the middle. Season with salt and pepper. Add the grated ginger, tomatoes, and shallots. Fold the parchment paper to create a pouch and crimp the edges.
3. Place the parchment paper containing the fish.

4.	Lock the lid. Select the Steam mode and cook for 10 minutes at Low Pressure.
5.	Once cooking is complete, do a quick pressure release. Carefully open the lid.
6.	Serve warm.

Red Curry Halibut

Prep time: 3 mins, Cook time: 10 mins, Servings: 4

- 2 tbsps. chopped cilantro
- 4 skinless halibut fillets
- 3 green curry leaves
- 1 cup chopped tomatoes
- 1 tbsp. freshly squeezed lime juice
- Salt and pepper, to taste

1.	Place all ingredients in the Instant Pot. Give a good stir to combine the ingredients.
2.	Lock the lid. Select the Manual mode and cook for 10 minutes at Low Pressure.
3.	Do a quick pressure release.

Thyme-Sesame Crusted Halibut

Prep time: 6 mins, Cook time: 8 mins, Servings: 4

- 1 cup water
- 1 tsp. dried thyme leaves
- 1 tbsp. toasted sesame seeds
- 8 oz. halibut, sliced
- Salt and pepper, to taste
- 1 tbsp. freshly squeezed lemon juice

1.	Set a trivet in the Instant Pot and pour the water into the pot.
2.	Season the halibut with lemon juice, salt, and pepper. Sprinkle with dried thyme leaves and sesame seeds.
3.	Place the fish on the trivet.
4.	Lock the lid. Select the Steam mode and cook for 8 minutes at Low Pressure.
5.	Once cooking is complete, do a quick pressure release. Carefully open the lid.
6.	Serve warm.

Tuna Fillets with Lemon Butter

Prep time: 5 minutes | Cook time: 3 minutes | Serves 4

1 cup water
$^1/_3$ cup lemon juice
2 sprigs fresh thyme
2 sprigs fresh parsley
2 sprigs fresh rosemary
1 pound (454 g) tuna fillets
4 cloves garlic, pressed
Sea salt, to taste
¼ teaspoon black pepper, or more to taste
2 tablespoons butter, melted
1 lemon, sliced

1.	Pour the water into your Instant Pot. Add the lemon juice, thyme, parsley, and rosemary and insert a steamer basket.
2.	Put the tuna fillets in the basket. Top with the garlic and season with the salt and black pepper.
3.	Drizzle the melted butter over the fish fillets and place the lemon slices on top.

4.	Lock the lid. Select the Manual mode and set the cooking time for 3 minutes at Low Pressure.
5.	When the timer beeps, perform a quick pressure release. Carefully remove the lid.
6.	Serve immediately.

Lemony Tilapia Fillets with Arugula

Prep time: 5 minutes | Cook time: 4 minutes | Serves 4

1 lemon, juiced
1 cup water
1 pound (454 g) tilapia fillets
½ teaspoon cayenne pepper, or more to taste
2 teaspoons butter, melted
Sea salt and ground black pepper, to taste
½ teaspoon dried basil
2 cups arugula

1.	Pour the fresh lemon juice and water into your Instant Pot and insert a steamer basket.
2.	Brush the fish fillets with the melted butter.
3.	Sprinkle with the cayenne pepper, salt, and black pepper. Place the tilapia fillets in the basket. Sprinkle the dried basil on top.
4.	Lock the lid. Select the Manual mode and set the cooking time for 4 minutes at Low Pressure.
5.	When the timer beeps, perform a quick pressure release. Carefully remove the lid.
6.	Serve with the fresh arugula.

Cheesy Fish Bake with Veggies

Prep time: 10 minutes | Cook time: 5 minutes | Serves 4

1½ cups water
Cooking spray
2 ripe tomatoes, sliced
2 cloves garlic, minced
1 teaspoon dried oregano
1 teaspoon dried basil
½ teaspoon dried rosemary
1 red onion, sliced
1 head cauliflower, cut into florets
1 pound (454 g) tilapia fillets, sliced
Sea salt, to taste
1 tablespoon olive oil
1 cup crumbled feta cheese
$^1/_3$ cup Kalamata olives, pitted and halved

1.	Pour the water into your Instant Pot and insert a trivet.
2.	Spritz a casserole dish with cooking spray. Add the tomato slices to the dish. Scatter the top with the garlic, oregano, basil, and rosemary.
3.	Mix in the onion and cauliflower. Arrange the fish fillets on top. Sprinkle with the salt and drizzle with the olive oil.
4.	Place the feta cheese and Kalamata olives on top. Lower the dish onto the trivet.
5.	Lock the lid. Select the Manual mode and set the cooking time for 5 minutes at High Pressure.
6.	When the timer beeps, perform a quick pressure release. Carefully remove the lid.
7.	Allow to cool for 5 minutes before serving.

Halibut Stew with Bacon and Cheese

Prep time: 10 minutes | Cook time: 10 minutes | Serves 4

4 slices bacon, chopped
1 celery, chopped
½ cup chopped shallots
1 teaspoon garlic, smashed
1 pound (454 g) halibut
2 cups fish stock
1 tablespoon coconut oil, softened
¼ teaspoon ground allspice
Sea salt and crushed black peppercorns, to taste
1 cup Cottage cheese, at room temperature
1 cup heavy cream

1. Set the Instant Pot to Sauté. Cook the bacon until crispy.
2. Add the celery, shallots, and garlic and sauté for another 2 minutes, or until the vegetables are just tender.
3. Mix in the halibut, stock, coconut oil, allspice, salt, and black peppercorns. Stir well.
4. Lock the lid. Select the Manual mode and set the cooking time for 7 minutes at Low Pressure.
5. When the timer beeps, perform a natural pressure release for 10 minutes, then release any remaining pressure. Carefully remove the lid.
6. Stir in the cheese and heavy cream. Select the Sauté mode again and let it simmer for a few minutes until heated through.
7. Serve immediately.

Lemony Mahi-Mahi fillets with Peppers

Prep time: 10 minutes | Cook time: 3 minutes | Serves 3

2 sprigs fresh rosemary
2 sprigs dill, tarragon
1 sprig fresh thyme
1 cup water
1 lemon, sliced
3 mahi-mahi fillets
2 tablespoons coconut oil, melted
Sea salt and ground black pepper, to taste
1 serrano pepper, seeded and sliced
1 green bell pepper, sliced
1 red bell pepper, sliced

1. Add the herbs, water, and lemon slices to the Instant Pot and insert a steamer basket.
2. Arrange the mahi-mahi fillets in the steamer basket.
3. Drizzle the melted coconut oil over the top and season with the salt and black pepper.
4. Lock the lid. Select the Manual mode and set the cooking time for 3 minutes at Low Pressure.
5. When the timer beeps, perform a natural pressure release for 10 minutes, then release any remaining pressure. Carefully remove the lid.
6. Place the peppers on top. Select the Sauté mode and let it simmer for another 1 minute.
7. Serve immediately.

Aromatic Monkfish Stew

Prep time: 5 minutes | Cook time: 6 minutes | Serves 6

Juice of 1 lemon
1 tablespoon fresh basil
1 tablespoon fresh parsley
1 tablespoon olive oil
1 teaspoon garlic, minced
1½ pounds (680 g) monkfish
1 tablespoon butter
1 bell pepper, chopped
1 onion, sliced
½ teaspoon cayenne pepper
½ teaspoon mixed peppercorns
¼ teaspoon turmeric powder
¼ teaspoon ground cumin
Sea salt and ground black pepper, to taste
2 cups fish stock
½ cup water
¼ cup dry white wine
2 bay leaves
1 ripe tomato, crushed

1. Stir together the lemon juice, basil, parsley, olive oil, and garlic in a ceramic dish. Add the monkfish and marinate for 30 minutes.
2. Set your Instant Pot to Sauté. Add and melt the butter. Once hot, cook the bell pepper and onion until fragrant.
3. Stir in the remaining ingredients.
4. Lock the lid. Select the Manual mode and set the cooking time for 6 minutes at High Pressure.
5. When the timer beeps, perform a quick pressure release. Carefully remove the lid.
6. Discard the bay leaves and divide your stew into serving bowls.
7. Serve hot.

Chunky Fish Soup with Tomatoes

Prep time: 10 minutes | Cook time: 8 minutes | Serves 4

2 teaspoons olive oil
1 yellow onion, chopped
1 bell pepper, sliced
1 celery, diced
2 garlic cloves, minced
3 cups fish stock
2 ripe tomatoes, crushed
¾ pound (340 g) haddock fillets
1 cup shrimp
1 tablespoon sweet Hungarian paprika
1 teaspoon hot Hungarian paprika
½ teaspoon caraway seeds

1. Set the Instant Pot to Sauté. Add and heat the oil. Once hot, add the onions and sauté until soft and fragrant.
2. Add the pepper, celery, and garlic and continue to sauté until soft.
3. Stir in the remaining ingredients.
4. Lock the lid. Select the Manual mode and set the cooking time for 5 minutes at High Pressure.

5.   When the timer beeps, perform a quick pressure release. Carefully remove the lid.
6.   Divide into serving bowls and serve hot.

Haddock and Veggie Foil Packets

Prep time: 5 minutes | Cook time: 10 minutes | Serves 4
1½ cups water
1 lemon, sliced
2 bell peppers, sliced
1 brown onion, sliced into rings
4 sprigs parsley
2 sprigs thyme
2 sprigs rosemary
4 haddock fillets
Sea salt, to taste
$^1/_3$ teaspoon ground black pepper, or more to taste
2 tablespoons extra-virgin olive oil
1.   Pour the water and lemon into your Instant Pot and insert a steamer basket.
2.   Assemble the packets with large sheets of heavy-duty foil.
3.   Place the peppers, onion rings, parsley, thyme, and rosemary in the center of each foil. Place the fish fillets on top of the veggies.
4.   Sprinkle with the salt and black pepper and drizzle the olive oil over the fillets. Place the packets in the steamer basket.
5.   Lock the lid. Select the Manual mode and set the cooking time for 10 minutes at Low Pressure.
6.   When the timer beeps, perform a quick pressure release. Carefully remove the lid.
7.   Serve warm.

Herb-Crusted Cod Steaks

Prep time: 5 minutes | Cook time: 4 minutes | Serves 4
1½ cups water
2 tablespoons garlic-infused oil
4 cod steaks, 1½-inch thick
Sea salt, to taste
½ teaspoon mixed peppercorns, crushed
2 sprigs thyme
1 sprig rosemary
1 yellow onion, sliced
1.   Pour the water into your Instant Pot and insert a trivet.
2.   Rub the garlic-infused oil into the cod steaks and season with the salt and crushed peppercorns.
3.   Lower the cod steaks onto the trivet, skin-side down. Top with the thyme, rosemary, and onion.
4.   Lock the lid. Select the Manual mode and set the cooking time for 4 minutes at High Pressure.
5.   When the timer beeps, perform a quick pressure release. Carefully remove the lid.
6.   Serve immediately.

Lemony Fish and Asparagus

Prep time: 5 minutes | Cook time: 3 minutes | Serves 4
2 lemons
2 cups cold water
2 tablespoons extra-virgin olive oil
4 (4-ounce / 113-g) white fish fillets, such as cod or haddock
1 teaspoon fine sea salt
1 teaspoon ground black pepper
1 bundle asparagus, ends trimmed
2 tablespoons lemon juice
Fresh dill, for garnish
1.   Grate the zest off the lemons until you have about 1 tablespoon and set the zest aside. Slice the lemons into ⅛-inch slices.
2.   Pour the water into the Instant Pot. Add 1 tablespoon of the olive oil to each of two stackable steamer pans.
3.   Sprinkle the fish on all sides with the lemon zest, salt, and pepper.
4.   Arrange two fillets in each steamer pan and top each with the lemon slices and then the asparagus. Sprinkle the asparagus with the salt and drizzle the lemon juice over the top.
5.   Stack the steamer pans in the Instant Pot. Cover the top steamer pan with its lid.
6.   Lock the lid. Select the Manual mode and set the cooking time for 3 minutes at High Pressure.
7.   Once cooking is complete, do a natural pressure release for 7 minutes, then release any remaining pressure. Carefully open the lid.
8.   Lift the steamer pans out of the Instant Pot.
9.   Transfer the fish and asparagus to a serving plate. Garnish with the lemon slices and dill.
10.   Serve immediately.

Fish Packets with Pesto and Cheese

Prep time: 8 minutes | Cook time: 6 minutes | Serves 4
1½ cups cold water.
4 (4-ounce / 113-g) white fish fillets, such as cod or haddock
1 teaspoon fine sea salt
½ teaspoon ground black pepper
1 (4-ounce / 113-g) jar pesto
½ cup shredded Parmesan cheese (about 2 ounces / 57 g)
Halved cherry tomatoes, for garnish
1.   Pour the water into your Instant Pot and insert a steamer basket.
2.   Sprinkle the fish on all sides with the salt and pepper. Take four sheets of parchment paper and place a fillet in the center of each sheet.
3.   Dollop 2 tablespoons of the pesto on top of each fillet and sprinkle with 2 tablespoons of the Parmesan cheese.
4.   Wrap the fish in the parchment by folding in the edges and folding down the top like an envelope to close tightly.

5.	Stack the packets in the steamer basket, seam-side down.
6.	Lock the lid. Select the Manual mode and set the cooking time for 6 minutes at Low Pressure.
7.	Once cooking is complete, do a natural pressure release for 10 minutes, then release any remaining pressure. Carefully open the lid.
8.	Remove the fish packets from the pot. Transfer to a serving plate and garnish with the cherry tomatoes.
9.	Serve immediately.

Cod Fillets with Cherry Tomatoes

Prep time: 2 minutes | Cook time: 15 minutes | Serves 4

2 tablespoons butter
¼ cup diced onion
1 clove garlic, minced
1 cup cherry tomatoes, halved
¼ cup chicken broth
¼ teaspoon dried thyme
¼ teaspoon salt
⅛ teaspoon pepper
4 (4-ounce / 113-g) cod fillets
1 cup water
¼ cup fresh chopped Italian parsley
1.	Set your Instant Pot to Sauté. Add and melt the butter. Once hot, add the onions and cook until softened. Add the garlic and cook for another 30 seconds.
2.	Add the tomatoes, chicken broth, thyme, salt, and pepper. Continue to cook for 5 to 7 minutes, or until the tomatoes start to soften.
3.	Pour the sauce into a glass bowl. Add the fish fillets. Cover with foil.
4.	Pour the water into the Instant Pot and insert a trivet. Place the bowl on top.
5.	Lock the lid. Select the Manual mode and set the cooking time for 3 minutes at Low Pressure.
6.	Once cooking is complete, do a quick pressure release. Carefully open the lid.
7.	Sprinkle with the fresh parsley and serve.

Garam Masala Fish

Prep time: 10 minutes | Cook time: 10 minutes | Serves 4

2 tablespoons sesame oil
½ teaspoon cumin seeds
½ cup chopped leeks
1 teaspoon ginger-garlic paste
1 pound (454 g) cod fillets, boneless and sliced
2 ripe tomatoes, chopped
1½ tablespoons fresh lemon juice
½ teaspoon garam masala
½ teaspoon turmeric powder
1 tablespoon chopped fresh dill leaves
1 tablespoon chopped fresh curry leaves
1 tablespoon chopped fresh parsley leaves
Coarse sea salt, to taste
½ teaspoon smoked cayenne pepper
¼ teaspoon ground black pepper, or more to taste
1.	Set the Instant Pot to Sauté. Add and heat the sesame oil until hot. Sauté the cumin seeds for 30 seconds.
2.	Add the leeks and cook for another 2 minutes until translucent. Add the ginger-garlic paste and cook for an additional 40 seconds.
3.	Stir in the remaining ingredients.
4.	Lock the lid. Select the Manual mode and set the cooking time for 6 minutes at Low Pressure.
5.	When the timer beeps, perform a quick pressure release. Carefully remove the lid.
6.	Serve immediately.

Snapper in Spicy Tomato Sauce

Prep time: 5 minutes | Cook time: 5 minutes | Serves 6

2 teaspoons coconut oil, melted
1 teaspoon celery seeds
½ teaspoon fresh grated ginger
½ teaspoon cumin seeds
1 yellow onion, chopped
2 cloves garlic, minced
1½ pounds (680 g) snapper fillets
¾ cup vegetable broth
1 (14-ounce / 113-g) can fire-roasted diced tomatoes
1 bell pepper, sliced
1 jalapeño pepper, minced
Sea salt and ground black pepper, to taste
¼ teaspoon chili flakes
½ teaspoon turmeric powder
1.	Set the Instant Pot to Sauté. Add and heat the sesame oil until hot. Sauté the celery seeds, fresh ginger, and cumin seeds.
2.	Add the onion and continue to sauté until softened and fragrant.
3.	Mix in the minced garlic and continue to cook for 30 seconds. Add the remaining ingredients and stir well.
4.	Lock the lid. Select the Manual mode and set the cooking time for 3 minutes at Low Pressure.
5.	When the timer beeps, perform a quick pressure release. Carefully remove the lid.
6.	Serve warm

Perch Fillets with Red Curry

Prep time: 5 minutes | Cook time: 6 minutes | Serves 4

1 cup water
2 sprigs rosemary
1 large-sized lemon, sliced
1 pound (454 g) perch fillets
1 teaspoon cayenne pepper
Sea salt and ground black pepper, to taste
1 tablespoon red curry paste
1 tablespoons butter
1.	Add the water, rosemary, and lemon slices to the Instant Pot and insert a trivet.

2. Season the perch fillets with the cayenne pepper, salt, and black pepper. Spread the red curry paste and butter over the fillets.
3. Arrange the fish fillets on the trivet.
4. Lock the lid. Select the Manual mode and set the cooking time for 6 minutes at Low Pressure.
5. When the timer beeps, perform a quick pressure release. Carefully remove the lid.
6. Serve with your favorite keto sides.

Lemony Salmon with Tomatoes

Prep time: 7 minutes | Cook time: 21 minutes | Serves 4

1 tablespoon unsalted butter
3 cloves garlic, minced
¼ cup lemon juice
1¼ cups fresh or canned diced tomatoes
1 tablespoon chopped fresh flat-leaf parsley, plus more for garnish
¼ teaspoon ground black pepper
4 (6-ounce / 170-g) skinless salmon fillets
1 teaspoon fine sea salt
Lemon wedges, for garnish
1. Add the butter to your Instant Pot and select the Sauté mode. Once melted, add the garlic (if using) and sauté for 1 minute.
2. Add the roasted garlic, lemon juice, tomatoes, parsley, and pepper. Let simmer for 5 minutes, or until the liquid has reduced a bit.
3. Meanwhile, rinse the salmon and pat dry with a paper towel. Sprinkle on all sides with the salt.
4. Using a spatula, push the reduced sauce to one side of the pot and place the salmon on the other side. Spoon the sauce over the salmon.
5. Sauté uncovered for another 15 minutes, or until the salmon flakes easily with a fork. The timing will depend on the thickness of the fillets.
6. Transfer the salmon to a serving plate. Serve with the sauce and garnish with the parsley and lemon wedges.

Salmon Fillets and Bok Choy

Prep time: 5 minutes | Cook time: 8 minutes | Serves 4

1½ cups water
2 tablespoons unsalted butter
4 (1-inch thick) salmon fillets
½ teaspoon cayenne pepper
Sea salt and freshly ground pepper, to taste
2 cups Bok choy, sliced
1 cup chicken broth
3 cloves garlic, minced
1 teaspoon grated lemon zest
½ teaspoon dried dill weed
1. Pour the water into your Instant Pot and insert a trivet.
2. Brush the salmon with the melted butter and season with the cayenne pepper, salt, and black pepper on all sides.

3. Lock the lid. Select the Manual mode and set the cooking time for 3 minutes at Low Pressure.
4. When the timer beeps, perform a quick pressure release. Carefully remove the lid.
5. Add the remaining ingredients.
6. Lock the lid. Select the Manual mode and set the cooking time for 5 minutes at High Pressure.
7. When the timer beeps, perform a quick pressure release. Carefully remove the lid.
8. Serve the poached salmon with the veggies on the side.

Salmon Steaks with Garlicky Yogurt

Prep time: 2 minutes | Cook time: 4 minutes | Serves 4

1 cup water
2 tablespoons olive oil
4 salmon steaks
Coarse sea salt and ground black pepper, to taste
Garlicky Yogurt:
1 (8-ounce / 227-g) container full-fat Greek yogurt
2 cloves garlic, minced
2 tablespoons mayonnaise
$1/_3$ teaspoon Dijon mustard
1. Pour the water into the Instant Pot and insert a trivet.
2. Rub the olive oil into the fish and sprinkle with the salt and black pepper on all sides. Put the fish on the trivet.
3. Lock the lid. Select the Manual mode and set the cooking time for 4 minutes at High Pressure.
4. When the timer beeps, perform a quick pressure release. Carefully remove the lid.
5. Meanwhile, stir together all the ingredients for the garlicky yogurt in a bowl.
6. Serve the salmon steaks alongside the garlicky yogurt.

Foil-Packet Salmon

Prep time: 2 minutes | Cook time: 7 minutes | Serves 2

2 (3-ounce / 85-g) salmon fillets
¼ teaspoon garlic powder
1 teaspoon salt
¼ teaspoon pepper
¼ teaspoon dried dill
½ lemon
1 cup water
1. Place each filet of salmon on a square of foil, skin-side down.
2. Season with garlic powder, salt, and pepper and squeeze the lemon juice over the fish.
3. Cut the lemon into four slices and place two on each filet. Close the foil packets by folding over edges.
4. Add the water to the Instant Pot and insert a trivet. Place the foil packets on the trivet.
5. Secure the lid. Select the Steam mode and set the cooking time for 7 minutes at Low Pressure.

6. Once cooking is complete, do a quick pressure release. Carefully open the lid.
7. Check the internal temperature with a meat thermometer to ensure the thickest part of the filets reached at least 145ºF (63ºC). Salmon should easily flake when fully cooked.
8. Serve immediately.

Pesto Salmon with Almonds

Prep time: 5 minutes | Cook time: 12 minutes | Serves 4

1 tablespoon butter
¼ cup sliced almonds
4 (3-ounce / 85-g) salmon fillets
½ cup pesto
¼ teaspoon pepper
½ teaspoon salt
1 cup water
1. Press the Sauté button on the Instant Pot and add the butter and almonds.
2. Sauté for 3 to 5 minutes until they start to soften. Remove and set aside.
3. Brush salmon fillets with pesto and season with salt and pepper.
4. Pour the water into Instant Pot and insert the trivet. Place the salmon fillets on the trivet.
5. Secure the lid. Select the Steam mode and set the cooking time for 7 minutes at High Pressure.
6. Once cooking is complete, do a quick pressure release. Carefully open the lid.
7. Serve the salmon with the almonds sprinkled on top.

Avocado Salmon Burgers

Prep time: 5 minutes | Cook time: 5 minutes | Serves 4

2 tablespoons coconut oil
1 pound (454 g) salmon fillets
$^1/_3$ cup finely ground pork rinds
2 tablespoons finely diced onion
2 tablespoons mayonnaise
½ teaspoon salt
¼ teaspoon chili powder
¼ teaspoon garlic powder
1 egg
1 avocado, pitted
Juice of ½ lime
1. Set your Instant Pot to Sauté. Add and heat the coconut oil.
2. Remove skin from the salmon filets. Finely mince the salmon and add to a large bowl.
3. Stir in the remaining ingredients except the avocado and lime and form 4 patties.
4. Place the burgers into the pot and sear for about 3 to 4 minutes per side, or until the center feels firm and reads at least 145ºF (63ºC) on a meat thermometer.
5. Scoop flesh out of the avocado. In a small bowl, mash the avocado with a fork and squeeze the lime juice over the top.

6. Divide the mash into four sections and place on top of salmon burgers. Serve warm.

Lemony Salmon with Avocados

Prep time: 10 minutes | Cook time: 7 minutes | Serves 2

2 (3-ounce / 85-g) salmon fillets
½ teaspoon salt
¼ teaspoon pepper
1 cup water
$^1/_3$ cup mayonnaise
Juice of ½ lemon
2 avocados
½ teaspoon chopped fresh dill
1. Season the salmon fillets on all sides with the salt and pepper. Add the water to the Instant Pot and insert a trivet.
2. Arrange the salmon fillets on the trivet, skin-side down.
3. Secure the lid. Select the Steam mode and set the cooking time for 7 minutes at Low Pressure.
4. Once cooking is complete, do a quick pressure release. Carefully open the lid. Set aside to cool.
5. Mix together the mayonnaise and lemon juice in a large bowl. Cut the avocados in half. Remove the pits and dice the avocados. Add the avocados to the large bowl and gently fold into the mixture.
6. Flake the salmon into bite-sized pieces with a fork and gently fold into the mixture.
7. Serve garnished with the fresh dill.

Easy Salmon Packets

Prep time: 8 minutes | Cook time: 6 minutes | Serves 4

1½ cups cold water
4 (5-ounce / 142-g) salmon fillets
½ teaspoon fine sea salt
¼ teaspoon ground black pepper
1 lime, thinly sliced
4 teaspoons extra-virgin olive oil, divided
Fresh thyme leaves
1. Pour the cold water into the Instant Pot and insert a steamer basket.
2. Sprinkle the fish on all sides with the salt and pepper.
3. Take four sheets of parchment paper and place 3 lime slices on each sheet. Top the lime slices with a piece of fish.
4. Drizzle with 1 teaspoon of olive oil and place a few thyme leaves on top. Cover each fillet with the parchment by folding in the edges and folding down the top like an envelope to close tightly.
5. Stack the packets in the steamer basket, seam-side down.
6. Secure the lid. Select the Manual mode and set the cooking time for 6 minutes at Low Pressure.

7. When the timer beeps, perform a natural pressure release for 10 minutes, then release any remaining pressure. Carefully remove the lid.
8. Remove the fish packets from the pot.
9. Serve the fish garnished with the fresh thyme.

Crispy Salmon Fillets

Prep time: 5 minutes | Cook time: 5 minutes | Serves 2

1 tablespoon avocado oil
2 (3-ounce / 85-g) salmon fillets
1 teaspoon paprika
½ teaspoon salt
¼ teaspoon dried thyme
¼ teaspoon onion powder
¼ teaspoon pepper
⅛ teaspoon cayenne pepper
1. Drizzle the avocado oil over salmon fillets. Combine the remaining ingredients in a small bowl and rub all over fillets.
2. Press the Sauté button on the Instant Pot. Add the salmon fillets and sear for 2 to 5 minutes until the salmon easily flakes with a fork.
3. Serve warm.

Lemon-Dill Salmon

Prep time: 3 minutes | Cook time: 5 minutes | Serves 2

2 (3-ounce / 85-g) salmon fillets, 1-inch thick
1 teaspoon chopped fresh dill
½ teaspoon salt
¼ teaspoon pepper
1 cup water
2 tablespoons lemon juice
½ lemon, sliced
1. Season salmon with dill, salt, and pepper.
2. Pour the water into the Instant Pot and insert the trivet. Place the salmon on the trivet, skin-side down. Squeeze lemon juice over fillets and scatter the lemon slices on top.
3. Lock the lid. Select the Steam mode and set the cooking time for 5 minutes at High Pressure.
4. Once cooking is complete, do a quick pressure release. Carefully open the lid.
5. Serve warm.

Smoky Paprika Chicken

Prep time: 5mins, Cook time: 15 mins, Servings: 6
- 2 tbsps. smoked paprika
- 2 lbs. chicken breasts
- Salt and pepper, to taste
- 1 tbsp. olive oil
- ½ cup water

1. Press the Sauté button on the Instant Pot and heat the olive oil.
2. Stir in the chicken breasts and smoked paprika and cook for 3 minutes until lightly golden.
3. Season with salt and pepper and add ½ cup water.
4. Lock the lid. Select the Manual mode and cook for 12 minutes at High Pressure.
5. Once cooking is complete, do a natural pressure release for 8 minutes, then release any remaining pressure. Carefully open the lid.
6. Garnish with cilantro or scallions, if desired.

Spiced Chicken Drumsticks

Prep time: 6 mins, Cook time: 15 mins, Servings: 10 to 12
- ¼ tsp. dried thyme
- 1½ tbsps. paprika
- Salt and pepper, to taste
- ½ tsp. onion powder
- 12 chicken drumsticks
- 2 cups water

1. On a clean work surface, rub the chicken drumsticks generously with the spices. Season with salt and pepper.
2. Transfer the chicken to the Instant Pot and add the water.
3. Lock the lid. Select the Poultry mode and cook for 15 minutes at High Pressure.
4. Once cooking is complete, do a natural pressure release for 8 minutes, then release any remaining pressure. Carefully open the lid.
5. Remove from the pot to a plate and serve.

Chili Lime Chicken

Prep time: 12 mins, Cook time: 6 mins, Servings:5
- 6 garlic cloves, minced
- 1 tbsp. chili powder
- 1 tsp. cumin
- 1 lb. skinless and boneless chicken breasts
- 1 ½ limes, juiced
- 1 cup water

1. In the Instant Pot, add the chicken breasts, garlic, chili powder, cumin, lime juice, salt, pepper, and water.
2. Lock the lid. Select the Manual mode and cook for 6 minutes at High Pressure.
3. Once cooking is complete, do a natural pressure release for 5 minutes, then release any remaining pressure. Carefully open the lid.
4. Cool for 5 minutes and serve warm.

Lemony Fennel Chicken

Prep time: 12 mins, Cook time: 12 mins, Servings: 8
- 3 tbsps. freshly squeezed lemon juice
- 1 tsp. cinnamon
- ¼ cup fennel bulb
- 4 garlic cloves, minced
- 2 lbs. boneless and skinless chicken thighs
- Salt and pepper, to taste
- ½ cup water

1. Place lemon juice, cinnamon, fennel bulb, garlic, and chicken thighs in the Instant Pot. Sprinkle pepper and salt for seasoning. Add ½ cup of water for moisture.
2. Lock the lid. Select the Manual mode and cook for 12 minutes at High Pressure.
3. Once cooking is complete, do a natural pressure release for 8 minutes, then release any remaining pressure. Carefully open the lid.
4. Remove the chicken from the pot and shred it, then serve.

Creamy Chicken with Mushrooms

Prep time: 12 mins, Cook time: 13 mins, Servings: 6
- 4 garlic cloves, minced
- 1 onion, chopped
- 1 cup mushrooms, sliced
- 6 boneless chicken breasts, halved
- ½ cup coconut milk
- ½ cup water

1. Press the Sauté button on the Instant Pot and stir in the chicken breasts.
2. Fold in the onions and garlic and sauté for at least 3 minutes until tender. Season with salt and pepper. Add the remaining ingredients to the Instant Pot and whisk well.
3. Lock the lid. Select the Poultry mode and cook for 8 minutes at High Pressure.
4. Once cooking is complete, do a natural pressure release for 5 minutes, then release any remaining pressure. Carefully open the lid.
5. Allow to cool for 5 minutes before serving.

Thai Peanut Chicken

Prep time: 6 mins, Cook time: 12 mins, Servings: 6
- 2 tbsps. chopped scallions
- Salt and pepper, to taste
- 1½ cups toasted peanuts, divided
- 2 garlic cloves, minced
- 1½ lbs. chicken breasts
- 1 cup water

1. Place 1 cup of toasted peanuts in a food processor and pulse until smooth. This will serve as your peanut butter.
2. On a flat work surface, chop the remaining toasted peanuts finely and set aside.

3.   Press the Sauté button on the Instant Pot and add the chicken breasts and garlic. Keep on stirring for 3 minutes until the meat has turned lightly golden. Sprinkle pepper and salt for seasoning.
4.   Pour in the prepared peanut butter and water. Give the mixture a good stir.
5.   Lock the lid. Select the Poultry mode and set the cooking time for 8 minutes at High Pressure.
6.   Once cooking is complete, do a natural pressure release for 5 minutes, then release any remaining pressure. Carefully open the lid.
7.   Garnish with chopped peanuts and scallions before serving.

Chinese Steamed Chicken

Prep time: 6 mins, Coo time: 10 mins, Servings: 6
- 1 tsp. grated ginger
- 1½ lbs. chicken thighs
- 1 tbsp. five-spice powder
- ¼ cup soy sauce
- 3 tbsps. sesame oil
- 1 cup water
- Salt and pepper, to taste

1.   In the Instant Pot, stir in all the ingredients.
2.   Lock the lid. Select the Poultry mode and set the cooking time for 10 minutes at High Pressure.
3.   Once cooking is complete, do a natural pressure release for 7 minutes, then release any remaining pressure. Carefully open the lid.
4.   Serve the chicken thighs while warm.

Chicken Stew with Tomatoes and Spinach

Prep time: 13 mins, Cook time: 10 mins, Servings: 6
- 1 ginger, sliced
- 3 garlic cloves, minced
- 2 cups spinach leaves
- 1 cup chopped tomatoes
- 1 lb. chicken breasts
- 1 cup water
- Salt and pepper, to taste

1.   Press the Sauté button on the Instant Pot and add the chicken and garlic. Stir-fry for 3 minutes until the garlic becomes fragrant.
2.   Add the ginger, tomatoes, spinach, and water. Season with salt and pepper.
3.   Lock the lid. Select the Manual mode and set the cooking time for 6 minutes at High Pressure.
4.   Once cooking is complete, do a natural pressure release for 5 minutes, then release any remaining pressure. Carefully open the lid.
5.   Cool for a few minutes and serve warm.

Crispy Chicken Wings

Prep time: 15 mins, Cook time: 15 mins, Servings: 8
- 1 tbsp. paprika
- 1 tsp. rosemary leaves
- Salt and pepper, to taste
- 2 lbs. chicken wings
- 1 cup water

1.   Put all the ingredients in the Instant Pot and stir well.
2.   Lock the lid. Select the Manual mode and set the cooking time for 15 minutes at High Pressure.
3.   Once cooking is complete, do a natural pressure release for 10 minutes, then release any remaining pressure. Carefully open the lid.
4.   Transfer to a plate and serve.

Basil and Tomatoes Chicken Soup

Prep time: 6 mins, Cook time: 20 mins, Servings: 4
- ¼ cup fresh basil leaves
- 8 chopped plum tomatoes
- 4 skinless chicken breasts, halved
- Salt and pepper, to taste
- 5 cups water

1.   Place all ingredients into the Instant Pot. Give a good stir to mix everything.
2.   Lock the lid. Select the Manual mode and set the timer to 20 minutes at High Pressure.
3.   Once cooking is complete, do a natural pressure release for 10 minutes, then release any remaining pressure. Carefully open the lid.
4.   Let the soup cool for 10 minutes and serve warm.

Mexican Shredded Chicken

Prep time: 12 mins, Cook time: 18 mins, Servings: 4
- ½ tsp. paprika
- 3 lbs. chicken breasts
- ½ tsp. dried oregano
- 1 tbsp. chili powder
- ¼ tsp. cumin powder
- Salt and pepper, to taste
- 2 cups water

1.   Place all ingredients in the Instant Pot and whisk well.
2.   Lock the lid. Select the Poultry mode and set the cooking time for 18 minutes at High Pressure.
3.   Once cooking is complete, do a natural pressure release for 12 minutes, then release any remaining pressure. Carefully open the lid.
4.   Remove the chicken breasts from the pot and shred them. Serve immediately.

Sesame Chicken

Prep time: 6 mins, Cook time: 25 mins, Servings: 12
- 1½ cup soy sauce
- 1 bay leaf
- 2 packets dried star anise flowers
- 5 lbs. chicken breasts or thighs
- 2 tbsps. toasted sesame seeds
- 2 cups water

1.   Place the chicken breasts, soy sauce, star anise flowers, and bay leaf into the Instant Pot.
2.   Lock the lid. Select the Manual mode and set the cooking time for 25 minutes at High Pressure.

3.	Once cooking is complete, do a natural pressure release for 15 minutes, then release any remaining pressure. Carefully open the lid.
4.	Allow the chicken breasts cool for 5 minutes and serve.

Eggplant and Chicken Sauté

Prep time: 6 mins, Cook time: 10 mins, Servings: 6

- 3 eggplants, sliced
- 1 tbsp. coconut oil
- 1 tsp. red pepper flakes
- 1 lb. ground chicken
- Salt and pepper, to taste

1.	Press the Sauté button on the Instant Pot and heat the coconut oil.
2.	Stir in the ground chicken and cook for 3 minutes until lightly golden.
3.	Add the remaining ingredients and stir to combine.
4.	Lock the lid. Select the Poultry mode and set the cooking time for 6 minutes at High Pressure.
5.	Once cooking is complete, do a quick pressure release. Carefully open the lid.
6.	Transfer to a large plate and serve warm.

Cheesy Jalapeño Chicken

Prep time: 15 mins, Cook Time: 12 mins, Servings: 3

- 1 lb. boneless chicken breast
- 3 jalapeños, sliced
- 8 oz. Cheddar cheese
- ¾ cup sour cream
- 8 oz. cream cheese
- Salt and pepper, to taste
- ½ cup water

1.	Add ½ cup water, cream cheese, jalapeños, chicken breast, salt, and pepper to the pot. Stir to combine well.
2.	Lock the lid. Select the Manual mode and set the cooking time for 12 minutes at High Pressure.
3.	Once cooking is complete, do a natural pressure release for 8 minutes, then release any remaining pressure. Carefully open the lid.
4.	Mix in the sour cream and Cheddar cheese, and serve warm!

BBQ Chicken

Prep time: 12 mins, Cook Time: 12 mins, Servings: 3

- ½ cup barbecue sauce
- 2 lbs. chicken breasts
- 1 cup water
- 2½ tbsps. honey
- ½ cup chopped onion
- Salt and pepper, to taste

1.	In the Instant Pot, add all the ingredients and stir well.
2.	Lock the lid. Select the Manual mode and set the timer to 12 minutes at High Pressure.

3.	Once cooking is complete, do a natural pressure release for 5 minutes, then release any remaining pressure. Carefully open the lid.
4.	Cook for a few minutes to thicken the sauce. Serve warm.

Broccoli Chicken with Parmesan

Prep time: 8 mins, Cook Time: 5 mins, Servings: 2 to 3

- ⅓ cup grated Parmesan cheese
- 1 cup chicken broth
- 2 cups broccoli florets
- ½ cup heavy cream
- 3 cups cooked and shredded chicken
- Salt and pepper, to taste

1.	In the Instant pot, add the broth, broccoli, chicken, salt, and pepper. Using a spatula, stir the ingredients.
2.	Lock the lid. Select the Steam mode and cook for 3 minutes at High Pressure.
3.	Once cooking is complete, do a quick pressure release. Carefully open the lid.
4.	Set your Instant Pot to Sauté and stir in the cream.
5.	Cook for 2 minutes. Transfer to a large plate and serve.

Ginger Chicken Congee

Prep time: 12 mins, Cook Time: 25 mins, Servings: 4

- 2 cups rice
- 8 medium chicken breasts
- 4 cups water
- 4-inch minced ginger piece
- 1 chicken stock cube
- Salt and pepper, to taste

1.	Add the rice, water, chicken breasts, chicken stock, and ginger to the Instant Pot. Season with salt and pepper.
2.	Lock the lid. Select the Poultry mode and set the cooking time for 25 minutes at High Pressure.
3.	Once cooking is complete, do a natural pressure release for 10 minutes, then release any remaining pressure. Carefully open the lid. Serve warm.

Chicken Yogurt Salsa

Prep time: 15 mins, Cook Time: 15 mins, Servings: 4

- 1 medium jar salsa
- ½ cup water
- 1 cup plain Greek yogurt
- 4 chicken breasts

1.	Add all the ingredients to the Instant Pot. Using a spatula, gently stir to combine well.
2.	Lock the lid. Select the Poultry mode and set the cooking time for 15 minutes at High Pressure.
3.	Once cooking is complete, do a natural pressure release for 8 minutes, then release any remaining pressure. Carefully open the lid.
4.	Transfer the cooked mixture to a salad bowl and serve warm.

Lemon Garlic Chicken

Prep time: 1 hour 20 mins, Cook time: 12 mins, Servings: 6
- 3 tbsps. olive oil, divided
- 2 tsps. dried parsley
- 6 chicken breasts
- 3 minced garlic cloves
- 1 tbsp. lemon juice
- Salt and pepper, to taste

1. Mix together 2 tablespoons olive oil, chicken breasts, parsley, garlic cloves, and lemon juice in a large bowl. Place in the refrigerator to marinate for 1 hour.
2. Press the Sauté button on the Instant Pot and heat the remaining olive oil.
3. Cook the chicken breasts for 5 to 6 minutes per side until cooked through.
4. Allow to cool for 5 minutes before serving.

Broccoli Chicken with Black Beans

Prep time: 10 mins, Cook Time: 25 mins, Servings: 4
- 1 tbsp. olive oil
- 2 chicken breasts, skinless and boneless
- 1 cup broccoli florets
- 1½ cups chicken stock
- 2 tbsps. tomato sauce
- 1 cup black beans, soaked overnight and drained
- A pinch of salt and black pepper

1. Set your Instant Pot to Sauté and heat the olive oil. Add the chicken breasts and sauté for 5 minutes until lightly browned.
2. Add the remaining ingredients to the pot and stir well.
3. Lock the lid. Select the Poultry mode and cook for 20 minutes at High Pressure.
4. Once cooking is complete, do a natural pressure release for 10 minutes, then release any remaining pressure. Carefully open the lid.
5. Remove from the pot and serve on plates.

Thyme Chicken with Brussels Sprouts

Prep time: 10 mins, Cook Time: 25 mins, Servings: 4
- 1 tbsp. olive oil
- 2 chicken breasts, skinless, boneless and halved
- 2 cups Brussels sprouts, halved
- 1 cup chicken stock
- 2 thyme springs, chopped
- A pinch of salt and black pepper

1. Set your Instant Pot to Sauté and heat the olive oil. Add the chicken breasts and brown for 5 minutes.
2. Add the remaining ingredients to the pot and whisk to combine.
3. Lock the lid. Select the Poultry mode and set the cooking time for 20 minutes at High Pressure.
4. Once cooking is complete, do a natural pressure release for 10 minutes, then release any remaining pressure. Carefully open the lid.
5. Divide the chicken and Brussels sprouts among four plates and serve.

Fennel Chicken

Prep time: 10 mins, Cook Time: 25 mins, Servings: 4
- 2 tbsps. olive oil
- 2 tbsps. grated ginger
- 2 chicken breasts, skinless, boneless and halved
- 1 cup chicken stock
- 2 fennel bulbs, sliced
- 1 tbsp. basil, chopped
- A pinch of salt and black pepper

1. Set your Instant Pot to Sauté and heat the olive oil. Cook the ginger and chicken breasts for 5 minutes until evenly browned.
2. Add the remaining ingredients to the pot and mix well.
3. Lock the lid. Select the Poultry mode and cook for 20 minutes at High Pressure.
4. Once cooking is complete, do a natural pressure release for 10 minutes, then release any remaining pressure. Carefully open the lid.
5. Allow the chicken cool for 5 minutes before serving.

Filipino Chicken Adobo

Prep time: 3 mins, Cook Time: 30 mins, Servings:4
Ingredients
- 4 chicken legs
- ⅓ cup soy sauce
- ¼ cup white vinegar
- ¼ cup sugar
- 5 cloves garlic, crushed
- 2 bay leaves
- 1 onion, chopped
- Salt and pepper, to taste

1. Add all the ingredients to your Instant Pot and stir to combine well.
2. Lock the lid. Select the Poultry mode and cook for 30 minutes at High Pressure.
3. Once cooking is complete, do a natural pressure release for 10 minutes, then release any remaining pressure. Carefully open the lid.
4. Divide the chicken legs among four plates and serve warm.

Paprika Chicken with Tomatoes

Prep time: 10 mins, Cook Time: 20 mins, Servings:4
- 1 tbsp. avocado oil
- 1½ lbs. chicken breast, skinless, boneless, and cubed
- 1 cup tomatoes, cubed
- 1 cup chicken stock
- 1 tbsp. smoked paprika
- 1 tsp. cayenne pepper
- A pinch of salt and black pepper

1.	Set your Instant Pot to Sauté and heat the oil. Cook the cubed chicken in the hot oil for 2 to 3 minutes until lightly browned.
2.	Add the remaining ingredients to the pot and stir well.
3.	Lock the lid. Select the Poultry mode and set the cooking time for 18 minutes at High Pressure.
4.	Once cooking is complete, do a natural pressure release for 10 minutes, then release any remaining pressure. Carefully open the lid.
5.	Serve the chicken and tomatoes in bowls while warm.

Chicken with Artichokes and Bacon

Prep time: 10 mins, Cook Time: 25 mins, Servings:4

•	2 chicken breasts, skinless, boneless, and halved
•	2 cups canned artichokes, drained, and chopped
•	1 cup bacon, cooked and crumbled
•	1 cup water
•	2 tbsps. tomato paste
•	1 tbsp. chives, chopped
•	Salt, to taste

1.	Mix all the ingredients in your Instant Pot until well combined.
2.	Lock the lid. Select the Poultry mode and set the cooking time for 25 minutes at High Pressure.
3.	Once cooking is complete, do a natural pressure release for 10 minutes, then release any remaining pressure. Carefully open the lid.
4.	Remove from the pot to a large plate and serve.

Crispy Chicken with Herbs

Prep time: 10 mins, Cook Time: 30 mins, Servings: 2 to 3

•	2 tbsps. butter, softened
•	½ head of garlic, crushed
•	1 thyme sprig, crushed
•	1 rosemary sprig, crushed
•	½ tbsp. paprika
•	Salt and ground black pepper, to taste
•	1½ lbs. whole chicken, patted dry
•	2 cups water

1.	Mix together the butter, garlic, thyme, rosemary, paprika, salt, and pepper in a shallow dish, and stir to incorporate.
2.	Slather the butter mixture all over the chicken until well coated. Add the water and chicken to the Instant Pot.
3.	Lock the lid. Select the Manual mode and cook for 20 minutes at High Pressure.
4.	Once cooking is complete, do a natural pressure release for 10 minutes, then release any remaining pressure. Carefully open the lid.
5.	Remove the chicken from the pot and place it under the broiler for 10 minutes, or until the skin is just lightly crisped. Serve warm.

BLT Chicken Salad

Prep time: 15 minutes | Cook time: 17 minutes | Serves 4

4 slices bacon
2 (6-ounce / 170-g) chicken breasts
1 teaspoon salt
½ teaspoon garlic powder
¼ teaspoon dried parsley
¼ teaspoon pepper
¼ teaspoon dried thyme
1 cup water
2 cups chopped romaine lettuce
Sauce:
$^1/_3$ cup mayonnaise
1 ounce (28 g) chopped pecans
½ cup diced Roma tomatoes
½ avocado, diced
1 tablespoon lemon juice

1.	Press the Sauté button to heat your Instant Pot.
2.	Add the bacon and cook for about 7 minutes, flipping occasionally, until crisp. Remove and place on a paper towel to drain. When cool enough to handle, crumble the bacon and set aside.
3.	Sprinkle the chicken with salt, garlic powder, parsley, pepper, and thyme.
4.	Pour the water into the Instant Pot. Use a wooden spoon to ensure nothing is stuck to the bottom of the pot. Add the trivet to the pot and place the chicken on top of the trivet.
5.	Secure the lid. Select the Manual mode and set the cooking time for 10 minutes at High Pressure.
6.	Meanwhile, whisk together all the ingredients for the sauce in a large salad bowl.
7.	Once cooking is complete, do a quick pressure release. Carefully open the lid.
8.	Remove the chicken and let sit for 10 minutes. Cut the chicken into cubes and transfer to the salad bowl, along with the cooked bacon. Gently stir until the chicken is thoroughly coated. Mix in the lettuce right before serving.

Easy Kung Pao Chicken

Prep time: 5 minutes | Cook time: 17 minutes | Serves 5

2 tablespoons coconut oil
1 pound (454 g) boneless, skinless chicken breasts, cubed
1 cup cashews, chopped
6 tablespoons hot sauce
½ teaspoon chili powder
½ teaspoon finely grated ginger
½ teaspoon kosher salt
½ teaspoon freshly ground black pepper

1.	Set the Instant Pot to Sauté and melt the coconut oil.
2.	Add the remaining ingredients to the Instant Pot and mix well.
3.	Secure the lid. Select the Manual mode and set the cooking time for 17 minutes at High Pressure.
4.	Once cooking is complete, do a quick pressure release. Carefully open the lid.
5.	Serve warm.

<u>**Crack Chicken Breasts**</u>
<u>Prep time: 5 minutes | Cook time: 15 minutes |</u>
<u>Serves 2</u>
½ pound (227 g) boneless, skinless chicken breasts
2 ounces (57 g) cream cheese, softened
½ cup grass-fed bone broth
¼ cup tablespoons keto-friendly ranch dressing
½ cup shredded full-fat Cheddar cheese
3 slices bacon, cooked and chopped into small pieces
1. Combine all the ingredients except the Cheddar cheese and bacon in the Instant Pot.
2. Secure the lid. Select the Manual mode and set the cooking time for 15 minutes at High Pressure.
3. Once cooking is complete, do a quick pressure release. Carefully open the lid.
4. Add the Cheddar cheese and bacon and stir well, then serve.

Bruschetta Chicken

Prep time: 5 minutes | Cook time: 20 minutes |
Serves 2
2 boneless, skinless chicken breasts
½ cup filtered water
1 (14-ounce / 397-g) can sugar-free or low-sugar crushed tomatoes
¼ teaspoon dried basil
½ cup shredded full-fat Cheddar cheese
¼ cup heavy whipping cream
1. Combine all the ingredients except the cheese and whipping cream in the Instant Pot.
2. Secure the lid. Select the Manual mode and set the cooking time for 20 minutes at High Pressure.
3. Once cooking is complete, do a quick pressure release. Carefully open the lid.
4. Stir in the cheese and whipping cream until the cheese melts, and serve.

Baked Cheesy Mushroom Chicken

Prep time: 5 minutes | Cook time: 15 minutes |
Serves 4
1 tablespoon butter
2 cloves garlic, smashed
½ cup chopped yellow onion
1 pound (454 g) chicken breasts, cubed
10 ounces (283 g) button mushrooms, thinly sliced
1 cup chicken broth
½ teaspoon shallot powder
½ teaspoon turmeric powder
½ teaspoon dried basil
½ teaspoon dried sage
½ teaspoon cayenne pepper
$^1/_3$ teaspoon ground black pepper
Kosher salt, to taste
½ cup heavy cream
1 cup shredded Colby cheese
1. Set your Instant Pot to Sauté and melt the butter.
2. Add the garlic, onion, chicken, and mushrooms and sauté for about 4 minutes, or until the vegetables are softened.
3. Add the remaining ingredients except the heavy cream and cheese to the Instant Pot and stir to incorporate.

4. Lock the lid. Select the Meat/Stew mode and set the cooking time for 6 minutes at High Pressure.
5. When the timer beeps, perform a natural pressure release for 10 minutes, then release any remaining pressure. Carefully remove the lid.
6. Stir in the heavy cream until heated through. Pour the mixture into a baking dish and scatter the cheese on top.
7. Bake in the preheated oven at 400ºF (205ºC) until the cheese bubbles.
8. Allow to cool for 5 minutes and serve.

Chicken and Bacon Ranch Casserole

Prep time: 5 minutes | Cook time: 30 minutes |
Serves 4
4 slices bacon
4 (6-ounce / 170-g) boneless, skinless chicken breasts, cut into 1-inch cubes
½ teaspoon salt
¼ teaspoon pepper
1 tablespoon coconut oil
½ cup <u>chicken broth</u>
½ cup ranch dressing
½ cup shredded Cheddar cheese
2 ounces (57 g) cream cheese
1. Press the Sauté button to heat your Instant Pot.
2. Add the bacon slices and cook for about 7 minutes until crisp, flipping occasionally.
3. Remove from the pot and place on a paper towel to drain. Set aside.
4. Season the chicken cubes with salt and pepper.
5. Set your Instant Pot to Sauté and melt the coconut oil.
6. Add the chicken cubes and brown for 3 to 4 minutes until golden brown.
7. Stir in the broth and ranch dressing.
8. Secure the lid. Select the Manual mode and set the cooking time for 20 minutes at High Pressure.
9. Once cooking is complete, do a quick pressure release. Carefully open the lid.
10. Stir in the Cheddar and cream cheese. Crumble the cooked bacon and scatter on top. Serve immediately.

Chicken Tacos with Fried Cheese Shells

Prep time: 5 minutes | Cook time: 25 minutes |
Serves 6
Chicken:
4 (6-ounce / 170-g) boneless, skinless chicken breasts
1 cup <u>chicken broth</u>
1 teaspoon salt
¼ teaspoon pepper
1 tablespoon chili powder
2 teaspoons garlic powder
2 teaspoons cumin
Cheese Shells:
1½ cups shredded whole-milk Mozzarella cheese
1. Combine all ingredients for the chicken in the Instant Pot.

2.	Secure the lid. Select the Manual mode and set the cooking time for 20 minutes at High Pressure.
3.	Once cooking is complete, do a quick pressure release. Carefully open the lid.
4.	Shred the chicken and serve in bowls or cheese shells.
5.	Make the cheese shells: Heat a nonstick skillet over medium heat.
6.	Sprinkle ¼ cup of Mozzarella cheese in the skillet and fry until golden. Flip and turn off the heat. Allow the cheese to get brown. Fill with chicken and fold. The cheese will harden as it cools. Repeat with the remaining cheese and filling.
7.	Serve warm.

Chicken Piccata

Prep time: 5 minutes | Cook time: 25 minutes | Serves 4
4 (6-ounce / 170-g) boneless, skinless chicken breasts
½ teaspoon salt
½ teaspoon garlic powder
¼ teaspoon pepper
2 tablespoons coconut oil
1 cup water
2 cloves garlic, minced
4 tablespoons butter
Juice of 1 lemon
¼ teaspoon xanthan gum
1.	Sprinkle the chicken with salt, garlic powder, and pepper.
2.	Set your Instant Pot to Sauté and melt the coconut oil.
3.	Add the chicken and sear each side for about 5 to 7 minutes until golden brown.
4.	Remove the chicken and set aside on a plate.
5.	Pour the water into the Instant Pot. Using a wooden spoon, scrape the bottom if necessary to remove any stuck-on seasoning or meat. Insert the trivet and place the chicken on the trivet.
6.	Secure the lid. Select the Manual mode and set the cooking time for 10 minutes at High Pressure.
7.	Once cooking is complete, do a natural pressure release for 10 minutes, then release any remaining pressure. Carefully open the lid.
8.	Remove the chicken and set aside. Strain the broth from the Instant Pot into a large bowl and return to the pot.
9.	Set your Instant Pot to Sauté again and add the remaining ingredients. Cook for at least 5 minutes, stirring frequently, or until the sauce is cooked to your desired thickness.
10.	Pour the sauce over the chicken and serve warm.

Keto Chicken Enchilada Bowl

Prep time: 10 minutes | Cook time: 35 minutes | Serves 4
2 (6-ounce / 170-g) boneless, skinless chicken breasts
2 teaspoons chili powder
½ teaspoon garlic powder
½ teaspoon salt
¼ teaspoon pepper
2 tablespoons coconut oil
¾ cup red enchilada sauce
¼ cup chicken broth
1 (4-ounce / 113-g) can green chilies
¼ cup diced onion
2 cups cooked cauliflower rice
1 avocado, diced
½ cup sour cream
1 cup shredded Cheddar cheese
1.	Sprinkle the chili powder, garlic powder, salt, and pepper on chicken breasts.
2.	Set your Instant Pot to Sauté and melt the coconut oil. Add the chicken breasts and sear each side for about 5 minutes until golden brown.
3.	Pour the enchilada sauce and broth over the chicken. Using a wooden spoon or rubber spatula, scrape the bottom of pot to make sure nothing is sticking. Stir in the chilies and onion.
4.	Secure the lid. Select the Manual mode and set the cooking time for 25 minutes at High Pressure.
5.	Once cooking is complete, do a quick pressure release. Carefully open the lid.
6.	Remove the chicken and shred with two forks. Serve the chicken over the cauliflower rice and place the avocado, sour cream, and Cheddar cheese on top.

Chicken and Mixed Greens Salad

Prep time: 5 minutes | Cook time: 20 minutes | Serves 4
Chicken:
2 tablespoons avocado oil
1 pound (454 g) chicken breast, cubed
½ cup filtered water
½ teaspoon ground turmeric
½ teaspoon dried parsley
½ teaspoon dried basil
½ teaspoon kosher salt
½ teaspoon freshly ground black pepper
Salad:
1 avocado, mashed
1 cup chopped arugula
1 cup chopped Swiss chard
1 cup chopped kale
½ cup chopped spinach
2 tablespoons pine nuts, toasted
1.	Combine all the chicken ingredients in the Instant Pot.
2.	Secure the lid. Select the Manual mode and set the cooking time for 20 minutes at High Pressure.
3.	Meanwhile, toss all the salad ingredients in a large salad bowl.
4.	Once cooking is complete, do a quick pressure release. Carefully open the lid.
5.	Remove the chicken to the salad bowl and serve.

Cheesy Pesto Chicken

Prep time: 5 minutes | Cook time: 25 minutes | Serves 2
2 (6-ounce / 170-g) boneless, skinless chicken breasts, butterflied

½ teaspoon salt
¼ teaspoon pepper
¼ teaspoon dried parsley
¼ teaspoon garlic powder
2 tablespoons coconut oil
1 cup water
¼ cup whole-milk ricotta cheese
¼ cup pesto
¼ cup shredded whole-milk Mozzarella cheese
Chopped parsley, for garnish (optional)
1.	Sprinkle the chicken breasts with salt, pepper, parsley, and garlic powder.
2.	Set your Instant Pot to Sauté and melt the coconut oil.
3.	Add the chicken and brown for 3 to 5 minutes. Remove the chicken from the pot to a 7-cup glass bowl.
4.	Pour the water into the Instant Pot and use a wooden spoon or rubber spatula to make sure no seasoning is stuck to bottom of pot.
5.	Scatter the ricotta cheese on top of the chicken. Pour the pesto over chicken, and sprinkle the Mozzarella cheese over chicken. Cover with aluminum foil. Add the trivet to the Instant Pot and place the bowl on the trivet.
6.	Secure the lid. Select the Manual mode and set the cooking time for 20 minutes at High Pressure.
7.	Once cooking is complete, do a natural pressure release for 10 minutes, then release any remaining pressure. Carefully open the lid.
8.	Serve the chicken garnished with the chopped parsley, if desired.

Chicken Alfredo with Bacon

Prep time: 10 minutes | Cook time: 27 minutes | Serves 4
2 (6-ounce / 170-g) boneless, skinless chicken breasts, butterflied
½ teaspoon garlic powder
¼ teaspoon dried parsley
¼ teaspoon dried thyme
¼ teaspoon salt
⅛ teaspoon pepper
2 tablespoons coconut oil
1 cup water
1 stick butter
2 cloves garlic, finely minced
¼ cup heavy cream
½ cup grated Parmesan cheese
¼ cup cooked crumbled bacon
1.	Sprinkle the chicken breasts with the garlic powder, parsley, thyme, salt, and pepper.
2.	Set your Instant Pot to Sauté and melt the coconut oil.
3.	Add the chicken and sear for 3 to 5 minutes until golden brown on both sides.
4.	Remove the chicken with tongs and set aside.
5.	Pour the water into the Instant Pot and insert the trivet. Place the chicken on the trivet.
6.	Secure the lid. Select the Manual mode and set the cooking time for 20 minutes at High Pressure.
7.	Once cooking is complete, do a quick pressure release. Carefully open the lid.

8.	Remove the chicken from the pot to a platter and set aside.
9.	Pour the water out of the Instant Pot, reserving ½ cup; set aside.
10.	Set your Instant Pot to Sauté again and melt the butter.
11.	Add the garlic, heavy cream, cheese, and reserved water to the Instant Pot. Cook for 3 to 4 minutes until the sauce starts to thicken, stirring frequently.
12.	Stir in the crumbled bacon and pour the mixture over the chicken. Serve immediately.

Stuffed Chicken with Spinach and Feta

Prep time: 10 minutes | Cook time: 25 minutes | Serves 4
½ cup frozen spinach
¹/₃ cup crumbled feta cheese
1¼ teaspoons salt, divided
4 (6-ounce / 170-g) boneless, skinless chicken breasts, butterflied
¼ teaspoon pepper
¼ teaspoon dried oregano
¼ teaspoon dried parsley
¼ teaspoon garlic powder
2 tablespoons coconut oil
1 cup water
1.	Combine the spinach, feta cheese, and ¼ teaspoon of salt in a medium bowl. Divide the mixture evenly and spoon onto the chicken breasts.
2.	Close the chicken breasts and secure with toothpicks or butcher's string. Sprinkle the chicken with the remaining 1 teaspoon of salt, pepper, oregano, parsley, and garlic powder.
3.	Set your Instant Pot to Sauté and heat the coconut oil.
4.	Sear each chicken breast until golden brown, about 4 to 5 minutes per side.
5.	Remove the chicken breasts and set aside.
6.	Pour the water into the Instant Pot and scrape the bottom to remove any chicken or seasoning that is stuck on. Add the trivet to the Instant Pot and place the chicken on the trivet.
7.	Secure the lid. Select the Manual mode and set the cooking time for 15 minutes at High Pressure.
8.	Once cooking is complete, do a natural pressure release for 15 minutes, then release any remaining pressure. Carefully open the lid. Serve warm.

Instant Pot Ranch Chicken

Prep time: 5 minutes | Cook time: 20 minutes | Serves 6
1 teaspoon salt
½ teaspoon garlic powder
¼ teaspoon pepper
¼ teaspoon dried oregano
3 (6-ounce / 170-g) skinless chicken breasts
1 stick butter
8 ounces (227 g) cream cheese
1 dry ranch packet
1 cup chicken broth

1.	In a small bowl, combine the salt, garlic powder, pepper, and oregano. Rub this mixture over both sides of chicken breasts.
2.	Place the chicken breasts into the Instant Pot, along with the butter, cream cheese, ranch seasoning, and chicken broth.
3.	Secure the lid. Select the Manual mode and set the cooking time for 20 minutes at High Pressure.
4.	Once cooking is complete, do a natural pressure release for 10 minutes, then release any remaining pressure. Carefully open the lid.
5.	Remove the chicken and shred with two forks, then return to the Instant Pot. Use a rubber spatula to stir and serve on a plate.

Simple Shredded Chicken

Prep time: 5 minutes | Cook time: 14 minutes | Serves 4
½ teaspoon salt
½ teaspoon pepper
½ teaspoon dried oregano
½ teaspoon dried basil
½ teaspoon garlic powder
2 (6-ounce / 170-g) boneless, skinless chicken breasts
1 tablespoon coconut oil
1 cup water
1.	In a small bowl, combine the salt, pepper, oregano, basil, and garlic powder. Rub this mix over both sides of the chicken.
2.	Set your Instant Pot to Sauté and heat the coconut oil until sizzling.
3.	Add the chicken and sear for 3 to 4 minutes until golden on both sides.
4.	Remove the chicken and set aside.
5.	Pour the water into the Instant Pot and use a wooden spoon or rubber spatula to make sure no seasoning is stuck to bottom of pot.
6.	Add the trivet to the Instant Pot and place the chicken on top.
7.	Secure the lid. Select the Manual mode and set the cooking time for 10 minutes at High Pressure.
8.	Once cooking is complete, do a natural pressure release for 5 minutes, then release any remaining pressure. Carefully open the lid.
9.	Remove the chicken and shred, then serve.

Chicken Fajita Bowls

Prep time: 5 minutes | Cook time: 10 minutes | Serves 2
1 pound (454 g) boneless, skinless chicken breasts, cut into 1-inch pieces
2 cups chicken broth
1 cup salsa
1 teaspoon paprika
1 teaspoon fine sea salt, or more to taste
1 teaspoon chili powder
½ teaspoon ground cumin
½ teaspoon ground black pepper
1 lime, halved
1.	Combine all the ingredients except the lime in the Instant Pot.

2.	Lock the lid. Select the Manual mode and set the cooking time for 10 minutes at High Pressure.
3.	When the timer beeps, perform a quick pressure release. Carefully remove the lid.
4.	Shred the chicken with two forks and return to the Instant Pot. Squeeze the lime juice into the chicken mixture. Taste and add more salt, if needed. Give the mixture a good stir.
5.	Ladle the chicken mixture into bowls and serve.

Prosciutto-Wrapped Chicken

Prep time: 5 minutes | Cook time: 15 minutes | Serves 5
1½ cups water
5 chicken breast halves, butterflied
2 garlic cloves, halved
1 teaspoon marjoram
Sea salt, to taste
½ teaspoon red pepper flakes
¼ teaspoon ground black pepper, or more to taste
10 strips prosciutto
1.	Pour the water into the Instant Pot and insert the trivet.
2.	Rub the chicken breast halves with garlic. Sprinkle with marjoram, salt, red pepper flakes, and black pepper. Wrap each chicken breast into 2 prosciutto strips and secure with toothpicks. Put the chicken on the trivet.
3.	Lock the lid. Select the Poultry mode and set the cooking time for 15 minutes at High Pressure.
4.	When the timer beeps, perform a natural pressure release for 10 minutes, then release any remaining pressure. Carefully remove the lid.
5.	Remove the toothpicks and serve warm.

Creamy Chicken Cordon Bleu

Prep time: 12 minutes | Cook time: 15 minutes | Serves 6
4 boneless, skinless chicken breast halves, butterflied
4 (1-ounce / 28-g) slices Swiss cheese
8 (1-ounce / 28-g) slices ham
1 cup water
Chopped fresh flat-leaf parsley, for garnish
Sauce:
1½ ounces (43 g) cream cheese (3 tablespoons)
¼ cup chicken broth
1 tablespoon unsalted butter
¼ teaspoon ground black pepper
¼ teaspoon fine sea salt
1.	Lay the chicken breast halves on a clean work surface. Top each with a slice of Swiss cheese and 2 slices of ham. Roll the chicken around the ham and cheese, then secure with toothpicks. Set aside.
2.	Whisk together all the ingredients for the sauce in a small saucepan over medium heat, stirring until the cream cheese melts and the sauce is smooth.
3.	Place the chicken rolls, seam-side down, in a casserole dish. Pour half of the sauce over the chicken rolls. Set the remaining sauce aside.
4.	Pour the water into the Instant Pot and insert the trivet. Place the dish on the trivet.

5.	Lock the lid. Select the Manual mode and set the cooking time for 15 minutes at High Pressure.
6.	When the timer beeps, perform a natural pressure release for 10 minutes, then release any remaining pressure. Carefully remove the lid.
7.	Remove the chicken rolls from the Instant Pot to a plate. Pour the remaining sauce over them and serve garnished with the parsley.

Cheesy Chicken Drumsticks

Prep time: 3 minutes | Cook time: 23 minutes | Serves 5

1 tablespoon olive oil
5 chicken drumsticks
½ cup chicken stock
¼ cup unsweetened coconut milk
¼ cup dry white wine
2 garlic cloves, minced
1 teaspoon shallot powder
½ teaspoon marjoram
½ teaspoon thyme
6 ounces (170 g) ricotta cheese
4 ounces (113 g) Cheddar cheese
½ teaspoon cayenne pepper
¼ teaspoon ground black pepper
Sea salt, to taste
1.	Set your Instant Pot to Sauté and heat the olive oil until sizzling.
2.	Add the chicken drumsticks and brown each side for 3 minutes.
3.	Stir in the chicken stock, milk, wine, garlic, shallot powder, marjoram, thyme.
4.	Lock the lid. Select the Manual mode and set the cooking time for 15 minutes at High Pressure.
5.	When the timer beeps, perform a natural pressure release for 10 minutes, then release any remaining pressure. Carefully remove the lid.
6.	Shred the chicken with two forks and return to the Instant Pot.
7.	Set your Instant Pot to Sauté again and add the remaining ingredients and stir well.
8.	Cook for another 2 minutes, or until the cheese is melted. Taste and add more salt, if desired. Serve immediately.

Jamaican Curry Chicken Drumsticks

Prep time: 5 minutes | Cook time: 20 minutes | Serves 4

1½ pounds (680 g) chicken drumsticks
1 tablespoon Jamaican curry powder
1 teaspoon salt
1 cup chicken broth
½ medium onion, diced
½ teaspoon dried thyme
1.	Sprinkle the salt and curry powder over the chicken drumsticks.
2.	Place the chicken drumsticks into the Instant Pot, along with the remaining ingredients.
3.	Secure the lid. Select the Manual mode and set the cooking time for 20 minutes at High Pressure.
4.	Once cooking is complete, do a quick pressure release. Carefully open the lid. Serve warm.

Parmesan Drumsticks

Prep time: 5 minutes | Cook time: 25 minutes | Serves 4

2 pounds (907 g) chicken drumsticks (about 8 pieces)
1 teaspoon salt
1 teaspoon dried parsley
½ teaspoon garlic powder
½ teaspoon dried oregano
¼ teaspoon pepper
1 cup water
1 stick butter
2 ounces (57 g) cream cheese, softened
½ cup grated Parmesan cheese
½ cup chicken broth
¼ cup heavy cream
⅛ teaspoon pepper
1.	Sprinkle the salt, parsley, garlic powder, oregano, and pepper evenly over the chicken drumsticks.
2.	Pour the water into the Instant Pot and insert the trivet. Arrange the drumsticks on the trivet.
3.	Secure the lid. Select the Manual mode and set the cooking time for 15 minutes at High Pressure.
4.	Once cooking is complete, do a quick pressure release. Carefully open the lid.
5.	Transfer the drumsticks to a foil-lined baking sheet and broil each side for 3 to 5 minutes, or until the skin begins to crisp.
6.	Meanwhile, pour the water out of the Instant Pot. Set your Instant Pot to Sauté and melt the butter.
7.	Add the remaining ingredients to the Instant Pot and whisk to combine. Pour the sauce over the drumsticks and serve warm.

Chicken Legs with Mayo Sauce

Prep time: 5 minutes | Cook time: 20 minutes | Serves 4

4 chicken legs, bone-in, skinless
2 garlic cloves, peeled and halved
½ teaspoon coarse sea salt
½ teaspoon crushed red pepper flakes
¼ teaspoon ground black pepper, or more to taste
1 tablespoon olive oil
¼ cup chicken broth
Dipping Sauce:
¾ cup mayonnaise
2 tablespoons stone ground mustard
1 teaspoon fresh lemon juice
½ teaspoon Sriracha
For Garnish:
¼ cup roughly chopped fresh cilantro
1.	Rub the chicken legs with the garlic. Sprinkle with salt, red pepper flakes, and black pepper.
2.	Set your Instant Pot to Sauté and heat the olive oil.
3.	Add the chicken legs and brown for 4 to 5 minutes. Add a splash of chicken broth to deglaze the bottom of the pot.
4.	Pour the remaining chicken broth into the Instant Pot and mix well.

5.	Lock the lid. Select the Manual mode and set the cooking time for 14 minutes at High Pressure.
6.	Meanwhile, whisk together all the sauce ingredients in a small bowl.
7.	When the timer beeps, perform a natural pressure release for 10 minutes, then release any remaining pressure. Carefully remove the lid.
8.	Sprinkle the cilantro on top for garnish and serve with the prepared dipping sauce.

Chicken With Cheese Mushroom Sauce

Prep time: 8 minutes | Cook time: 14 minutes | Serves 4

2 tablespoons unsalted butter or coconut oil
2 cloves garlic, minced
¼ cup diced onions
2 cups sliced button or cremini mushrooms
4 boneless, skinless chicken breast halves
½ cup chicken broth
¼ cup heavy cream
1 teaspoon fine sea salt
1 teaspoon dried tarragon leaves
½ teaspoon dried thyme leaves
½ teaspoon ground black pepper
2 bay leaves
½ cup grated Parmesan cheese
Fresh thyme leaves, for garnish
1.	Set your Instant Pot to Sauté and melt the butter.
2.	Add the garlic, onions, and mushrooms and sauté for 4 minutes, stirring often, or until the onions are softened.
3.	Add the remaining ingredients except the Parmesan cheese and thyme leaves to the Instant Pot and stir to combine.
4.	Lock the lid. Select the Manual mode and set the cooking time for 10 minutes at High Pressure.
5.	When the timer beeps, perform a natural pressure release for 10 minutes, then release any remaining pressure. Carefully remove the lid.
6.	Discard the bay leaves and transfer the chicken to a serving platter.
7.	Add the Parmesan cheese to the Instant Pot with the sauce and stir until the cheese melts.
8.	Pour the mushroom sauce from the pot over the chicken. Serve garnished with the fresh thyme leaves.

Chicken Cacciatore

Prep time: 5 minutes | Cook time: 22 minutes | Serves 4 to 5

6 tablespoons coconut oil
5 chicken legs
1 bell pepper, diced
½ onion, chopped
1 (14-ounce / 397-g) can sugar-free or low-sugar diced tomatoes
½ teaspoon dried basil
½ teaspoon dried parsley
½ teaspoon kosher salt
½ teaspoon freshly ground black pepper
½ cup filtered water

1.	Press the Sauté button on the Instant Pot and melt the coconut oil.
2.	Add the chicken legs and sauté until the outside is browned.
3.	Remove the chicken and set aside.
4.	Add the bell pepper, onion, tomatoes, basil, parsley, salt, and pepper to the Instant Pot and cook for about 2 minutes.
5.	Pour in the water and return the chicken to the pot.
6.	Lock the lid. Select the Manual mode and set the cooking time for 18 minutes at High Pressure.
7.	Once cooking is complete, do a quick pressure release. Carefully open the lid. Serve warm.

Salsa Chicken Legs

Prep time: 5 minutes | Cook time: 16 minutes | Serves 5

5 chicken legs, skinless and boneless
½ teaspoon sea salt
Salsa Sauce:
1 cup puréed tomatoes
1 cup onion, chopped
1 jalapeño, chopped
2 bell peppers, deveined and chopped
2 tablespoons minced fresh cilantro
3 teaspoons lime juice
1 teaspoon granulated garlic
1.	Press the Sauté button to heat your Instant Pot.
2.	Add the chicken legs and sear each side for 2 to 3 minutes until evenly browned. Season with sea salt.
3.	Thoroughly combine all the ingredients for the salsa sauce in a mixing bowl. Spoon the salsa mixture evenly over the browned chicken legs.
4.	Lock the lid. Select the Manual mode and set the cooking time for 10 minutes at High Pressure.
5.	When the timer beeps, perform a natural pressure release for 10 minutes, then release any remaining pressure. Carefully remove the lid. Serve warm.

Curried Mustard Chicken Legs

Prep time: 10 minutes | Cook time: 20 minutes | Serves 5

5 chicken legs, boneless, skin-on
2 garlic cloves, halved
Sea salt, to taste
½ teaspoon smoked paprika
¼ teaspoon ground black pepper
2 teaspoons olive oil
1 tablespoon yellow mustard
1 teaspoon curry paste
4 strips pancetta, chopped
1 shallot, peeled and chopped
1 cup vegetable broth
1.	Rub the chicken legs with the garlic halves. Sprinkle with salt, paprika, and black pepper.
2.	Set your Instant Pot to Sauté and heat the olive oil.

3.	Add the chicken legs and brown for 4 to 5 minutes. Add a splash of chicken broth to deglaze the bottom of the pot.
4.	Spread the chicken legs with mustard and curry paste.
5.	Add the pancetta strips, shallot, and remaining vegetable broth to the Instant Pot.
6.	Lock the lid. Select the Manual mode and set the cooking time for 14 minutes at High Pressure.
7.	When the timer beeps, perform a natural pressure release for 10 minutes, then release any remaining pressure. Carefully remove the lid.
8.	Serve warm.

Buffalo Wings

Prep time: 5 minutes | Cook time: 12 minutes | Serves 4
2 pounds (907 g) chicken wings, patted dry
1 teaspoon seasoned salt
¼ teaspoon pepper
½ teaspoon garlic powder
¼ cup buffalo sauce
¾ cup chicken broth
$^1/_3$ cup blue cheese crumbles
¼ cup cooked bacon crumbles
2 stalks green onion, sliced
1.	Season the chicken wings with salt, pepper, and garlic powder.
2.	Pour the buffalo sauce and broth into the Instant Pot. Stir in the chicken wings.
3.	Lock the lid. Select the Manual mode and set the cooking time for 12 minutes at High Pressure.
4.	Once cooking is complete, do a quick pressure release. Carefully open the lid. Gently stir to coat wings with the sauce.
5.	If you prefer crispier wings, you can broil them for 3 to 5 minutes until the skin is crispy.
6.	Remove the chicken wings from the pot to a plate. Brush them with the leftover sauce and serve topped with the blue cheese, bacon, and green onions.

Barbecue Wings

Prep time: 5 minutes | Cook time: 12 minutes | Serves 4
1 pound (454 g) chicken wings
1 teaspoon salt
½ teaspoon pepper
¼ teaspoon garlic powder
1 cup sugar-free barbecue sauce, divided
1 cup water
1.	Toss the chicken wings with the salt, pepper, garlic powder, and half of barbecue sauce in a large bowl until well coated.
2.	Pour the water into the Instant Pot and insert the trivet. Place the wings on the trivet.
3.	Secure the lid. Select the Manual mode and set the cooking time for 12 minutes at High Pressure.
4.	Once cooking is complete, do a quick pressure release. Carefully open the lid.
5.	Transfer the wings to a serving bowl and toss with the remaining sauce. Serve immediately.

Butter-Parmesan Wings

Prep time: 5 minutes | Cook time: 12 minutes | Serves 4
2 pounds (907 g) chicken wings, patted dry
1 teaspoon seasoned salt
½ teaspoon garlic powder
½ teaspoon pepper
1 cup water
3 tablespoons butter
1 teaspoon lemon pepper
¼ cup grated Parmesan cheese
1.	Season the chicken wings with the salt, garlic powder, and pepper.
2.	Pour the water into the Instant Pot and insert the trivet. Arrange the wings on the trivet.
3.	Secure the lid. Select the Manual mode and set the cooking time for 10 minutes at High Pressure.
4.	Once cooking is complete, do a quick pressure release. Carefully open the lid.
5.	Remove the chicken wings and set aside on a plate.
6.	For crispy wings, you can place them on a foil-lined baking sheet and broil for 3 to 5 minutes, or until the skin is crispy.
7.	Pour the water out of the Instant Pot. Set your Instant Pot to Sauté and melt the butter.
8.	Stir in the lemon pepper and return the wings to the pot, tossing to coat. Scatter with the cheese and serve warm.

Chicken Wingettes with Cilantro Sauce

Prep time: 5 minutes | Cook time: 6 minutes | Serves 6
12 chicken wingettes
10 fresh cayenne peppers, trimmed and chopped
3 garlic cloves, minced
1½ cups white vinegar
1 teaspoon sea salt
1 teaspoon onion powder
½ teaspoon black pepper
2 tablespoons olive oil
Dipping Sauce:
½ cup sour cream
½ cup mayonnaise
½ cup cilantro, chopped
2 cloves garlic, minced
1 teaspoon smoked paprika
1.	In a large bowl, toss the chicken wingettes, cayenne peppers, garlic, white vinegar, salt, onion powder, and black pepper. Cover and marinate for 1 hour in the refrigerator.
2.	When ready, transfer the chicken wingettes to the Instant Pot, along with the marinade and olive oil.
3.	Lock the lid. Select the Manual mode and set the cooking time for 6 minutes at High Pressure.
4.	Meanwhile, thoroughly combine all the sauce ingredients in a mixing bowl.
5.	When the timer beeps, perform a quick pressure release. Carefully remove the lid.
6.	Serve the chicken warm alongside the dipping sauce.

Chicken Fillets with Cheese Sauce

Prep time: 5 minutes | Cook time: 10 minutes | Serves 4

1 tablespoon olive oil
1 pound (454 g) chicken fillets
½ teaspoon dried basil
Salt and freshly ground black pepper, to taste
1 cup chicken broth
Cheese Sauce:
3 teaspoons butter, at room temperature
$^{1}/_{3}$ cup grated Gruyère cheese
$^{1}/_{3}$ cup Neufchâtel cheese, at room temperature
$^{1}/_{3}$ cup heavy cream
3 tablespoons unsweetened coconut milk
1 teaspoon shallot powder
½ teaspoon granulated garlic
1.   Set your Instant Pot to Sauté and heat the olive oil until sizzling.
2.   Add the chicken and sear each side for 3 minutes. Sprinkle with the basil, salt, and black pepper.
3.   Pour the broth into the Instant Pot and stir well.
4.   Lock the lid. Select the Manual mode and set the cooking time for 6 minutes at High Pressure.
5.   When the timer beeps, perform a natural pressure release for 10 minutes, then release any remaining pressure. Carefully remove the lid.
6.   Transfer the chicken to a platter and set aside.
7.   Clean the Instant Pot. Press the Sauté button and melt the butter.
8.   Add the cheeses, heavy cream, milk, shallot powder, and garlic, stirring until everything is heated through.
9.   Pour the cheese sauce over the chicken and serve.

Chicken Liver Pâté

Prep time: 5 minutes | Cook time: 15 minutes | Serves 8

2 tablespoons olive oil
1 pound (454 g) chicken livers
2 garlic cloves, crushed
½ cup chopped leeks
1 tablespoon poultry seasonings
1 teaspoon dried rosemary
½ teaspoon paprika
½ teaspoon dried marjoram
½ teaspoon red pepper flakes
½ teaspoon ground black pepper
¼ teaspoon dried dill weed
Salt, to taste
1 cup water
1 tablespoon stone ground mustard
1.   Set your Instant Pot to Sauté and heat the olive oil.
2.   Add the chicken livers and sauté for about 3 minutes until no longer pink.
3.   Add the remaining ingredients except the mustard to the Instant Pot and stir to combine.
4.   Lock the lid. Select the Manual mode and set the cooking time for 10 minutes at High Pressure.
5.   When the timer beeps, perform a quick pressure release. Carefully remove the lid.
6.   Transfer the cooked mixture to a food processor, along with the mustard. Pulse until the mixture is smooth. Serve immediately.

CHAPTER 10 BEEF

Apricot Preserved Flank Steak

Prep time: 10 minutes | Cook time: 45 minutes | Serves 4

¼ cup apricot preserves
⅛ cup apple cider vinegar
¼ cup ketchup
⅛ cup honey
¼ cup soy sauce
1 teaspoon ground mustard
⅛ teaspoon cayenne pepper
¼ teaspoon ground black pepper
1 (2-pound / 907-g) flank steak
2 tablespoons avocado oil, divided
1 large sweet onion, peeled and sliced
1½ cups beef broth

1. In a small bowl, combine the preserves, vinegar, ketchup, honey, soy sauce, mustard, cayenne pepper, and pepper. Spread half of the mixture on all sides of the flank steak on a clean work surface. Set the remaining mixture aside.
2. Press the Sauté button on Instant Pot. Heat 1 tablespoon of avocado oil. Add and sear the meat on each side for about 5 minutes. Remove the meat and set aside.
3. Add remaining 1 tablespoon of avocado oil and onions. Sauté for 3 to 5 minutes or until translucent.
4. Pour in the beef broth. Set meat on the onions. Pour the remaining preserve mixture over. Lock the lid.
5. Press the Meat / Stew button and set the cooking time for 35 minutes at High Pressure.
6. When timer beeps, let pressure release naturally for 15 minutes, then release any remaining pressure. Unlock the lid.
7. Transfer the meat to a serving platter. Thinly slice and serve immediately.

Beef and Bacon Fig Chutney

Prep time: 20 minutes | Cook time: 35 minutes | Serves 4

3 bacon slices, chopped
1 teaspoon olive oil
4 pounds (1.8 kg) beef short ribs
Salt and black pepper, to taste
1 pound (454 g) cherry tomatoes, halved
1 medium white onion, chopped
3 garlic cloves, minced
1 cup Marsala wine
¼ cup fig preserves
2 cups beef broth
3 tablespoons thyme leaves

1. Set the Instant Pot to Sauté mode and brown the bacon for 5 minutes until crispy. Place the bacon on a paper towel-lined plate and set aside.
2. Heat the olive oil, then season beef ribs with salt, and pepper. Sear the beef in the pot for 5 minutes on both sides or until brown. Transfer the beef next to bacon.
3. Add the cherry tomatoes, onion, and garlic to Instant Pot, then sauté for 5 minutes or until soft.
4. Stir in Marsala wine, fig preserves, beef broth, and thyme. Return beef and bacon to the pot.
5. Seal the lid, then select the Manual mode and set the time for 20 minutes at High Pressure.
6. Once cooking is complete, allow a natural release for 10 minutes, then release any remaining pressure. Unlock the lid.
7. Serve immediately.

Beef and Broccoli

Prep time: 15 minutes | Cook time: 25 minutes | Serves 4

½ cup grass-fed bone broth
1 pound (454 g) chuck steak, sliced
1 jalapeño pepper, sliced
1 green onion, chopped
½ teaspoon ginger, grated
½ teaspoon garlic
2 tablespoons coconut oil
½ teaspoon crushed red pepper
½ teaspoon kosher salt
½ teaspoon freshly ground black pepper
½ teaspoon dried parsley
1 cup broccoli, chopped
1 teaspoon sesame seeds

1. Pour the bone broth into the Instant Pot, then add the steak, jalapeño, green onion, ginger, garlic, coconut oil, red pepper, salt, black pepper, and parsley.
2. Close the lid and select the Manual mode. Set the cooking time for 20 minutes on High Pressure.
3. When timer beeps, let the pressure naturally release for about 10 minutes, then release any remaining pressure. Carefully open the lid.
4. Transfer the steak mixture on a plate. Add the broccoli and set to the Sauté mode. Cook for 5 minutes or until tender. Remove the broccoli from the pot.
5. Top the beef with the sesame seeds, serve with the broccoli.

Beef and Lush Vegetable Pot

Prep time: 15 minutes | Cook time: 21 minutes | Serves 4

2 tablespoons olive oil
1 pound (454 g) ground beef
¾ cup chopped baby Bella mushrooms
1 carrot, peeled and chopped
1 small onion, finely chopped
1 celery stick, chopped
1 garlic clove, minced
1 tablespoon Worcestershire Sauce
2 tablespoons tomato paste
1 teaspoon cinnamon powder
2 cups beef stock
2 sweet potatoes, chopped

1. Set the Instant Pot to the Sauté mode, then heat the olive oil.

2.	Brown the beef in the pot for 5 minutes. Mix in mushrooms, carrot, onion, celery, and garlic. Sauté for 5 minutes or until softened.
3.	Mix in Worcestershire sauce, tomato paste, and cinnamon. Cook for 1 minute.
4.	Pour in the beef stock and add the potatoes. Seal the lid, then select the Manual mode and set the cooking time for 10 minutes.
5.	Once cooking is complete, allow a natural release for 5 minutes, then release any remaining pressure and unlock the lid.
6.	Serve warm.

Beef and Spinach Tagliatelle

Prep time: 15 minutes | Cook time: 18 minutes | Serves 4

1 tablespoon olive oil
1 pound (454 g) ground beef
1 cup sliced cremini mushrooms
1 small yellow onion, chopped
2 garlic cloves, minced
8 ounces (227 g) tagliatelle
2 (26-ounce / 737-g) jars tomato pasta sauce
1 tablespoon Italian seasoning
1 teaspoon dried basil
6 cups water
Salt and black pepper, to taste
1 cup baby spinach
1.	Set the Instant Pot to Sauté mode, heat the olive oil and brown the beef for 5 minutes.
2.	Add the mushrooms, onion, garlic, and sauté for 3 minutes or until soft.
3.	Stir in tagliatelle, tomato sauce, Italian seasoning, basil, water, salt, and pepper.
4.	Seal the lid, then select the Manual mode and set the time for 5 minutes at High Pressure.
5.	Once cooking is complete, do a quick release, then unlock the lid.
6.	Select the Sauté mode and add the spinach. Cook for 5 minutes or until wilted. Serve warm.

Beef and Yogurt Pitas

Prep time: 15 minutes | Cook time: 28 minutes | Serves 4

1 tablespoon olive oil
1 pound (454 g) beef stew meat, cut into strips
Salt and black pepper, to taste
1 small white onion, chopped
3 garlic cloves, minced
2 teaspoons hot sauce
1 cup beef broth
1 cucumber, deseeded and chopped
1 medium tomato, chopped
4 whole pita bread, warmed
1 cup Greek yogurt
1 teaspoon chopped dill
1.	Set the Instant Pot to Sauté mode, then heat the olive oil until shimmering.
2.	Season the beef with salt, pepper, and brown the beef in the pot for 5 minutes. Remove the beef from the pot and set aside.
3.	Add the onion and garlic to oil and sauté for 3 minutes or until softened,. Return the beef to the pot, stir in hot sauce and beef broth.
4.	Seal the lid, then select the Manual mode and set the time for 20 minutes at High Pressure.
5.	Once cooking is complete, allow a natural release for 5 minutes, then release any remaining pressure. Unlock the lid.
6.	Transfer the beef into a bowl. Mix in the cucumber, tomatoes, and spoon the beef mixture into pita bread.
7.	In a medium bowl, mix yogurt and dill. Top beef with yogurt mixture and serve immediately.

Beef Empanadas

Prep time: 20 minutes | Cook time: 20 minutes | Serves 4

2 tablespoons olive oil, divided
¼ pound (113 g) ground beef
1 garlic clove, minced
½ white onion, chopped
6 green olives, pitted and chopped
¼ teaspoon cumin powder
¼ teaspoon paprika
¼ teaspoon cinnamon powder
2 small tomatoes, chopped
1 cup water
8 square wonton wrappers
1 egg, beaten
1.	Select the Sauté mode of the Instant Pot and heat 1 tablespoon of olive oil.
2.	Add and sauté the ground beef, garlic, and onion for 5 minutes or until fragrant and the beef is no longer pink.
3.	Stir in olives, cumin, paprika, and cinnamon, and cook for 3 minutes.
4.	Add the tomatoes and water, and cook for 1 minute.
5.	Seal the lid, then select the Manual mode and set the time for 8 minutes on High Pressure.
6.	When timer beeps, allow a natural release for 10 minutes, then release any remaining pressure. Carefully open the lid.
7.	Spoon the beef mixture onto a plate and let cool for a few minutes. Lay the wonton wrappers on a flat surface.
8.	Place 2 tablespoons of the beef mixture in the middle of each wrapper. Brush the edges of the wrapper with egg and fold in half to form a triangle. Pinch the edges together to seal.
9.	Heat the remaining oil in the Instant Pot and fry the empanadas for a minute each. Work in batches to avoid overcrowding.
10.	Remove to paper towels to soak up excess fat before serving.

Beef Lasagna

Prep time: 20 minutes | Cook time: 20 minutes | Serves 4

1 cup water
1 pound (454 g) ground beef
1 cup spinach, chopped
1 (14-ounce / 397-g) can fire roasted tomatoes

1 egg
¼ (4-ounce / 113-g) small onion, sliced
¾ cup Mozzarella cheese, shredded
½ cup Parmesan cheese, grated
1½ cups whole milk ricotta cheese
2 tablespoons coconut oil
½ teaspoon garlic
½ teaspoon dried basil
½ teaspoon fennel seeds
½ teaspoon dried parsley
½ teaspoon dried oregano
1. Pour the water into the Instant Pot, then insert the trivet.
2. In a large bowl, combine the remaining ingredients in the pot. Transfer the mixture into a baking pan.
3. Place the pan onto the trivet, and cover with aluminum foil.
4. Close the lid, then select the Manual mode. Set the cooking time for 20 minutes on High Pressure.
5. When timer beeps, naturally release the pressure for about 10 minutes, then release any remaining pressure. Carefully open the lid.
6. Let cool and serve.

Beef Meatballs with Roasted Tomatoes

Prep time: 15 minutes | Cook time: 16 minutes | Serves 4
2 tablespoons avocado oil
1 pound (454 g) ground beef
½ teaspoon dried basil
½ teaspoon crushed red pepper
½ teaspoon ground cayenne pepper
½ teaspoon kosher salt
½ teaspoon freshly ground black pepper
2 (14-ounce / 397-g) cans fire roasted tomatoes
1. Set the Instant Pot to Sauté mode and heat the avocado oil.
2. In a large bowl, mix the remaining ingredients, except for the tomatoes. Form the mixture into 1½-inch meatballs and place them into the Instant Pot. Spread the tomatoes evenly over the meatballs.
3. Close the lid. Select the Manual mode, set the cooking time for 16 minutes on High Pressure.
4. When timer beeps, perform a natural pressure release for 5 minutes, then release any remaining pressure.
5. Open the lid and serve.

Beef Rice Noodles

Prep time: 15 minutes | Cook time: 16 minutes | Serves 4
6 cups boiled water
8 ounces (227 g) rice noodles
1 tablespoon sesame oil
1 pound (454 g) ground beef
2 cups sliced shitake mushrooms
½ cup julienned carrots
1 yellow onion, sliced
1 cup shredded green cabbage
¼ cup sliced scallions, for garnish
Sesame seeds, for garnish

Sauce:
¼ cup tamarind sauce
1 tablespoon hoisin sauce
1 teaspoon grated ginger
1 teaspoon maple syrup
1. In a medium bowl, whisk together the ingredients for the sauce. Set aside.
2. Pour boiling water into a bowl and add rice noodles. Cover the bowl and allow the noodles to soften for 5 minutes. Drain and set aside.
3. Set the Instant Pot to Sauté mode and heat the sesame oil.
4. Cook the beef in the pot for 5 minutes or until browned.
5. Stir in the mushrooms, carrots, onion, and cabbage. Cook for 5 minutes or until softened.
6. Add the noodles. Top with the sauce and mix well. Cook for 1 more minute. Garnish with scallions and sesame seeds and serve immediately.

Beef Roast with Cauliflower

Prep time: 10 minutes | Cook time: 15 minutes | Serves 2
2 teaspoons sesame oil
12 ounces (340 g) sliced beef roast
Freshly ground black pepper, to taste
½ small onion, chopped
3 garlic cloves, minced
½ cup beef stock
¼ cup soy sauce
2 tablespoons brown sugar
Pinch red pepper flakes
1 tablespoon cornstarch
8 ounces (227 g) fresh cauliflower, cut into florets
1. Set the Instant Pot pot on Sauté mode. Add the sesame oil, beef, and black pepper. Sear for 2 minutes on all sides. Transfer the beef to a plate and set aside.
2. Add the onion and garlic to the pot and sauté for 2 minutes or until softened.
3. Stir in the stock, soy sauce, brown sugar, and red pepper flakes. Stir until the sugar is dissolved, then return the beef to the pot.
4. Secure the lid and set to the Manual mode. Set the cooking time for 10 minutes on High Pressure.
5. When timer beeps, quick release the pressure and open the lid. Set to the Sauté mode.
6. Transfer 2 tablespoons of liquid from the pot to a small bowl. Whisk it with the cornstarch, then add back to the pot along with the cauliflower.
7. Cover the lid and let simmer for 3 to 4 minutes, or until the sauce is thickened and the cauliflower is softened.
8. Serve the beef and cauliflower.

Beef Steaks with Mushrooms

Prep time: 15 minutes | Cook time: 25 minutes | Serves 2
2 beef steaks, boneless
Salt and black pepper, to taste
2 tablespoons olive oil
4 ounces (113 g) mushrooms, sliced
½ onion, chopped

1 garlic clove, minced
1 cup vegetable soup
1½ tablespoons cornstarch
1 tablespoon half-and-half
1. Rub the beef steaks with salt and pepper on a clean work surface.
2. Set the Instant Pot to Sauté mode and warm the olive oil until shimmering.
3. Sear the beef for 2 minutes per side until browned. Transfer to a plate.
4. Add the mushrooms and sauté for 5 minutes or until soft. Add the onion and garlic and sauté for 2 minutes until fragrant.
5. Return the steaks to the pot and pour in the soup. Seal the lid, select the Manual mode, and set the time to 15 minutes on High Pressure.
6. When cooking is complete, do a quick pressure release and unlock the lid and transfer the chops to a plate. Press the Sauté button.
7. In a bowl, combine the cornstarch and half-and-half and mix well. Pour the mixture into the pot and cook until the sauce is thickened. Serve warm.

Beef Tips with Portobello Mushrooms

Prep time: 20 minutes | Cook time: 16 minutes | Serves 4

2 teaspoons olive oil
1 beef top sirloin steak (1-pound / 454-g), cubed
½ teaspoon salt
¼ teaspoon ground black pepper
$^1/_3$ cup dry red wine
½ pound (227 g) sliced baby portobello mushrooms
1 small onion, halved and sliced
2 cups beef broth
1 tablespoon Worcestershire sauce
3 to 4 tablespoons cornstarch
¼ cup cold water
1. Select the Sauté setting of the Instant Pot. Add the olive oil.
2. Sprinkle the beef with salt and pepper. Brown meat in batches in the pot for 10 minutes. Flip constantly. Transfer meat to a bowl.
3. Add the wine to the pot. Return beef to the pot and add mushrooms, onion, broth, and Worcestershire sauce.
4. Lock the lid. Select the Manual setting and set the cooking time for 15 minutes at High Pressure.
5. When timer beeps, quick release the pressure. Carefully open the lid.
6. Select the Sauté setting and bring to a boil.
7. Meanwhile, in a small bowl, mix cornstarch and water until smooth.
8. Gradually stir the cornstarch into beef mixture. Sauté for 1 more minute or until sauce is thickened. Serve immediately.

Beef with Red and Green Cabbage

Prep time: 20 minutes | Cook time: 22 minutes | Serves 4

1 tablespoon olive oil
1 pound (454 g) ground beef
1 tablespoon grated ginger
3 garlic cloves, minced
Salt and black pepper, to taste
1 medium red cabbage, shredded
1 medium green cabbage, shredded
1 red bell pepper, chopped
1 cup water
2 tablespoons tamarind sauce
½ tablespoon honey
1 tablespoon hot sauce
1 tablespoon sesame oil
2 tablespoons walnuts
1 teaspoon toasted sesame seeds
1. Set the Instant Pot to Sauté mode and heat the olive oil.
2. Add the beef, then season with ginger, garlic, salt, black pepper. Cook for 5 minutes.
3. Add the red and green cabbage, bell pepper, and sauté for 5 minutes.
4. Pour in the water and seal the lid. Select the Manual mode and set the time to 10 minutes on High Pressure.
5. When timer beeps, allow a natural release for 10 minutes, then release any remaining pressure. Unlock the lid.
6. Meanwhile, in a bowl, combine the tamarind sauce, honey, hot sauce, and sesame oil. Stir in the pot, add walnuts, and cook for 1 to 2 minutes on Sauté mode.
7. Dish out and garnish with sesame seeds. Serve warm.

Beery Back Ribs

Prep time: 20 minutes | Cook time: 50 minutes | Serves 2 to 4

½ pound (227 g) back ribs
4 ounces (113 g) beers
½ cup BBQ sauce
½ red chili, sliced
½ onion, chopped
1 garlic clove, minced
1-inch piece fresh ginger, minced
2 tablespoons tamari
1 tablespoon agave nectar
Sea salt and ground black pepper, to taste
1 teaspoon toasted sesame seeds
1. Place the back ribs, beers, BBQ sauce, red chili, onion, garlic, and ginger in the Instant Pot.
2. Secure the lid. Choose the Manual mode and set the cooking time for 40 minutes at High pressure.
3. Once cooking is complete, perform a natural pressure release for 10 minutes, then release any remaining pressure. Carefully open the lid.
4. Add the tamari sauce, agave, salt and pepper and place the beef ribs under the broiler.
5. Broil ribs for 10 minutes or until well browned. Serve with sesame seeds.

Cheesy and Creamy Delmonico Steak

Prep time: 10 minutes | Cook time: 20 minutes | Serves 4

1 tablespoon butter
1 pound (454 g) Delmonico steak, cubed
½ cup double cream
½ cup beef broth

1 clove garlic, minced
¼ cup sour cream
1 teaspoon cayenne pepper
Sea salt and ground black pepper, to taste
¼ cup gorgonzola cheese, shredded
1.	Press the Sauté button of the Instant Pot. Melt the butter and brown the beef cubes in batches for about 4 minutes per batch.
2.	Add the double cream, broth, garlic, and sour cream to the Instant Pot, then season with cayenne pepper, salt, and black pepper.
3.	Secure the lid. Choose the Manual mode and set the cooking time for 10 minutes at High pressure.
4.	Once cooking is complete, use a quick pressure release. Carefully open the lid.
5.	Top with gorgonzola cheese and serve.

Citrus Beef Carnitas

Prep time: 15 minutes | Cook time: 25 minutes | Serves 8

2½ pounds (1.1 kg) bone-in country ribs
Salt, to taste
¼ cup orange juice
1½ cups beef stock
1 onion, cut into wedges
2 garlic cloves, smashed and peeled
1 teaspoon chili powder
1 cup shredded Jack cheese
1.	Season the ribs with salt on a clean work surface.
2.	In the Instant Pot, combine the orange juice and stock. Fold in the onion and garlic. Put the ribs in the pot. Sprinkle with chili powder.
3.	Seal the lid, select the Manual mode and set the cooking time for 25 minutes at High Pressure.
4.	Once cooking is complete, do a natural pressure release for 10 minutes, then release any remaining pressure. Carefully open the lid. Transfer beef to a plate to cool.
5.	Remove and discard the bones. Shred the ribs with two forks. Top the beef with the sauce remains in the pot. Sprinkled with cheese and serve.

Classic Sloppy Joes

Prep time: 10 minutes | Cook time: 19 minutes | Serves 4

1 pound (454 g) ground beef, divided
½ cup chopped onion
½ cup chopped green bell pepper
¼ cup water
2 teaspoons Worcestershire sauce
1 garlic clove, minced
1 tablespoon Dijon mustard
¾ cup ketchup
2 teaspoons brown sugar
¼ teaspoon sea salt
½ teaspoon hot sauce
4 soft hamburger buns
1.	Select the Sauté mode of the Instant Pot. Put about ½ cup of the ground beef in the pot and cook for about 4 minutes or until browned.

2.	Stir in the onion, bell pepper, and water. Add the remaining beef and cook for about 3 minutes or until well browned.
3.	Mix in the Worcestershire sauce, garlic, mustard, ketchup, brown sugar, and salt.
4.	Lock the lid. Select the Manual mode. Set the time for 12 minutes at High Pressure.
5.	When timer beeps, quick release the pressure, then unlock the lid.
6.	Stir in the hot sauce. Select the Sauté mode and simmer until lightly thickened. Spoon the meat and sauce into the buns. Serve immediately.

Easy Japanese Beef Shanks

Prep time: 15 minutes | Cook time: 30 minutes | Serves 4

1 pound (454 g) beef shank
½ teaspoon Five-spice powder
1 teaspoon instant dashi granules
½ teaspoon garlic, minced
1 tablespoon tamari or soy sauce
¼ cup rice wine
1 clove star anise
½ dried red chili, sliced
1 tablespoon sesame oil
¾ cup water
1.	Combine all ingredients to the Instant Pot.
2.	Secure the lid. Choose the Manual mode and set the cooking time for 30 minutes at High pressure.
3.	Once cooking is complete, use a natural pressure release for 10 minutes, then release any remaining pressure. Carefully open the lid.
4.	Slice the beef shank and serve hot.

Greek Beef and Spinach Ravioli

Prep time: 15 minutes | Cook time: 20 minutes | Serves 4

1 cup cheese ravioli
3 cups water
Salt, to taste
1 tablespoon olive oil
1 pound (454 g) ground beef
1 cup canned diced tomatoes
1 tablespoon dried mixed herbs
3 cups chicken broth
1 cup baby spinach
¼ cup Kalamata olives, sliced
¼ cup crumbled feta cheese
1.	Put ravioli, water, and salt in Instant Pot. Seal the lid, select the Manual mode and set the time for 3 minutes at High Pressure.
2.	Once cooking is complete, do a quick pressure release. Carefully open the lid. Drain the ravioli through a colander and set aside.
3.	Set the pot to Sauté mode, then heat the olive oil. Add and brown the beef for 5 minutes.
4.	Mix in the tomatoes, mixed herbs, and chicken broth. Seal the lid, select the Manual mode and set cooking time for 10 minutes on High Pressure.
5.	When timer beeps, do a quick pressure release. Carefully open the lid.

6. Set the pot to Sauté mode, then mix in ravioli, spinach, olives and cook for 2 minutes or until spinach wilts. Stir in the feta cheese and serve.

Ground Beef and Mushroom Stroganoff

Prep time: 25 minutes | Cook time: 20 minutes | Serves 8

2 pounds (907 g) ground beef, divided
1½ teaspoons salt, divided
1 teaspoon ground black pepper, divided
½ pound (227 g) sliced fresh mushrooms
1 tablespoon butter
2 medium onions, chopped
2 garlic cloves, minced
1 (10½-ounce / 298-g) can condensed beef consomme, undiluted
$^1/_3$ cup all-purpose flour
2 tablespoons tomato paste
1½ cups sour cream
Hot cooked noodles, for serving

1. Select the Sauté setting of the Instant Pot. Add half of ground beef, salt and pepper. Sauté for 8 minutes or until no longer pink. Remove the beef. Repeat with remaining ground beef, salt and pepper.
2. Add mushrooms, butter, and onions to Instant Pot. Sauté for 6 minutes or until mushrooms are tender. Add garlic and sauté for 1 minute more until fragrant. Return the beef to the pot.
3. Lock the lid. Select the Manual setting and set the cooking time for 5 minutes at High Pressure.
4. When timer beeps, quick release pressure. Carefully open the lid. Select the Sauté setting.
5. In a small bowl, whisk together consomme, flour and tomato paste. Pour over the beef and stir to combine.
6. Sauté for 3 more minutes or until thickened. Stir in sour cream; cook for a minute more until heated through. Serve with noodles.

Herbed Beef Ribs with Leek

Prep time: 40 minutes | Cook time: 1 hour 40 minutes | Serves 4

1 pound (454 g) beef short ribs, bone-in
½ medium leek, sliced
½ teaspoon celery seeds
1 teaspoon onion soup mix
1 clove garlic, sliced
1 sprig thyme
1 sprig rosemary
1 tablespoon olive oil
Sea salt and ground black pepper, to taste
1 cup water

1. Place all ingredients in the Instant Pot.
2. Secure the lid. Choose the Manual mode and set the cooking time for 90 minutes at High pressure.
3. Once cooking is complete, do a natural pressure release for 30 minutes, then release any remaining pressure. Carefully open the lid.
4. Transfer the short ribs in the broiler and broil for 10 minutes or until crispy.
5. Transfer the ribs to a platter and serve.

Hot Sirloin with Snap Peas

Prep time: 15 minutes | Cook time: 8 minutes | Serves 4

½ teaspoon hot sauce
1 teaspoon balsamic vinegar
1 cup chicken stock
¼ cup soy sauce
2 tablespoons sesame oil, divided
2 tablespoons maple syrup
½ cup plus 2 teaspoons cornstarch, divided
1 pound (454 g) beef sirloin, sliced
2 cups snap peas
3 garlic cloves, minced
3 scallions, sliced

1. In a bowl, combine the hot sauce, vinegar, stock, soy sauce, 1 tablespoon of sesame oil, maple syrup, and 2 tablespoons of cornstarch. Set aside.
2. Pour the remaining cornstarch on a plate. Season beef with salt, and pepper; toss lightly in cornstarch.
3. Set the Instant Pot to Sauté mode, heat the remaining sesame oil and fry the beef in batches for 5 minutes or until browned and crispy. Remove the beef from the pot and set aside.
4. Wipe the Instant Pot clean and pour in hot sauce mixture. Return meat to the pot, then add snow peas and garlic.
5. Seal the lid, select the Manual mode and set the time for 3 minutes on High Pressure.
6. When cooking is complete, perform natural pressure release for 10 minutes, then release the remaining pressure. Unlock the lid.
7. Dish out and garnish with scallions.

Indian Spicy Beef with Basmati

Prep time: 15 minutes | Cook time: 15 minutes | Serves 4

1 tablespoon olive oil
1 pound (454 g) beef stew meat, cubed
Salt and black pepper, to taste
½ teaspoon garam masala powder
½ teaspoon grated ginger
2 white onions, sliced
2 garlic cloves, minced
1 tablespoon cilantro leaves
½ teaspoon red chili powder
1 teaspoon cumin powder
¼ teaspoon turmeric powder
1 cup basmati rice
1 cup grated carrots
2 cups beef broth
¼ cup cashew nuts
¼ cup coconut yogurt, for serving

1. Set the Instant Pot to Sauté mode, then heat the olive oil.
2. Season the beef with salt and pepper, and brown both sides for 5 minutes. Transfer to a plate and set aside.
3. Add and sauté the garam masala, ginger, onions, garlic, cilantro, red chili, cumin, turmeric, salt, and pepper for 2 minutes.
4. Stir in beef, rice, carrots, and broth. Seal the lid, select the Manual mode, and set the time to 6 minutes on High Pressure.

5. When cooking is complete, do a natural pressure release for 5 minutes, then release any remaining pressure. Unlock the lid.
6. Fluff the rice and stir in cashews. Serve with coconut yogurt.

Korean Flavor Beef Ribs

Prep time: 10 minutes | Cook time: 15 minutes | Serves 6

3 pounds (1.4 kg) beef short ribs
1 cup beef broth
2 green onions, sliced
1 tablespoon toasted sesame seeds
Sauce:
½ teaspoon gochujang
½ cup rice wine
½ cup soy sauce
½ teaspoon garlic powder
½ teaspoon ground ginger
½ cup pure maple syrup
1 teaspoon white pepper
1 tablespoon sesame oil

1. In a large bowl, combine the ingredients for the sauce. Dunk the rib in the bowl and press to coat well. Cover the bowl in plastic and refrigerate for at least an hour.
2. Add the beef broth to the Instant Pot. Insert a trivet. Arrange the ribs standing upright over the trivet. Lock the lid.
3. Press the Manual button and set the cooking time for 25 minutes at High Pressure.
4. When timer beeps, let pressure release naturally for 10 minutes, then release any remaining pressure. Unlock the lid.
5. Transfer ribs to a serving platter and garnish with green onions and sesame seeds. Serve immediately.

Lemongrass Beef and Rice Pot

Prep time: 45 minutes | Cook time: 15 minutes | Serves 4

1 pound (454 g) beef stew meat, cut into cubes
2 tablespoons olive oil
1 green bell pepper, chopped
1 red bell pepper, chopped
1 lemongrass stalk, sliced
1 onion, chopped
2 garlic cloves, minced
1 cup jasmine rice
2 cups chicken broth
2 tablespoons chopped parsley, for garnish
Marinade:
1 tablespoon rice wine
½ teaspoon Five-spice
½ teaspoon miso paste
1 teaspoon garlic purée
1 teaspoon chili powder
1 teaspoon cumin powder
1 tablespoon soy sauce
1 teaspoon plus ½ tablespoon ginger paste, divided
½ teaspoon sesame oil
Salt and black pepper, to taste

1. In a bowl, add beef and top with the ingredients for the marinade. Mix and wrap the bowl in plastic. Marinate in the refrigerate for 30 minutes.
2. Set the Instant Pot to Sauté mode, then heat the olive oil.
3. Drain beef from marinade and brown in the pot for 5 minutes. Flip frequently.
4. Stir in bell peppers, lemongrass, onion, and garlic. Sauté for 3 minutes.
5. Stir in rice, cook for 1 minute. Pour in the broth. Seal the lid, select the Manual mode and set the time for 5 minutes on High Pressure.
6. When timer beeps, perform a quick pressure release. Carefully open the lid.
7. Dish out and garnish with parsley. Serve warm.

Mexican Beef Shred

Prep time: 20 minutes | Cook time: 30 minutes | Serves 4

1 pound (454 g) tender chuck roast, cut into half
3 tablespoons chipotle sauce
1 (8-ounce / 227-g) can tomato sauce
1 cup beef broth
½ cup chopped cilantro
1 lime, zested and juiced
2 teaspoons cumin powder
1 teaspoon cayenne pepper
Salt and ground black pepper, to taste
½ teaspoon garlic powder
1 tablespoon olive oil

1. In the Instant Pot, add the beef, chipotle sauce, tomato sauce, beef broth, cilantro, lime zest, lime juice, cumin powder, cayenne pepper, salt, pepper, and garlic powder.
2. Seal the lid, then select the Manual mode and set the cooking time for 30 minutes at High Pressure.
3. Once cooking is complete, allow a natural pressure release for 10 minutes, then release any remaining pressure.
4. Unlock the lid and using two forks to shred the beef into strands. Stir in the olive oil. Serve warm.

Mongolian Arrowroot Glazed Beef

Prep time: 15 minutes | Cook time: 20 minutes | Serves 4

1 tablespoon sesame oil
1 (2-pound / 907-g) skirt steak, sliced into thin strips
½ cup pure maple syrup
¼ cup soy sauce
4 cloves garlic, minced
1-inch knob fresh ginger root, peeled and grated
½ cup plus 2 tablespoons water, divided
2 tablespoons arrowroot powder

1. Press the Sauté button on the Instant Pot. Heat the sesame oil.
2. Add and sear the steak strips for 3 minutes on all sides.
3. In a medium bowl, whisk together maple syrup, soy sauce, garlic, ginger, and ½ cup water. Pour the mixture over beef. Lock the lid.

4. Press the Manual button and set the cooking time for 10 minutes at High Pressure.
5. When timer beeps, quick release the pressure, then unlock the lid.
6. Meanwhile, in a small dish, whisk together the arrowroot and 2 tablespoons water until smooth and chunky.
7. Stir the arrowroot into the beef mixture. Press the Sauté button and simmer for 5 minutes or until the sauce thickens.
8. Ladle the beef and sauce on plates and serve.

New York Strip with Heavy Cream

Prep time: 15 minutes | Cook time: 30 minutes | Serves 4

1 tablespoon sesame oil
1 pound (454 g) New York strip, sliced into thin strips
½ leek, sliced
1 carrot, sliced
$^1/_3$ cup dry red wine
½ tablespoon tamari
½ cup cream of mushroom soup
1 clove garlic, sliced
Kosher salt and ground black pepper, to taste
¼ cup heavy cream
1. Press the Sauté button of the Instant Pot. Heat the sesame oil until sizzling.
2. Add and brown the beef strips in batches for 4 minutes. Stir in the remaining ingredients, except for the heavy cream.
3. Secure the lid. Choose the Manual mode and set the cooking time for 20 minutes at High pressure.
4. Once cooking is complete, use a quick pressure release. Carefully open the lid.
5. Transfer the beef on a serving plate. Mash the vegetables in the pot with a potato masher.
6. Press the Sauté button. Bring to a boil, then Stir in the heavy cream.
7. Spoon the mixture over the New York strip and serve immediately.

Philly Steak Sub

Prep time: 20 minutes | Cook time: 13 minutes | Serves 4

1½ pounds (680 g) flat iron steak
1 tablespoon olive oil
4 teaspoons garlic seasoning
1 cup beef broth
1 large red bell pepper, cut into 1-inch-wide strips
2 tablespoons soy sauce
4 crusty sub sandwich rolls, split lengthwise
4 slices provolone cheese
1. Select the Sauté mode. Brush the steak with the olive oil and rub with garlic seasoning.
2. Add the steaks in batches to the pot and cook for 8 minutes until well browned. Flip the steaks halfway through.
3. Transfer the steaks to a cutting board and slice into ¼- to ½-inch-thick slices. Return the meat to the pot. Add the broth, bell peppers, and soy sauce.

4. Lock the lid, select the Manual function, and set the cooking time for 5 minutes on High Pressure.
5. When timer beeps, let the pressure release naturally for 10 minutes, then release any remaining pressure. Carefully open the lid.
6. Remove the beef and vegetables from the pot. Mound the beef and peppers on the rolls. Top with slices of cheese and serve.

Ribeye Steak with Cauliflower Rice

Prep time: 15 minutes | Cook time: 20 minutes | Serves 4

1 cup water
1 ribeye steak
½ teaspoon dried parsley
½ teaspoon ground cumin
½ teaspoon ground turmeric
½ teaspoon paprika
½ teaspoon freshly ground black pepper
½ teaspoon kosher salt
1 head cauliflower, riced
2 tablespoons butter, softened
1. Pour the water into the Instant Pot, then insert a trivet.
2. In a small bowl, mix the parsley, cumin, turmeric, paprika, black pepper, and salt. Coat the steak evenly with the mixture.
3. Place the steak into a greased baking pan. Arrange the cauliflower rice beside the steak.
4. Place the pan onto the trivet, and cover with aluminum foil. Close the lid, then select the Manual mode. Set the cooking time for 20 minutes on High Pressure.
5. When timer beeps, naturally release the pressure for about 10 minutes, then release any remaining pressure. Carefully open the lid.
6. Remove the pan. Add the butter to the steak. Serve immediately.

Saucy Italian Beef Chuck

Prep time: 10 minutes | Cook time: 19 minutes | Serves 6

1 tablespoon olive oil
1 pound (454 g) 95% lean ground chuck
1 medium yellow onion, chopped
3 tablespoons tomato paste
3 medium garlic cloves, chopped
2 teaspoons Italian seasoning
1 (28-ounce / 794-g) can tomatoes, chopped, with juice
½ cup beef broth
Salt and freshly ground black pepper, to taste
1. Put the olive oil in the pot, select the Sauté mode.
2. Add the ground beef and onion and sauté for 8 minutes or until the beef is browned.
3. Push the meat and onion mixture to one side of the pot. Add the tomato paste, garlic, and Italian seasoning to the other side of the pot and sauté for 1 minute or until fragrant.
4. Add the tomatoes and the broth to the pot. Lock on the lid, select the Manual function, and set the cooking time for 10 minutes on High Pressure.

5. When the cooking time is up, quick release the pressure. Season with salt and pepper and serve.

Saucy Short Ribs

Prep time: 20 minutes | Cook time: 40 minutes | Serves 4

2 tablespoons olive oil
1½ pounds (680 g) large beef short ribs
Salt and ground black pepper, to taste
3 garlic cloves, minced
1 medium onion, finely chopped
½ cup apple cider vinegar
1 tablespoon honey
1 cup beef broth
2 tablespoons tomato paste
1 tablespoon cornstarch

1. Select the Sauté mode of the Instant Pot, then heat the olive oil.
2. Season ribs with salt and pepper, and fry in the pot for 8 minutes or until browned. Remove from the pot and set aside.
3. Sauté the garlic, onion, and cook for 4 minutes until fragrant.
4. Stir in apple cider vinegar, honey, broth, tomato paste. Bring to a simmer.
5. Add ribs. Seal the lid, then select the Manual mode and set the time for 25 minutes at High Pressure.
6. Once cooking is complete, allow a natural pressure release for 10 minutes, then release any remaining pressure. Unlock the lid.
7. Transfer the ribs to serving plates. Stir cornstarch into the sauce in the pot and stir for 1 minute or until thickened, on Sauté mode.
8. Spoon sauce over ribs and serve.

Simple Herbed Beef Chuck Roast

Prep time: 15 minutes | Cook time: 1 hour | Serves 8

2 tablespoons coconut oil
3 pounds (1.4 kg) beef chuck roast
1 cup water
½ teaspoon dried parsley
½ teaspoon dried basil
½ teaspoon chili powder
½ teaspoon fresh paprika
1 cup butter
½ teaspoon kosher salt
½ teaspoon freshly ground black pepper

1. Set the Instant Pot to Sauté mode and melt the coconut oil.
2. Add and sear the roast for 4 minutes or until browned on both sides. Flip the roast halfway through, then remove from the pot.
3. Pour the water into the Instant Pot, then add the parsley, basil, chili powder, paprika, butter, salt, and black pepper. Return the beef to the pot.
4. Close the lid. Select the Manual mode, set the cooking time for 55 minutes on High Pressure.
5. When timer beeps, naturally release the pressure for about 10 minutes, then release any remaining pressure. Open the lid.
6. Serve immediately.

Steak and Bell Pepper Fajitas

Prep time: 15 minutes | Cook time: 45 minutes | Serves 6

1 (2-pound / 907-g) skirt steak
1 medium red bell pepper, deseeded and diced
1 medium green bell pepper, deseeded and diced
1 small onion, diced
1 cup beef broth
Sauce:
1 tablespoon fish sauce
¼ cup soy sauce
1 teaspoon ground cumin
2 tablespoons tomato paste
1 teaspoon chili powder
½ teaspoon sea salt
⅛ cup avocado oil

1. In a small bowl, combine the ingredients for the sauce. Spread ¾ of the sauce on all sides of the beef on a clean work surface. Reserve the remaining sauce.
2. Press the Sauté button on Instant Pot. Add skirt steak and sear on each side for about 5 minutes. Remove the meat and set aside.
3. Add the bell peppers and onion with reserved sauce. Sauté for 3 to 5 minutes or until the onions are translucent.
4. Pour in the beef broth. Set the beef over the onion and peppers. Lock the lid.
5. Press the Meat / Stew button and set the cooking time for 35 minutes at High Pressure.
6. When timer beeps, let the pressure release naturally for 15 minutes, then release any remaining pressure. Unlock the lid.
7. Using a slotted spoon, remove the meat and vegetables to a serving platter. Thinly slice the skirt steak and serve.

Steak, Pepper, and Lettuce Salad

Prep time: 20 minutes | Cook time: 25 minutes | Serves 4

¾ pound (340 g) steak
¼ cup red wine
½ teaspoon red pepper flakes
Sea salt and ground black pepper, to taste
¾ cup water
2 tablespoons olive oil
1 tablespoon wine vinegar
1 sweet pepper, cut into strips
½ red onion, sliced
1 butterhead lettuce, separate into leaves
¼ cup feta cheese, crumbled
¼ cup black olives, pitted and sliced

1. Add the steak, red wine, red pepper, salt, black pepper, and water to the Instant Pot.
2. Secure the lid. Choose the Manual mode and set the cooking time for 25 minutes at High pressure.
3. Once cooking is complete, perform a natural pressure release for 10 minutes. Carefully open the lid.
4. Thinly slice the steak and transfer to a salad bowl. Toss with the olive oil and vinegar.

5.	Add the peppers, red onion, and lettuce, then toss to combine well. Top with cheese and olives and serve.

Sumptuous Beef and Tomato Biryani

Prep time: 10 minutes | Cook time: 25 minutes | Serves 6

1 tablespoon ghee
1 small onion, sliced
1 pound (454 g) top round, cut into strips
1 (28-ounce / 794-g) can whole stewed tomatoes, with juice
1 cup plain Greek yogurt
1 tablespoon minced fresh ginger root
2 cloves garlic, minced
½ teaspoon ground cloves
½ teaspoon ground cumin
½ teaspoon ground coriander
½ teaspoon ground cinnamon
½ teaspoon ground cardamom
1 teaspoon salt
½ teaspoon ground black pepper
2 cups cooked basmati rice

1.	Press the Sauté button on Instant Pot. Melt the ghee.
2.	Add the onion and sauté for 3 to 5 minutes or until translucent.
3.	Add the remaining ingredients, except for the rice, to the Instant Pot. Lock the lid.
4.	Press the Manual button and set the cooking time for 10 minutes at High Pressure.
5.	When timer beeps, quick release the pressure, then unlock the lid.
6.	Press the Sauté button and simmer for about 10 minutes or until most of the liquid has evaporated. Serve over cooked basmati rice.

Tequila Short Ribs

Prep time: 3 hours 25 minutes | Cook time: 35 minutes | Serves 4

1 pound (454 g) chuck short ribs
1 shot tequila
½ tablespoon stone ground mustard
½ tablespoon Sriracha sauce
½ cup apple cider
1 tablespoon tomato paste
1 tablespoon honey
½ teaspoon marjoram
½ teaspoon garlic powder
½ teaspoon shallot powder
½ teaspoon paprika
Kosher salt and cracked black pepper, to taste
¾ cup beef bone broth

1.	Place all ingredients, except for the beef broth, in a large bowl. Cover with a foil and let it marinate for 3 hours in the refrigerator.
2.	Pour the beef along with the marinade in the Instant Pot. Pour in the beef bone broth.
3.	Secure the lid. Choose the Meat / Stew mode and set the cooking time for 35 minutes at High pressure.

4.	Once cooking is complete, do a natural pressure release for 15 minutes, then release any remaining pressure. Carefully open the lid.
5.	Serve immediately.

Thai Coconut Beef with Snap Peas

Prep time: 30 minutes | Cook time: 40 minutes | Serves 10

1 (3-pound / 1.4-kg) boneless beef chuck roast, halved
1 teaspoon salt
1 teaspoon ground black pepper
2 tablespoons canola oil
1 (14-ounce / 397-g) can coconut milk
½ cup creamy peanut butter
¼ cup red curry paste
2 tablespoons honey
¾ cup beef stock
2 tablespoons soy sauce
2 teaspoons minced fresh ginger root
1 large sweet red pepper, sliced
½ pound (227 g) fresh sugar snap peas, trimmed
¼ cup minced fresh cilantro

1.	Sprinkle the beef with salt and pepper on a clean work surface. Select the Sauté setting of the Instant Pot. Add the canola oil and heat.
2.	Add one roast half. Brown on all sides for about 5 minutes. Remove and repeat with remaining beef half.
3.	Meanwhile, in a bowl, whisk the coconut milk with peanut butter, curry paste, honey, beef stock, soy sauce, and ginger root.
4.	Put all the beef halves into the Instant Pot, then add red pepper and pour the coconut milk mixture over the beef.
5.	Lock the lid. Select the Manual setting and set the cooking time for 35 minutes at High Pressure.
6.	When timer beeps, quick release the pressure. Carefully open the lid.
7.	Add the sugar snap peas and set the cooking time for 5 minutes at High Pressure.
8.	When timer beeps, naturally release the pressure for 10 minutes, then release any remaining pressure. Unlock the lid.
9.	Remove beef from the pot. Skim fat from cooking juices. Shred beef with forks. Stir in cilantro and serve.

Winter Beef Roast Pot

Prep time: 15 minutes | Cook time: 40 minutes | Serves 6

2 tablespoons olive oil
1 (3-pound / 1.4-kg) chuck roast
½ cup dry red wine
1 (1-pound / 454-g) butternut squash, chopped
2 carrots, chopped
¾ cup pearl onions
1 teaspoon dried oregano leaves
1 bay leaf
1½ cups beef broth
Salt and black pepper, to taste
1 small red onion, quartered

1.   Select the Sauté mode of the Instant Pot and heat the olive oil.
2.   Season the beef with salt and sear in the pot for 3 minutes per side or until well browned.
3.   Mix in the wine. Bring to a boil and cook for 2 more minutes or until the wine has reduced by half.
4.   Mix in the butternut squash, carrots, pearl onions, oregano, bay leaf, broth, black pepper, and red onion. Stir to combine and add the beef.
5.   Seal the lid, then select the Manual mode and set the time for 35 minutes on High Pressure.
6.   Once cooking is complete, do a quick pressure release. Carefully open the lid.
7.   Remove the beef and slice. Spoon over the sauce and vegetables to serve.

Beef and Cauliflower

Prep time: 12 mins, Cook Time: 30 mins, Servings: 4

- 1 tbsp. extra virgin olive oil
- 1½ lbs. ground beef
- 1 tsp salt
- 1 cup puréed tomato
- 6 cups cauliflower, cut into florets
- 1 cup water

1.   Set the Instant Pot to Sauté setting, then add the olive oil and heat until shimmering.
2.   Add the beef and sauté for 4 or 5 minutes or until browned.
3.   Add the rest of the ingredients.
4.   Lock the lid. Select the Manual setting and set the timer at 30 minutes on High Pressure.
5.   When the timer beeps, press Cancel, then use a quick pressure release.
6.   Carefully open the lid and allow to cool for a few minutes. Serve warm.

Beef and Corn Chili

Prep time: 12 mins, Cook Time: 30 mins, Servings: 4

- 1 tbsp. olive oil
- 2 small onions, chopped
- 2 small chili peppers, diced
- ¼ cup canned corn
- 10 oz. lean ground beef
- 3 cups water
- Salt and pepper, to taste

1.   Press Sauté on the Instant Pot. Heat the olive oil in the pot.
2.   Add the onions, chili peppers, corn, and beef. Sauté for 2 to 3 minutes or until the onions are translucent and the peppers are softened.
3.   Add the water to the Instant Pot, and sprinkle with salt and pepper. Mix to combine well.
4.   Lock the lid. Press Meat/Stew. Set the timer to 20 minutes at High Pressure.
5.   Once cooking is complete, press Cancel, then use a quick pressure release.
6.   Open the lid, transfer them on 4 plates and serve.

Beef Meatballs with Tomato

Prep time: 12 mins, Cook Time: 10 mins, Servings: 4

- 1 lb. lean ground beef
- 2 large eggs
- 3 tbsps. all-purpose flour
- Salt and pepper, to taste
- 1 tbsp. olive oil
- 2 cups diced tomatoes
- 1 cup water

1.   In a large bowl, thoroughly mix the beef, eggs, and flour, then sprinkle with salt and pepper. Mix well and make 6 meatballs of 1½ inch.
2.   Grease a baking dish with olive oil and add the meatballs. Add the tomatoes and tightly wrap with a foil.
3.   Pour the water in the Instant pot. Arrange the trivet or steamer basket inside, then place the dish on the trivet/basket.
4.   Lock the lid. Press Manual. Set the timer to 10 minutes at High Pressure.
5.   When the timer goes off, press Cancel, then use a quick pressure release.
6.   Carefully open the lid. Allow to cool for a few minutes, then serve warm.

Beef Tenderloin with Cauliflower

Prep time: 20 mins, Cook Time: 25 mins, Servings: 4

- 1½ lbs. beef tenderloin
- 1 tsp. sea salt
- 1 tbsp. extra virgin olive oil
- 4 garlic cloves, finely chopped
- 4 cups cauliflower florets

1.   On a clean work surface, slice the beef tenderloin into 1-inch thick slices and rub with salt.
2.   Put the olive oil in the Instant Pot, set the Sauté setting.
3.   Add and brown the beef for 4 to 5 minutes, then add the garlic and sauté for a minute.
4.   Add the cauliflower.
5.   Lock the lid. Set the Instant Pot to Manual mode and set the cooking time for 20 minutes at High Pressure.
6.   Once cooking is complete, use a quick pressure release.
7.   Carefully open the lid. Allow to cool for a few minutes. Transfer them on a large plate and serve immediately.

Bell Pepper and Beef

Prep time: 12 mins, Cook time: 30 mins, Servings: 4

- 1½ lbs. beef tenderloin
- 1 tsp. sea salt
- 4 green bell peppers, deseeded and stems removed
- 1 tbsp. extra virgin olive oil
- 1 red onion, peeled and diced
- 1 cup water

1.   On a clean work surface, cut the beef into 1-inch thick slices, sprinkle with salt
2.   Cut the bell peppers into ¼-inch slices.

3.   Set Instant Pot to Sauté setting, then add extra virgin olive oil and heat until hot.
4.   Add the beef and cook for 4 to 5 minutes or until browned.
5.   Add peppers and onion, and sauté for 2 minutes. Pour in the water.
6.   Lock the lid. Set the Instant Pot to the Manual setting and set the timer at 30 minutes at High Pressure.
7.   When the timer beeps, press Cancel, then use a quick pressure release.
8.   Carefully open the lid and allow to cool for a few minutes. Serve warm.

Big Papa's Roast

Prep time: 12 mins, Coo Time: 1 hour, Servings: 6
- 3 lbs. beef chuck roast
- 2 tsps. salt
- 6 peppercorns, crushed
- 2 tbsps. extra virgin olive oil
- 2 cups beef stock

1.   On a clean work surface, rub the beef with salt and peppercorns.
2.   Coat the Instant Pot with olive oil and set the Sauté setting. Heat the oil until shimmering.
3.   Add and brown the beef roast for 4 to 5 minutes.
4.   Pour in the beef stock.
5.   Lock the lid. Set to Manual mode, set the cooking time for 60 minutes at High Pressure.
6.   Once cooking is complete, use a natural pressure release for 10 minutes, then release any remaining pressure.
7.   Carefully open the lid. Allow to cool for a few minutes. Transfer them on a large plate and serve immediately.

Corned Beef

Prep time: 6 mins, Cook Time: 1 hour 30 mins, Servings: 4
- 12 oz. beer
- 1 cup water
- 3 garlic cloves, minced
- 3 lbs. corned beef brisket
- Salt and pepper, to taste

1.   Pour the beer and water into the Instant Pot. Add the garlic and mix to combine well.
2.   Put the steamer basket inside.
3.   Add the beef to the basket and season with salt and pepper.
4.   Cover the pot. Select the Meat/Stew mode and cook at High Pressure for 90 minutes.
5.   Once cooking is complete, do a quick pressure release for 10 minutes, and then release any remaining pressure. Carefully open the lid.
6.   Transfer the beef to a baking pan and cover it with foil.
7.   Let it rest for 15 minutes before slicing to serve.

Garlic Prime Rib

Prep time: 12 mins, Cook Time: 1 hour, Servings: 10
- 2 tbsps. olive oil
- 10 garlic cloves, minced
- 4 lbs. prime rib roast
- 2 tsps. dried thyme
- Salt and pepper, to taste
- 1 cup water

1.   Press the Sauté button on the Instant Pot and heat the oil.
2.   Add and sauté the garlic for 1 to 2 minutes until fragrant.
3.   Add the prime rib roast and sear on all sides for 3 minutes until lightly browned.
4.   Sprinkle with thyme, salt and pepper.
5.   Pour in the water and remove the browning at the bottom.
6.   Lock the lid. Set the pot to Meat/Stew mode and set the timer to 1 hour at High Pressure.
7.   Once cooking is complete, use a natural pressure release for 10 minutes, then release any remaining pressure.
8.   Carefully open the lid. Allow to cool for a few minutes. Transfer them on a large plate and serve immediately.

Garlicky Beef

Prep time: 12 mins, Cook time: 10 mins, Servings: 4
- 1½ lbs. beef sirloin
- 1 tbsp. sea salt
- 1 tbsp. extra virgin olive oil
- 5 garlic cloves, chopped
- 1 cup heavy cream

1.   On a clean work surface, rub the beef with salt.
2.   Set the Instant Pot to Sauté mode. Add the olive oil and heat until shimmering.
3.   Add the beef and sear for 3 minutes until lightly browned.
4.   Add garlic and sauté for 30 seconds or until fragrant.
5.   Mix in the heavy cream.
6.   Lock the lid. Set the pot to Manual setting and set the timer for 10 minutes at High Pressure.
7.   When the timer beeps, press Cancel, then use a natural pressure release for 10 minutes, and then release any remaining pressure.
8.   Carefully open the lid. Allow to cool for a few minutes. Transfer them on a large plate and serve immediately.

Ginger Short Ribs

Prep time: 12 mins, Cook Time: 25 mins, Servings: 6
- 4 beef short ribs
- 1 tsp. salt
- 3 tbsps. extra virgin olive oil, plus 1 tbsp. for coating
- 1 large onion, diced
- 2-inch knob of ginger, grated
- ¾ cup water

1.   On a clean work surface, rub the ribs with salt.

2. Lightly coat the Instant Pot with olive oil and set the setting to Sauté.
3. Add the onion and ginger, then sauté for a minute
4. Add the ribs and brown for 4 to 5 minutes. Pour in the water.
5. Lock the lid. Set to Manual mode and set the cooking time for 25 minutes at High Pressure.
6. Once cooking is complete, use a natural pressure release for 10 minutes, then release any remaining pressure.
7. Carefully open the lid. Allow to cool for a few minutes. Transfer them on a large plate and serve immediately.

Gingered Beef Tenderloin

Prep time: 12 mins, Cook Time: 1 hour, Servings: 8

- 2 tbsps. olive oil
- 2 tbsps. minced garlic
- 2 tbsps. thinly sliced ginger
- 4 fillet mignon steaks
- ¼ cup soy sauce
- Salt and pepper, to taste
- 1 cup water

1. Press the Sauté button on the Instant Pot and heat the olive oil.
2. Sauté the garlic for 1 minute until fragrant.
3. Add the ginger and fillet mignon and allow to sear for 4 minutes or until lightly browned.
4. Drizzle with the soy sauce. Add salt and pepper to taste. Pour in a cup of water.
5. Lock the lid and select the Meat/Stew mode and set the timer to 1 hour at High Pressure.
6. Once cooking is complete, use a natural pressure release for 10 minutes, then release any remaining pressure.
7. Carefully open the lid. Allow to cool for a few minutes. Transfer them on a large plate and discard the bay leaf, then serve.

Herbed Sirloin Tip Roast

Prep time: 5 mins, Cook Time: 1 hour 30 mins, Servings: 6

- 2 tbsps. mixed herbs
- 1 tsp. garlic powder
- 3 lbs. sirloin tip roast
- 1¼ tsps. paprika
- 1 cup water
- Salt and pepper, to taste

1. In the Instant Pot, combine all the ingredients. Stir to mix well.
2. Lock the lid. Set the pot to Meat/Stew mode and set the timer to 1 hour 30 minutes at High Pressure.
3. Once cooking is complete, use a natural pressure release for 10 minutes, then release any remaining pressure.
4. Carefully open the lid. Allow to cool for a few minutes. Transfer them on a large plate and discard the bay leaf, then serve.

Instant Pot Rib Roast

Prep time: 6 mins, Cook Time: 2 hours 30 mins, Servings: 12

- 5 lbs. beef rib roast
- 1 tsp. garlic powder
- 1 bay leaf
- 1 tbsp. olive oil
- Salt and pepper, to taste
- 1 cup water

1. Put all the ingredients in the Instant Pot. Stir to mix well.
2. Lock the lid. Set the pot to Meat/Stew mode and set the timer to 2 hours 30 minutes at High Pressure.
3. Once cooking is complete, use a natural pressure release for 10 to 20 minutes, then release any remaining pressure.
4. Carefully open the lid. Allow to cool for a few minutes. Transfer them on a large plate and discard the bay leaf, then serve.

Lemon Beef Meal

Prep time: 12 mins, Cook Time: 10 mins, Servings: 2

- 1 tbsp. olive oil
- 2 beef steaks
- ½ tsp. garlic salt
- 1 garlic clove, crushed
- 2 tbsps. lemon juice

1. Press Sauté on the Instant Pot. Heat the olive oil in the pot until shimmering.
2. Add the beef and garlic salt and sauté for 4 to 5 minutes to evenly brown.
3. Add the garlic and sauté for 1 minute until fragrant.
4. Serve with lemon juice on top.

Mushroom and Beef Meal

Prep time: 12 mins, Cook Time: 40 mins, Servings: 4

- 1 lb. fat removed beef ribs
- Salt, to taste
- 3 cups low-sodium beef stock
- 1 bacon slice, chopped
- 2 cups button mushrooms slices

1. On a clean work surface, rub the beef ribs with salt.
2. Add the ribs and stock to the Instant Pot. Stir to combine well.
3. Lock the lid. Press Manual. Set the timer to 30 minutes at High Pressure.
4. When the timer goes off, press Cancel, then use a natural pressure release for 10 minutes, and then release any remaining pressure.
5. Take out the beef and shred with a knife.
6. Put the shredded beef back to the pot, add the bacon and mushrooms; gently stir to combine.
7. Lock the lid. Press Manual. Set the timer to 7 minutes at High Pressure.
8. Once the timer goes off, press Cancel, then use a quick pressure release.

9.	Open the lid, transfer them on 4 plates and serve.

Sautéed Beef and Green Beans

Prep time: 12 mins, Cook Time: 5 mins, Servings: 4

- 1 tbsp. olive oil
- 10 oz. fat removed beef sirloin
- 2 spring onions, chopped
- 7 oz. canned green beans
- 2 tbsps. soy sauce
- Salt and pepper, to taste

1.	Press Sauté on the Instant Pot. Grease the pot with the olive oil.
2.	Add the beef and sauté for 2 to 3 minutes to evenly brown.
3.	Add the onions, green beans, and soy sauce, then sauté for another 2 to 3 minutes until the beans are soft. Sprinkle with salt and pepper.
4.	Serve warm.

Super Beef Chili

Prep time: 12 mins, Cook Time: 8 mins, Servings: 4

- 1 lb. ground beef
- 1½ tsps. sea salt
- 1 medium onion, chopped
- 2 cups tomato purée
- 2 cups zucchini, peeled and rinsed, cut into 1-inch bites
- 1 cup water
- 1 tsp. chili spice powder

1.	Select the Instant Pot to Sauté setting. Coat the pot with olive oil and heat until shimmering.
2.	Add the beef, salt and onion, then sauté for 4 minutes or until the beef is lightly browned.
3.	Add the tomato purée, zucchini, water and chili spice powder. Stir to mix well.
4.	Lock the lid. Set the Instant Pot to Manual setting and set the timer for 8 minutes at High Pressure.
5.	Once cooking is complete, use a quick pressure release.
6.	Carefully open the lid. Allow to cool for a few minutes. Transfer them on a large plate and serve immediately.

Sweet Apricot Beef

Prep time: 12 mins, Cook Time: 30 mins, Servings: 4

- 1½ lbs. beef tenderloin
- 1 tsp. sea salt
- 1 tbsp. coconut oil
- 4 apricots, pitted and sliced thinly
- ½ cup chopped almonds
- 1 cup water

1.	On a clean work surface, sprinkle the beef with salt and cut into 1-inch thick slices.
2.	Set the Instant Pot to Sauté setting, then add coconut oil and heat until melted.
3.	Add the beef and sauté for 4 to 5 minutes or until browned.
4.	Add the apricot and sauté for a minute. Add the chopped almonds. Pour in the water.
5.	Lock the lid. Press the Manual setting and set the timer at 30 minutes at High Pressure.
6.	When the timer beeps, press Cancel, then use a quick pressure release.
7.	Carefully open the lid and allow to cool for a few minutes. Serve warm.

Sweet Potato Beef

Prep time: 12 mins, Cook Time: 40 mins, Servings: 4

- 1 tbsp. olive oil
- 1 lb. lean beef stew meat
- 4 cups low-sodium beef stock
- 1 small sweet potato, diced
- 1 tomato, roughly chopped
- 2 bell peppers, sliced
- Salt and pepper, to taste

1.	Press Sauté on Instant Pot. Grease the pot with the olive oil.
2.	Add the beef and sauté for 4 to 5 minutes to evenly brown.
3.	Mix in the remaining ingredients.
4.	Lock the lid. Press Manual. Set the timer to 35 minutes at High Pressure.
5.	When the timer beeps, press Cancel, then use a quick pressure release.
6.	Open the lid, transfer them in 4 plates and serve warm.

Beef and Sausage Medley

Prep time: 10 minutes | Cook time: 27 minutes | Serves 8

1 teaspoon butter
2 beef sausages, casing removed and sliced
2 pounds (907 g) beef steak, cubed
1 yellow onion, sliced
2 fresh ripe tomatoes, puréed
1 jalapeño pepper, chopped
1 red bell pepper, chopped
1½ cups roasted vegetable broth
2 cloves garlic, minced
1 teaspoon Old Bay seasoning
2 bay leaves
1 sprig thyme
1 sprig rosemary
½ teaspoon paprika
Sea salt and ground black pepper, to taste

1.	Press the Sauté button to heat up the Instant Pot. Melt the butter and cook the sausage and steak for 4 minutes, stirring periodically. Set aside.
2.	Add the onion and sauté for 3 minutes or until softened and translucent. Add the remaining ingredients, including reserved beef and sausage.
3.	Secure the lid. Choose Manual mode and set time for 20 minutes on High Pressure.
4.	Once cooking is complete, use a quick pressure release. Carefully remove the lid.
5.	Serve immediately.

Beef Back Ribs with Barbecue Glaze

Prep time: 10 minutes | Cook time: 35 minutes | Serves 4
½ cup water
1 (3-pound / 1.4-kg) rack beef back ribs, prepared with rub of choice
¼ cup unsweetened tomato purée
¼ teaspoon Worcestershire sauce
¼ teaspoon garlic powder
2 teaspoons apple cider vinegar
¼ teaspoon liquid smoke
¼ teaspoon smoked paprika
3 tablespoons Swerve
Dash of cayenne pepper
1.	Pour the water in the pot and place the trivet inside.
2.	Arrange the ribs on top of the trivet.
3.	Close the lid. Select Manual mode and set cooking time for 25 minutes on High Pressure.
4.	Meanwhile, prepare the glaze by whisking together the tomato purée, Worcestershire sauce, garlic powder, vinegar, liquid smoke, paprika, Swerve, and cayenne in a medium bowl. Heat the broiler.
5.	When timer beeps, quick release the pressure. Open the lid. Remove the ribs and place on a baking sheet.
6.	Brush a layer of glaze on the ribs. Put under the broiler for 5 minutes.
7.	Remove from the broiler and brush with glaze again. Put back under the broiler for 5 more minutes, or until the tops are sticky.
8.	Serve immediately.

Beef Big Mac Salad

Prep time: 10 minutes | Cook time: 9 minutes | Serves 2
5 ounces (142 g) ground beef
1 teaspoon ground black pepper
1 tablespoon sesame oil
1 cup lettuce, chopped
¼ cup Monterey Jack cheese, shredded
2 ounces (57 g) dill pickles, sliced
1 ounce (28 g) scallions, chopped
1 tablespoon heavy cream
1.	In a mixing bowl, combine the ground beef and ground black pepper.shape the mixture into mini burgers.
2.	Pour the sesame oil in the Instant Pot and heat for 3 minutes on Sauté mode.
3.	Place the mini hamburgers in the hot oil and cook for 3 minutes on each side.
4.	Meanwhile, in a salad bowl, mix the chopped lettuce, shredded cheese, dill pickles, scallions, and heavy cream. Toss to mix well.
5.	Top the salad with cooked mini burgers. Serve immediately.

Beef Bourguignon

Prep time: 15 minutes | Cook time: 35 minutes | Serves 6
3 ounces (85 g) bacon, chopped
1 pound (454 g) beef tenderloin, chopped
¼ cup apple cider vinegar
¼ teaspoon ground coriander
¼ teaspoon xanthan gum
1 teaspoon dried oregano
1 teaspoon unsweetened tomato purée
1 cup beef broth
1.	Put the bacon in the Instant Pot and cook for 5 minutes on Sauté mode. Flip the bacon with a spatula every 1 minute.
2.	Add the chopped beef tenderloin, apple cider vinegar, ground coriander, xanthan gum, and dried oregano.
3.	Add the tomato purée and beef broth. Stir to mix well and close the lid.
4.	Select Manual mode and set cooking time for 30 minutes on High Pressure.
5.	When timer beeps, make a quick pressure release. Open the lid.
6.	Serve immediately.

Beef Brisket with Cabbage

Prep time: 15 minutes | Cook time: 1 hour 7 minutes | Serves 8
3 pounds (1.4 kg) corned beef brisket
4 cups water
3 garlic cloves, minced
2 teaspoons yellow mustard seed
2 teaspoons black peppercorns
3 celery stalks, chopped
½ large white onion, chopped
1 green cabbage, cut into quarters
1.	Add the brisket to the Instant Pot. Pour the water into the pot. Add the garlic, mustard seed, and black peppercorns.
2.	Lock the lid. Select Meat/Stew mode and set cooking time for 50 minutes on High Pressure.
3.	When cooking is complete, allow the pressure to release naturally for 20 minutes, then release any remaining pressure. Open the lid and transfer only the brisket to a platter.
4.	Add the celery, onion, and cabbage to the pot.
5.	Lock the lid. Select Soup mode and set cooking time for 12 minutes on High Pressure.
6.	When cooking is complete, quick release the pressure. Open the lid, add the brisket back to the pot and let warm in the pot for 5 minutes.
7.	Transfer the warmed brisket back to the platter and thinly slice. Transfer the vegetables to the platter. Serve hot.

Beef Carne Guisada

Prep time: 10 minutes | Cook time: 20 minutes | Serves 4
2 tomatoes, chopped
1 red bell pepper, chopped
½ onion, chopped
3 garlic cloves, chopped
1 teaspoon ancho chili powder
1 tablespoon ground cumin
½ teaspoon dried oregano
1 teaspoons salt
1 teaspoon freshly ground black pepper
1 teaspoon smoked paprika

1 pound (454 g) beef chuck, cut into large pieces
¾ cup water, plus 2 tablespoons
¼ teaspoon xanthan gum
1.	In a blender, purée the tomatoes, bell pepper, onion, garlic, chili powder, cumin, oregano, salt, pepper, and paprika.
2.	Put the beef pieces in the Instant Pot. Pour in the blended mixture.
3.	Use ¾ cup of water to wash out the blender and pour the liquid into the pot.
4.	Lock the lid. Select Manual mode and set cooking time for 20 minutes on High Pressure.
5.	When cooking is complete, quick release the pressure. Unlock the lid.
6.	Switch the pot to Sauté mode. Bring the stew to a boil.
7.	Put the xanthan gum and 2 tablespoons of water into the boiling stew and stir until it thickens.
8.	Serve immediately.

Beef Cheeseburger Pie

Prep time: 15 minutes | Cook time: 30 minutes | Serves 6

1 tablespoon olive oil
1 pound (454 g) ground beef
3 eggs (1 beaten)
½ cup unsweetened tomato purée
2 tablespoons golden flaxseed meal
1 garlic clove, minced
½ teaspoon Italian seasoning blend
½ teaspoon sea salt
½ teaspoon smoked paprika
½ teaspoon onion powder
2 tablespoons heavy cream
½ teaspoon ground mustard
¼ teaspoon ground black pepper
2 cups water
½ cup grated Cheddar cheese
1.	Coat a round cake pan with the olive oil.
2.	Select Sauté mode. Once the pot is hot, add the ground beef and sauté for 5 minutes or until the beef is browned.
3.	Transfer the beef to a large bowl.
4.	Add the 1 beaten egg, tomato purée, flaxseed meal, garlic, Italian seasoning, sea salt, smoked paprika, and onion powder to the bowl. Mix until well combined.
5.	Transfer the meat mixture to the prepared cake pan and use a knife to spread the mixture into an even layer. Set aside.
6.	In a separate medium bowl, combine the 2 remaining eggs, heavy cream, ground mustard, and black pepper. Whisk until combined.
7.	Pour the egg mixture over the meat mixture. Tightly cover the pan with a sheet of aluminum foil.
8.	Place the trivet in the Instant Pot and add the water to the bottom of the pot. Place the pan on the trivet.
9.	Lock the lid. Select Manual mode and set cooking time for 20 minutes on High Pressure.
10.	When cooking is complete, allow the pressure to release naturally for 10 minutes and then release the remaining pressure. Allow the pie to rest in the pot for 5 minutes.
11.	Preheat the oven broiler to 450°F (235°C).
12.	Open the lid, remove the pan from the pot. Remove the foil and sprinkle the Cheddar over top of the pie.
13.	Place the pie in the oven and broil for 2 minutes or until the cheese is melted and the top becomes golden brown. Slice into six equal-sized wedges. Serve hot.

Beef Clod Vindaloo

Prep time: 15 minutes | Cook time: 15 minutes | Serves 2

½ Serrano pepper, chopped
¼ teaspoon cumin seeds
¼ teaspoon minced ginger
¼ teaspoon cayenne pepper
¼ teaspoon salt
¼ teaspoon ground paprika
1 cup water
9 ounces (255 g) beef clod, chopped
1.	Put Serrano pepper, cumin seeds, minced ginger, cayenne pepper, salt, ground paprika, and water in a food processor. Blend the mixture until smooth.
2.	Transfer the mixture in a bowl and add the chopped beef clod. Toss to coat well.
3.	Transfer the beef clod and the mixture in the Instant Pot and close the lid.
4.	Select Manual mode and set cooking time for 15 minutes on High Pressure.
5.	When timer beeps, use a natural pressure release for 10 minutes, then release any remaining pressure. Open the lid.
6.	Serve immediately.

Beef Masala Curry

Prep time: 10 minutes | Cook time: 20 minutes | Serves 4

2 tomatoes, quartered
1 small onion, quartered
4 garlic cloves, chopped
½ cup fresh cilantro leaves
1 teaspoon garam masala
½ teaspoon ground coriander
1 teaspoon ground cumin
½ teaspoon cayenne
1 teaspoon salt
1 pound (454 g) beef chuck roast, cut into 1-inch cubes
1.	In a blender, combine the tomatoes, onion, garlic, and cilantro.
2.	Process until the vegetables are puréed. Add the garam masala, coriander, cumin, cayenne, and salt. Process for several more seconds.
3.	To the Instant Pot, add the beef and pour the vegetable purée on top.
4.	Lock the lid. Select Manual mode and set cooking time for 20 minutes on High Pressure.
5.	When timer beeps, let the pressure release naturally for 10 minutes, then release any remaining pressure. Unlock the lid.
6.	Stir and serve immediately.

Beef Ribs with Radishes

Prep time: 20 minutes | Cook time: 56 minutes | Serves 4

¼ teaspoon ground coriander
¼ teaspoon ground cumin
1 teaspoon kosher salt, plus more to taste
½ teaspoon smoked paprika
Pinch of ground allspice (optional)
4 (8-ounce / 227-g) bone-in beef short ribs
2 tablespoons avocado oil
1 cup water
2 radishes, ends trimmed, leaves rinsed and roughly chopped
Freshly ground black pepper, to taste

1. In a small bowl, mix together the coriander, cumin, salt, paprika, and allspice. Rub the spice mixture all over the short ribs.
2. Set the Instant Pot to Sauté mode and add the oil to heat. Add the short ribs, bone side up. Brown for 4 minutes on each side.
3. Pour the water into the Instant Pot. Secure the lid. Press the Manual button and set cooking time for 45 minutes on High Pressure.
4. When timer beeps, allow the pressure to release naturally for 10 minutes, then release any remaining pressure. Open the lid.
5. Remove the short ribs to a serving plate.
6. Add the radishes to the sauce in the pot. Place a metal steaming basket directly on top of the radishes and place the radish leaves in the basket.
7. Secure the lid. Press the Manual button and set cooking time for 3 minutes on High Pressure.
8. When timer beeps, quick release the pressure. Open the lid. Transfer the leaves to a serving bowl. Sprinkle with with salt and pepper.
9. Remove the radishes and place on top of the leaves. Serve hot with the short ribs.

Beef Shami Kabob

Prep time: 15 minutes | Cook time: 35 minutes | Serves 4

1 pound (454 g) beef chunks, chopped
1 teaspoon ginger paste
½ teaspoon ground cumin
2 cups water
¼ cup almond flour
1 egg, beaten
1 tablespoon coconut oil

1. Put the beef chunks, ginger paste, ground cumin, and water in the Instant Pot.
2. Select Manual mode and set cooking time for 30 minutes on High Pressure.
3. When timer beeps, make a quick pressure release. Open the lid.
4. Drain the water from the meat. Transfer the beef in the blender. Add the almond flour and beaten egg. Blend until smooth. Shape the mixture into small meatballs.
5. Heat the coconut oil on Sauté mode and put the meatballs inside.
6. Cook for 2 minutes on each side or until golden brown.
7. Serve immediately.

Beef Shawarma and Veggie Salad Bowls

Prep time: 10 minutes | Cook time: 19 minutes | Serves 4

2 teaspoons olive oil
1½ pounds (680 g) beef flank steak, thinly sliced
Sea salt and freshly ground black pepper, to taste
1 teaspoon cayenne pepper
½ teaspoon ground bay leaf
½ teaspoon ground allspice
½ teaspoon cumin, divided
½ cup Greek yogurt
2 tablespoons sesame oil
1 tablespoon fresh lime juice
2 English cucumbers, chopped
1 cup cherry tomatoes, halved
1 red onion, thinly sliced
½ head romaine lettuce, chopped

1. Press the Sauté button to heat up the Instant Pot. Then, heat the olive oil and cook the beef for about 4 minutes.
2. Add all seasonings, 1½ cups of water, and secure the lid.
3. Choose Manual mode. Set the cook time for 15 minutes on High Pressure.
4. Once cooking is complete, use a natural pressure release. Carefully remove the lid.
5. Allow the beef to cool completely.
6. To make the dressing, whisk Greek yogurt, sesame oil, and lime juice in a mixing bowl.
7. Then, divide cucumbers, tomatoes, red onion, and romaine lettuce among four serving bowls. Dress the salad and top with the reserved beef flank steak. Serve warm.

Beef Shoulder Roast

Prep time: 15 minutes | Cook time: 46 minutes | Serves 6

2 tablespoons peanut oil
2 pounds (907 g) shoulder roast
¼ cup coconut aminos
1 teaspoon porcini powder
1 teaspoon garlic powder
1 cup beef broth
2 cloves garlic, minced
2 tablespoons champagne vinegar
½ teaspoon hot sauce
1 teaspoon celery seeds
1 cup purple onions, cut into wedges
1 tablespoon flaxseed meal, plus 2 tablespoons water

1. Press the Sauté button to heat up the Instant Pot. Then, heat the peanut oil and cook the beef shoulder roast for 3 minutes on each side.
2. In a mixing dish, combine coconut aminos, porcini powder, garlic powder, broth, garlic, vinegar, hot sauce, and celery seeds.
3. Pour the broth mixture into the Instant Pot. Add the onions to the top.
4. Secure the lid. Choose Meat/Stew mode and set cooking time for 40 minutes on High Pressure.
5. Once cooking is complete, use a natural pressure release for 15 minutes, then release any remaining pressure. Carefully remove the lid.

6. Make the slurry by mixing flaxseed meal with 2 tablespoons of water. Add the slurry to the Instant Pot.
7. Press the Sauté button and allow it to cook until the cooking liquid is reduced and thickened slightly. Serve warm.

Beef Stuffed Kale Rolls

Prep time: 15 minutes | Cook time: 30 minutes | Serves 4

8 ounces (227 g) ground beef
1 teaspoon chives
¼ teaspoon cayenne pepper
4 kale leaves
1 tablespoon cream cheese
¼ cup heavy cream
½ cup chicken broth

1. In the mixing bowl, combine the ground beef, chives, and cayenne pepper.
2. Then fill and roll the kale leaves with ground beef mixture.
3. Place the kale rolls in the Instant Pot.
4. Add cream cheese, heavy cream, and chicken broth. Close the lid.
5. Select Manual mode mode and set cooking time for 30 minutes on High Pressure
6. When timer beeps, make a quick pressure release. Open the lid.
7. Serve warm.

Beef, Bacon and Cauliflower Rice Casserole

Prep time: 15 minutes | Cook time: 26 minutes | Serves 5

2 cups fresh cauliflower florets
1 pound (454 g) ground beef
5 slices uncooked bacon, chopped
8 ounces (227 g) unsweetened tomato purée
1 cup shredded Cheddar cheese, divided
1 teaspoon garlic powder
½ teaspoon paprika
½ teaspoon sea salt
¼ teaspoon ground black pepper
¼ teaspoon celery seed
1 cup water
1 medium Roma tomato, sliced

1. Spray a round soufflé dish with coconut oil cooking spray. Set aside.
2. Add the cauliflower florets to a food processor and pulse until a riced. Set aside.
3. Select Sauté mode. Once the pot is hot, crumble the ground beef into the pot and add the bacon. Sauté for 6 minutes or until the ground beef is browned and the bacon is cooked through.
4. Transfer the beef, bacon, and rendered fat to a large bowl.
5. Add the cauliflower rice, tomato purée, ½ cup Cheddar cheese, garlic powder, paprika, sea salt, black pepper, and celery seed to the bowl with the beef and bacon. Mix well to combine.
6. Add the mixture to the prepared dish and use a spoon to press and smooth the mixture into an even layer.

7. Place the trivet in the Instant Pot and add the water to the bottom of the pot. Place the dish on top of the trivet.
8. Lock the lid. Select Manual mode and set cooking time for 20 minutes on High Pressure.
9. When cooking is complete, quick release the pressure.
10. Open the lid. Arrange the tomato slices in a single layer on top of the casserole and sprinkle the remaining cheese over top.
11. Secure the lid and let the residual heat melt the cheese for 5 minutes.
12. Open the lid, remove the dish from the pot.
13. Transfer the casserole to a serving plate and slice into 5 equal-sized wedges. Serve warm.

Braised Tri-Tip Steak

Prep time: 20 minutes | Cook time: 54 minutes | Serves 4

2 pounds (907 g) tri-tip steak, patted dry
2 teaspoons coarse sea salt
3 tablespoons avocado oil
½ medium onion, diced
2 cloves garlic, smashed
1 tablespoon unsweetened tomato purée
1½ cups dry red wine
½ tablespoon dried thyme
2 bay leaves
1 Roma (plum) tomato, diced
1 stalk celery, including leaves, chopped
1 small turnip, chopped
½ cup water

1. Season the tri-tip with the coarse salt. Set the Instant Pot to Sauté mode and heat the avocado oil until shimmering.
2. Cook the steak in the pot for 2 minutes per side or until well browned. Remove the steak from the pot and place it in a shallow bowl. Set aside.
3. Add the onion to the pot and sauté for 3 minutes. Add the garlic and sauté for 1 minute. Add the unsweetened tomato purée and cook for 1 minute, stirring constantly.
4. Pour in the red wine. Stir in the thyme and bay leaves.
5. Return the tri-tip steak to the pot. Scatter the tomato, celery, and turnip around the steak. Pour in the water.
6. Secure the lid. Press the Manual button and set cooking time for 35 minutes on High Pressure.
7. When timer beeps, allow the pressure to release naturally for 20 minutes, then release any remaining pressure. Open the lid. Discard the bay leaves.
8. Remove the steak and place in a dish. Press the Sauté button and bring the braising liquid to a boil. Cook for 10 minutes or until the liquid is reduced by about half.
9. Slice the steak thinly and serve with braising liquid over.

Cheesy Bacon Stuffed Meatloaf

Prep time: 15 minutes | Cook time: 32 minutes | Serves 4

1 pound (454 g) ground beef
1 large egg, beaten
½ cup unsweetened tomato purée
2 tablespoons golden flaxseed meal
1 teaspoon garlic powder
1 teaspoon sea salt
½ teaspoon paprika
¼ teaspoon ground black pepper
4 slices uncooked bacon
$^1/_3$ cup shredded Cheddar cheese
1 cup water
For The Glaze:
$^1/_3$ cup unsweetened tomato purée
1 teaspoon apple cider vinegar
¼ teaspoon onion powder
¼ teaspoon garlic powder
2 teaspoons erythritol
⅛ teaspoon sea salt
⅛ teaspoon allspice
1. In a large bowl, combine the ground beef, egg, tomato purée, flaxseed meal, garlic powder, sea salt, paprika, and black pepper. Mix to combine well.
2. Place a sheet of aluminum foil on a flat surface. Place half of the meat mixture in the center of the foil sheet and use the hands to mold the mixture into a flat oval shape that is about 6 inches long.
3. Place the bacon slices on top of the meat and sprinkle the Cheddar over. Place the remaining meat mixture on top and shape the mixture into an oval-shaped loaf.
4. Fold the sides of the foil up and around the sides of the meatloaf to form a loaf pan. Set aside.
5. Make the tomato glaze by combining the tomato purée, vinegar, onion powder, garlic powder, erythritol, sea salt, and allspice in a small bowl. Mix well. Spoon the glaze over the meatloaf.
6. Add the water to the Instant Pot. Place the loaf on the trivet and lower the trivet into the pot.
7. Lock the lid. Select Manual mode and set cooking time for 30 minutes on High Pressure.
8. While the meatloaf is cooking, preheat the oven broiler to 550°F (288°C).
9. When cooking time is complete, quick release the pressure, then open the lid and carefully remove the meatloaf from the pot.
10. Transfer the loaf pan to a large baking sheet. Place the meatloaf under the broiler to brown for 2 minutes or until the glaze is bubbling.
11. Transfer the browned meatloaf to a serving plate, discard the foil, and cut the loaf into 8 equal-sized slices. Serve hot.

Classic and Sumptuous Pot Roast

Prep time: 15 minutes | Cook time: 1 hour 8 minutes | Serves 6
¼ cup dry red wine
1 tablespoon dried thyme
1½ cups beef broth
½ tablespoon dried rosemary
1 teaspoon paprika
1 teaspoon garlic powder
1½ teaspoons sea salt
½ teaspoon ground black pepper

3 pounds (1.4 kg) boneless chuck roast
1½ tablespoons avocado oil
2 tablespoons unsalted butter
½ medium yellow onion, chopped
2 garlic cloves, minced
1 cup sliced mushrooms
4 stalks celery, chopped
2 sprigs fresh thyme
1 bay leaf
1. In a medium bowl, combine the wine, dried thyme, beef broth, and dried rosemary. Stir to combine. Set aside.
2. In a small bowl, combine the paprika, garlic powder, sea salt, and black pepper. Mix well. Generously rub the dry spice mixture into the roast. Set aside.
3. Select Sauté mode. Once the pot becomes hot, add the avocado oil and butter and heat until the butter is melted, about 2 minutes.
4. Add the roast to the pot. Sauté for 3 minutes per side or until a crust is formed. Transfer the browned roast to a plate and set aside.
5. Add the onions and garlic to the pot. Sauté for 3 minutes or until the onions soften and the garlic becomes fragrant.
6. Add half the broth and wine mixture to the pot.
7. Place the trivet in the Instant Pot and place the roast on top of the trivet. Add the mushrooms and celery to the pot, and pour the remaining broth and wine mixture over the roast. Place the thyme sprigs and bay leaf on top of the roast.
8. Lock the lid. Select Manual mode and set cooking time for 1 hour on High Pressure.
9. When cooking is complete, allow the pressure to release naturally for 10 minutes and then release the remaining pressure.
10. Open the lid, discard the bay leaf and thyme sprigs. Transfer the roast to a serving platter.
11. Transfer the vegetables to the platter and spoon the remaining broth over the roast and vegetables.
12. Slice the roast and ladle ¼ cup of the broth over each serving. Serve hot.

Classic Osso Buco with Gremolata

Prep time: 35 minutes | Cook time: 1 hour 2 minutes | Serves 6
4 bone-in beef shanks
Sea salt, to taste
2 tablespoons avocado oil
1 small turnip, diced
1 medium onion, diced
1 medium stalk celery, diced
4 cloves garlic, smashed
1 tablespoon unsweetened tomato purée
½ cup dry white wine
1 cup chicken broth
1 sprig fresh rosemary
2 sprigs fresh thyme
3 Roma tomatoes, diced
For the Gremolata:
½ cup loosely packed parsley leaves
1 clove garlic, crushed

Grated zest of 2 lemons
1. On a clean work surface, season the shanks all over with salt.
2. Set the Instant Pot to Sauté and add the oil. When the oil shimmers, add 2 shanks and sear for 4 minutes per side. Remove the shanks to a bowl and repeat with the remaining shanks. Set aside.
3. Add the turnip, onion, and celery to the pot and cook for 5 minutes or until softened.
4. Add the garlic and unsweetened tomato purée and cook 1 minute more, stirring frequently.
5. Deglaze the pot with the wine, scraping the bottom with a wooden spoon to loosen any browned bits. Bring to a boil.
6. Add the broth, rosemary, thyme, and shanks, then add the tomatoes on top of the shanks.
7. Secure the lid. Press the Manual button and set cooking time for 40 minutes on High Pressure.
8. Meanwhile, for the gremolata: In a small food processor, combine the parsley, garlic, and lemon zest and pulse until the parsley is finely chopped. Refrigerate until ready to use.
9. When timer beeps, allow the pressure to release naturally for 20 minutes, then release any remaining pressure. Open the lid.
10. To serve, transfer the shanks to large, shallow serving bowl. Ladle the braising sauce over the top and sprinkle with the gremolata.

Slow Cooked Beef Pizza Casserole

Prep time: 15 minutes | Cook time: 3 hours 4 minutes | Serves 6
2 tablespoons olive oil, divided
1 pound (454 g) ground beef
2 cups shredded whole Mozzarella cheese, divided
1 tablespoon Italian seasoning blend, divided
1 teaspoon garlic powder, divided
½ cup unsweetened tomato purée
¼ teaspoon dried oregano
¼ teaspoon sea salt
15 slices pepperoni
2 tablespoons sliced black olives

1. Select Sauté mode. Once the pot is hot, add 1 tablespoon olive oil and crumble the ground beef into the pot. Sauté for 4 minutes until the meat is browned.
2. Place a colander over a large bowl. Transfer the meat to the colander to drain and then transfer the drained meat to a large mixing bowl.
3. To the bowl with the meat, add 1 cup Mozzarella, ½ tablespoon Italian seasoning, and ½ teaspoon garlic powder. Mix until well combined. Set aside.
4. In a small bowl, combine the tomato purée, remaining Italian seasoning, remaining garlic powder, oregano, and sea salt. Mix well. Set aside.
5. Coat the bottom of the Instant Pot with the remaining olive oil. Press the meat mixture into the bottom of the pot.
6. Add the tomato purée mixture to the pot and use a spoon to evenly distribute the sauce over the meat. Add the pepperoni over the sauce. Sprinkle the remaining Mozzarella over and then top with the olives.
7. Lock the lid. Select Slow Cook mode and set cooking time for 3 hours on Normal.
8. When cooking is complete, open the lid and transfer the casserole to a serving platter. Slice into six equal-sized wedges. Serve hot.

Slow Cooked Beef Steak

Prep time: 10 minutes | Cook time: 7 hours | Serves 4
½ cup butter, softened
1 pound (454 g) beef steak
1 teaspoon ground nutmeg
½ teaspoon salt
1. Heat the butter in the Instant Pot on Sauté mode.
2. When the butter is melted, add beef steak, ground nutmeg, and salt.
3. Close the lid and select Slow Cook mode and set cooking time for 7 hours on Less.
4. When cooking is complete, allow to cool for half an hour and serve warm.

CHAPTER 11 PORK

Pork Chops with Sauerkraut

Prep time: 15 minutes | Cook time: 30 minutes | Serves 4

2 tablespoons olive oil
4 (1-inch-thick) bone-in pork loin chops
1 teaspoon sea salt
½ teaspoon ground black pepper
4 slices bacon, diced
3 large carrots, peeled and sliced
1 large onion, peeled and diced
1 stalk celery, finely chopped
1 clove garlic, peeled and minced
1 (12-ounce / 340-g) bottle lager
2 medium red apples, peeled, cored, and quartered
4 medium red potatoes, peeled and quartered
1 (1-pound / 454-g) bag high-quality sauerkraut, rinsed and drained
1 tablespoon caraway seeds

1. Set your Instant Pot to Sauté. Add and heat the olive oil.
2. Sprinkle the pork chops with the salt and pepper. Working in batches, sear the pork chops for 1 to 2 minutes on each side. Set aside.
3. Add the bacon, carrots, onion, and celery to the Instant Pot. Sauté for 3 to 5 minutes, or until the onions are translucent.
4. Fold in the garlic and cook for an additional 1 minute. Pour in the beer and deglaze the bottom of the pot by scraping out any browned bits from the pot. Let simmer uncovered for 5 minutes.
5. Mix in the apples, potatoes, and sauerkraut. Sprinkle the caraway seeds on top. Slightly prop pork chops up against the sides of the pot to avoid crowding the pork.
6. Secure the lid. Select the Manual function and cook for 15 minutes on High Pressure.
7. Once the timer goes off, do a natural pressure release for 5 minutes and release any remaining pressure. Carefully remove the lid.
8. Transfer to a serving plate and serve immediately.

Pork Chops in Mushroom Sauce

Prep time: 10 minutes | Cook time: 15 minutes | Serves 2

1 tablespoon oil
2 bone-in, medium-cut pork chops
Kosher salt and freshly ground black pepper, to taste
4 ounces (113 g) cremini mushrooms, sliced
2 garlic cloves, minced
½ small onion, sliced
Splash of dry white wine
1 cup chicken stock
1 tablespoon cornstarch
1 tablespoon butter
¾ cup sour cream

1. Set your Instant Pot to Sauté. Add and heat the oil.
2. Sprinkle the pork chops generously with the salt and pepper. Sear the pork chops on both sides and transfer to a plate.
3. Add the mushrooms, garlic, and onion and sauté for 3 minutes until soft. Add the white wine and deglaze the pot by scraping up any browned bits on the bottom with a wooden spoon.
4. Stir in the stock. Add the seared pork chops to the pot.
5. Lock the lid. Select the Manual mode and cook for 8 minutes on High Pressure.
6. Once cooking is complete, do a natural pressure release for about 10 minutes. Carefully open the lid.
7. Select the Sauté mode.
8. Transfer the pork chops to a plate. Remove 1 tablespoon of the cooking liquid from the pot and pour in a small bowl with the cornstarch. Stir well and transfer the mixture back to the pot.
9. Mix in the butter and sour cream and stir until mixed. Let simmer for 4 to 5 minutes until thickened. Sprinkle with the salt and pepper if necessary.
10. Transfer to a serving plate and serve.

Vinegary Pork Chops with Figs and Pears

Prep time: 10 minutes | Cook time: 10 minutes | Serves 2

2 (1-inch-thick) bone-in pork chops
1 teaspoon sea salt
1 teaspoon ground black pepper
¼ cup chicken broth
¼ cup balsamic vinegar
1 tablespoon dried mint
2 tablespoons avocado oil
5 dried figs, stems removed and halved
3 pears, peeled, cored, and diced large
1 medium sweet onion, peeled and sliced

1. Pat the pork chops dry with a paper towel and sprinkle both sides generously with the salt and pepper. Set aside.
2. Stir together the broth, vinegar, and mint in a small bowl. Set aside.
3. Set the Instant Pot to Sauté. Add and heat the oil. Sear the pork chops for 5 minutes on each side and transfer to a plate.
4. Pour in the broth mixture and deglaze the Instant Pot, scraping any browned bits from the pot.
5. Add the onions to the pot and scatter the figs and pears on top. Return the pork chops to the pot.
6. Secure the lid. Select the Steam function and cook for 3 minutes on High Pressure.
7. Once the timer goes off, do a natural pressure release for 10 minutes and then release any remaining pressure. Carefully open the lid.
8. Transfer to a serving dish with a slotted spoon. Serve immediately.

Pork Chops with Bell Peppers

Prep time: 10 minutes | Cook time: 35 minutes | Serves 4

2 tablespoons olive oil
4 pork chops
1 red onion, chopped
3 garlic cloves, minced
1 red bell pepper, roughly chopped
1 green bell pepper, roughly chopped
2 cups beef stock
A pinch of salt and black pepper
1 tablespoon parsley, chopped
1. Press the Sauté on your Instant Pot. Add and heat the oil. Brown the pork chops for 2 minutes.
2. Fold in the onion and garlic and brown for an additional 3 minutes.
3. Stir in the bell peppers, stock, salt, and pepper.
4. Lock the lid. Select the Manual mode and cook for 30 minutes on High Pressure.
5. Once cooking is complete, use a natural pressure release for 10 minutes and then release any remaining pressure. Carefully open the lid.
6. Divide the mix among the plates and serve topped with the parsley.

Cinnamon and Orange Pork

Prep time: 10 minutes | Cook time: 35 minutes | Serves 4

4 pork chops
1 tablespoon cinnamon powder
3 garlic cloves, minced
½ cup beef stock
Juice of 1 orange
1 tablespoon grated ginger
1 teaspoon dried rosemary
A pinch of salt and black pepper
1. Stir together all the ingredients in your Instant Pot.
2. Secure the lid. Press the Manual button on the Instant Pot and set the cooking time for 35 minutes on High Pressure.
3. Once cooking is complete, perform a natural pressure release for 10 minutes and then release any remaining pressure. Carefully open the lid.
4. Divide the mix among the plates and serve immediately.

Cocoa and Chili Pork

Prep time: 10 minutes | Cook time: 30 minutes | Serves 4

4 pork chops
2 tablespoons hot sauce
2 tablespoons cocoa powder
2 teaspoons chili powder
1 cup beef stock
¼ teaspoon ground cumin
1 tablespoon chopped parsley
A pinch of salt and black pepper
1. Stir together all the ingredients in your Instant Pot.
2. Secure the lid. Press the Manual button on the Instant Pot and set the cooking time for 30 minutes on High Pressure.

3. Once cooking is complete, perform a natural pressure release for 10 minutes and then release any remaining pressure. Carefully open the lid.
4. Divide the mix among the plates and serve with a side salad.

Pork Chops with Brussels Sprouts

Prep time: 10 minutes | Cook time: 30 minutes | Serves 4

1½ pound (680 g) pork chops
1 pound (454 g) Brussels sprouts, trimmed and halved
2 tablespoons Cajun seasoning
1 cup beef stock
A pinch of salt and black pepper
1 tablespoon parsley, chopped
1. Stir together all the ingredients in your Instant Pot.
2. Secure the lid. Press the Manual button on the Instant Pot and set the cooking time for 30 minutes on High Pressure.
3. Once cooking is complete, perform a natural pressure release for 10 minutes and then release any remaining pressure. Carefully open the lid.
4. Divide the mix among the plates and serve immediately.

Pork with Cherry Sauce

Prep time: 5 minutes | Cook time: 25 minutes | Serves 4

4 pork chops
A pinch of salt and black pepper
1 cup beef stock
1 cup cherries, pitted
1 tablespoon chopped parsley
1 tablespoon balsamic vinegar
1 tablespoon avocado oil
1. Press the Sauté button on the Instant Pot. Add and heat the oil.
2. Brown the pork chops for 2 minutes per side.
3. Stir in the remaining the ingredients. Secure the lid. Press the Manual button and cook for 20 minutes on High Pressure.
4. When the timer goes off, perform a natural pressure release for 5 minutes and then release any remaining pressure. Carefully open the lid.
5. Divide the mix among the plates and serve immediately.

Maple-Glazed Spareribs

Prep time: 40 minutes | Cook time: 30 minutes | Serves 6

2 racks (about 3 pounds / 1.4 kg) baby back pork ribs, cut into 2-rib sections
1 teaspoon instant coffee crystals
1 teaspoon sea salt
½ teaspoon ground cumin
½ teaspoon chili powder
½ teaspoon ground mustard
½ teaspoon cayenne pepper
½ teaspoon onion powder
½ teaspoon garlic powder

¼ teaspoon ground coriander
¼ cup soy sauce
¼ cup pure maple syrup
2 tablespoons tomato paste
1 tablespoon apple cider vinegar
1 tablespoon olive oil
1 medium onion, peeled and large diced
1. Mix together the coffee, salt, cumin, chili powder, mustard, cayenne pepper, onion powder, garlic powder, and coriander in a mixing bowl. Rub the mixture into the rib sections with your hands. Refrigerate for at least 30 minutes, covered. Set aside.
2. Stir together the soy sauce, maple syrup, tomato paste, and apple cider vinegar in a small mixing bowl.
3. Set your Instant Pot to Sauté and heat the olive oil. Add the onions and sauté for 3 to 5 minutes until translucent.
4. Stir in the soy sauce mixture. Add a few ribs at a time with tongs and gently stir to coat. Arrange the ribs standing upright, meat-side outward. Secure the lid.
5. Select the Manual function and cook for 25 minutes on High Pressure.
6. Once cooking is complete, use a natural pressure release for 10 minutes and then release any remaining pressure. Carefully open the lid.
7. Transfer the ribs to a serving plate and serve warm.

Honey Barbecue Baby Back Ribs

Prep time: 10 minutes | Cook time: 25 minutes | Serves 4

2 racks baby back ribs (3 pounds / 1.4 kg; about 4 ribs each), cut into 5- to 6-inch portions
2 tablespoons chili powder
2 tablespoons toasted sesame oil
3 tablespoons grainy mustard
1 tablespoon red wine vinegar
1 cup ketchup
$^1/_3$ cup honey
½ cup chicken broth
1. Rub the ribs all over with the chili powder.
2. Mix together the remaining ingredients in your Instant Pot and stir until the honey has dissolved.
3. Dip the ribs in the sauce to coat. Using tongs, arrange the ribs standing upright against the sides of the pot.
4. Secure the lid. Select the Manual function and cook for 25 minutes on High Pressure.
5. Preheat the broiler and adjust an oven rack so that it is 4 inches below the broiler element. Line a baking sheet with aluminum foil.
6. When the timer beeps, use a natural pressure release for 15 minutes and then release any remaining pressure. Carefully open the lid.
7. Transfer the ribs with tongs to the prepared baking sheet, meaty side up.
8. Stir the cooking liquid and pour over the ribs with a spoon. Broil the ribs for 5 minutes until browned in places.
9. Transfer the ribs to a serving plate and serve warm.

Pork Tenderloin with Cherry and Rosemary

Prep time: 5 minutes | Cook time: 25 minutes | Serves 6

2 tablespoons avocado oil
2 (3-pound / 1.4 kg) pork tenderloins, halved
½ cup balsamic vinegar
¼ cup cherry preserves
¼ cup finely chopped fresh rosemary
¼ cup olive oil
½ teaspoon sea salt
¼ teaspoon ground black pepper
4 garlic cloves, minced
1. Set your Instant Pot to Sauté. Add and heat the oil. Add the pork and brown for about 2 minutes on each side.
2. Stir together the remaining ingredients in a small bowl and pour over the pork. Secure the lid.
3. Select the Manual function and cook for 20 minutes on High Pressure.
4. Once cooking is complete, use a natural pressure release for 5 minutes and then release any remaining pressure. Carefully open the lid.
5. Remove the tenderloin from the Instant Pot to a cutting board. Let stand for 5 minutes.
6. Cut into medallions before serving.

Pork Tenderloin in Salsa

Prep time: 20 minutes | Cook time: 15 minutes | Serves 8

2 teaspoons grapeseed oil
3 pounds (1.4 kg) pork tenderloin, cut into slices
1 teaspoon granulated garlic
½ teaspoon dried marjoram
½ teaspoon dried thyme
1 teaspoon paprika
1 teaspoon ground cumin
Sea salt and ground black pepper, to taste
1 cup water
1 avocado, pitted, peeled, and sliced
Salsa:
1 cup puréed tomatoes
1 teaspoon granulated garlic
2 bell peppers, deveined and chopped
1 cup chopped onion
2 tablespoons minced fresh cilantro
3 teaspoons lime juice
1 minced jalapeño, chopped
Avocado slices, for serving
1. Press the Sauté button on your Instant Pot. Add and hear the oil. Sear the pork until nicely browned on all sides.
2. Stir in the garlic, seasonings, and water.
3. Lock the lid. Select the Manual mode and set the cooking time for 12 minutes at High Pressure.
4. Once the timer beeps, use a natural pressure release for 10 minutes. Carefully open the lid.
5. Remove the tenderloin. Shred with two forks and reserve.
6. Meanwhile, stir together all the ingredients for the salsa in a mixing bowl.
7. Spoon the salsa over the prepared pork.

8.	Divide the pork among bowls and serve garnished with the avocado slices.

Curry Pork Steak

Prep time: 15 minutes | Cook time: 15 minutes | Serves 6

1 teaspoon cumin seeds
1 teaspoon fennel seeds
½ teaspoon mustard seeds
2 chili peppers, deseeded and minced
1 teaspoon mixed peppercorns
½ teaspoon ground bay leaf
1 tablespoon sesame oil
1½ pounds (680 g) pork steak, sliced
1 cup chicken broth
3 tablespoons coconut cream
2 tablespoons balsamic vinegar
2 tablespoons chopped scallions
2 cloves garlic, finely minced
1 teaspoon curry powder
1 teaspoon grated fresh ginger
¼ teaspoon crushed red pepper flakes
¼ teaspoon ground black pepper
1 cup vegetable broth
Sea salt, to taste

1.	Heat a skillet over medium-high heat and roast the cumin seeds, fennel seeds, mustard seeds, peppers, peppercorns, and ground bay leaf and until aromatic.
2.	Set the Instant Pot to Sauté. Add and heat the sesame oil until sizzling. Sear the pork steak until nicely browned.
3.	Stir in the roasted seasonings and the remaining ingredients.
4.	Lock the lid. Select the Manual mode and set the cooking time for 8 minutes at High Pressure.
5.	When the timer beeps, do a quick pressure release. Carefully open the lid.
6.	Divide the mix among bowls and serve immediately.

Pork Cutlets with Creamy Mustard Sauce

Prep time: 20 minutes | Cook time: 13 minutes | Serves 6

6 pork cutlets
½ teaspoon dried rosemary
½ teaspoon dried marjoram
¼ teaspoon paprika
¼ teaspoon cayenne pepper
Kosher salt and ground black pepper, to taste
2 tablespoons olive oil
½ cup water
½ cup vegetable broth
1 tablespoon butter
1 cup heavy cream
1 tablespoon yellow mustard
½ cup shredded Cheddar cheese

1.	Sprinkle both sides of the pork cutlets with rosemary, marjoram, paprika, cayenne pepper, salt, and black pepper.
2.	Press the Sauté button on the Instant Pot and heat the olive oil until sizzling.

3.	Add the pork cutlets and sear both sides for about 3 minutes until lightly browned.
4.	Pour in the water and vegetable broth.
5.	Secure the lid. Select the Manual mode and set the cooking time for 8 minutes at High Pressure.
6.	When the timer beeps, perform a quick pressure release. Carefully open the lid. Transfer the pork cutlets to a plate and set aside.
7.	Press the Sauté button again and melt the butter.
8.	Stir in the heavy cream, mustard, and cheese and cook for another 2 minutes until heated through.
9.	Add the pork cutlets to the sauce, turning to coat.
10.	Remove from the Instant Pot and serve.

Pork, Green Beans, and Corn

Prep time: 10 minutes | Cook time: 35 minutes | Serves 4

2 pounds (907 g) pork shoulder, boneless and cubed
1 cup green beans, trimmed and halved
1 cup corn
1 cup beef stock
2 garlic cloves, minced
1 teaspoon ground cumin
A pinch of salt and black pepper

1.	Combine all the ingredients in the Instant Pot.
2.	Secure the lid. Select the Manual mode and set the cooking time for 35 minutes at High Pressure.
3.	Once cooking is complete, do a natural pressure release for 10 minutes, then release any remaining pressure. Carefully open the lid.
4.	Divide the mix among four plates and serve.

Pork Shoulder and Celery

Prep time: 10 minutes | Cook time: 30 minutes | Serves 4

2 tablespoons avocado oil
4 garlic cloves, minced
2 pounds (907 g) pork shoulder, boneless and cubed
1½ cups beef stock
2 celery stalks, chopped
2 tablespoons chili powder
1 tablespoon chopped sage
A pinch of salt and black pepper

1.	Press the Sauté button on the Instant Pot and heat the avocado oil.
2.	Add the garlic and sauté for 2 minutes until fragrant.
3.	Stir in the pork and brown for another 3 minutes.
4.	Add the remaining ingredients to the Instant Pot and mix well.
5.	Secure the lid. Select the Manual mode and set the cooking time for 25 minutes at High Pressure.
6.	Once cooking is complete, do a natural pressure release for 10 minutes, then release any remaining pressure. Carefully open the lid.
7.	Serve warm.

Pork Roast with Sweet Potatoes

Prep time: 10 minutes | Cook time: 40 minutes | Serves 4

1 tablespoon olive oil
2 red onions, chopped
2 pounds (907 g) pork shoulder, sliced
2 sweet potatoes, peeled and cubed
1 cup beef stock
1 teaspoon chili powder
½ teaspoon chopped rosemary
A pinch of salt and black pepper
1 cup coconut cream
1 tablespoon chopped parsley
1. Press the Sauté button on the Instant Pot and heat the olive oil.
2. Add the onions and pork and brown for 5 minutes.
3. Stir in the sweet potatoes, beef stock, chili powder, rosemary, salt, and black pepper.
4. Secure the lid. Select the Manual mode and set the cooking time for 25 minutes at High Pressure.
5. Once cooking is complete, do a natural pressure release for 10 minutes, then release any remaining pressure. Carefully open the lid.
6. Press the Sauté button again and add the coconut cream, toss, and cook for an additional 10 minutes.
7. Serve with the parsley sprinkled on top.

Paprika Pork and Brussels Sprouts

Prep time: 10 minutes | Cook time: 30 minutes | Serves 4

2 tablespoons olive oil
2 pounds (907 g) pork shoulder, cubed
2 cups Brussels sprouts, trimmed and halved
1½ cups beef stock
1 tablespoon sweet paprika
1 tablespoon chopped parsley
1. Press the Sauté button on the Instant Pot and heat the olive oil.
2. Add the pork and brown for 5 minutes. Stir in the remaining ingredients.
3. Secure the lid. Select the Manual mode and set the cooking time for 25 minutes at High Pressure.
4. Once cooking is complete, do a natural pressure release for 10 minutes, then release any remaining pressure. Carefully open the lid.
5. Divide the mix between plates and serve warm.

Carolina-Style Pork Barbecue

Prep time: 10 minutes | Cook time: 40 minutes | Serves 4 to 6

1 (4-pound / 1.8-kg) boneless pork shoulder or pork butt roast
3 tablespoons packed brown sugar
1½ teaspoons smoked paprika
1 tablespoon seasoning salt
1 cup ketchup
½ cup water
½ cup cider vinegar
1. On a clean work surface, trim any excess fat off the outside of the pork shoulder, then cut the pork into four large pieces.

2. Mix together the brown sugar, paprika, and seasoning salt in a small bowl. Rub this mixture all over the pork pieces.
3. Place the ketchup, water, and vinegar into the Instant Pot and stir well. Add the pork pieces to the pot, turning to coat.
4. Secure the lid. Select the Manual mode and set the cooking time for 40 minutes at High Pressure.
5. Once cooking is complete, do a natural pressure release for 5 minutes, then release any remaining pressure. Carefully open the lid.
6. Remove the pork pieces from the pot to a cutting board. Using two forks to shred them and discard any large chunks of fat.
7. Spoon the sauce over the pork and serve immediately.

Jamaican Pork Roast

Prep time: 10 minutes | Cook time: 55 minutes | Serves 6

¼ cup Jamaican jerk spice blend
¾ tablespoon olive oil
2 pounds (907 g) pork shoulder
¼ cup beef broth
1. Rub the jerk spice blend and olive oil all over the pork shoulder and set aside to marinate for 10 minutes.
2. When ready, press the Sauté button on the Instant Pot and add the pork.
3. Sear for 4 minutes. Flip the pork and cook for 4 minutes.
4. Pour the beef broth into the Instant Pot.
5. Secure the lid. Select the Manual mode and set the cooking time for 45 minutes at High Pressure.
6. Once cooking is complete, do a natural pressure release for 10 minutes, then release any remaining pressure. Carefully open the lid.
7. Serve hot.

Easy Chinese Pork

Prep time: 10 mins, Cook Time: 25 mins, Servings: 4

- 4 tbsps. coconut oil
- 4 garlic cloves, minced
- 1 tbsp. fresh ginger
- 4 boneless pork chops
- 2 tbsps. soy sauce
- Salt and pepper, to taste
- 1 cup water
1. Press the Sauté button on the Instant Pot and heat the coconut oil until melted.
2. Add and sauté the garlic and ginger for 1 minutes or until fragrant.
3. Add the pork and sauté for 3 minutes or until lightly browned.
4. Pour in the soy sauce and water, then sprinkle salt and pepper for seasoning.
5. Lock the lid. Press the Meat/Stew button and set the cooking time to 20 minutes at High Pressure.
6. Once cooking is complete, perform a natural pressure release for 10 minutes, and then release any remaining pressure. Carefully open the lid.

7. Press the Sauté button and allow to simmer for 3 to 5 minutes or until the sauce has thickened. Keep stirring.
8. Allow to cool for a few minutes. Remove them from the pot and serve warm.

Garlicky Pork Tenderloin

Prep time: 6 mins, Cook Time: 8 hours, Servings: 10

- 3 tbsps. extra virgin olive oil
- ¼ cup butter
- 1 tsp. thyme
- 1 garlic clove, minced
- 3 lbs. pork tenderloin
- 1 cup water
- Salt and pepper, to taste

1. Set the Instant Pot on Sauté. Heat the olive oil and butter until the butter is melted.
2. Add and sauté the garlic and thyme for 1 minute or until fragrant.
3. Add the pork tenderloin and sauté for 3 minutes or until lightly browned.
4. Pour in the water and sprinkle salt and pepper for seasoning.
5. Lock the lid. Press the Slow Cook button and set the cooking time to 8 hours at High Pressure.
6. Once cooking is complete, perform a natural pressure release for 10 minutes, and then release any remaining pressure. Carefully open the lid.
7. Allow to cool for a few minutes. Remove the pork from the pot and serve warm.

Indian Roasted Pork

Prep time: 6 mins, Cook Time: 8 hours, Servings: 3

- 1 tbsp. olive oil
- 1 lb. pork loin
- 1 tsp. cumin
- 2 garlic cloves, roughly chopped
- 1 onion, sliced
- Salt and pepper, to taste

1. Coat the Instant Pot with olive oil and add the pork loin. Set aside.
2. In a food processor, place the remaining ingredients.
3. Pulse until smooth then pour the mixture over the pork loin.
4. Lock the lid. Press the Slow Cook button and set the cooking time to 8 hours at High Pressure.
5. Once cooking is complete, perform a natural pressure release for 10 minutes, and then release any remaining pressure. Carefully open the lid.
6. Allow to cool for a few minutes. Remove them from the pot and serve warm.

Instant Pot Rib

Prep time: 6 mins, Cook Time: 8 hours, Servings: 3

- 1 rack baby back rib
- 1 tbsp. smoked paprika
- 2 tbsps. olive oil
- 1 tbsp. onion powder
- 1 tbsp. garlic powder
- Salt and pepper, to taste
- ½ cup water

1. Prepare a baking sheet. Lay on the ribs. Rub with paprika, olive oil, onion powder, garlic powder, salt, and pepper.
2. Place the well-coated rib in the Instant Pot. Pour in the water.
3. Lock the lid. Press the Slow Cook button and set the cooking time to 8 hours at High Pressure.
4. Once cooking is complete, perform a natural pressure release for 10 minutes, and then release any remaining pressure. Carefully open the lid.
5. Allow to cool for a few minutes. Remove the rib from the pot and serve warm.

Italian Pork Cutlets

Prep time: 6 mins, Cook Time: 20 mins, Servings: 6

- 4 tbsps. olive oil
- 6 pork cutlets
- Salt and pepper, to taste
- 1 tbsp. Italian herb mix
- 1½ cups water

1. In the Instant Pot, add all the ingredients. Stir to combine well.
2. Lock the lid. Press the Meat/Stew button and set the cooking time to 20 minutes at High Pressure.
3. Once cooking is complete, do a natural pressure release for 10 minutes, and then release any remaining pressure. Carefully open the lid.
4. Remove the meat and serve immediately.

Mexican Chili Pork

Prep time: 6 mins, Cook Time: 35 mins, Servings: 6

- 3 tbsps. olive oil
- 2 tsps. minced garlic
- 2 lbs. pork sirloin, sliced
- 2 tsps. ground cumin
- 1 tbsp. red chili flakes
- 1 cup water
- Salt and pepper, to taste

1. Press the Sauté button on the Instant pot and heat the olive oil until shimmering.
2. Add and sauté the garlic for 30 seconds or until fragrant.
3. Add the pork sirloin and sauté for 3 minutes or until lightly browned.
4. Add the cumin and chili flakes.
5. Pour in the water and sprinkle salt and pepper for seasoning.
6. Lock the lid. Press the Meat/Stew button and set the cooking time to 30 minutes at High Pressure.
7. Once cooking is complete, perform a natural pressure release for 10 minutes, and then release any remaining pressure. Carefully open the lid.
8. Remove the pork from the pot and serve warm.

Mexican Pulled Pork

Prep time: 6 mins, Cook Time: 1 hour, Servings: 12

- 4 lbs. pork shoulder
- 1 tsp. cinnamon
- 2 tsps. garlic powder
- 5 tbsps. coconut oil
- 1 tsp. cumin powder
- 1½ cups water
- Salt and pepper, to taste

1. In the Instant Pot, add all the ingredients. Stir to combine well.
2. Lock the lid. Press the Meat/Stew button and set the cooking time to 1 hour at High Pressure.
3. Once cooking is complete, do a natural pressure release for 10 minutes, and then release any remaining pressure. Carefully open the lid.
4. Remove the meat and shred with two forks to serve.

Mustard Pork and Mushrooms

Prep time: 6 mins, Cook Time: 35 mins, Servings: 6

- 3 tbsps. butter
- 2 lbs. pork shoulder
- 3 tbsps. yellow mustard
- 1 cup water
- 1 cup sliced mushrooms
- Salt and pepper, to taste

1. Press the Sauté button on the Instant Pot and heat the butter until melted.
2. Add the pork shoulder and mustard. Sauté for 3 minutes or until the pork is lightly browned.
3. Stir in water and mushrooms. Sprinkle salt and pepper for seasoning.
4. Lock the lid. Press the Meat/Stew button and set the cooking time to 30 minutes at High Pressure.
5. Once cooking is complete, perform a natural pressure release for 10 minutes, and then release any remaining pressure. Carefully open the lid.
6. Remove the pork from the pot and serve warm.

Paprika Pork Loin Roast

Prep time: 6 mins, Cook Time: 50 mins, Servings: 9

- 4 tbsps. olive oil
- 4 garlic cloves
- ½ cup chopped paprika
- 3 lbs. pork loin roast
- Salt and pepper, to taste
- 1 cup water

1. Press the Sauté button on the Instant Pot. Coat the pot with olive oil.
2. Add and sauté the garlic and paprika for 1 minute or until fragrant.
3. Add the pork loin roast and sear on all sides for 3 minutes or until lightly browned.
4. Sprinkle salt and pepper for seasoning. Pour in the water.

5. Lock the lid. Press the Meat/Stew button and set the cooking time to 45 minutes at High Pressure.
6. Once cooking is complete, perform a natural pressure release for 10 minutes, and then release any remaining pressure. Carefully open the lid.
7. Allow to cool for a few minutes. Remove the pork from the pot and baste with the juice remains in the pot before serving.

Pear and Pork Butt

Prep time: 12 mins, Cook time: 50 mins, Servings: 12

- 4 lbs. pork butt
- 2 tbsps. sea salt
- 3 tbsps. extra virgin olive oil
- 4 pears, peeled, stem removed, deseeded, and cut into ½-inch chunks
- 1½ cups chicken broth

1. On a clean work surface, rub the pork butt with salt.
2. Set the Instant Pot to Sauté setting, then add and heat the olive oil.
3. Place pork in pot and brown for 5 minutes per side.
4. Add pears and chicken broth. Stir to mix well.
5. Lock the lid. Set the pot to Manual setting and set the timer for 45 minutes at High Pressure.
6. When the timer beeps, press Cancel, then use a quick pressure release.
7. Carefully open the lid and allow to cool for a few minutes. Serve warm.

Pine Nut Pork

Prep time: 20 mins, Cook Time: 25 mins, Servings: 4

- 1½ lbs. pork tenderloin
- 1 tsp. sea salt
- 1 tbsp. extra virgin olive oil
- 1 medium onion, finely sliced
- ½ cup pine nuts
- 1 cup pesto sauce

1. On a clean work surface, cut the pork tenderloin into 1-inch thick slices and rub with salt.
2. Place the olive oil in Instant Pot, then set to Sauté setting.
3. Add and brown the pork for 3 minutes, then add onion and sauté for a minute or until translucent.
4. Add the pine nuts and pesto sauce.
5. Lock the lid. Set the pot to Manual mode and set the timer to 20 minutes at High Pressure.
8. Once cooking is complete, use a natural pressure release for 10 minutes, then release any remaining pressure.
6. Carefully open the lid. Allow to cool for a few minutes. Transfer them on a large plate and serve immediately.

Pork and Sweet Potato

Prep time: 20 mins, Cook Time: 25 mins, Servings: 8

- 2 tbsps. extra virgin olive oil

- 2 lbs. pork tenderloin, slice into 1-inch bites
- 1 tsp. sea salt
- 2 sweet potatoes, peeled and quartered
- 4 cups beef broth

1. Lightly coat the Instant Pot with the olive oil and set the Sauté mode.
2. Add the pork along with salt and brown for 3 minutes on all sides.
3. Add sweet potatoes with beef broth to the pot.
4. Set the setting to Manual mode and set the cooking time for 25 minutes at High Pressure.
5. Once cooking is complete, use a quick pressure release.
6. Carefully open the lid. Allow to cool for a few minutes. Transfer them on a large plate and serve immediately.

Pork Chops and Peas

Prep time: 12 mins, Cook time: 10 mins, Servings: 4

- 1 tbsp. olive oil
- 4 pork chops
- 1 medium onion, chopped
- 1 cup peas
- ½ tsp. salt
- 1 tsp. curry powder

1. Coat the Instant Pot with olive oil and set to Sauté setting.
2. Add the pork chops and sear for 3 minutes or until lightly browned.
3. Add the onion and sauté for 1 to 2 minutes or until soft.
4. Add peas, salt and curry powder and sauté for 3 to 5 minutes or until peas are tender.
5. Serve them warm on a large plate.

Pork Chops with Onions

Prep time: 6 mins, Cook Time: 25 mins, Servings: 4

- 3 tbsps. butter
- 4 boneless pork chops
- 3 onions, chopped
- ½ cup beef broth
- Salt and pepper, to taste
- ¼ cup heavy cream

1. Press the Sauté button on the Instant Pot.
2. Heat the butter until melted and add the pork chops and onion.
3. Sauté for 3 minutes or until the pork is seared.
4. Stir in the broth and sprinkle salt and pepper for seasoning.
5. Lock the lid. Press the Meat/Stew button and set the cooking time to 20 minutes at High Pressure.
6. Once cooking is complete, perform a natural pressure release for 10 minutes, and then release any remaining pressure. Carefully open the lid.
7. Add the heavy cream. Press the Sauté button and allow to simmer for 5 minutes.

8. Allow to cool for a few minutes. Remove the pork from the pot and serve warm.

Pork Coconut Curry

Prep time: 6 mins, Cook Time: 35 mins, Servings: 6

- 3 tbsps. coconut oil
- 3 garlic cloves, minced
- 1 tbsp. garam masala
- 2 lbs. pork shoulders, sliced
- 1 cup freshly squeezed coconut milk
- Salt and pepper, to taste

1. Press the Sauté button on the Instant Pot and heat the coconut oil until melted.
2. Add and sauté the garlic and garam masala until fragrant.
3. Add the pork and allow to sear on all sides for 3 minutes or until lightly browned.
4. Pour in the coconut milk. Sprinkle with salt and pepper.
5. Lock the lid. Press the Meat/Stew button and set the cooking time to 30 minutes at High pressure.
6. Once cooking is complete, perform a natural pressure release for 10 minutes, and then release any remaining pressure. Carefully open the lid.
7. Remove the pork from the pot and serve warm.

Pork Medallions and Mushrooms

Prep time: 12 mins, Cook time: 8 mins, Servings: 4

- 2 tsps. extra virgin olive oil
- 4 pork medallions, rinsed and trimmed
- 1 tsp. salt
- 12 oyster mushrooms, quartered
- 1 onion, diced
- 1 cup water

1. Set the Instant Pot to Sauté setting, then add the extra virgin olive oil and heat until the oil is shimmering.
2. Add the pork medallions and brown for 3 to 4 minutes.
3. Add the remaining ingredients.
4. Lock the lid. Select the Manual setting and set the timer to 8 minutes at High Pressure.
5. When the timer beeps, press Cancel, then use a quick pressure release.
6. Carefully open the lid. Allow to cool for a few minutes. Transfer them on a large plate and serve immediately.

Pork Potato Lunch

Prep time: 12 mins, Cook Time: 25 mins, Servings: 4

- 1 tbsp. olive oil
- 1 onion, chopped
- 10 oz. fat removed pork neck
- 3 cups low-sodium beef stock
- 1 medium sweet potato, chopped
- Salt and pepper, to taste

1.	Press the Sauté bottom on the Instant Pot. Grease the pot with the olive oil.
2.	Add the onion and sauté for 2 minutes until translucent and softened.
3.	Add the beef and sauté for 4 to 5 minutes to evenly brown.
4.	Add the stock and potatoes. Sprinkle with salt and pepper. Stir to mix well.
5.	Lock the lid. Press Manual. Set the timer to 20 minutes at High Pressure.
6.	When the timer beeps, press Cancel, then use a quick pressure release.
7.	Open the lid, transfer them in a large plate and serve warm.

Pork Tenderloin with Celery

Prep time: 12 mins, Cook Time: 25 mins, Servings: 4

- 1½ lbs. pork tenderloin
- 2 tsps. sea salt
- ½ tsp. rosemary
- 1 cup heavy cream
- 4 celery stalks, rinsed, sliced into ½-inch pieces
- 1 cup water

1.	On a clean work surface, rub the pork with salt and rosemary.
2.	Slice the well-coated tenderloin into 1-inch thick slices.
3.	Set the Instant Pot to Sauté setting.
4.	Add the pork and brown for 3 minutes.
5.	Add the celery, heavy cream, and water. Stir to combine well.
6.	Lock the lid. Set the Instant Pot to Manual mode and set the timer for 20 minutes at High Pressure.
7.	Once cooking is complete, use a natural pressure release for 10 minutes, then release any remaining pressure.
8.	Carefully open the lid. Allow to cool for a few minutes. Transfer them on a large plate and serve immediately.

Pork Vindaloo (Curry Pork)

Prep time: 6 mins, Cook Time: 35 mins, Servings: 6

- ¼ cup coconut oil
- 2 lbs. pork shoulder, sliced
- 1 tbsp. garam masala
- 3 tbsps. freshly squeezed lemon juice
- 1 cup water
- Salt and pepper, to taste

1.	Press the Sauté button on the Instant Pot and heat the coconut oil until melted.
2.	Add and sear the pork loin on all sides for 3 minutes or until lightly browned.
3.	Add the garam masala and continue sauté for 2 more minutes.
4.	Stir in the lemon juice and water. Sprinkle with salt and pepper.
5.	Lock the lid. Press the Meat/Stew button and set the cooking time to 30 minutes at High Pressure.

6.	Once cooking is complete, perform a natural pressure release for 10 minutes, and then release any remaining pressure. Carefully open the lid.
7.	Remove the pork from the pot and serve warm.

Pork with Coconut Meat

Prep time: 12 mins, Cook Time: 6 mins, Servings: 4

- 1 tbsp. olive oil
- ½ lb. ground pork
- 1 tsp. salt
- 6 garlic cloves
- 2 cups tomato sauce
- 1 cup water
- 2 cups coconut meat

1.	Set the Instant Pot to Sauté function. Coat the pot with olive oil and heat until the oil is shimmering.
2.	Add pork to Instant Pot along with salt and garlic, then sauté for 3 minutes until lightly browned.
3.	Add the tomato sauce and water.
4.	Lock the lid. Set the Instant Port to Manual function and set the cooking time for 6 minutes at High Pressure.
5.	Once cooking is complete, use a natural pressure release for 10 minutes, then release any remaining pressure.
6.	Carefully open the lid. Allow to cool for a few minutes. Transfer them on a large plate and serve with coconut meat on top.

Albóndigas Sinaloenses

Prep time: 15 minutes | Cook time: 10 minutes | Serves 6

1 pound (454 g) ground pork
½ pound (227 g) Italian sausage, crumbled
2 tablespoons yellow onion, finely chopped
½ teaspoon dried oregano
1 sprig fresh mint, finely minced
½ teaspoon ground cumin
2 garlic cloves, finely minced
¼ teaspoon fresh ginger, grated
Seasoned salt and ground black pepper, to taste
1 tablespoon olive oil
½ cup yellow onions, finely chopped
2 chipotle chilies in adobo
2 tomatoes, puréed
2 tablespoons tomato passata
1 cup chicken broth

1.	In a mixing bowl, combine the pork, sausage, 2 tablespoons of yellow onion, oregano, mint, cumin, garlic, ginger, salt, and black pepper.
2.	Roll the mixture into meatballs and reserve.
3.	Press the Sauté button to heat up the Instant Pot. Heat the olive oil and cook the meatballs for 4 minutes, stirring continuously.
4.	Stir in ½ cup of yellow onions, chilies in adobo, tomatoes passata, and broth. Add reserved meatballs.
5.	Secure the lid. Choose the Manual mode and set cooking time for 6 minutes at High pressure.

6. Once cooking is complete, use a quick pressure release. Carefully remove the lid.
7. Serve immediately.

Apple and Pumpkin Ham

Prep time: 10 minutes | Cook time: 10 minutes | Serves 6

1 cup apple cider vinegar
1 pound (454 g) ham, cooked
2 tablespoons erythritol
1 tablespoon avocado oil
2 tablespoons butter
½ teaspoon pumpkin pie spices

1. Pour apple cider vinegar in the Instant Pot and insert the trivet.
2. Rub the ham with erythritol avocado oil,, butter, and pumpkin pie spices.
3. Put the ham on the trivet. Close the lid.
4. Select Manual mode and set cooking time for 10 minutes on High Pressure.
5. When timer beeps, use a natural pressure release for 5 minutes, then release any remaining pressure and open the lid.
6. Slice the ham and serve.

Aromatic Pork Steak Curry

Prep time: 15 minutes | Cook time: 8 minutes | Serves 6

½ teaspoon mustard seeds
1 teaspoon fennel seeds
1 teaspoon cumin seeds
2 chili peppers, deseeded and minced
½ teaspoon ground bay leaf
1 teaspoon mixed peppercorns
1 tablespoon sesame oil
1½ pounds (680 g) pork steak, sliced
2 cloves garlic, finely minced
2 tablespoons scallions, chopped
1 teaspoon fresh ginger, grated
1 teaspoon curry powder
1 cup chicken broth
2 tablespoons balsamic vinegar
3 tablespoons coconut cream
¼ teaspoon red pepper flakes, crushed
Sea salt, to taste
¼ teaspoon ground black pepper

1. Heat a skillet over medium-high heat. Once hot, roast the mustard seeds, fennel seeds, cumin seeds, chili peppers, ground bay leaf, and peppercorns for 1 or 2 minutes or until aromatic.
2. Press the Sauté button to heat up the Instant Pot. Heat the sesame oil until sizzling. Sear pork steak for 5 minutes or until browned.
3. Add the remaining ingredients, including roasted seasonings. Stir to mix well.
4. Secure the lid. Choose the Manual mode and set cooking time for 8 minutes on High pressure.
5. Once cooking is complete, use a quick pressure release. Carefully remove the lid.
6. Serve immediately.

Bacon-Wrapped Pork Bites

Prep time: 15 minutes | Cook time: 20 minutes | Serves 4

3 tablespoons butter
10 ounces (283 g) pork tenderloin, cubed
6 ounces (170 g) bacon, sliced
½ teaspoon white pepper
¾ cup chicken stock

1. Melt the butter on Sauté mode in the Instant Pot.
2. Meanwhile, wrap the pork tenderloin cubes in the sliced bacon and sprinkle with white pepper. Secure with toothpicks, if necessary.
3. Put the wrapped pork tenderloin in the melted butter and cook for 3 minutes on each side.
4. Add the chicken stock and close the lid.
5. Select Manual mode and set cooking time for 14 minutes on High Pressure.
6. When timer beeps, use a natural pressure release for 5 minutes, then release any remaining pressure. Open the lid.
7. Discard the toothpicks and serve immediately.

Beery Boston-Style Butt

Prep time: 10 minutes | Cook time: 1 hour 1 minutes | Serves 4

1 tablespoon butter
1 pound (454 g) Boston-style butt
½ cup leeks, chopped
¼ cup beer
½ cup chicken stock
Pinch of grated nutmeg
Sea salt, to taste
¼ teaspoon ground black pepper
¼ cup water

1. Press the Sauté button to heat up the Instant Pot. Once hot, melt the butter.
2. Cook the Boston-style butt for 3 minutes on each side. Remove from the pot and reserve.
3. Sauté the leeks for 5 minutes or until fragrant. Add the remaining ingredients and stir to combine.
4. Secure the lid. Choose the Manual mode and set cooking time for 50 minutes on High pressure.
5. Once cooking is complete, use a natural pressure release for 20 minutes, then release any remaining pressure. Carefully remove the lid.
6. Serve immediately.

Blade Pork with Sauerkraut

Prep time: 15 minutes | Cook time: 37 minutes | Serves 6

2 pounds (907 g) blade pork steaks
Sea salt and ground black pepper, to taste
½ teaspoon cayenne pepper
½ teaspoon dried parsley flakes
1 tablespoon butter
1½ cups water
2 cloves garlic, thinly sliced
2 pork sausages, casing removed and sliced
4 cups sauerkraut

1. Season the blade pork steaks with salt, black pepper, cayenne pepper, and dried parsley.

2.	Press the Sauté button to heat up the Instant Pot. Melt the butter and sear blade pork steaks for 5 minutes or until browned on all sides.
3.	Clean the Instant Pot. Add water and trivet to the bottom of the Instant Pot.
4.	Place the blade pork steaks on the trivet. Make small slits over entire pork with a knife. Insert garlic pieces into each slit.
5.	Secure the lid. Choose the Meat/Stew mode and set cooking time for 30 minutes on High pressure.
6.	Once cooking is complete, use a natural pressure release for 15 minutes, then release any remaining pressure. Carefully remove the lid.
7.	Add the sausage and sauerkraut. Press the Sauté button and cook for 2 minutes more or until heated through.
8.	Serve immediately.

Blue Pork

Prep time: 5 minutes | Cook time: 20 minutes | Serves 2

1 teaspoon coconut oil
2 pork chops
2 ounces (57 g) blue cheese, crumbled
1 teaspoon lemon juice
¼ cup heavy cream
1.	Heat the coconut oil in the Instant Pot on Sauté mode.
2.	Put the pork chops in the Instant Pot and cook on Sauté mode for 5 minutes on each side.
3.	Add the lemon juice and crumbled cheese. Stir to mix well.
4.	Add heavy cream and close the lid.
5.	Select Manual mode and set cooking time for 10 minutes on High Pressure.
6.	When timer beeps, perform a natural pressure release for 5 minutes, then release any remaining pressure. Open the lid.
7.	Serve immediately.

Bo Ssäm

Prep time: 10 minutes | Cook time: 8 minutes | Serves 6

1 tablespoon vegetable oil
1 pound (454 g) ground pork
2 tablespoons gochujang
1 tablespoon Doubanjiang
½ teaspoon ground Sichuan peppercorns
1 tablespoon minced fresh ginger
1 tablespoon minced garlic
1 tablespoon coconut aminos
1 teaspoon hot sesame oil
1 teaspoon salt
¼ cup water
1 bunch bok choy, chopped (about 4 to 6 cups)
1.	Preheat the Instant Pot on Sauté mode. Add the oil and heat until it is shimmering.
2.	Add the ground pork, breaking up all lumps, and cook for 4 minutes or until the pork is no longer pink.

3.	Add the gochujang, doubanjiang, peppercorns, ginger, garlic, coconut aminos, sesame oil, and salt. Stir to combine.
4.	Add the water and bok choy.
5.	Lock the lid. Select Manual mode. Set cooking time for 4 minutes on High Pressure.
6.	When cooking is complete, quick-release the pressure. Unlock the lid.
7.	Serve immediately.

Cheesy Pork Taco Casserole

Prep time: 15 minutes | Cook time: 30 minutes | Serves 6

½ cup water
2 eggs
3 ounces (85 g) Cottage cheese, at room temperature
¼ cup heavy cream
1 teaspoon taco seasoning
6 ounces (170 g) Cotija cheese, crumbled
¾ pound (340 g) ground pork
½ cup tomatoes, puréed
1 tablespoon taco seasoning
3 ounces (85 g) chopped green chilies
6 ounces (170 g) Queso Manchego cheese, shredded
1.	Add the water in the Instant Pot and place in the trivet.
2.	In a mixing bowl, combine the eggs, Cottage cheese, heavy cream, and taco seasoning.
3.	Lightly grease a casserole dish. Spread the Cotija cheese over the bottom. Stir in the egg mixture.
4.	Lower the casserole dish onto the trivet.
5.	Secure the lid. Choose Manual mode and set cooking time for 20 minutes on High Pressure.
6.	Once cooking is complete, use a quick pressure release. Carefully remove the lid.
7.	In the meantime, heat a skillet over a medium-high heat. Brown the ground pork, crumbling with a fork.
8.	Add the tomato purée, taco seasoning, and green chilies. Spread the mixture over the prepared cheese crust.
9.	Top with shredded Queso Manchego.
10.	Secure the lid. Choose Manual mode and set cooking time for 10 minutes on High Pressure.
11.	Once cooking is complete, use a quick pressure release. Carefully remove the lid.
12.	Serve immediately.

Chile Verde Pulled Pork with Tomatillos

Prep time: 15 minutes | Cook time: 1 hour 3 minutes | Serves 6

2 pounds (907 g) pork shoulder, cut into 6 equal-sized pieces
1 teaspoon sea salt
½ teaspoon ground black pepper
2 jalapeño peppers, deseeded and stemmed
1 pound (454 g) tomatillos, husks removed and quartered
3 garlic cloves
1 tablespoon lime juice
3 tablespoons fresh cilantro, chopped
1 medium white onion, chopped
1 teaspoon ground cumin

½ teaspoon dried oregano
1²/₃ cups chicken broth
1½ tablespoons olive oil
1.	Season the pork pieces with the salt and pepper. Gently rub the seasonings into the pork cuts. Set aside.
2.	Combine the jalapeños, tomatillos, garlic cloves, lime juice, cilantro, onions, cumin, oregano, and chicken broth in the blender. Pulse until well combined. Set aside.
3.	Select Sauté mode and add the olive oil to the pot. Once the oil is hot, add the pork cuts and sear for 4 minutes per side or until browned.
4.	Pour the jalapeño sauce over the pork and lightly stir to coat well.
5.	Lock the lid. Select Manual mode and set cooking time for 55 minutes on High Pressure.
6.	When cooking is complete, allow the pressure to release naturally for 10 minutes and then release the remaining pressure.
7.	Open the lid. Transfer the pork pieces to a cutting board and use two forks to shred the pork.
8.	Transfer the shredded pork back to the pot and stir to combine the pork with the sauce. Transfer to a serving platter. Serve warm.

Classic Pork and Cauliflower Keema

Prep time: 15 minutes | Cook time: 8 minutes | Serves 6

1 tablespoon sesame oil
½ cup yellow onion, chopped
1 garlic cloves, minced
1 (1-inch) piece fresh ginger, minced
1½ pounds (680 g) ground pork
1 cup cauliflower, chopped into small florets
1 ripe tomatoes, puréed
1 jalapeño pepper, seeded and minced
4 cloves, whole
1 teaspoon garam masala
½ teaspoon ground cumin
¼ teaspoon turmeric powder
1 teaspoon brown mustard seeds
½ teaspoon hot paprika
Sea salt and ground black pepper, to taste
1 cup water
1.	Press the Sauté button to heat up the Instant Pot. Heat the sesame oil. Once hot, sauté yellow onion for 3 minutes or until softened.
2.	Stir in garlic and ginger; cook for an additional minute. Add the remaining ingredients.
3.	Secure the lid. Choose the Manual mode and set cooking time for 5 minutes on High pressure.
4.	Once cooking is complete, use a quick pressure release. Carefully remove the lid.
5.	Serve immediately.

Coconut Pork Muffins

Prep time: 5 minutes | Cook time: 9 minutes | Serves 2

1 egg, beaten
2 tablespoons coconut flour
1 teaspoon parsley
¼ teaspoon salt
1 tablespoon coconut cream
4 ounces (113 g) ground pork, fried
1 cup water
1.	Whisk together the egg, coconut flour, parsley, salt, and coconut cream. Add the fried ground pork. Mix the the mixture until homogenous.
2.	Pour the mixture into a muffin pan.
3.	Pour the water in the Instant Pot and place in the trivet.
4.	Lower the muffin pan on the trivet and close the Instant Pot lid.
5.	Set the Manual mode and set cooking time for 4 minutes on High Pressure.
6.	When timer beeps, perform a natural pressure release for 5 minutes, then release any remaining pressure. Open the lid.
7.	Serve warm.

Creamy Pork Liver

Prep time: 5 minutes | Cook time: 7 minutes | Serves 3

14 ounces (397 g) pork liver, chopped
1 teaspoon salt
1 teaspoon butter
½ cup heavy cream
3 tablespoons scallions, chopped
1.	Rub the liver with the salt on a clean work surface.
2.	Put the butter in the Instant Pot and melt on the Sauté mode.
3.	Add the heavy cream, scallions, and liver.
4.	Stir and close the lid. Select Manual mode and set cooking time for 12 minutes on High Pressure.
5.	When timer beeps, perform a natural pressure release for 5 minutes, then release any remaining pressure. Open the lid.
6.	Serve immediately.

Easy Braised Pork Belly

Prep time: 15 minutes | Cook time: 37 minutes | Serves 4

1 pound (454 g) pork belly
1 tablespoon olive oil
Salt and ground black pepper to taste
1 clove garlic, minced
1 cup dry white wine
Rosemary sprig
1.	Select the Sauté mode on the Instant Pot and heat the oil.
2.	Add the pork belly and sauté for 2 minutes per side, until starting to brown.
3.	Season the meat with salt and pepper, add the garlic.
4.	Pour in the wine and add the rosemary sprig. Bring to a boil.
5.	Select the Manual mode and set the cooking time for 35 minutes at High pressure.
6.	Once cooking is complete, use a natural pressure release for 10 minutes, then release any remaining pressure. Open the lid.
7.	Slice the meat and serve.

Easy Ginger Pork Meatballs

Prep time: 10 minutes | Cook time: 7 minutes | Serves 3

11 ounces (312 g) ground pork
1 teaspoon ginger paste
1 teaspoon lemon juice
¼ teaspoon chili flakes
1 tablespoon butter
¼ cup water
1.   Combine the ground pork and ginger paste in a large bowl.
2.   Mix in the lemon juice and chili flakes.
3.   Put the butter in the Instant Pot and melt on Sauté mode.
4.   Meanwhile, shape the mixture into small meatballs.
5.   Place the meatballs in the Instant Pot and cook for 2 minutes on each side.
6.   Add water and lock the lid.
7.   Set the Manual mode and set cooking time for 3 minutes on High Pressure.
8.   When timer beeps, perform a quick pressure release. Open the lid.
9.   Serve warm.

Easy Pork Steaks with Pico de Gallo

Prep time: 15 minutes | Cook time: 12 minutes | Serves 6

1 tablespoon butter
2 pounds (907 g) pork steaks
1 bell pepper, deseeded and sliced
½ cup shallots, chopped
2 garlic cloves, minced
¼ cup dry red wine
1 cup chicken bone broth
¼ cup water
Salt, to taste
¼ teaspoon freshly ground black pepper, or more to taste
Pico de Gallo:
1 tomato, chopped
1 chili pepper, seeded and minced
½ cup red onion, chopped
2 garlic cloves, minced
1 tablespoon fresh cilantro, finely chopped
Sea salt, to taste
1.   Press the Sauté button to heat up the Instant Pot. Melt the butter and sear the pork steaks about 4 minutes or until browned on both sides.
2.   Add bell pepper, shallot, garlic, wine, chicken bone broth, water, salt, and black pepper to the Instant Pot.
3.   Secure the lid. Choose the Manual mode and set cooking time for 8 minutes at High pressure.
4.   Meanwhile, combine the ingredients for the Pico de Gallo in a small bowl. Refrigerate until ready to serve.
5.   Once cooking is complete, use a quick pressure release. Carefully remove the lid.
6.   Serve warm pork steaks with the chilled Pico de Gallo on the side.

Egg Meatloaf

Prep time: 20 minutes | Cook time: 25 minutes | Serves 6

1 tablespoon avocado oil
1½ cup ground pork
1 teaspoon chives
1 teaspoon salt
½ teaspoon ground black pepper
2 tablespoons coconut flour
3 eggs, hard-boiled, peeled
1 cup water
1.   Brush a loaf pan with avocado oil.
2.   In the mixing bowl, mix the ground pork, chives, salt, ground black pepper, and coconut flour.
3.   Transfer the mixture in the loaf pan and flatten with a spatula.
4.   Fill the meatloaf with hard-boiled eggs.
5.   Pour water and insert the trivet in the Instant Pot.
6.   Lower the loaf pan over the trivet in the Instant Pot. Close the lid.
7.   Select Manual mode and set cooking time for 25 minutes on High Pressure.
8.   When timer beeps, use a natural pressure release for 10 minutes, then release any remaining pressure. Open the lid.
9.   Serve immediately.

Eggplant Pork Lasagna

Prep time: 20 minutes | Cook time: 30 minutes | Serves 6

2 eggplants, sliced
1 teaspoon salt
10 ounces (283 g) ground pork
1 cup Mozzarella, shredded
1 tablespoon unsweetened tomato purée
1 teaspoon butter, softened
1 cup chicken stock
1.   Sprinkle the eggplants with salt and let sit for 10 minutes, then pat dry with paper towels.
2.   In a mixing bowl, mix the ground pork, butter, and tomato purée.
3.   Make a layer of the sliced eggplants in the bottom of the Instant Pot and top with ground pork mixture.
4.   Top the ground pork with Mozzarella and repeat with remaining ingredients.
5.   Pour in the chicken stock. Close the lid. Select Manual mode and set cooking time for 30 minutes on High Pressure.
6.   When timer beeps, use a natural pressure release for 10 minutes, then release the remaining pressure and open the lid.
7.   Cool for 10 minutes and serve.

Golden Bacon Sticks

Prep time: 5 minutes | Cook time: 6 minutes | Serves 4

6 ounces (170 g) bacon, sliced
2 tablespoons almond flour
1 tablespoon water
¾ teaspoon chili pepper
1.   Sprinkle the sliced bacon with the almond flour and drizzle with water. Add the chili pepper.

2.	Put the bacon in the Instant Pot.
3.	Cook on Sauté mode for 3 minutes per side.
4.	Serve immediately.

Hawaiian Pulled Pork Roast with Cabbage

Prep time: 10 minutes | Cook time: 1 hour 2 minutes minutes | Serves 6

1½ tablespoons olive oil
3 pounds (1.4 kg) pork shoulder roast, cut into 4 equal-sized pieces
3 cloves garlic, minced
1 tablespoon liquid smoke
2 cups water, divided
1 tablespoon sea salt
2 cups shredded cabbage

1.	Select Sauté mode and add the olive oil to the Instant Pot. Once the oil is hot, add the pork cuts and sear for 5 minutes per side or until browned. Once browned, transfer the pork to a platter and set aside.
2.	Add the garlic, liquid smoke, and 1½ cups water to the Instant Pot. Stir to combine.
3.	Return the pork to the pot and sprinkle the salt over top.
4.	Lock the lid. Select Manual mode and set cooking time for 1 hour on High Pressure.
5.	When cooking is complete, allow the pressure to release naturally for 20 minutes, then release any remaining pressure.
6.	Open the lid and transfer the pork to a large platter. Using two forks, shred the pork. Set aside.
7.	Add the shredded cabbage and remaining water to the liquid in the pot. Stir.
8.	Lock the lid. Select Manual mode and set cooking time for 2 minutes on High Pressure. When cooking is complete, quick release the pressure.
9.	Transfer the cabbage to the serving platter with the pork. Serve warm.

CHAPTER 12 LAMB

Black Bean Minced Lamb

Prep time: 10 minutes | Cook time: 25 minutes | Serves 4 to 6

1 pound (454 g) ground lamb
2 tablespoons vegetable oil
½ cup chopped onion
½ teaspoon salt
2 cans drained black beans
1 can undrained diced tomatoes
1 can chopped and undrained green chillies
1½ cups chicken broth
1½ tablespoons tomato paste
1½ tablespoons chili powder
2 teaspoons cumin
½ teaspoon cayenne

1. Set the Instant Pot to the Sauté mode and heat the oil. Add the lamb, onion and salt to the pot and sauté for 5 minutes, stirring constantly. Add the remaining ingredients to the pot and stir well.
2. Select the Manual setting and set the cooking time for 20 minutes on High Pressure. Once the timer goes off, use a natural pressure release for 10 minutes, then release any remaining pressure. Carefully open the lid.
3. Serve immediately.

Braised Lamb Ragout

Prep time: 10 minutes | Cook time: 1 hour 8 minutes | Serves 4 to 6

1½ pounds (680 g) lamb, bone-in
1 teaspoon vegetable oil
4 tomatoes, chopped
2 carrots, sliced
½ pound (227 g) mushrooms, sliced
1 small yellow onion, chopped
6 cloves garlic, minced
2 tablespoons tomato paste
1 teaspoon dried oregano
Water, as needed
Salt and ground black pepper, to taste
Handful chopped parsley

1. Press the Sauté button on the Instant Pot and heat the olive oil. Add the lamb and sear for 4 minutes per side, or until browned.
2. Stir in the tomatoes, carrots, mushrooms, onion, garlic, tomato paste, oregano and water. Season with salt and pepper.
3. Set the lid in place. Select the Manual mode and set the cooking time for 60 minutes on High Pressure. Once cooking is complete, perform a quick pressure release. Carefully open the lid.
4. Transfer the lamb to a plate. Discard the bones and shred the meat. Return the shredded lamb to the pot, add the parsley and stir.
5. Serve warm.

Garlicky Lamb Leg

Prep time: 35 minutes | Cook time: 50 minutes | Serves 6

2 pounds (907 g) lamb leg
6 garlic cloves, minced
1 teaspoon sea salt
1½ teaspoons black pepper
2½ tablespoons olive oil
1½ small onions
1½ cups bone broth
¾ cup orange juice
6 sprigs thyme

1. In a bowl, whisk together the garlic, salt and pepper. Add the lamb leg to the bowl and marinate for 30 minutes.
2. Press the Sauté button on the Instant Pot and heat the olive oil. Add the onions and sauté for 4 minutes. Transfer the onions to a separate bowl.
3. Add the marinated lamb to the pot and sear for 3 minutes on each side, or lightly browned. Whisk in the cooked onions, broth, orange juice and thyme.
4. Close and secure the lid. Set the Instant Pot to the Meat/Stew mode and set the cooking time for 40 minutes on High Pressure. When the timer beeps, use a natural pressure release for 10 minutes, then release any remaining pressure. Carefully open the lid.
5. Divide the dish among 6 serving bowls and serve hot.

Greek Lamb Loaf

Prep time: 5 minutes | Cook time: 15 minutes | Serves 2

1 pound (454 g) ground lamb meat
4 garlic cloves
½ small onion, chopped
1 teaspoon ground marjoram
1 teaspoon rosemary
¾ teaspoon salt
¼ teaspoon black pepper
¾ cup water

1. In a blender, combine the lamb meat, garlic, onions, marjoram, rosemary, salt and pepper. Pulse until well mixed. Shape the lamb mixture into a compact loaf and cover tightly with aluminium foil. Use a fork to make some holes.
2. Pour the water into the Instant Pot and put a trivet in the pot. Place the lamb loaf on the trivet and lock the lid.
3. Select the Manual mode and set the cooking time for 15 minutes on High Pressure. When the timer goes off, use a quick pressure release.
4. Carefully open the lid. Serve warm.

Indian Lamb Curry

Prep time: 15 minutes | Cook time: 1 hour 3 minutes | Serves 4

2 tablespoons olive oil
1 pound (454 g) lamb meat, cubed
2 tomatoes, chopped
1 onion, chopped
1-inch piece ginger, grated
2 garlic cloves, minced
½ tablespoon ground cumin

½ tablespoon chili flakes
½ tablespoon ground turmeric
½ teaspoon garam masala
1 cup chicken stock
½ cup coconut milk
¼ cup rice, rinsed
1 tablespoon fish sauce
¼ cup chopped cilantro
1.	Set the Instant Pot on the Sauté mode. Heat the olive oil and sear the lamb shoulder on both sides for 8 minutes, or until browned. Transfer the lamb to a plate and set aside.
2.	Add the tomatoes, onion, ginger and garlic to the pot and sauté for 5 minutes. Stir in the cumin, chili flakes, turmeric and garam masala. Cook for 10 minutes, or until they form a paste. Whisk in the chicken stock, coconut milk, rice and fish sauce. Return the lamb back to the pot.
3.	Lock the lid. Select Meat/Stew mode and set the cooking time for 35 minutes on High Pressure. Once cooking is complete, do a natural pressure release for 10 minutes, then release any remaining pressure. Open the lid and select the Sauté mode. Cook the curry for 5 minutes, or until thickened.
4.	Top with the chopped cilantro and serve warm in bowls.

Instant Pot Lamb Meatballs

Prep time: 10 minutes | Cook time: 38 minutes | Serves 3
¾ pound (340 g) ground lamb meat
1 teaspoon adobo seasoning
½ tablespoon olive oil
2 small tomatoes, chopped roughly
5 mini bell peppers, deseeded and halved
2 garlic cloves, peeled
½ small yellow onion, chopped roughly
½ cup sugar-free tomato sauce
¼ teaspoon crushed red pepper flakes,
Salt and freshly ground black pepper, to taste
1.	Mix the lamb meat and adobo seasoning in a bowl until well combined. Shape the meat mixture into small meatballs.
2.	Set the Instant Pot on the Sauté mode and heat the olive oil. Add the meatballs to the pot and cook for 3 minutes, or until golden brown. Transfer the meatballs to bowls.
3.	Stir together all the remaining ingredients in the pot. Lock the lid. Select the Meat/Stew mode and set the cooking time for 35 minutes on High Pressure. When the timer beeps, use a natural pressure release for 10 minutes, then release any remaining pressure.
4.	Carefully open the lid. Transfer the vegetable mixture to a blender and pulse until smooth. Spread the vegetable paste over the meatballs and serve hot.

Lamb Biryani with Raisins

Prep time: 45 minutes | Cook time: 16 to 17 minutes | Serves 4
1 pound (454 g) lamb leg steak, cut into cubes
1 large brown onion, thinly sliced
1 green bell pepper, sliced
Juice of ½ lime
½ cup Greek yogurt
4 tablespoons ghee, divided
1 tablespoon garlic paste
1 tablespoon grated ginger
3 teaspoons garam masala
1 teaspoon paprika
¼ teaspoon cayenne pepper
½ teaspoon cardamom powder
½ teaspoon turmeric
Salt, to taste
2 cups warm water
1 cup basmati rice, rinsed
½ cup chopped cilantro
½ teaspoon saffron, soaked in 3 tablespoons of hot water
2 tablespoons red raisins
1.	In a bowl, stir together the lamb, brown onion and bell pepper.
2.	In another bowl, whisk together the lime juice, yogurt, 2 tablespoons of the ghee, garlic, ginger, garam masala, paprika, cayenne pepper, cardamom, turmeric and salt.
3.	Spread the mixture over the meat and vegetables. Stir and cover in plastic. Let marinate in the refrigerator for 30 minutes.
4.	Remove the meat from the refrigerator and drain the marinade.
5.	Press the Sauté button on the Instant Pot and melt the remaining 2 tablespoons of the ghee. Add the lamb and sear for 6 to 7 minutes, or lightly browned. Add the warm water, basmati rice, cilantro and saffron liquid to the pot. Do not stir.
6.	Close and secure the lid. Select the Manual mode and set the cooking time for 10 minutes on High Pressure. When the timer goes off, use a natural pressure release for 10 minutes, then release any remaining pressure.
7.	Carefully open the lid and stir in raisins. Serve immediately.

Lamb Chops in Picante Sauce

Prep time: 5 minutes | Cook time: 40 minutes | Serves 6
6 lamb chops, bone-in
3 tablespoons all-purpose flour
1¼ apples, peeled and sliced
1¼ cups Picante sauce
3 tablespoons brown sugar
3 tablespoons olive oil
1.	In a bowl, place the flour and dip the lamb chops in it to coat well.
2.	In another bowl, combine the apples, Picante sauce and brown sugar until well mixed.
3.	Press the Sauté button on the Instant Pot and heat the olive oil. Add the coated chops to the pot and sear for 5 minutes, or until lightly browned.
4.	Lock the lid. Select the Meat/Stew mode and set the cooking time for 35 minutes on High Pressure.
5.	When the timer beeps, use a natural pressure release for 10 minutes, then release any remaining pressure.

6. Open the lid and serve warm.

Lamb Curry with Tomatoes

Prep time: 15 minutes | Cook time: 59 minutes | Serves 4

¼ cup olive oil, divided
2 pounds (907 g) lamb shoulder, cubed
4 green onions, sliced
2 tomatoes, peeled and chopped
2 tablespoons garlic paste
1 tablespoon ginger paste
1½ cups vegetable stock
2 teaspoons ground coriander
2 teaspoons allspice
1 teaspoon ground cumin
½ teaspoon ground red chili pepper
½ teaspoon curry powder
1 large carrot, sliced
1 potato, cubed
2 bay leaves
Salt, to taste
2 tablespoons mint leaves, chopped

1. Press the Sauté button on the Instant Pot and heat 2 tablespoons of the olive oil. Add the green onions and sauté for 3 minutes, or until softened, stirring constantly. Transfer the green onions to a blender. Mix in the tomatoes, garlic paste and ginger paste. Blend until smooth.
2. Heat the remaining 2 tablespoons of the olive oil in the pot and add the lamb to the pot. Cook for 6 minutes. Stir in the vegetable stock, coriander, allspice, cumin, red chili pepper, curry powder, carrot, potato, bay leaves and salt.
3. Lock the lid. Select the Manual function and set the cooking time for 50 minutes on High Pressure. When the timer beeps, use a natural pressure release for 10 minutes, then release any remaining pressure. Open the lid. Discard the bay leaves.
4. Top with the mint leaves and serve immediately.

Lamb Curry with Zucchini

Prep time: 40 minutes | Cook time: 25 minutes | Serves 3

1 pound (454 g) cubed lamb stew meat
2 garlic cloves, minced
½ cup coconut milk
1 tablespoon grated fresh ginger
½ teaspoon lime juice
¼ teaspoon salt
¼ teaspoon black pepper
1 tablespoon olive oil
1½ medium carrots, sliced
½ medium onion, diced
¾ cup diced tomatoes
½ teaspoon turmeric powder
½ medium zucchini, diced

1. In a bowl, stir together the garlic, coconut milk, ginger, lime juice, salt and pepper. Add the lamb to the bowl and marinate for 30 minutes.
2. Combine the remaining ingredients, except for the zucchini, in the Instant Pot. Add the meat and the marinade to the pot.
3. Set the lid in place. Select the Manual mode and set the cooking time for 20 minutes on High Pressure. Once the timer goes off, use a natural pressure release for 15 minutes, then release any remaining pressure.
4. Open the lid. Add the zucchini to the pot. Select the Sauté mode and cook for 5 minutes.
5. Serve hot.

Lamb Tagine with Carrots

Prep time: 15 minutes | Cook time: 32 to 34 minutes | Serves 4

2 tablespoons ghee
1½ pounds (680 g) lamb stew meat, cubed
4 large carrots, peeled and chopped
1 large red onion, chopped
6 cloves garlic, minced
2 teaspoons coriander powder
2 teaspoons ginger powder
2 teaspoons cumin powder
½ teaspoon turmeric
¼ teaspoon clove powder
¼ teaspoon cinnamon powder
¼ teaspoon red chili flakes
2 bay leaves
1 lemon, zested and juiced
Salt and black pepper, to taste
2 cups vegetable stock
2 cups green olives, pitted
3 tablespoons chopped parsley

1. Select the Sauté setting. Melt the ghee and add the lamb to the pot. Cook for 6 to 7 minutes, or until the lamb is lightly browned. Stir in the carrots, onion and garlic and cook for 5 minutes, or until the vegetables are tender.
2. Add the coriander, ginger, cumin, turmeric, clove, cinnamon, red chili flakes, bay leaves, lemon zest, lemon juice, salt and pepper to the pot. Cook for 1 to 2 minutes, or until fragrant. Pour the vegetable stock into the pot.
3. Lock the lid. Select Manual mode and set the cooking time for 20 minutes on High Pressure. Once cooking is complete, use a natural pressure release for 10 minutes, then release any remaining pressure. Open the lid. Discard the bay leaves and stir in the green olives and parsley.
4. Divide the dish among 4 serving bowls and serve warm.

Lamb with Peppers and Tomatoes

Prep time: 10 minutes | Cook time: 30 minutes | Serves 10

2 tablespoons olive oil
2 pounds (907 g) boneless lamb, trimmed
Salt and black pepper, to taste
4 cups chopped tomatoes
3 cups sugar-free tomato sauce
2 cups water
2 teaspoons crushed dried rosemary
6 garlic cloves, minced

2 large yellow bell peppers, deseeded and sliced
2 large red bell peppers, deseeded and sliced
2 large green bell peppers, deseeded and sliced
1.	Press the Sauté button on the Instant Pot and heat the olive oil. Add the lamb meat to the pot and season with salt and pepper. Cook for 5 minutes. Transfer the lamb meat to a plate.
2.	Stir together all the remaining ingredients in the pot and add the lamb meat.
3.	Lock the lid. Select the Manual function and set the cooking time for 25 minutes at High Pressure.
4.	Once cooking is complete, use a quick pressure release. Open the lid. Serve hot.

Milky Lamb with Potatoes

Prep time: 10 minutes | Cook time: 1 hour | Serves 4

2 pounds (907 g) boneless lamb shoulder, cubed
1 pound (454 g) potatoes, cubed
3 carrots, cubed
5 garlic cloves
2 rosemary sprigs
4 cups milk
2 cups water
1 tablespoon Vegeta seasoning
Salt and black pepper, to taste
1.	Add all the ingredients to the Instant Pot and stir to combine.
2.	Lock the lid. Select the Manual mode and set the cooking time for 60 minutes on High Pressure. Once cooking is complete, use a natural pressure release for 10 minutes, then release any remaining pressure.
3.	Carefully open the lid. Remove and discard the rosemary springs. Divide the dish among four serving bowls and serve warm.

Sauce Glazed Lamb Chops

Prep time: 10 minutes | Cook time: 29 minutes | Serves 2

1½ tablespoons butter
1 pound (454 g) lamb loin chops
½ small onion, sliced
1 garlic clove, crushed
1 cup carrots, peeled and sliced
¾ cup diced sugar-free tomatoes
½ cup bone broth
¾ teaspoon crushed dried rosemary
Salt and black pepper, to taste
1 tablespoon arrowroot starch
½ tablespoon cold water
1.	Select the Sauté mode and heat the butter in the Instant Pot. Add the lamb chops to the pot and cook for 3 minutes on each side, or until lightly browned. Transfer the lamb chops to plates.
2.	Add the onion and garlic to the pot and cook for 3 minutes. Stir in the carrots, tomatoes, bone broth, rosemary, salt and pepper.
3.	Lock the lid. Select the Manual mode and set the cooking time for 15 minutes at High Pressure. When the timer goes off, do a quick pressure release. Carefully open the lid.

4.	In a small bowl, whisk together the arrowroot starch and water. Pour the slurry in the pot. Select the Sauté mode and cook for 5 minutes.
5.	Spread the sauce over the cooked chops and serve hot.

Slow Cooked Lamb Shanks

Prep time: 10 minutes | Cook time: 55 minutes | Serves 4

2 tablespoons olive oil
2 pounds (907 g) lamb shanks
Salt and black pepper, to taste
6 garlic cloves, minced
1 cup chicken broth
¾ cup red wine
2 cups crushed tomatoes
1 teaspoon dried oregano
¼ cup chopped parsley, for garnish
1.	Press the Sauté button on the Instant Pot. Heat the olive oil and add the lamb to the pot. Season with salt and pepper. Sear the lamb on both sides for 6 minutes, or until browned. Transfer the lamb to a plate and set aside.
2.	Add the garlic to the pot and sauté for 30 seconds, or until fragrant. Stir in the chicken broth and red wine and cook for 2 minutes, stirring constantly. Add the tomatoes and oregano. Stir and cook for 2 minutes. Return the lamb to the pot and baste with the chicken broth mixture.
3.	Lock the lid. Select the Manual setting and set the cooking time for 45 minutes on High Pressure.
4.	When the timer beeps, do a natural pressure release for 15 minutes, then release any remaining pressure. Open the lid. Top with the chopped parsley and adjust the taste with salt and pepper.
5.	Divide among 4 plates and serve warm.

Spicy Lamb Shoulder

Prep time: 10 minutes | Cook time: 50 minutes | Serves 4

2 pounds (907 g) lamb shoulder
1 cup chopped fresh thyme
¼ cup rice wine
¼ cup chicken stock
1 tablespoon turmeric
1 tablespoon ground black pepper
1 teaspoon oregano
1 teaspoon paprika
1 teaspoon sugar
1 tablespoon olive oil
½ cup water
4 tablespoons butter
1.	In a large bowl, whisk together the thyme, rice wine, chicken stock, turmeric, black pepper, oregano, paprika and sugar. Rub all sides of the lamb shoulder with the spice mix.
2.	Press the Sauté button on the Instant Pot and heat the oil. Add the lamb to the pot and sear for 5 minutes on both sides, or until browned. Add the remaining spice mixture, water and butter to the pot. Stir until the butter is melted.

3.	Lock the lid. Select the Manual mode and set the cooking time for 45 minutes on High Pressure. Once cooking is complete, do a natural pressure release for 10 minutes, then release any remaining pressure. Carefully open the lid.
4.	Serve hot.

Spicy Lamb with Anchovies

Prep time: 10 minutes | Cook time: 1 hour 5 minutes | Serves 4

2 tablespoons olive oil
2 pounds (907 g) boneless lamb shoulder, cut into 4 pieces
2 cups chicken stock
6 tinned anchovies, chopped
1 teaspoon garlic purée
3 green chilies, minced
1 sprig rosemary
1 teaspoon dried oregano
Salt, to taste
2 tablespoons chopped parsley
1.	Press the Sauté button on the Instant Pot. Heat the olive oil and sear the lamb shoulder on both sides for 5 minutes, or until browned. Transfer the lamb to a plate and set aside.
2.	Pour the chicken stock into the Instant Pot and add the anchovies and garlic. Return the lamb to the pot and sprinkle the green chilies, rosemary, oregano and salt on top.
3.	Set the lid in place, select the Manual mode and set the cooking time for 60 minutes on High Pressure.
4.	When the timer goes off, use a natural pressure release for 15 minutes, then release any remaining pressure.
5.	Open the lid, shred the lamb with two forks and top with the chopped parsley. Serve warm.

Spicy Minced Lamb Meat

Prep time: 10 minutes | Cook time: 20 minutes | Serves 2

½ pound (227 g) ground lamb meat
½ cup onion, chopped
½ tablespoon minced ginger
½ tablespoon garlic
½ teaspoon salt
¼ teaspoon ground coriander
¼ teaspoon cayenne pepper
¼ teaspoon cumin
¼ teaspoon turmeric
1.	Press the Sauté button on the Instant Pot. Add the onion, ginger and garlic to the pot and sauté for 5 minutes. Add the remaining ingredients to the pot and lock the lid.
2.	Select the Manual mode and set the cooking time for 15 minutes on High Pressure. Once the timer goes off, perform a natural pressure release for 15 minutes.
3.	Open the lid and serve immediately.

Sumptuous Lamb Casserole

Prep time: 15 minutes | Cook time: 41 minutes | Serves 2 to 4

1 pound (454 g) lamb stew meat, cubed
1 tablespoon olive oil
3 cloves garlic, minced
2 tomatoes, chopped
2 carrots, chopped
1 onion, chopped
1 pound (454 g) baby potatoes
1 celery stalk, chopped
2 cups chicken stock
2 tablespoons red wine
2 tablespoons ketchup
1 teaspoon ground cumin
1 teaspoon sweet paprika
¼ teaspoon dried rosemary
¼ teaspoon dried oregano
Salt and ground black pepper, to taste
1.	Press the Sauté button on the Instant Pot and heat the oil. Add the lamb to the pot and sear for 5 minutes, or until lightly browned. Add the garlic and sauté for 1 minute. Add all the remaining ingredients to the pot.
2.	Set the lid in place. Select the Manual mode and set the cooking time for 35 minutes on High Pressure. Once cooking is complete, perform a natural pressure release for 10 minutes, then release any remaining pressure. Carefully open the lid.
3.	Serve hot.

Traditional Lamb Rogan Josh

Prep time: 15 minutes | Cook time: 35 to 37 minutes | Serves 4

2 tablespoons ghee
1 large onion, chopped
2 pounds (907 g) boneless lamb shoulder, cubed
4 teaspoons chili powder
3 teaspoons coriander powder
2 teaspoons minced ginger
1 teaspoon garam masala
1 teaspoon turmeric
½ teaspoon cinnamon powder
½ teaspoon cardamom powder
¼ teaspoon ground cloves
¼ teaspoon cumin powder
10 garlic cloves, minced
1 bay leaf
Salt and black pepper, to taste
1 (15-ounce / 425-g) can tomato sauce
8 tablespoons plain yogurt
1 cup water
3 tablespoons chopped cilantro
1.	Select the Sauté mode. Melt the ghee and add the onion and lamb to the pot. Cook for 6 to 7 minutes, or until the lamb is lightly browned.
2.	Add the chili powder, coriander, ginger, garam masala, turmeric, cinnamon, cardamom, cloves, cumin, garlic, bay leaf, salt and pepper to the pot. Cook for 3 minutes, or until fragrant.
3.	Stir in the tomato sauce and cook for 2 to 3 minutes. Add the yogurt, 1 tablespoon at a time, stirring to combine. Pour the water in the pot.
4.	Lock the lid. Select Manual mode and set the cooking time for 20 minutes on High Pressure.
5.	When the timer goes off, do a natural pressure release for 10 minutes, then release any

remaining pressure. Open the lid and select the Sauté mode. Cook for another 4 minutes to boil off some liquid until the consistency is stew-like.
6.	Divide the dish among 4 bowls. Top with the chopped cilantro and serve warm.

Creamy Lamb Curry

Prep time: 10 minutes | Cook time: 30 minutes | Serves 4

1 teaspoon curry paste
2 tablespoons coconut cream
¼ teaspoon chili powder
1 pound (454 g) lamb shoulder, chopped
1 tablespoon fresh cilantro, chopped
½ cup heavy cream
1.	In a bowl, mix the curry paste and coconut cream.
2.	Add the chili powder and chopped lamb shoulder. Toss to coat the lamb in the curry mixture well.
3.	Transfer the lamb and all remaining curry paste mixture in the Instant Pot. Add cilantro and heavy cream.
4.	Close the lid and select Manual mode. Set cooking time for 30 minutes on High Pressure.
5.	When timer beeps, do a quick pressure release. Open the lid.
6.	Serve warm.

Easy Lamb Burgers

Prep time: 10 minutes | Cook time: 14 minutes | Serves 2

10 ounces (283 g) ground lamb
½ teaspoon chili powder
1 teaspoon dried cilantro
1 teaspoon garlic powder
½ teaspoon salt
¼ cup water
1 tablespoon coconut oil
1.	In a mixing bowl, mix the ground lamb, chili powder, dried cilantro, garlic powder, salt, and water.
2.	Shape the mixture into 2 burgers.
3.	Melt the coconut oil on Sauté mode.
4.	Put the burgers in the hot oil and cook for 7 minutes on each side or until well browned.
5.	Serve immediately.

Greek Lamb Leg

Prep time: 10 minutes | Cook time: 50 minutes | Serves 4

1 pound (454 g) lamb leg
½ teaspoon dried thyme
1 teaspoon paprika powder
¼ teaspoon cumin seeds
1 tablespoon softened butter
2 garlic cloves
¼ cup water
1.	Rub the lamb leg with dried thyme, paprika powder, and cumin seeds on a clean work surface.
2.	Brush the leg with softened butter and transfer to the Instant Pot. Add garlic cloves and water.

3.	Close the lid. Select Manual mode and set cooking time for 50 minutes on High Pressure.
4.	When timer beeps, use a quick pressure release. Open the lid.
5.	Serve warm.

Harissa Lamb

Prep time: 30 minutes | Cook time: 40 minutes | Serves 4

1 tablespoon keto-friendly Harissa sauce
1 teaspoon dried thyme
½ teaspoon salt
1 pound (454 g) lamb shoulder
2 tablespoons sesame oil
2 cups water
1.	In a bowl, mix the Harissa, dried thyme, and salt.
2.	Rub the lamb shoulder with the Harissa mixture and brush with sesame oil.
3.	Heat the the Instant Pot on Sauté mode for 2 minutes and put the lamb shoulder inside.
4.	Cook the lamb for 3 minutes on each side, then pour in the water.
5.	Close the lid. Select Manual mode and set cooking time for 40 minutes on High Pressure.
6.	When timer beeps, use a natural pressure release for 25 minutes, then release any remaining pressure. Open the lid.
7.	Serve warm.

Icelandic Lamb with Turnip

Prep time: 5 minutes | Cook time: 45 minutes | Serves 4

12 ounces (340 g) lamb fillet, chopped
4 ounces (113 g) turnip, chopped
3 ounces (85 g) celery ribs, chopped
1 teaspoon unsweetened tomato purée
¼ cup scallions, chopped
½ teaspoon salt
½ teaspoon ground black pepper
4 cups water
1.	Put all ingredients in the Instant Pot and stir well.
2.	Close the lid. Select Manual mode and set cooking time for 45 minutes on High Pressure.
3.	When timer beeps, use a quick pressure release. Open the lid.
4.	Serve hot.

Indian Lamb Korma

Prep time: 15 minutes | Cook time: 25 minutes | Serves 6

1 (6-inch) Anaheim chile, minced
1 clove garlic, grated
½ medium onion, chopped
2 tablespoons coconut oil
½ teaspoon grated fresh ginger
1 teaspoon garam masala
¼ teaspoon ground cardamom
Pinch of ground cinnamon
2 teaspoons ground cumin
1 teaspoon coriander seeds
1 teaspoon sea salt

½ teaspoon cayenne pepper
½ tablespoon unsweetened tomato purée
1 cup chicken broth
3 pounds (1.4 kg) lamb shoulder, cut into 1-inch cubes
¼ cup full-fat coconut milk
½ cup full-fat Greek yogurt
1.	Preheat the Instant Pot on Sauté mode. Add the chile, garlic, onion, coconut oil, and ginger and sauté for 2 minutes.
2.	Add the garam masala, cardamom, cinnamon, cumin, coriander seeds, salt, cayenne, and unsweetened tomato purée and sauté for a minute or until fragrant.
3.	Pour in the broth. Add the lamb and stir well.
4.	Secure the lid. Press the Manual button and set cooking time for 15 minutes on High Pressure.
5.	When timer beeps, quick release the pressure. Open the lid.
6.	Stir in the coconut milk and yogurt. Switch to Sauté mode and bring the mixture to a simmer for 5 minutes, stirring occasionally until thickened.
7.	Serve hot.

Herbed Lamb Shank

Prep time: 15 minutes | Cook time: 35 minutes | Serves 2

2 lamb shanks
1 rosemary spring
1 teaspoon coconut flour
¼ teaspoon onion powder
¼ teaspoon chili powder
¾ teaspoon ground ginger
½ cup beef broth
½ teaspoon avocado oil
1.	Put all ingredients in the Instant Pot. Stir to mix well.
2.	Close the lid. Select Manual mode and set cooking time for 35 minutes on High Pressure.
3.	When timer beeps, use a natural pressure release for 15 minutes, then release any remaining pressure. Open the lid.
4.	Discard the rosemary sprig and serve warm.

Lamb and Tomato Bhuna

Prep time: 15 minutes | Cook time: 20 minutes | Serves 2

¼ teaspoon minced ginger
¼ teaspoon garlic paste
1 teaspoon coconut oil
¼ cup crushed tomatoes
10 ounces (283 g) lamb fillet, chopped
2 ounces (57 g) scallions, chopped
¼ cup water
1.	Put the minced ginger, garlic paste, coconut oil, and crushed tomatoes in the Instant Pot. Sauté for 10 minutes on Sauté mode.
2.	Add the chopped lamb fillet, scallions, and water.
3.	Select Manual mode and set cooking time for 10 minutes on High Pressure.

4.	When timer beeps, use a natural pressure release for 15 minutes, then release any remaining pressure. Open the lid.
5.	Serve warm.

Lamb Kleftiko with Turnip

Prep time: 25 minutes | Cook time: 50 minutes | Serves 6

¼ cup apple cider vinegar
½ cup chicken broth
1 tablespoon lemon juice
½ teaspoon lemon zest
½ teaspoon fresh thyme
1 pound (454 g) lamb shoulder, chopped
½ cup turnip, chopped
1.	In the mixing bowl, mix the apple cider vinegar, chicken broth, lemon juice, lemon zest, and thyme.
2.	Put the lamb shoulder in the Instant Pot. Add the lemon juice mixture and turnip.
3.	Close the lid. Select Manual mode and set cooking time for 50 minutes on High Pressure.
4.	When the time is over, use a natural pressure release for 20 minutes, then release any remaining pressure. Open the lid.
5.	Serve warm.

Lamb Koobideh

Prep time: 15 minutes | Cook time: 30 minutes | Serves 4

1 pound (454 g) ground lamb
1 egg, beaten
1 tablespoon lemon juice
1 teaspoon ground turmeric
½ teaspoon garlic powder
1 teaspoon chives, chopped
½ teaspoon ground black pepper
1 cup water
1.	In a mixing bowl, combine all the ingredients except for water.
2.	Shape the mixture into meatballs and press into ellipse shape.
3.	Pour the water and insert the trivet in the Instant Pot.
4.	Put the prepared ellipse meatballs in a baking pan and transfer on the trivet.
5.	Close the lid and select Manual mode. Set cooking time for 30 minutes on High Pressure.
6.	When timer beeps, make a quick pressure release. Open the lid.
7.	Serve immediately.

Lamb Kofta Curry

Prep time: 15 minutes | Cook time: 20 minutes | Serves 4

1 pound (454 g) ground lamb
4 ounces (113 g) scallions, chopped
1 tablespoon curry powder, divided
½ teaspoon chili flakes
1 tablespoon dried cilantro
1 tablespoon coconut oil
1 cup chicken broth
$^1/_3$ cup coconut cream

1. In a mixing bowl, mix the ground lamb, scallions, and ½ tablespoon of curry powder.
2. Add chili flakes and dried cilantro. Stir the mixture until homogenous and shape the mixture into medium size koftas (meatballs).
3. Heat the coconut oil in the Instant Pot on Sauté mode until melted.
4. Put the koftas in the hot oil and cook for 2 minutes on each side.
5. Meanwhile, mix the chicken broth, coconut cream and remaining curry powder in a small bowl.
6. Pour the mixture over the koftas.
7. Select Manual mode and set timer for 12 minutes on High Pressure.
8. When timer beeps, use a natural pressure release for 10 minutes, then release any remaining pressure. Open the lid.
9. Serve warm.

Lamb Rostelle

Prep time: 20 minutes | Cook time: 30 minutes | Serves 4

1 pound (454 g) lamb loin, slice into strips
½ teaspoon apple cider vinegar
1 teaspoon ground black pepper
1 teaspoon olive oil
½ teaspoon salt
1 cup water, for cooking
1. Combine the apple cider vinegar, ground black pepper, olive oil, and salt in a bowl. Stir to mix well.
2. Put the lamb strips in the bowl and toss to coat well.
3. Run the lamb strips through four skewers and put in a baking pan.
4. Pour water in the Instant Pot and then insert the trivet.
5. Put the baking pan on the trivet. Close the lid.
6. Select Manual mode and set cooking time for 30 minutes on High Pressure.
7. When timer beeps, use a natural pressure release for 10 minutes, then release any remaining pressure. Open the lid.
8. Serve immediately.

Lamb Sirloin Masala

Prep time: 10 minutes | Cook time: 25 minutes | Serves 3

12 ounces (340 g) lamb sirloin, sliced
1 tablespoon garam masala
1 tablespoon lemon juice
1 tablespoon olive oil
¼ cup coconut cream
1. Sprinkle the sliced lamb sirloin with garam masala, lemon juice, olive oil, and coconut cream in a large bowl. Toss to mix well.
2. Transfer the mixture in the Instant Pot. Cook on Sauté mode for 25 minutes. Flip the lamb for every 5 minutes.
3. When cooking is complete, allow to cool for 10 minutes, then serve warm.

Simple Roast Lamb Leg

Prep time: 10 minutes | Cook time: 25 minutes | Serves 3

14 ounces (397 g) lamb leg, roughly chopped
1 teaspoon dried thyme
1 teaspoon ground black pepper
1 tablespoon sesame oil
¼ cup beef broth
½ cup water
1. Rub the lamb leg with thyme, ground black pepper, and sesame oil on a clean work surface.
2. Put the leg in the Instant Pot, add beef broth and water.
3. Close the lid. Select Manual mode and set cooking time for 25 minutes on High Pressure.
4. When timer beeps, make a quick pressure release. Open the lid.
5. Serve warm.

Pesto Lamb Rack

Prep time: 15 minutes | Cook time: 45 minutes | Serves 4

1 pound (454 g) lamb rack
2 tablespoons pesto sauce
1 teaspoon chili powder
1 tablespoon coconut oil
1 cup water
1. Rub the lamb rack with pesto sauce and chili powder. Let sit for 15 minutes to marinate.
2. Heat the coconut oil in the Instant Pot on Sauté mode for 3 minutes.
3. Put the marinated lamb in the hot oil and cook on Sauté mode for 4 minutes on each side. Pour in the water.
4. Close the lid. Select Manual mode and set cooking time for 45 minutes on High Pressure.
5. When timer beeps, use a quick pressure release. Open the lid.
6. Serve immediately.

CHAPTER 13 SOUPS, STEWS, AND CHILIS

Authentic Pozole

Prep time: 20 minutes | Cook time: 53 minutes | Serves 6

2½ pounds (1.1 kg) boneless pork shoulder, cut into pieces
1 teaspoon salt, divided
1 teaspoon ground black pepper, divided
2 tablespoons vegetable oil
2 medium yellow onions, peeled and chopped
2 medium poblano peppers, deseeded and diced
1 chipotle pepper in adobo, minced
4 cloves garlic, peeled and minced
1 cinnamon stick
1 tablespoon smoked paprika
2 teaspoons chili powder
1 teaspoon dried oregano
1 teaspoon ground cumin
½ teaspoon ground coriander
1 (12-ounce / 340-g) can lager-style beer
4 cups chicken broth
2 (15-ounce / 425-g) cans hominy, drained and rinsed
1 tablespoon lime juice
½ cup chopped cilantro
1.　　Season the pork pieces with ½ teaspoon of the salt and ½ teaspoon of the pepper.
2.　　Press the Sauté button on the Instant Pot and heat the oil. Add half the pork to the pot in an even layer, making sure there is space between pieces to prevent steam from forming. Sear the pork for 3 minutes on each side, or until lightly browned. Remove the pork to a plate. Repeat with the remaining pork.
3.　　Add the onions and poblano peppers to the pot and sauté for 5 minutes, or until just softened. Add the chipotle pepper, garlic, cinnamon, paprika, chili powder, oregano, cumin and coriander to the pot. Sauté for 1 minute, or until fragrant.
4.　　Return the pork to the pot and turn to coat with the spices. Pour in the beer and chicken broth.
5.　　Lock the lid. Select the Manual mode and set the cooking time for 35 minutes on High Pressure. When the timer beeps, perform a natural pressure release for 20 minutes, then release any remaining pressure. Carefully open the lid.
6.　　Season with the remaining ½ teaspoon of the salt and ½ teaspoon of the pepper. Stir in the hominy, lime juice and cilantro. Serve hot.

Bean and Carrot Chili

Prep time: 10 minutes | Cook time: 41 minutes | Serves 4

1 tablespoon olive oil
1 small red onion, peeled and diced
1 medium green bell pepper, deseeded and diced
1 large carrot, peeled and diced
4 cloves garlic, peeled and minced
1 small jalapeño, deseeded and diced
1 (28-ounce / 794-g) can diced tomatoes, undrained
1 (15-ounce / 425-g) can cannellini beans, drained and rinsed
1 (15-ounce / 425-g) can kidney beans, drained and rinsed
1 (15-ounce / 425-g) can black beans, drained and rinsed
2 tablespoons chili powder
1 teaspoon ground cumin
1 teaspoon salt
¼ cup vegetable broth
1.　　Press the Sauté button on the Instant Pot and heat the oil. Add the onion, bell pepper and carrot to the pot and sauté for 5 minutes, or until the onion is translucent. Add the garlic and sauté for 1 minute.
2.　　Stir in the remaining ingredients.
3.　　Set the lid in place. Select the Meat/Stew setting and set the cooking time for 35 minutes on High Pressure. When the timer goes off, perform a natural pressure release for 15 minutes, then release any remaining pressure. Open the lid.
4.　　Ladle the chili into 4 bowls and serve warm.

Beef and Mushroom Chili

Prep time: 15 minutes | Cook time: 40 minutes | Serves 6

1 tablespoon olive oil
1 pound (454 g) beef stew cubes
1 medium onion, peeled and diced
4 cloves garlic, minced
½ cup beef broth
1 (16-ounce / 454-g) can chili beans, undrained
1 (14.5-ounce / 411-g) can diced tomatoes, undrained
2 cups sliced mushrooms
2 tablespoons tomato paste
2 tablespoons chili powder
1 tablespoon Italian seasoning
1 teaspoon red pepper flakes
1 teaspoon sea salt
½ teaspoon ground black pepper
1.　　Press the Sauté button on the Instant Pot and heat the oil. Add the beef stew cubes and onion to the pot and sauté for 3 minutes, or until the beef is lightly browned and the onion is translucent. Add the garlic to the pot and sauté for 2 minutes.
2.　　Pour in the beef broth and deglaze by scraping any of the bits from the bottom and sides of the pot. Stir in the remaining ingredients.
3.　　Set the lid in place. Select the Meat/Stew setting and set the cooking time for 35 minutes on High Pressure. Once cooking is complete, do a natural pressure release for 15 minutes, then release any remaining pressure. Open the lid.
4.　　Ladle the chili into individual bowls and serve warm.

Beef and Vegetable Stew

Prep time: 15 minutes | Cook time: 46 minutes | Serves 6

2 tablespoons olive oil

2 pounds (907 g) beef stew cubes
1 medium sweet onion, peeled and diced
4 cloves garlic, peeled and minced
3 cups beef broth
½ cup dry red wine
1 (14.5-ounce / 411-g) can crushed tomatoes, undrained
2 medium carrots, peeled and diced
2 medium Russet potatoes, scrubbed and small-diced
1 stalk celery, chopped
2 tablespoons chopped fresh rosemary
1 teaspoon salt
½ teaspoon ground black pepper
2 tablespoons gluten-free all-purpose flour
4 tablespoons water
¼ cup chopped fresh Italian flat-leaf parsley
1.	Press the Sauté button on the Instant Pot and heat the oil. Add the beef and onion to the pot and sauté for 5 minutes, or until the beef is seared and the onion is translucent. Add the garlic and sauté for 1 minute.
2.	Pour in the beef broth and wine and deglaze the pot by scraping up any bits from the sides and bottom of the pot.
3.	Stir in the tomatoes with juice, carrots, potatoes, celery, rosemary, salt and pepper.
4.	Set the lid in place. Select the Meat/Stew setting and set the cooking time for 35 minutes on High Pressure. When the timer goes off, perform a natural pressure release for 10 minutes, then release any remaining pressure. Open the lid.
5.	Create a slurry by whisking together the flour and water in a small bowl. Add the slurry to the pot. Select the Sauté mode and let simmer for 5 minutes, stirring constantly.
6.	Ladle the stew into 6 bowls and serve topped with the parsley.

Beef and Pork Chili

Prep time: 10 minutes | Cook time: 40 minutes | Serves 4

1 tablespoon olive oil
½ pound (227 g) ground beef
½ pound (227 g) ground pork
1 medium onion, peeled and diced
1 (28-ounce / 794-g) can puréed tomatoes, undrained
1 large carrot, peeled and diced
1 small green bell pepper, deseeded and diced
1 small jalapeño, deseeded and diced
3 cloves garlic, minced
2 tablespoons chili powder
1 teaspoon sea salt
2 teaspoons ground black pepper
1.	Press the Sauté button on the Instant Pot and heat the olive oil. Add the ground beef, ground pork and onion to the pot and sauté for 5 minutes, or until the pork is no longer pink.
2.	Stir in the remaining ingredients.
3.	Close and secure the lid. Select the Meat/Stew setting and set the cooking time for 35 minutes on High Pressure. Once cooking is complete, use a natural pressure release for 15 minutes, then release any remaining pressure. Open the lid.

4.	Serve warm.

Beef Chili with Onions

Prep time: 20 minutes | Cook time: 19 minutes | Serves 8

2 pounds (907 g) 90% lean ground beef
3 large yellow onions, peeled and diced, divided
3 cloves garlic, peeled and minced
2 (16-ounce / 454-g) cans kidney beans, rinsed and drained
1 (15-ounce / 425-g) can tomato sauce
1 cup beef broth
2 tablespoons semisweet chocolate chips
2 tablespoons honey
2 tablespoons red wine vinegar
2 tablespoons chili powder
1 tablespoon pumpkin pie spice
1 teaspoon ground cumin
½ teaspoon ground cardamom
½ teaspoon salt
½ teaspoon freshly cracked black pepper
¼ teaspoon ground cloves
1 pound (454 g) cooked spaghetti
4 cups shredded Cheddar cheese
1.	Press the Sauté button on the Instant Pot. Add the ground beef and ¾ of the diced onions to the pot and sauté for 8 minutes, or until the beef is browned and the onions are transparent. Drain the beef mixture and discard any excess fat. Add the garlic to the pot and sauté for 30 seconds.
2.	Stir in the remaining ingredients, except for the reserved onions, spaghetti and cheese. Cook for 1 minute, or until fragrant.
3.	Set the lid in place. Select the Manual mode and set the cooking time for 10 minutes on High Pressure. When the timer goes off, perform a quick pressure release. Carefully open the lid.
4.	Serve over the cooked spaghetti and top with the reserved onions and cheese.

Beef Chili with Pinto Beans

Prep time: 20 minutes | Cook time: 40 minutes | Serves 8

1 pound (454 g) 80% lean ground beef
1 medium onion, peeled and chopped
2 cloves garlic, peeled and minced
¼ cup chili powder
2 tablespoons brown sugar
1 teaspoon ground cumin
½ teaspoon ground coriander
½ teaspoon salt
½ teaspoon ground black pepper
1 (14.5-ounce / 411-g) can diced tomatoes
2 cups dried pinto beans, soaked overnight in water and drained
2 cups beef broth
1 tablespoon lime juice
1.	Press the Sauté button on the Instant Pot and brown the beef for 10 minutes, or until no pink remains. Add the onion, garlic, chili powder, brown sugar, cumin, coriander, salt and pepper to the pot and sauté for 10 minutes, or until the onion is just softened.

2.	Stir in the tomatoes, soaked beans and beef broth.
3.	Lock the lid. Select the Manual mode and set the cooking time for 20 minutes on High Pressure. When the timer goes off, do a natural pressure release for 20 minutes, then release any remaining pressure. Carefully open the lid.
4.	Add the lime juice and stir well. Serve hot.

Beer Chipotle Chili

Prep time: 15 minutes | Cook time: 55 minutes | Serves 8

2 pounds (907 g) chili meat, made from chuck roast
1 medium onion, peeled and chopped
3 cloves garlic, peeled and minced
3 tablespoons minced chipotle in adobo
2 tablespoons chili powder
2 tablespoons light brown sugar
1 teaspoon ground cumin
½ teaspoon ground coriander
½ teaspoon salt
½ teaspoon ground black pepper
2 cups beef broth
1 (12-ounce / 340-g) bottle lager-style beer
½ cup water
¼ cup corn masa
1 tablespoon lime juice
1.	Press the Sauté button on the Instant Pot and brown the chili meat for 10 minutes. Add the onion, garlic, chipotle, chili powder, brown sugar, cumin, coriander, salt and pepper to the pot and cook for 10 minutes, or until the onion is just softened.
2.	Pour in the beef broth and beer and stir well.
3.	Lock the lid. Select the Bean/Chili mode and set the cooking time for 30 minutes on High Pressure. When the timer goes off, perform a quick pressure release. Carefully open the lid.
4.	Select the Sauté mode. Whisk in the water and masa and cook for 5 minutes, stirring constantly, or until it starts to thicken.
5.	Stir in the lime juice. Serve hot.

Black Bean and Quinoa Chili

Prep time: 10 minutes | Cook time: 16 minutes | Serves 6

1 tablespoon vegetable oil
1 medium onion, peeled and chopped
1 medium red bell pepper, deseeded and chopped
2 cloves garlic, peeled and minced
3 tablespoons chili powder
1 teaspoon ground cumin
½ teaspoon salt
½ teaspoon ground black pepper
2 cups vegetable broth
1 cup water
¾ cup quinoa
2 (15-ounce / 425-g) cans black beans, drained and rinsed
1.	Press the Sauté button on the Instant Pot and heat the oil. Add the onion and bell pepper to the pot and sauté for 5 minutes, or until tender. Add the

garlic, chili powder, cumin, salt and black pepper to the pot and sauté for 1 minute, or until fragrant.
2.	Stir in the remaining ingredients.
3.	Lock the lid. Select the Manual mode and set the cooking time for 10 minutes on High Pressure. When the timer goes off, do a quick pressure release. Carefully open the lid.
4.	Serve hot.

Carrot and Cabbage Beef Stew

Prep time: 10 minutes | Cook time: 19 minutes | Serves 4 to 6

3 tablespoons extra-virgin olive oil
2 large carrots, peeled and sliced into ¼-inch disks and then quartered
1 large Spanish onion, diced
2 pounds (907 g) ground beef
3 cloves garlic, minced
1 (46-ounce / 1.3-kg) can tomato juice
2 cups vegetable broth
Juice of 2 lemons
1 head cabbage, cored and roughly chopped
½ cup jasmine rice
¼ cup dark brown sugar
1 tablespoon Worcestershire sauce
2 teaspoons seasoned salt
1 teaspoon black pepper
3 bay leaves
1.	Set the Instant Pot to the Sauté mode and heat the oil for 3 minutes. Add the carrots and onion to the pot and sauté for 3 minutes, or until just tender. Add the ground beef and garlic to the pot and sauté for 3 minutes, or until the beef is lightly browned. Stir in the remaining ingredients.
2.	Lock the lid. Select the Manual mode and set the cooking time for 10 minutes on High Pressure. When the timer goes off, perform a quick pressure release. Carefully open the lid.
3.	Let rest for 5 minutes to thicken and cool before serving.

Cheesy Beef Soup

Prep time: 10 minutes | Cook time: 16 minutes | Serves 4

1 tablespoon olive oil
1 pound (454 g) ground beef
1 medium yellow onion, peeled and diced
1 small green bell pepper, deseeded and diced
1 medium carrot peeled and shredded
1 (15-ounce / 425-g) can diced tomatoes, undrained
2 teaspoons yellow mustard
1 teaspoon garlic powder
1 teaspoon smoked paprika
½ teaspoon salt
4 cups beef broth
2 cups shredded iceberg lettuce
1 cup shredded Cheddar cheese, divided
½ cup diced dill pickles
1.	Set the Instant Pot to the Sauté mode and heat the olive oil for 30 seconds. Add the beef, onion and green bell pepper to the pot and sauté for 5 minutes, or until the beef is lightly browned. Add the carrot and sauté for 1 minute.

2.	Stir in the tomatoes with juice, mustard, garlic powder, paprika, salt and beef broth.
3.	Close and secure the lid. Select the Manual mode and set the cooking time for 7 minutes on High Pressure. When the timer goes off, use a quick pressure release. Carefully open the lid.
4.	Whisk in the lettuce and ½ cup of the cheese. Select the Sauté mode and cook for 3 minutes.
5.	Divide the soup among 4 bowls and serve topped with the remaining ½ cup of the cheese and dill pickles.

Cheesy Veggie Orzo Soup

Prep time: 15 minutes | Cook time: 10 minutes | Serves 4

1 medium potato, peeled and small-diced
1 medium zucchini, diced
1 small carrot, peeled and diced
1 small yellow onion, peeled and diced
2 stalks celery, diced
1 (15-ounce / 425-g) can diced tomatoes, undrained
2 cloves garlic, peeled and minced
½ cup gluten-free orzo
5 cups vegetable broth
2 teaspoons dried oregano leaves
2 teaspoons dried thyme leaves
1 teaspoon salt
1 teaspoon ground black pepper
3 cups fresh baby spinach
4 tablespoons grated Parmesan cheese

1.	Add all the ingredients, except for the spinach and Parmesan cheese, to the Instant Pot.
2.	Lock the lid. Select the Manual setting and set the cooking time for 10 minutes at High Pressure. Once the timer goes off, use a quick pressure release. Carefully open the lid.
3.	Stir in the spinach until wilted.
4.	Ladle the soup into four bowls and garnish with the Parmesan cheese. Serve warm.

Chicken Soup with Egg Noodles

Prep time: 15 minutes | Cook time: 24 minutes | Serves 8

1 (3½-pound / 1.5-kg) chicken, cut into pieces
4 cups low-sodium chicken broth
3 stalks celery, chopped
2 medium carrots, peeled and chopped
1 medium yellow onion, peeled and chopped
1 clove garlic, and smashed
1 bay leaf
1 teaspoon poultry seasoning
½ teaspoon dried thyme
1 teaspoon salt
¼ teaspoon ground black pepper
4 ounces (113 g) dried egg noodles

1.	Add all the ingredients, except for the egg noodles, to the Instant Pot and stir to combine.
2.	Set the lid in place. Select the Soup mode and set the cooking time for 20 minutes at High Pressure. Once cooking is complete, use a natural pressure release for 20 to 25 minutes, then release any remaining pressure. Carefully open the lid.

3.	Remove and discard the bay leaf. Transfer the chicken to a clean work surface. Shred chicken and discard the skin and bones. Return the shredded chicken to the pot and stir to combine. Stir in the noodles.
4.	Lock the lid. Select the Manual mode and set the cooking time for 4 minutes at High Pressure. Once cooking is complete, use a quick pressure release. Carefully open the lid.
5.	Serve hot.

Chickpea and Lamb Soup

Prep time: 10 minutes | Cook time: 13 minutes | Serves 4

1 tablespoon olive oil
1 pound (454 g) ground lamb
1 medium red onion, peeled and diced
1 medium carrot, peeled and shredded
3 cloves garlic, peeled and minced
1 (15-ounce / 425-g) can diced tomatoes, undrained
1 (15.5-ounce / 439-g) can chickpeas, rinsed and drained
4 cups chicken broth
½ teaspoon ground ginger
½ teaspoon turmeric
½ teaspoon salt
¼ teaspoon ground cinnamon
½ cup chopped fresh cilantro
4 tablespoons plain full-fat Greek yogurt

1.	Set the Instant Pot to the Sauté mode and heat the olive oil. Add the lamb and onion to the pot and sauté for 5 minutes, or until the lamb is lightly browned. Add the carrot and garlic to the pot and sauté for 1 minute.
2.	Stir in the remaining ingredients, except for the cilantro and Greek yogurt.
3.	Set the lid in place. Select the Manual mode and set the cooking time for 7 minutes on High Pressure. When the timer goes off, perform a quick pressure release. Carefully open the lid.
4.	Ladle the soup into 4 bowls and garnish with the cilantro and yogurt. Serve warm.

Chinese Pork Belly Stew

Prep time: 10 minutes | Cook time: 42 minutes | Serves 8

½ cup plus 2 tablespoons soy sauce, divided
¼ cup Chinese cooking wine
½ cup packed light brown sugar
2 pounds (907 g) pork belly, skinned and cubed
12 scallions, cut into pieces
3 cloves garlic, minced
3 tablespoons vegetable oil
1 teaspoon Chinese five-spice powder
2 cups vegetable broth
4 cups cooked white rice

1.	In a large bowl, whisk together ½ cup of the soy sauce, wine and brown sugar. Place the pork into the bowl and turn to coat evenly. Cover in plastic and refrigerate for at least 4 hours. Drain the pork and pat dry. Reserve the marinade.
2.	Press the Sauté button on the Instant Pot and heat the oil. Add half the pork to the pot in an

even layer, making sure there is space between pork cubes to prevent steam from forming. Sear the pork for 3 minutes on each side, or until lightly browned. Transfer the browned pork to a plate. Repeat with the remaining pork.
3.	Stir in the remaining ingredients, except for the rice. Return the browned pork to the pot with the reserved marinade.
4.	Lock the lid. Select the Manual mode and set the cooking time for 30 minutes on High Pressure. When the timer beeps, perform a natural pressure release for 20 minutes, then release any remaining pressure. Carefully open the lid.
5.	Serve hot over cooked rice.

Coconut Red Bean Soup

Prep time: 10 minutes | Cook time: 50 minutes | Serves 4

2 teaspoons olive oil
3 slices bacon, diced
2 large carrots, peeled and diced
5 green onions, sliced
1 stalk celery, chopped
1 Scotch bonnet, deseeded, veins removed and minced
1 (15-ounce / 425-g) can diced tomatoes, undrained
½ pound (227 g) dried small red beans
1 (13.5-ounce / 383-g) can coconut milk
2 cups chicken broth
1 tablespoon Jamaican jerk seasoning
1 teaspoon salt
4 cups cooked basmati rice
1 cup chopped fresh parsley
1 lime, quartered
1.	Press the Sauté button on the Instant Pot and heat the oil. Add the bacon, carrots, onions, celery and Scotch bonnet to the pot and sauté for 5 minutes, or until the onions are translucent.
2.	Stir in the tomatoes with juice, red beans, coconut milk, chicken broth, Jamaican jerk seasoning and salt.
3.	Lock the lid. Select the Manual mode and set the cooking time for 45 minutes on High Pressure. When the timer goes off, do a natural pressure release for 10 minutes, then release any remaining pressure. Carefully open the lid.
4.	Ladle the soup into four bowls over cooked rice and garnish with parsley. Squeeze a quarter of lime over each bowl. Serve warm.

Creamy Crab Soup

Prep time: 10 minutes | Cook time: 21 minutes | Serves 4

4 tablespoons unsalted butter
2 large carrots, peeled and diced
1 cup chopped leeks
2 stalks celery, chopped
4 cloves garlic, peeled and minced
2 teaspoons Italian seasoning
1 teaspoon salt
5 cups vegetable broth
1 pound (454 g) lump crabmeat, divided
2 tablespoons cooking sherry

¼ cup heavy cream
2 tablespoons fresh thyme leaves
1.	Press the Sauté button on the Instant Pot and melt the butter. Add the carrots, leeks and celery to the pot and sauté for 5 minutes, or until the leeks are translucent. Add the garlic and sauté for 1 minute.
2.	Stir in the Italian seasoning, salt, vegetable broth and ½ pound (227 g) of the crabmeat.
3.	Lock the lid, select the Manual mode and set the cooking time for 15 minutes on High Pressure. Once cooking is complete, use a natural pressure release for 10 minutes, then release any remaining pressure. Carefully open the lid.
4.	Use an immersion blender to blend the soup in the pot until smooth. Stir in the remaining ½ pound (227 g) of the crabmeat, sherry and heavy cream.
5.	Ladle soup into four bowls and serve garnished with the thyme

Creamy Broccoli Soup with Bacon

Prep time: 15 minutes | Cook time: 30 minutes | Serves 4

2 teaspoons unsalted butter
6 slices bacon, diced
1 large carrot, peeled and diced
1 medium sweet onion, peeled and diced
1 small Russet potato, scrubbed and diced
1 pound (454 g) fresh broccoli, chopped
¼ cup grated Cheddar cheese
1 tablespoon Dijon mustard
1 teaspoon salt
1 teaspoon ground black pepper
4 cups chicken broth
¼ cup whole milk
4 tablespoons sour cream
1.	Set the Instant Pot to the Sauté mode and melt the butter. Add the bacon to the pot and sear for 5 minutes, or until crispy. Transfer the bacon to a plate lined with paper towels and let rest for 5 minutes. Crumble the bacon when cooled.
2.	Add the carrot, onion and potato to the pot. Sauté for 5 minutes, or until the onion is translucent. Stir in the remaining ingredients, except for the milk and sour cream.
3.	Set the lid in place. Select the Soup mode and set the cooking time for 20 minutes at High Pressure. Once cooking is complete, use a quick pressure release. Carefully open the lid.
4.	Pour the milk into the pot. Use an immersion blender to blend the soup in the pot until it achieves the desired smoothness.
5.	Ladle the soup into 4 bowls and garnish with the crumbled bacon and sour cream. Serve warm.

Fish Stew with Carrot

Prep time: 10 minutes | Cook time: 14 minutes | Serves 4

1 tablespoon olive oil
1 large carrot, peeled and diced
1 stalk celery, diced
1 small yellow onion, peeled and diced

4 cloves garlic, peeled and minced
2 cups baby red potatoes, scrubbed and small-diced
1 (28-ounce / 794-g) can diced tomatoes, undrained
1 pound (454 g) skinless cod, cut into cubes
1 (8-ounce / 227-g) bottle clam juice
2 cups water
1 tablespoon Italian seasoning
1 teaspoon salt
1 bay leaf
1. Press the Sauté button on the Instant Pot and heat the oil. Add the carrot, celery and onion to the pot and sauté for 5 minutes, or until the onion is translucent. Add the garlic and sauté for 1 minute. Stir in the remaining ingredients.
2. Set the lid in place. Select the Manual setting and set the cooking time for 8 minutes on High Pressure. Once cooking is complete, perform a natural pressure release for 10 minutes, then release any remaining pressure. Open the lid.
3. Ladle the stew into 4 bowls and serve warm.

Tuscan Sausage and Kale Soup

Prep time: 15 minutes | Cook time: 13 minutes | Serves 3

1 bacon slice, chopped
6 ounces (170 g) Italian sausages, chopped
2 ounces (57 g) scallions, diced
½ teaspoon garlic powder
¼ cup cauliflower, chopped
1 cup kale, chopped
3 cups chicken broth
¼ cup heavy cream
1. Heat the the Instant Pot on Sauté mode for 3 minutes.
2. Add chopped bacon and cook for 2 minutes on Sauté mode until curls and buckles.
3. Mix in the Italian sausages, scallions, garlic powder, and cauliflower.
4. Cook for 5 minutes on Sauté mode.
5. Add kale, chicken broth, and heavy cream.
6. Select Manual mode and set cooking time for 6 minutes on High Pressure.
7. When timer beeps, make a quick pressure release. Open the lid.
8. Serve immediately.

Avocado and Serrano Chile Soup

Prep time: 10 minutes | Cook time: 7 minutes | Serves 4

2 avocados
1 small fresh tomatillo, quartered
2 cups chicken broth
2 tablespoons avocado oil
1 tablespoon butter
2 tablespoons finely minced onion
1 clove garlic, minced
½ Serrano chile, deseeded and ribs removed, minced, plus thin slices for garnish
¼ teaspoon sea salt
Pinch of ground white pepper
½ cup full-fat coconut milk
Fresh cilantro sprigs, for garnish

1. Scoop the avocado flesh into a food processor. Add the tomatillo and chicken broth and purée until smooth. Set aside.
2. Set the Instant Pot to Sauté mode and add the avocado oil and butter. When the butter melts, add the onion and garlic and sauté for a minute or until softened. Add the Serrano chile and sauté for 1 minute more.
3. Pour the puréed avocado mixture into the pot, add the salt and pepper, and stir to combine.
4. Secure the lid. Press the Manual button and set cooking time for 5 minutes on High Pressure.
5. When timer beeps, use a quick pressure release. Open the lid and stir in the coconut milk.
6. Serve hot topped with thin slices of Serrano chile, and cilantro sprigs.

Bacon Curry Soup

Prep time: 10 minutes | Cook time: 20 minutes | Serves 4

3 ounces (85 g) bacon, chopped
1 tablespoon chopped scallions
1 teaspoon curry powder
1 cup coconut milk
3 cups beef broth
1 cup Cheddar cheese, shredded
1. Heat the the Instant Pot on Sauté mode for 3 minutes and add bacon. Cook for 5 minutes. Flip constantly.
2. Add the scallions and curry powder. Sauté for 5 minutes more.
3. Pour in the coconut milk and beef broth. Add the Cheddar cheese and stir to mix well.
4. Select Manual mode and set cooking time for 10 minutes on High Pressure.
5. When timer beeps, use a quick pressure release. Open the lid.
6. Blend the soup with an immersion blender until smooth. Serve warm.

Bacon, Leek, and Cauliflower Soup

Prep time: 15 minutes | Cook time: 15 minutes | Serves 6

6 slices bacon
1 leek, remove the dark green end and roots, sliced in half lengthwise, rinsed, cut into ½-inch-thick slices crosswise
½ medium yellow onion, sliced
4 cloves garlic, minced
3 cups chicken broth
1 large head cauliflower, roughly chopped into florets
1 cup water
1 teaspoon kosher salt
1 teaspoon ground black pepper
$^2/_3$ cup shredded sharp Cheddar cheese, divided
½ cup heavy whipping cream
1. Set the Instant Pot to Sauté mode. When heated, place the bacon on the bottom of the pot and cook for 5 minutes or until crispy.
2. Transfer the bacon slices to a plate. Let stand until cool enough to handle, crumble it with forks.

3.   Add the leek and onion to the bacon fat remaining in the pot. Sauté for 5 minutes or until fragrant and the onion begins to caramelize. Add the garlic and sauté for 30 seconds more or until fragrant.
4.   Stir in the chicken broth, cauliflower florets, water, salt, pepper, and three-quarters of the crumbled bacon.
5.   Secure the lid. Press the Manual button and set cooking time for 3 minutes on High Pressure.
6.   When timer beeps, perform a quick pressure release. Open the lid.
7.   Stir in ½ cup of the Cheddar and the cream. Use an immersion blender to purée the soup until smooth.
8.   Ladle into bowls and garnish with the remaining Cheddar and crumbled bacon. Serve immediately.

Beef and Cauliflower Soup

Prep time: 10 minutes | Cook time: 14 minutes | Serves 4

1 cup ground beef
½ cup cauliflower, shredded
1 teaspoon unsweetened tomato purée
¼ cup coconut milk
1 teaspoon minced garlic
1 teaspoon dried oregano
½ teaspoon salt
4 cups water
1.   Put all ingredients in the Instant Pot and stir well.
2.   Close the lid. Select Manual mode and set cooking time for 14 minutes on High Pressure.
3.   When timer beeps, make a quick pressure release and open the lid.
4.   Blend with an immersion blender until smooth.
5.   Serve warm.

Beef and Eggplant Tagine

Prep time: 15 minutes | Cook time: 25 minutes | Serves 6

1 pound (454 g) beef fillet, chopped
1 eggplant, chopped
6 ounces (170 g) scallions, chopped
4 cups beef broth
1 teaspoon ground allspices
1 teaspoon erythritol
1 teaspoon coconut oil
1.   Put all ingredients in the Instant Pot. Stir to mix well.
2.   Close the lid. Select Manual mode and set cooking time for 25 minutes on High Pressure.
3.   When timer beeps, use a natural pressure release for 15 minutes, then release any remaining pressure. Open the lid.
4.   Serve warm.

Beef and Okra Stew

Prep time: 15 minutes | Cook time: 25 minutes | Serves 3

8 ounces (227 g) beef sirloin, chopped
¼ teaspoon cumin seeds

1 teaspoon dried basil
1 tablespoon avocado oil
¼ cup coconut cream
1 cup water
6 ounces (170 g) okra, chopped
1.   Sprinkle the beef sirloin with cumin seeds and dried basil and put in the Instant Pot.
2.   Add avocado oil and roast the meat on Sauté mode for 5 minutes. Flip occasionally.
3.   Add coconut cream, water, and okra.
4.   Close the lid and select Manual mode. Set cooking time for 25 minutes on High Pressure.
5.   When timer beeps, use a natural pressure release for 10 minutes, the release any remaining pressure. Open the lid.
6.   Serve warm.

Beef and Spinach Stew

Prep time: 20 minutes | Cook time: 30 minutes | Serves 4

1 pound (454 g) beef sirloin, chopped
2 cups spinach, chopped
3 cups chicken broth
1 cup coconut milk
1 teaspoon allspices
1 teaspoon coconut aminos
1.   Put all ingredients in the Instant Pot. Stir to mix well.
2.   Close the lid. Set the Manual mode and set cooking time for 30 minutes on High Pressure.
3.   When timer beeps, use a natural pressure release for 10 minutes, then release any remaining pressure. Open the lid.
4.   Blend with an immersion blender until smooth.
5.   Serve warm.

Beef Meatball Minestrone

Prep time: 5 minutes | Cook time: 35 minutes | Serves 6

1 pound (454 g) ground beef
1 large egg
1½ tablespoons golden flaxseed meal
$^{1}/_{3}$ cup shredded Mozzarella cheese
¼ cup unsweetened tomato purée
1½ tablespoons Italian seasoning, divided
1½ teaspoons garlic powder, divided
1½ teaspoons sea salt, divided
1 tablespoon olive oil
2 garlic cloves, minced
½ medium yellow onion, minced
¼ cup pancetta, diced
1 cup sliced yellow squash
1 cup sliced zucchini
½ cup sliced turnips
4 cups beef broth
14 ounces (397 g) can diced tomatoes
½ teaspoon ground black pepper
3 tablespoons shredded Parmesan cheese
1.   Preheat the oven to 400°F (205°C) and line a large baking sheet with aluminum foil.
2.   In a large bowl, combine the ground beef, egg, flaxseed meal, Mozzarella, unsweetened tomato

purée, ½ tablespoon of Italian seasoning, ½ teaspoon of garlic powder, and ½ teaspoon of sea salt. Mix the ingredients until well combined.
3.　　Make the meatballs by shaping 1 heaping tablespoon of the ground beef mixture into a meatball. Repeat with the remaining mixture and then transfer the meatballs to the prepared baking sheet.
4.　　Place the meatballs in the oven and bake for 15 minutes. When the baking time is complete, remove from the oven and set aside.
5.　　Select Sauté mode of the Instant Pot. Once the pot is hot, add the olive oil, garlic, onion, and pancetta. Sauté for 2 minutes or until the garlic becomes fragrant and the onions begin to soften.
6.　　Add the yellow squash, zucchini, and turnips to the pot. Sauté for 3 more minutes.
7.　　Add the beef broth, diced tomatoes, black pepper, and remaining garlic powder, sea salt, and Italian seasoning to the pot. Stir to combine and then add the meatballs.
8.　　Lock the lid. Select Manual mode and set cooking time for 15 minutes on High Pressure.
9.　　When cooking is complete, allow the pressure to release naturally for 10 minutes and then release the remaining pressure.
10.　　Open the lid and gently stir the soup. Ladle into serving bowls and top with Parmesan. Serve hot.

Beef T-Bone Broth

Prep time: 20 minutes | Cook time: 50 minutes | Serves 4
1 pound (454 g) T-bone beef steak, chopped
1 bay leaf
1 teaspoon peppercorns
1 teaspoon salt
3 cups water
1.　　Put all ingredients in the Instant Pot. Stir to mix well. Close the lid.
2.　　Set Manual mode and set cooking time for 50 minutes on High Pressure.
3.　　When timer beeps, use a natural pressure release for 15 minutes, then release the remaining pressure and open the lid.
4.　　Strain the cooked mixture and shred the meat. Serve the beef broth with the shredded beef.

Blue Cheese Mushroom Soup

Prep time: 15 minutes | Cook time: 20 minutes | Serves 4
2 cups chopped white mushrooms
3 tablespoons cream cheese
4 ounces (113 g) scallions, diced
4 cups chicken broth
1 teaspoon olive oil
½ teaspoon ground cumin
1 teaspoon salt
2 ounces (57 g) blue cheese, crumbled
1.　　Combine the mushrooms, cream cheese, scallions, chicken broth, olive oil, and ground cumin in the Instant Pot.
2.　　Seal the lid. Select Manual mode and set cooking time for 20 minutes on High Pressure.

3.　　When timer beeps, use a quick pressure release and open the lid.
4.　　Add the salt and blend the soup with an immersion blender.
5.　　Ladle the soup in the bowls and top with blue cheese. Serve warm.

Broccoli and Bacon Cheese Soup

Prep time: 6 minutes | Cook time: 10 minutes | Serves 6
3 tablespoons butter
2 stalks celery, diced
½ yellow onion, diced
3 garlic cloves, minced
3½ cups chicken stock
4 cups chopped fresh broccoli florets
3 ounces (85 g) block-style cream cheese, softened and cubed
½ teaspoon ground nutmeg
½ teaspoon sea salt
1 teaspoon ground black pepper
3 cups shredded Cheddar cheese
½ cup shredded Monterey Jack cheese
2 cups heavy cream
4 slices cooked bacon, crumbled
1 tablespoon finely chopped chives
1.　　Select Sauté mode. Once the Instant Pot is hot, add the butter and heat until the butter is melted.
2.　　Add the celery, onions, and garlic. Continue sautéing for 5 minutes or until the vegetables are softened.
3.　　Add the chicken stock and broccoli florets to the pot. Bring the liquid to a boil.
4.　　Lock the lid,. Select Manual mode and set cooking time for 5 minutes on High Pressure.
5.　　When cooking is complete, allow the pressure to release naturally for 10 minutes and then release the remaining pressure.
6.　　Open the lid and add the cream cheese, nutmeg, sea salt, and black pepper. Stir to combine.
7.　　Select Sauté mode. Bring the soup to a boil and then slowly stir in the Cheddar and Jack cheeses. Once the cheese has melted, stir in the heavy cream.
8.　　Ladle the soup into serving bowls and top with bacon and chives. Serve hot.

Broccoli and Red Feta Soup

Prep time: 10 minutes | Cook time: 25 minutes | Serves 4
1 cup broccoli, chopped
½ cup coconut cream
1 teaspoon unsweetened tomato purée
4 cups beef broth
1 teaspoon chili flakes
6 ounces (170 g) feta, crumbled
1.　　Put broccoli, coconut cream, tomato purée, and beef broth in the Instant Pot. Sprinkle with chili flakes and stir to mix well.
2.　　Close the lid and select Manual mode. Set cooking time for 8 minutes on High Pressure.
3.　　When timer beeps, make a quick pressure release and open the lid.

4.   Add the feta cheese and stir the soup on Sauté mode for 5 minutes or until the cheese melt.
5.   Serve immediately.

Buffalo Chicken Soup

Prep time: 7 minutes | Cook time: 10 minutes | Serves 2

1 ounce (28 g) celery stalk, chopped
4 tablespoons coconut milk
¾ teaspoon salt
¼ teaspoon white pepper
1 cup water
2 ounces (57 g) Mozzarella, shredded
6 ounces (170 g) cooked chicken, shredded
2 tablespoons keto-friendly Buffalo sauce
1.   Place the chopped celery stalk, coconut milk, salt, white pepper, water, and Mozzarella in the Instant Pot. Stir to mix well.
2.   Set the Manual mode and set timer for 7 minutes on High Pressure.
3.   When timer beeps, use a quick pressure release and open the lid.
4.   Transfer the soup on the bowls. Stir in the chicken and Buffalo sauce. Serve warm.

Cabbage and Pork Soup

Prep time: 10 minutes | Cook time: 12 minutes | Serves 3

1 teaspoon butter
½ cup shredded white cabbage
½ teaspoon ground coriander
½ teaspoon salt
½ teaspoon chili flakes
2 cups chicken broth
½ cup ground pork
1.   Melt the butter in the Instant Pot on Sauté mode.
2.   Add cabbage and sprinkle with ground coriander, salt, and chili flakes.
3.   Fold in the chicken broth and ground pork.
4.   Close the lid and select Manual mode. Set cooking time for 12 minutes on High Pressure.
5.   When timer beeps, use a quick pressure release. Open the lid.
6.   Ladle the soup and serve warm.

Cauliflower Rice and Chicken Thigh Soup

Prep time: 15 minutes | Cook time: 13 minutes | Serves 5

2 cups cauliflower florets
1 pound (454 g) boneless, skinless chicken thighs
4½ cups chicken broth
½ yellow onion, chopped
2 garlic cloves, minced
1 tablespoon unflavored gelatin powder
2 teaspoons sea salt
½ teaspoon ground black pepper
½ cup sliced zucchini
$^1/_3$ cup sliced turnips
1 teaspoon dried parsley
3 celery stalks, chopped
1 teaspoon ground turmeric
½ teaspoon dried marjoram
1 teaspoon dried thyme
½ teaspoon dried oregano
1.   Add the cauliflower florets to a food processor and pulse until a ricelike consistency is achieved. Set aside.
2.   Add the chicken thighs, chicken broth, onions, garlic, gelatin powder, sea salt, and black pepper to the pot. Gently stir to combine.
3.   Lock the lid. Select Manual mode and set cooking time for 10 minutes on High Pressure.
4.   When cooking is complete, quick release the pressure and open the lid.
5.   Transfer the chicken thighs to a cutting board. Chop the chicken into bite-sized pieces and then return the chopped chicken to the pot.
6.   Add the cauliflower rice, zucchini, turnips, parsley, celery, turmeric, marjoram, thyme, and oregano to the pot. Stir to combine.
7.   Lock the lid. Select Manual mode and set cooking time for 3 minutes on High Pressure.
8.   When cooking is complete, quick release the pressure.
9.   Open the lid. Ladle the soup into serving bowls. Serve hot.

Cheesy Cauliflower Soup

Prep time: 10 minutes | Cook time: 6 minutes | Serves 4

2 cups chopped cauliflower
2 tablespoons fresh cilantro
1 cup coconut cream
2 cups beef broth
3 ounces (85 g) Provolone cheese, chopped
1.   Put cauliflower, cilantro, coconut cream, beef broth, and cheese in the Instant Pot. Stir to mix well.
2.   Select Manual mode and set cooking time for 6 minutes on High Pressure.
3.   When timer beeps, allow a natural pressure release for 4 minutes, then release any remaining pressure. Open the lid.
4.   Blend the soup and ladle in bowls to serve.

Chicken and Zoodles Soup

Prep time: 25 minutes | Cook time: 15 minutes | Serves 2

2 cups water
6 ounces (170 g) chicken fillet, chopped
1 teaspoon salt
2 ounces (57 g) zucchini, spiralized
1 tablespoon coconut aminos
1.   Pour water in the Instant Pot. Add chopped chicken fillet and salt. Close the lid.
2.   Select Manual mode and set cooking time for 15 minutes on High Pressure.
3.   When cooking is complete, perform a natural pressure release for 10 minutes, then release any remaining pressure. Open the lid.
4.   Fold in the zoodles and coconut aminos.
5.   Leave the soup for 10 minutes to rest. Serve warm.

Chicken Chili Verde Soup

Prep time: 10 minutes | Cook time: 25 minutes | Serves 4

1 pound (454 g) chicken breast, skinless, boneless
5 cups chicken broth
½ cup Cheddar cheese, shredded
2 ounces (57 g) chili Verde sauce
1 tablespoon dried cilantro
1.   Put chicken breast and chicken broth in the Instant Pot.
2.   Add the cilantro, Close the lid. Select Manual mode and set cooking time for 15 minutes on High Pressure.
3.   When timer beeps, make a quick pressure release and open the lid.
4.   Shred the chicken breast with a fork.
5.   Add the Cheddar and chili Verde sauce in the soup and cook on Sauté mode for 10 minutes.
6.   Mix in the dried cilantro. Serve immediately.

Chicken Thigh and Shrimp Stock

Prep time: 10 minutes | Cook time: 15 minutes | Serves 4

2 chicken thighs, boneless, chopped
4 ounces (113 g) shrimps, peeled
3 ounces (85 g) sausages, chopped
½ bell pepper, chopped
1 cup beef broth
1 teaspoon unsweetened tomato purée
1 celery stalk, chopped
½ teaspoon Cajun seasonings
1.   Heat the the Instant Pot on Sauté mode for 3 minutes.
2.   Add the chicken thighs, shrimps, sausages, bell pepper, beef broth, unsweetened tomato purée, celery stalk, and Cajun seasonings.
3.   Gently mix the the ingredients and close the lid.
4.   Select Manual mode and set time to 15 minutes on High Pressure.
5.   When cooking is complete, use a quick pressure release and open the lid.
6.   Serve immediately.

Chicken Chipotle Stew

Prep time: 15 minutes | Cook time: 10 minutes | Serves 3

9 ounces (255 g) chicken fillet, chopped
2 chipotle chili in adobo sauce, chopped
2 tablespoons sesame seeds
1 ounce (28 g) fresh cilantro, chopped
1 teaspoon ground paprika
¼ teaspoon salt
1 cup chicken broth
1.   In a mixing bowl, combine the chicken fillet, chipotle chili, sesame seeds, cilantro, ground paprika, and salt.
2.   Transfer the mixture in the Instant Pot and pour in the chicken broth.
3.   Select Manual mode and set cooking time for 10 minutes on High Pressure.
4.   When timer beeps, use a natural pressure release for 10 minutes, then release any remaining pressure. Open the lid.

5.   Serve warm.

Swiss Chard and Leek Soup

Prep time: 12 mins, Cook Time: 6 mins, Servings: 4

•   8 cups chopped Swiss chard
•   3 leeks, chopped
•   Salt, to taste
•   1½ cups chicken stock
•   1 cup coconut milk
1.   In the Instant Pot, mix the chard with leeks, salt, stock and coconut milk, stir to combine well.
2.   Lock the lid. Select the Manual mode, then set the timer for 6 minutes at High Pressure.
3.   Once the timer goes off, do a quick pressure release.
4.   Carefully open the lid. Allow to cool for a few minutes, then pour the soup in an immersion blender and process until smooth. Ladle the soup into bowls and serve.

Thai Coconut Shrimp Soup

Prep time: 6 mins, Cook Time: 6 mins, Servings: 2

•   6 oz. shrimps, shelled and deveined
•   2 cups water
•   Juice of 3 kaffir limes
•   1½ cups coconut milk
•   1 cup fresh cilantro
1.   In the Instant Pot, add all the ingredients excluding cilantro.
2.   Lock the lid. Set on the Manual mode and set the timer to 6 minutes at Low Pressure.
3.   When the timer goes off, perform a quick release.
4.   Carefully open the lid. Garnish with the fresh cilantro and serve immediately.

Thai Tom Saap Pork Ribs Soup

Prep time: 6 mins, Cook Time: 30 mins, Servings: 4

•   1 lb. pork spare ribs
•   4 lemongrass stalks
•   10 galangal slices
•   10 kaffir lime leaves
•   6 cups water
•   Salt and pepper, to taste
•   1 tbsp. sesame oil
•   Cilantro, to taste
1.   In the Instant Pot, place the spare ribs, lemongrass, galangal, and kaffir lime leaves.
2.   Pour in the water and sprinkle salt and pepper for seasoning.
3.   Lock the lid. Set on the Manual mode, then set the timer to 30 minutes at High Pressure.
4.   When the timer goes off, do a natural pressure release, then release any remaining pressure.
5.   Carefully open the lid. Drizzle with sesame oil and garnish with cilantro before serving.

Turkey with Ginger and Turmeric Soup

Prep time: 6 mins, Cook Time: 17 mins, Servings: 4

- 1 tbsp. coconut oil
- 2 celery stalks, chopped
- 1 thumb-size ginger, sliced
- 1 tsp. turmeric powder
- 1 lb. turkey meat, chopped
- 3 cups water
- Salt and pepper, to taste

1. Press the Sauté button on the Instant Pot and heat the coconut oil.
2. Add the celery, ginger, and turmeric powder and sauté for 3 minutes or until fragrant and the celery is tender.
3. Add the turkey meat and stir for another 3 minutes until lightly browned.
4. Pour in the water and sprinkle salt and pepper for seasoning.
5. Lock the lid. Set on the Manual mode, then set the timer to 15 minutes at High Pressure.
6. When the timer goes off, do a natural pressure release, then release any remaining pressure.
7. Carefully open the lid. Serve warm.

Turmeric Chicken Soup

Prep time: 6 mins, Cook Time: 15 mins, Servings: 3

- 3 boneless chicken breasts
- 1 bay leaf
- ½ cup coconut milk
- 2½ tsps. turmeric powder
- 4 cups water

1. Place all the ingredients in the Instant Pot. Stir to combine well.
2. Lock the lid. Set to Poultry mode and set the timer to 15 minutes at High Pressure.
1. When the timer goes off, perform a natural pressure release for 10 minutes, then release any remaining pressure.
3. Carefully open the lid. Allow to cool for a few minutes, then serve immediately.

Salmon Head Soup

Prep time: 6 mins, Cook Time: 12 mins, Servings: 1

- 1 tsp. coconut oil
- 1 onion, sliced
- 3 cups water
- 1 salmon head
- 3-inch ginger piece, slivered
- Salt and pepper, to taste

1. Press the Sauté button on the Instant Pot and heat the coconut oil.
2. Sauté the onion for 3 minutes or until translucent.
3. Pour in the water, then add the salmon head and ginger.
4. Sprinkle salt and pepper for seasoning.
5. Lock the lid. Set on the Manual mode, then set the timer to 10 minutes at Low Pressure.

6. When the timer goes off, perform a quick release.
7. Carefully open the lid. Allow to cool before serving.

Simple Chicken and Kale Soup

Prep time: 6 mins, Cook Time: 20 mins, Servings: 4

- 1 tbsp. coconut oil
- 1 onion, diced
- 2 celery stalks, chopped
- 1 lb. boneless chicken breasts
- 3 cups water
- Salt and pepper, to taste
- 4 cups chopped kale

1. Press the Sauté button on the Instant Pot and heat the coconut oil.
2. Sauté the onions and celery for 2 minutes until soft.
3. Add the chicken breasts and sear for 2 minutes on each side or until lightly browned.
4. Pour in the water and sprinkle salt and pepper for seasoning.
5. Lock the lid. Set to Poultry mode and set the timer to 15 minutes at High Pressure.
6. When the timer goes off, do a natural pressure release for 10 minutes, then release any remaining pressure.
7. Carefully open the lid. Press the Sauté button and add the kale.
8. Allow to simmer for 3 minutes.
9. Serve warm.

Vegetable and Lentil Soup

Prep time: 30 mins, Cook Time: 20 mins, Servings: 5

- 1 tbsp. olive oil
- 6 cups chicken stock
- 1¼ cup green lentils
- 6 garlic cloves, minced
- 5 tbsps. mixed spices
- Salt, to taste
- 4 cups mixed vegetables

1. Set the Instant Pot to Sauté and heat the olive oil. Cook the garlic for 2 minutes or until fragrant.
2. Add the vegetables and spices. Season with salt and cook for 5 minutes more.
3. Add the stock and lentils and stir well.
4. Lock the lid. Select the Manual mode, then set the timer for 12 minutes at High Pressure.
5. Once the timer goes off, do a natural pressure release for 10 minutes, then release any remaining pressure. Carefully open the lid.
6. Serve immediately.

White Bean and Kale Soup

Prep time: 30 mins, Cook Time: 13 mins, Servings: 10

- 3 tbsps. olive oil
- 1 (28 oz) can diced tomatoes
- 4 cups kale

- 1 white onion, chopped
- 30 oz. white cannellini beans
- 4 cups vegetable stock

1. Set the Instant Pot to Sauté and heat the olive oil.
2. Sauté the white onion for 3 minutes, stirring occasionally.
3. Add the tomatoes, beans, and vegetable stock, and whisk well.
4. Lock the lid. Select the Manual mode, then set the timer for 10 minutes at High Pressure.
5. Once the timer goes off, do a quick pressure release. Carefully open the lid.
6. Stir in the kale.
7. Cover the pot and let rest for a few minutes until the kale is wilted. Serve warm.

Bean and Tomato Stew

Prep time: 12 mins, Cook Time: 20 mins, Servings: 4

- 1 tbsp. olive oil
- 1 large onion, chopped
- 2 large tomatoes, roughly chopped
- 1 lb. green beans
- 2 cups low-sodium chicken stock
- Salt and pepper, to taste
- ¼ cup Parmesan cheese

1. Press the Sauté bottom on the Instant Pot.
2. Add and heat the olive oil.
3. Add the onions and sauté for 2 minutes until translucent and softened.
4. Add the tomatoes and sauté for 3 to 4 minutes or until soft.
5. Add the beans and stock. Sprinkle with salt and pepper.
6. Lock the lid. Press Manual. Set the timer to 15 minutes at High Pressure.
7. Once the timer goes off, press Cancel. Do a quick pressure release.
8. Open the lid, transfer them in a large bowl and serve with Parmesan cheese on top.

Beef Tomato Stew

Prep time: 12 mins, Cook Time: 30 mins, Servings: 4

- 2 tsps. olive oil
- 1 lb. lean beef stew meat
- 2 cups diced tomatoes
- 2 spring onions, chopped
- 4 cups low-sodium beef broth
- Salt and pepper, to taste

1. Press the Sauté bottom on the Instant Pot.
2. Add and heat the olive oil.
3. Add the meat and sauté for 3 to 4 minutes to evenly brown.
4. Add the tomatoes and onions, then sauté for 3 to 4 minutes or until soft.
5. Pour in the broth. Sprinkle with salt and pepper.
6. Lock the lid. Press Meat/Stew bottom. Set the timer to 20 minutes at High Pressure.

7. Once the timer goes off, press Cancel. Do a quick pressure release.
8. Open the lid, transfer them in a large bowl and serve.

Calamari Stew

Prep time: 12 mins, Cook Time: 32 mins, Servings: 3

- 1 tbsp. olive oil
- 1 lb. separated calamari
- ¼ cup white wine
- ½ bunch parsley, chopped
- 7 oz. tomatoes, chopped

1. Set the Instant Pot to Sauté and add the oil and calamari. Stir to combine well.
2. Lock the lid. Select the Manual mode, then set the timer for 9 minutes at Low Pressure.
3. Once the timer goes off, do a quick pressure release. Carefully open the lid.
4. Add the wine, tomatoes and half of the parsley, and stir well.
5. Lock the lid. Select the Manual mode, then set the timer for 25 minutes at High Pressure.
6. Once the timer goes off, do a quick pressure release. Carefully open the lid.
7. Sprinkle the remaining parsley on top. Divide the soup into bowls and serve.

Chicken and Quinoa Stew

Prep time: 30 mins, Cook Time: 23 mins, Servings: 6

- 1¼ lbs. chicken thigh fillets
- 4 cups chicken stock
- 4 cups chopped butternut squash
- 1 cup chopped onion
- ½ cup uncooked quinoa

1. Put the chicken in the Instant Pot. Add the chicken thigh fillets, stock, squash and chopped onion.
2. Lock the lid. Select the Manual mode, then set the timer for 8 minutes at High Pressure.
3. Once the timer goes off, do a quick pressure release. Carefully open the lid.
4. Stir the quinoa into the stew.
5. Set the Instant Pot to Sauté and cook for about 15 minutes, stirring occasionally.
6. Serve the stew in a large serving bowl.

Chicken Tomato Stew

Prep time: 12 mins, Cook Time: 30 mins, Servings: 8

- 4 onions, chopped
- 1 tbsp. olive oil
- 10 oz. chicken breast
- 1 cup diced tomatoes
- 4 cups low-sodium chicken stock
- ¼ cup water

1. Press the Sauté bottom on the Instant Pot.
2. Add and heat the olive oil.
3. Add the onions and sauté for 1 to 2 minutes until turn translucent and softened.

4.	Add the chicken and evenly brown for 4 to 5 minutes.
5.	Add the tomatoes and sauté for 2 minutes or until soft.
6.	Pour in the stock and water.
7.	Lock the lid. Press Manual. Set the timer to 20 minutes at High Pressure.
8.	Once the timer goes off, press Cancel. Do a quick pressure release.
9.	Open the lid, transfer them in a large bowl and serve.

Kale and Veal Stew

Prep time: 12 mins, Cook Time: 35 mins, Servings: 6

- 1 tbsp. olive oil
- 2 large onions, finely chopped
- 1 small sweet potato, diced
- 4 cups low-sodium beef stock
- 10 oz. fat removed and chopped veal shoulder
- 1 lb. fresh kale, chopped
- Salt and pepper, to taste
1.	Press the Sauté bottom on the Instant Pot.
2.	Add and heat the olive oil.
3.	Add the onions and sauté for 3 minutes until turn translucent and softened.
4.	Add the sweet potato and ¼ cup of stock. Sauté for 5 minutes or until soft.
5.	Add the remaining stock, veal shoulder, and kale to the Instant Pot. Sprinkle with salt and pepper. Combine to mix well.
6.	Lock the lid. Press Manual. Set the timer to 25 minutes at High pressure.
7.	Once the timer goes off, press Cancel. Do a quick pressure release.
8.	Open the lid, transfer them in a large bowl and serve

Kidney Bean Stew

Prep time: 15 mins, Cook Time: 15 mins, Servings: 2

- 1 cup tomato passata
- 3 tbsps. Italian herbs
- 1lb. cooked kidney beans
- 1 cup low-sodium beef broth
1.	Mix all the ingredients in the Instant Pot.
2.	Lock the lid. Select the Bean/Chili mode, then set the timer for 15 minutes at High Pressure.
3.	Once the timer goes off, do a natural pressure release for 10 minutes, then release any remaining pressure. Carefully open the lid.
4.	Serve warm.

Salmon Stew

Prep time: 6 mins, Cook Time:13 mins, Servings: 9

- 2 tbsps. olive oil
- 3 garlic cloves, minced
- 3 cups water
- 3 lbs. salmon fillets
- Salt and pepper, to taste
- 3 cups spinach leaves
1.	Press the Sauté button on the Instant Pot and heat the olive oil.
2.	Sauté the garlic for a minute until fragrant.
3.	Add the water and salmon fillets. Sprinkle salt and pepper for seasoning.
4.	Lock the lid. Set on the Manual mode, then set the timer to 10 minutes at Low Pressure.
5.	When the timer goes off, perform a quick release.
6.	Carefully open the lid. Press the Sauté button and add the spinach.
7.	Allow to simmer for 3 minutes.
8.	Serve warm.

Slow-Cooked Cabbage and Chuck Roast Stew

Prep time: 6 mins, Cook Time: 36 mins, Servings: 10

- 2 tbsps. olive oil
- 2 onions, sliced
- 1 garlic clove, minced
- 3 lbs. chuck roast
- 6 cups water
- Salt and pepper, to taste
- 1 small cabbage head, chopped
1.	Press the Sauté button on the Instant Pot and heat the olive oil.
2.	Sauté the onions and garlic for 2 minutes until fragrant.
3.	Add the chuck roast and sauté for 3 minutes or until lightly browned.
4.	Pour in the water and sprinkle salt and pepper for seasoning.
5.	Lock the lid. Set on the Manual mode, then set the timer to 30 minutes at High Pressure.
6.	When the timer goes off, do a natural pressure release, then release any remaining pressure.
7.	Carefully open the lid. Press the Sauté button and add the cabbage.
8.	Allow to simmer for 3 minutes.
9.	Serve warm.

Veal and Buckwheat Groat Stew

Prep time: 12 mins, Cook Time: 50 mins, Servings: 4

- ¼ cup buckwheat groats
- 1 tsp. olive oil
- 1 onion, chopped
- 7 oz. veal shoulder
- 3 cups low-sodium beef stock
- Salt and pepper, to taste
1.	Add the buckwheat and pour in enough water to cover the buckwheat in the Instant Pot. Stir the ingredients to combine well.
2.	Lock the lid. Press Manual. Set the timer to 12 minutes at Low Pressure.
3.	Once the timer goes off, press Cancel. Do a natural pressure release, then release any remaining pressure.
4.	Drain water and set the buckwheat aside.

5. Press the Sauté bottom on the Instant Pot.
6. Add and heat the olive oil.
7. Add the onions and cook for 3 minutes until translucent.
8. Add the veal shoulder and sauté for 4 to 5 minutes to evenly brown.
9. Pour in the beef stock. Sprinkle with salt and pepper.
10. Lock the lid. Press Manual. Set the timer to 30 minutes at High Pressure.
11. Once the timer goes off, press Cancel. Do a natural pressure release for 8 to 10 minutes.
12. Open the lid, mix in the buckwheat and transfer them in a large bowl and serve.

Veggie Stew

Prep time: 40 mins, Cook Time: 20 mins, Servings: 4

- 1 tbsp. olive oil
- 1 onion, minced
- 1 package mixed frozen vegetables
- 4 cups vegetable broth
- 20 oz. tomato sauce
- 2 tsps. Italian seasoning
- Salt and pepper, to taste

1. Set the Instant Pot to Sauté and heat the olive oil.
2. Cook the onion for 1 minute until translucent. Add the frozen vegetables and cook for 5 minutes, stirring frequently.
3. Add the remaining ingredients and stir to combine.
4. Lock the lid. Select the Manual mode, then set the timer for 15 minutes at High Pressure.
5. Once the timer goes off, do a quick pressure release. Carefully open the lid.
6. Serve immediately.

Butternut Squash and Kale Chili

Prep time: 10 minutes | Cook time: 20 minutes | Serves 6

1 teaspoon vegetable oil
2 cloves garlic, minced
½ cup diced onion
¼ cup diced green bell pepper
3 cups diced butternut squash (½-inch cubes)
1 teaspoon chili powder
1½ teaspoons cumin
1 tablespoon Sriracha sauce
1 cup dried brown lentils, rinsed and drained
2 tomatoes, diced
3 cups vegetable broth
4 cups loosely packed kale, cut or torn into bite-size pieces
1 tablespoon lemon juice
Salt and ground black pepper, to taste
1. In the Instant Pot, heat the oil on Sauté mode.
2. Add the garlic, onion, and bell pepper and sauté for 2 minutes, until the onion softens.
3. Add the squash, chili powder, cumin, and Sriracha and sauté for 4 minutes. Stir in the lentils and tomatoes.

4. Add the vegetable broth to cover by 1 inch. Add the kale and stir to combine.
5. Cover the lid. Select Manual mode and set cooking time for 10 minutes on High Pressure.
6. When timer beeps, use a natural pressure release for 15 minutes, then release any remaining pressure.
7. Remove the lid. Stir in the lemon juice. Add salt and ground black pepper and serve.

Corn and Kidney Bean Chili

Prep time: 5 minutes | Cook time: 10 minutes | Serves 4

1 teaspoon olive oil
½ cup diced carrot
1 cup diced onion
3 cloves garlic, minced
½ cup chopped celery
1 (14.5-ounce / 411-g) can whole kernel corn, drained
1 cup diced green bell pepper
1 cup diced red bell pepper
1 teaspoon chili powder
½ teaspoon ground cumin
1 (28-ounce / 794-g) can diced tomatoes
2 tablespoons tomato paste
2 cups vegetable broth
1 fresh jalapeño, deseeded and finely diced
½ teaspoon cayenne pepper
1 teaspoon red pepper flakes
1 cup water
1½ cups red kidney beans, rinsed and drained
1. In the Instant Pot, heat the oil on Sauté mode.
2. Add the carrot, onion, garlic, and celery and sauté for 3 minutes.
3. Add the corn, bell peppers, chili powder, cumin, diced tomatoes, tomato paste, broth, jalapeño, cayenne, red pepper flakes, water, and beans.
4. Secure the lid. Select Manual mode and set cooking time for 6 minutes at Low Pressure.
5. When timer beeps, use a natural pressure release for 15 minutes, then release any remaining pressure. Open the lid.
6. Serve immediately.

Hearty Black-Eyed Pea and Collard Chili

Prep time: 10 minutes | Cook time: 20 minutes | Serves 4

1 teaspoon olive oil
½ cup diced red onion
3 cloves garlic, minced
2 cups chopped carrot
2 cups chopped celery
4 large collard green leaves, halved, center ribs removed, cut into ¼-inch wide strips
½ teaspoon ground coriander
1 teaspoon ground cinnamon
1 tablespoon dried oregano
2 tablespoons chili powder
1 teaspoon ground cumin
1 teaspoon deseeded and diced fresh jalapeño
2 cups dried black-eyed peas, rinsed and drained

1 (28-ounce / 794-g) can diced tomatoes
1 (8-ounce / 227-g) can tomato sauce
2 bay leaves
2 cups vegetable broth
1 cup water
¼ teaspoon sea salt
1.	In the Instant Pot heat the oil on Sauté mode.
2.	Add the onion and garlic and sauté for about 2 minutes until the onion begins to soften.
3.	Add the carrots and celery and continue to sauté for another 3 to 5 minutes.
4.	Add the collard greens, coriander, cinnamon, oregano, chili powder, cumin, and jalapeño and sauté for a minute.
5.	Add the black-eyed peas, diced tomatoes, tomato sauce, bay leaves, broth, and water. Stir to combine.
6.	Secure the lid. Select Manual mode and set cooking time for 10 minutes on High Pressure.
7.	When timer beeps, use a natural pressure release for 15 minutes, then release any remaining pressure.
8.	Remove the cover. Add salt to taste. Remove the bay leaves before serving.

Rich Acorn Squash Chili

Prep time: 15 minutes | Cook time: 16 minutes | Serves 6

1 tablespoon olive oil
½ cup chopped onion
1 cup sliced carrots
1 large celery stalks, chopped
2 cloves garlic, minced
1½ cups cubed acorn squash
10 ounces (283 g) can red kidney beans, drained
10 ounces (283 g) can cannellini beans, drained
2 (10-ounce / 283-g) can crushed tomatoes
¾ cup corn kernels
1 teaspoon Tabasco sauce
1 teaspoon mesquite powder
1 teaspoon chili flakes
1 teaspoon dried oregano
1 teaspoon ground cumin
1 teaspoon smoked paprika
1.	Heat the oil in the Instant pot on Sauté mode.
2.	Add the onion and carrots. Sauté for 3 minutes or until soft.
3.	Add the celery and sauté for 2 minutes. Add the garlic and sauté for 1 minute.
4.	Add the remaining ingredients and lock the lid.
5.	Select Manual mode and set cooking time for 10 minutes on High Pressure.
6.	When timer beeps, use a natural pressure release for 5 minutes, then release any remaining pressure. Open the lid.
7.	Serve warm.

Rich Brown Lentil and Millet Chili

Prep time: 10 minutes | Cook time: 20 minutes | Serves 6

2 tablespoons olive oil
1 cup finely diced yellow onion
2 cloves garlic, minced
1 seeded and finely diced fresh jalapeño
½ teaspoon ground cinnamon
1 teaspoon chili powder
1 teaspoon ground cumin
1 cup dried brown lentils, rinsed and drained
1 cup millet, rinsed and drained
½ cup diced summer squash
4 cups diced fresh tomatoes
2 cups bite-size pieces kale
1 bay leaf
2 cups vegetable broth
4 cups water
Juice of 1 lemon
1 tablespoon chopped fresh sweet basil
½ teaspoon sea salt
1.	Heat the olive oil in the Instant Pot. Add the onion and cook for 3 to 4 minutes, stirring occasionally, until softened.
2.	Add the garlic, stir, then add the jalapeño, cinnamon, chili powder, and cumin and sauté for a few minutes more, until the jalapeño softens.
3.	Add the lentils, millet, squash, tomatoes, kale, bay leaf, broth, and water and stir to combine.
4.	Cover the lid. Select Manual mode and set cooking time for 8 minutes on High Pressure.
5.	When timer beeps, use a natural pressure release for 15 minutes, then release any remaining pressure.
6.	Carefully remove the lid. Select Sauté mode and bring to a simmer, then add the lemon juice, basil, and salt.
7.	Stir and let simmer for a few minutes more. Serve immediately.

Ritzy Beans and Quinoa Chili

Prep time: 10 minutes | Cook time: 7 minutes | Serves 6

1 tablespoon olive oil
1 large yellow onion, diced
3 cloves garlic, minced
1 green bell pepper, deseeded and diced
1 cup peeled and diced sweet potato cubes (about 1 inch)
1 (15-ounce / 425-g) can black beans, drained and rinsed
1 (15-ounce / 425-g) can kidney beans, drained and rinsed
½ cup uncooked quinoa, rinsed and drained
1 (4-ounce / 113-g) can diced green chiles
1 (26-ounce / 737-g) box chopped or diced tomatoes
1½ tablespoons chili powder
1 tablespoon ground cumin
½ teaspoon smoked paprika
½ teaspoon sea salt
2 cups vegetable broth
Fresh cilantro leaves, for garnish
1 avocado, sliced, for garnish
1.	Select Sauté mode, and heat the oil in the Instant Pot until hot.

2.	Add the onion and sauté for 1 minute. Add the garlic, bell pepper, and sweet potatoes, and sauté 1 minute more.
3.	Add the black beans, kidney beans, quinoa, chiles, tomatoes, chili powder, cumin, paprika, salt, and broth, and stir.
4.	Lock the lid. Select Manual mode and set the cook time for 5 minutes on High Pressure.
5.	Once the cook time is complete, quick release the pressure and carefully remove the lid.
6.	Serve warm, garnished with cilantro and avocado.

Ritzy Summer Chili

Prep time: 10 minutes | Cook time: 15 minutes | Serves 6

2 tablespoons olive oil
1 poblano chile or green bell pepper, deseeded and diced
1 jalapeño chile, deseeded and diced
1 celery stalk, diced
2 cloves garlic, minced
1 yellow onion, diced
½ teaspoon fine sea salt, plus more as needed
2 tablespoons chili powder
1 teaspoon dried oregano
½ teaspoon ground cumin
¼ teaspoon cayenne pepper
2 zucchini, diced
1 (15-ounce / 425-g) can peruano beans, rinsed and drained
1 (12-ounce / 340-g) bag frozen corn
1 cup vegetable broth
1 (14.5-ounce / 411-g) can diced fire-roasted tomatoes
¼ cup chopped fresh cilantro
2 green onions, white and tender green parts, thinly sliced
1.	Select the Sauté setting on the Instant Pot, add the oil, and heat for 1 minute.
2.	Add the poblano and jalapeño chiles, celery, garlic, onion, and salt, and sauté for about 5 minutes, until the vegetables soften.
3.	Add the chili powder, oregano, cumin, and cayenne and sauté for about 1 minute more.
4.	Add the zucchini, beans, corn, and broth and stir to combine. Pour the tomatoes and their liquid over the top. Do not stir.
5.	Secure the lid. Select Manual mode and set the cooking time for 5 minutes at High Pressure.
6.	When timer beeps, perform a quick pressure release. Open the pot, give a stir.
7.	Ladle the chili into bowls and sprinkle with cilantro and green onions. Serve hot.

Ritzy Winter Chili

Prep time: 10 minutes | Cook time: 15 minutes | Serves 4 to 6

3 tablespoons olive oil
2 cloves garlic, minced
2 leeks, white and tender green parts, halved lengthwise and thinly sliced
2 jalapeño chiles, deseeded and diced
1 teaspoon fine sea salt
1 canned chipotle chile in adobo sauce, minced
3 tablespoons chili powder
1 cup vegetable broth
2 carrots, peeled and diced
1 (15-ounce / 425-g) can black beans, rinsed and drained
1 (1-pound / 454-g) delicata squash, deseeded and diced
1 (14.5-ounce / 411-g) can diced fire-roasted tomatoes
Chopped fresh cilantro, for serving
1.	Select the Sauté setting on the Instant Pot, add the oil and garlic, and heat for 2 minutes, until the garlic is bubbling.
2.	Add the leeks, jalapeños, and salt and sauté for 5 minutes, until the leeks are wilted.
3.	Add the chipotle chile and chili powder and sauté for 1 minute more. Stir in the broth.
4.	Add the carrots, beans and the squash. Pour the tomatoes and their liquid over the top. Do not stir.
5.	Secure the lid. Select Manual mode and set the cooking time for 5 minutes at High Pressure.
6.	When timer beeps, perform a quick pressure release. Open the pot, give a stir.
7.	Ladle the chili into bowls and sprinkle with cilantro. Serve hot.

Salsa Verde Cannellini Bean Chili

Prep time: 10 minutes | Cook time: 10 minutes | Serves 4 to 6

1 tablespoon olive oil
1 yellow onion, diced
1 green bell pepper, deseeded and diced
1 jalapeño pepper, deseeded and diced
1 clove garlic, grated
2 (15.5-ounce / 439-g) cans cannellini beans, drained and rinsed
1 cup salsa verde
1 teaspoon ground cumin
1 teaspoon ground coriander
¼ teaspoon cayenne pepper
4 cups vegetable stock
Salt and freshly ground black pepper, to taste
4 ounces (113 g) plant-based cheese, softened
1.	Press Sauté button on the Instant Pot and allow the pot to heat for 2 minutes.
2.	Add the oil, onion, bell pepper and jalapeño to the pot. Sauté for 3 minutes. Stir in the garlic.
3.	Add the beans, salsa verde, cumin, coriander, cayenne, stock, and salt and black pepper, to taste. Stir to combine.
4.	Secure the lid. Press Manual button and set cooking time for 5 minutes on High Pressure.
5.	When timer beeps, quick release the pressure. Remove the lid and mix in the plant-based cheese.
6.	Serve immediately.

Sumptuous Spring Veggie Chili

Prep time: 3 minutes | Cook time: 9 minutes | Serves 4

1 (8-ounce / 227-g) can cannellini beans, rinsed

2 radishes, trimmed, sliced
1 cup sliced carrots
1 cup fennel bulb, sliced
¼ cup onion, chopped
2 tablespoon shallots, chopped
¼ cup chopped celery
2 cloves garlic, chopped
1 cup tomato paste
1 teaspoon chipotle powder
½ cup vegetable broth
½ teaspoon cumin
1 teaspoon dried oregano
Pinch of rosemary
Pinch of cayenne
Salt and ground black pepper, to taste
1 medium zucchini, cubed
½ cup corn kernels
2 cherry tomatoes, quartered
1. Combine all ingredients, into the Instant pot, except the zucchinis, corn, and cherry tomatoes.
2. Lock the lid and select Manual mode. Set cooking time for 8 minutes on High Pressure.
3. When timer beeps, use a natural pressure release for 5 minutes, then release any remaining pressure. Open the lid.
4. Stir in the zucchinis, corn, and tomatoes. Lock the lid and set cooking time for 1 minute on High Pressure on Manual mode.
5. When timer beeps, perform a quick pressure release and open the lid.
6. Serve warm.

Black Bean, Pumpkin, and Kale Chili

Prep time: 10 minutes | Cook time: 12 minutes | Serves 4

¾ cup dried black beans, soaked in water overnight, rinsed and drained
2 cups chopped pumpkin
1 (28-ounce / 794-g) can crushed tomatoes
2 tablespoons chili powder
1 teaspoon onion powder
3 cups water
½ teaspoon garlic powder
2 cups finely shredded kale
½ teaspoon salt
1. Combine the black beans, pumpkin, tomatoes, chili powder, onion powder, water, and garlic powder.
2. Close the lid, then select Manual mode and set cooking time for 10 minutes on High Pressure.
3. Once the cook time is complete, let the pressure release naturally for about 20 minutes, then release any remaining pressure. Open the lid.
4. Stir in the kale to wilt on Sauté mode for 2 minutes more. Season with salt. Serve warm.

Butternut Squash and Cauliflower Soup

Prep time: 5 minutes | Cook time: 25 minutes | Serves 3

2 teaspoons olive oil
1 garlic clove, minced
½ medium onion, diced
1 cup vegetable broth
½ pound (227 g) frozen cauliflower
½ pound (227 g) frozen, cubed, butternut squash
½ teaspoon paprika
¼ teaspoon dried thyme
2 pinches of sea salt
½ cup coconut milk
1. Set your Instant Pot to Sauté and heat the olive oil.
2. Add the garlic and onion and cook for 2 minutes.
3. Add the broth, cauliflower, butternut, and all the spices to the Instant Pot, stirring well.
4. Secure the lid. Select the Manual mode and set the cooking time for 5 minutes at High Pressure.
5. Once cooking is complete, do a quick pressure release. Carefully open the lid.
6. Add the milk to the soup and blend with an immersion blender until creamy.
7. Serve hot.

Classic Borscht (Beet Soup)

Prep time: 15 minutes | Cook time: 15 minutes | Serves 7

4 tablespoons olive oil
2 medium white onions, chopped
2 large grated carrots
4 medium beets
4 large white potatoes, peeled and diced
½ medium white cabbage, thinly sliced
8 medium cloves garlic, diced
10 cups water
4 cups vegetable stock
½ cup dried porcini mushrooms
4 tablespoons apple cider vinegar
3 tablespoons tomato paste
2 teaspoons salt
1 teaspoon pepper
Fresh parsley, for garnish
1. Press the Sauté button on the Instant Pot and add the oil and onions. Cook for 3 minutes, stirring frequently.
2. Add the carrots, beets, potatoes, and cabbage, and sauté for 1 minute.
3. Add the remaining ingredients except the parsley to the Instant Pot and stir well.
4. Secure the lid. Select the Manual mode and set the cooking time for 10 minutes at High Pressure.
5. Once cooking is complete, do a natural pressure release for 10 minutes, then release any remaining pressure. Carefully open the lid.
6. Garnish with the parsley and serve.

Lentil Soup with Garam Masala

Prep time: 5 minutes | Cook time: 15 minutes | Serves 6

1 tablespoon vegetable oil
2 tablespoons finely diced shallot
1 cup diced carrots
1 cup diced celery
½ teaspoon garam masala
½ teaspoon ground cinnamon
½ teaspoon cumin
1 bay leaf

1¾ cups dried brown or green lentils, rinsed and drained
2 cups vegetable broth
3 cups water
¼ to ½ teaspoon sea salt (optional)
Freshly ground black pepper, to taste
1.	Set your Instant Pot to Sauté and heat the oil.
2.	Add the shallot, carrots, and celery and sauté for 3 to 5 minutes, until the shallot and celery are tender, stirring occasionally.
3.	Add the garam masala, cinnamon, cumin, bay leaf, and lentils and stir well. Pour in the vegetable broth and water and stir to mix well.
4.	Secure the lid. Select the Manual mode and set the cooking time for 8 minutes at High Pressure.
5.	Once cooking is complete, do a natural pressure release for 10 minutes, then release any remaining pressure. Carefully open the lid.
6.	Remove the bay leaf and sprinkle with salt (if desired). Season to taste with black pepper and serve.

White Beans and Greens Soup

Prep time: 5 minutes | Cook time: 20 minutes | Serves 6

1 tablespoon vegetable oil
4 large cloves garlic, minced
2 cups diced carrots
1 cup diced onion
1 cup diced celery
2 cups sliced cremini, shiitake, maitake, or baby bella mushrooms
2 tablespoons dried herbes de Provence
1 bay leaf
1 teaspoon red pepper flakes
½ teaspoon freshly ground black pepper, plus additional for serving
5 cups vegetable broth
2 cups water
¼ cup tomato paste
1½ cups dried cannellini beans, soaked for 12 hours or overnight, rinsed
8 cups loosely packed greens
Juice of 1 large lemon (about 3 tablespoons)
1 to 1½ teaspoons salt (optional)
1.	Press the Sauté button on the Instant Pot and heat the oil.
2.	Add the garlic, carrots, onion, and celery and sauté for 3 minutes.
3.	Add the mushrooms and seasonings and sauté for 3 to 5 minutes more. Add the vegetable broth, water, and tomato paste. Stir well.
4.	Stir in the beans and greens.
5.	Secure the lid. Select the Manual mode and set the cooking time for 8 minutes at High Pressure.
6.	Once cooking is complete, do a natural pressure release for 10 minutes, then release any remaining pressure. Carefully open the lid.
7.	Stir in the lemon juice and taste before adding salt. Remove the bay leaf and serve with additional black pepper.

Creamy Tofu Vegetable Soup

Prep time: 5 minutes | Cook time: 10 minutes | Serves 8

2 to 3 tablespoons butter
3 cloves garlic, minced
1 (14-ounce / 397-g) package soft tofu
1 cup almond milk
2 tablespoons lemon juice
1 teaspoon dried dill
½ teaspoon salt
4 cups diced potatoes
2 cups sliced mushrooms
2 cups sliced onion, cut into half-moons
1 cup chopped celery
1 cup chopped carrot
4 cups vegetable broth
Ground black pepper, to taste
1.	Set your Instant Pot to Sauté and melt the butter.
2.	Add the garlic and sauté for 1 minute.
3.	Pulse the tofu, almond milk, lemon juice, salt, and dill in a food processor until creamy.
4.	Add the potatoes, mushrooms, onion, carrots, and celery to the Instant Pot, stirring well. Pour the tofu mixture into the pot and stir in the vegetable broth.
5.	Secure the lid. Select the Manual mode and set the cooking time for 5 minutes at High Pressure.
6.	Once cooking is complete, do a quick pressure release. Carefully open the lid.
7.	Season to taste with black pepper and serve.

Miso Soup with Tofu and Kale

Prep time: 5 minutes | Cook time: 10 minutes | Serves 6

1 to 2 teaspoons vegetable oil
4 cloves garlic, cut in half
1 small sweet onion, quartered
2 medium carrots, cut into 2- to 3-inch pieces
4 cups low-sodium vegetable broth
1 (12-ounce / 340-g) package silken (light firm) tofu
1 bunch kale (off the stem), plus a few leaves for garnish
¼ cup yellow miso
Ground black pepper, to taste
1.	Press the Sauté button on the Instant Pot and heat the oil.
2.	Add the garlic, onion, and carrots and sauté for 5 minutes, stirring occasionally.
3.	Add the vegetable broth and tofu. Crumble the tofu into pieces with a spoon. Add the kale and stir to incorporate.
4.	Secure the lid. Select the Manual mode and set the cooking time for 4 minutes at High Pressure.
5.	Once cooking is complete, do a natural pressure release for 10 minutes, then release any remaining pressure. Carefully open the lid.
6.	Stir in the miso and blend the soup with an immersion blender until smooth.
7.	Season to taste with black pepper and serve garnished with extra kale.

Artichoke and Chickpea Soup

Prep time: 5 minutes | Cook time: 6 minutes | Serves 4

1 large potato, diced
3 cloves garlic, minced
½ package extra-firm tofu, pressed, drained, and diced
1 (14-ounce / 397-g) can artichoke hearts, drained
1 (14-ounce / 397-g) can chickpeas, rinsed and drained
5 cups vegetable broth
1 tomato, diced
2 stalks celery, chopped
1 teaspoon turmeric
1 teaspoon paprika
¼ teaspoon ground black pepper
¼ cup capers, for garnish

1.　　　Combine all the ingredients except the black pepper and capers in the Instant Pot.
2.　　　Secure the lid. Select the Manual mode and set the cooking time for 6 minutes at High Pressure.
3.　　　Once cooking is complete, do a quick pressure release. Carefully open the lid and stir in the black pepper.
4.　　　Garnish with the capers and serve hot.

White Bean and Swiss Chard Stew

Prep time: 6 minutes | Cook time: 10 minutes | Serves 4 to 6

1 tablespoon olive oil
2 carrots, sliced, with thicker end cut into half-moons
1 celery stalk, sliced
½ onion, cut into large dices
2 or 3 garlic cloves, minced
3 tomatoes, chopped
¼ to ½ teaspoon red pepper flakes
½ teaspoon dried oregano
½ teaspoon dried rosemary
½ teaspoon salt, plus more as needed
¼ teaspoon dried basil
Pinch freshly ground black pepper, plus more as needed
2 cups cooked great northern beans
1 small bunch Swiss chard leaves, chopped
Nutritional yeast, for sprinkling (optional)

1.　　　Set your Instant Pot to Sauté and heat the olive oil until it shimmers.
2.　　　Add the carrots, celery, and onion. Sauté for 2 to 3 minutes, stirring occasionally. Add the garlic and cook for 30 seconds more. Turn off the Instant Pot.
3.　　　Stir in the tomatoes, red pepper flakes, oregano, rosemary, salt, basil, black pepper, and beans.
4.　　　Secure the lid. Select the Manual mode and set the cooking time for 4 minutes at High Pressure.
5.　　　Once cooking is complete, do a quick pressure release. Carefully open the lid.
6.　　　Stir in the Swiss chard and let sit for 2 to 3 minutes until wilted. Taste and season with salt and pepper, as needed. Sprinkle the nutritional yeast over individual servings, if desired.

Quinoa Vegetable Stew

Prep time: 10 minutes | Cook time: 15 minutes | Serves 4

2 teaspoons corn oil
1 yellow onion, minced
3 Roma tomatoes, minced
¼ cup frozen corn kernels, thawed to room temperature
1 zucchini, cut into 1-inch chunks
½ cup chopped red bell pepper
1½ cups broccoli florets
¼ cup diced carrot
½ cup quinoa, rinsed
1 teaspoon ground coriander
½ teaspoon paprika
½ teaspoon ground cumin
1 (32-ounce / 907-g) container vegetable broth
2 teaspoons kosher salt
4 tablespoons minced fresh cilantro, divided

1.　　　Press the Sauté button on the Instant Pot and heat the oil. Once hot, add the onion and sauté 5 minutes, stirring occasionally.
2.　　　Add the tomatoes, corn, zucchini, bell pepper, broccoli, and carrot and mix well. Stir in the quinoa, coriander, paprika, cumin, broth, salt, and 2 tablespoons of cilantro.
3.　　　Secure the lid. Select the Manual mode and set the cooking time for 8 minutes at High Pressure.
4.　　　Once cooking is complete, do a natural pressure release for 5 minutes, then release any remaining pressure. Carefully open the lid.
5.　　　Stir in the remaining 2 tablespoons of cilantro and serve hot.

African Yam and Peanut Stew

Prep time: 20 minutes | Cook time: 60 minutes | Serves 4

3 yams, chopped
1 white onion, roughly chopped
1 teaspoon minced ginger root
1 teaspoon garlic, diced
1 tablespoon almond butter
1 teaspoon cilantro
1 teaspoon oregano
1 teaspoon cayenne pepper
1 teaspoon onion powder
1 teaspoon ground black pepper
1 teaspoon cumin
¼ cup peanuts, chopped
1 bell pepper, chopped
1 cup collard greens, chopped
3 tablespoons peanut butter
½ cup almond milk
2 cups water

1.　　　Select the Instant Pot to Sauté mode. Add the yams, onion, minced ginger root, and diced garlic with almond butter for 5 minutes. Stir constantly.
2.　　　Meanwhile, mix up together the cilantro, oregano, cayenne pepper, onion powder, ground black pepper, and cumin in a small bowl.
3.　　　Add the mixture in the Instant Pot, then add the peanuts, bell pepper, collard, and peanut butter. Add almond milk and water.
4.　　　Close the lid. Set Meat/Stew mode and set cooking time for 50 minutes on High Pressure.

5.	When timer beeps, use a quick pressure release. Open the lid.
6.	Let the stew sit for at least 15 minutes before serving.

Seitan and Rutabaga Stew

Prep time: 10 minutes | Cook time: 15 minutes | Serves 4 to 6

1 pound (454 g) seitan, patted dry
¼ teaspoon fine sea salt
½ teaspoon freshly ground black pepper
1 tablespoon avocado oil
1 yellow onion, diced
4 cloves garlic, minced
½ cup red wine
1 teaspoon fresh thyme leaves
1 teaspoon chopped fresh sage leaves
1 teaspoon chopped fresh rosemary
1 cup vegetable broth
2 teaspoons Dijon mustard
1 (1-pound / 454-g) large rutabaga, peeled and cut into 1-inch pieces
4 medium carrots (about 8 ounces / 227 g in total), peeled and sliced into 1-inch rounds
3 waxy potatoes (about 1 pound / 454 g in total), cut into 1-inch pieces
1 tablespoon tomato paste
1.	Sprinkle the seitan with the salt and pepper.
2.	Select the Sauté setting on the Instant Pot, add the oil, and heat for 2 minutes.
3.	Add the seitan and sear for 4 minutes until golden brown. Flip and sear for 3 minutes more. Transfer the seitan to a dish and set aside.
4.	Add the onion and garlic to the pot and sauté for 4 minutes until the onion softens.
5.	Stir in the wine. Let the wine simmer until it has mostly evaporated, about 4 minutes.
6.	Add the thyme, sage, and rosemary, and sauté for 1 minute more. Add the broth and mustard and stir to dissolve.
7.	Bring the mixture up to a simmer, then stir in the seitan, rutabaga, carrots, and potatoes. Add the tomato paste on top. Do not stir.
8.	Secure the lid. Select the Meat/Stew setting and set the cooking time for 4 minutes at High Pressure.
9.	When timer beeps, perform a quick pressure release. Open the pot and gently stir the stew to incorporate the tomato paste and make sure everything is coated with the cooking liquid.
10.	Ladle the stew into bowls and serve hot.

Super West African Chickpea Stew

Prep time: 5 minutes | Cook time: 7 minutes | Serves 6

1½ tablespoons refined coconut oil
1 large yellow onion, diced
6 garlic cloves, minced
2-inch piece fresh ginger, grated or minced
1 Scotch bonnet pepper, deseeded and minced
1 teaspoon ground coriander
1 teaspoon ground turmeric
¼ teaspoon ground cinnamon
½ teaspoon dried thyme
1½ teaspoons ground cumin
½ teaspoon freshly cracked black pepper
¼ teaspoon ground cloves
2 cups vegetable broth
1 pound (454 g) sweet potatoes, peeled and cut into ¾-inch cubes
1½ teaspoons kosher salt
½ cup peanut butter
1 (15-ounce / 425-g) can chickpeas, drained and rinsed
1 (28-ounce / 794-g) can crushed tomatoes
3 tablespoons tomato paste
4 cups kale, stems and midribs removed and sliced into strips
½ cup fresh cilantro, roughly chopped
1 tablespoon fresh lime juice
¹/₃ cup roasted peanuts, roughly chopped
1.	Select the Sauté setting on the Instant Pot and let the pot heat for a few minutes before adding the oil.
2.	Once the oil is hot, add the onion. Cook until the onion is softened, about 3 to 4 minutes.
3.	Add the garlic, ginger, and chile pepper and cook for 1 minute, tossing frequently.
4.	Add the coriander, turmeric, cinnamon, thyme, cumin, black pepper, and cloves. Stir the spices into the vegetables and cook until the mixture is fragrant, about 30 seconds.
5.	Pour in the vegetable broth to deglaze the pan, using a wooden spoon to scrape up any browned bits on the bottom of the pot.
6.	Add the sweet potatoes, salt, peanut butter, and chickpeas. Stir to combine.
7.	Pour the crushed tomatoes and tomato paste on top, but do not stir, allowing the tomatoes and paste to sit on top.
8.	Secure the lid. Select the Manual mode and set the cook time to 5 minutes on High Pressure.
9.	When timer beeps, allow a natural pressure release for 5 minutes, then release any remaining pressure.
10.	Open the pot and stir in the kale. Select the Sauté setting and cook until wilted and cooked through, about 2 minutes. Stir in the cilantro and lime juice.
11.	Transfer the stew to bowls and garnish with the roasted peanuts. Serve immediately.

Super Flageolet Bean and Millet Stew

Prep time: 10 minutes | Cook time: 20 minutes | Serves 6

1 teaspoon olive oil
¼ cup sliced shallot
1 apple, diced
½ cup diced parsnip
1 golden beet, diced
1½ cups dried flageolet beans, soaked in water overnight, rinsed and drained
½ cup millet
1 (14-ounce / 398-g) can diced tomatoes
1 bay leaf
1 teaspoon whole fennel seed, crumbled
1 teaspoon dried thyme

1 teaspoon dried sweet basil
2½ cups vegetable broth
2½ cups water
1 to 2 tablespoons lemon juice
¼ teaspoon black pepper
1. In the Instant Pot, heat the oil on Sauté mode.
2. Add the shallot and sauté for 1 minute to soften a bit.
3. Add the apple, parsnip, and beet and sauté for 4 minutes.
4. Add the beans, millet, diced tomatoes, bay leaf, fennel, thyme, and basil. Stir to combine.
5. Cover the vegetables and beans with broth and water by 3 inches.
6. Secure the lid. Select Manual mode and set cooking time for 10 minutes on High Pressure.
7. When timer beeps, use a natural pressure release for 15 minutes, then release any remaining pressure.
8. Remove the lid and stir in the lemon juice. Remove the bay leaf before serving. Add ground pepper and serve.

Sweet Potato and Black Bean Stew

Prep time: 5 minutes | Cook time: 30 minutes | Serves 6

2 tablespoons avocado oil
4 cups vegetable broth
½ cup chopped onion
4 cloves garlic, minced
2 carrots, chopped
1 large sweet potato, diced into equal, bite-size pieces
2 small tomatoes, diced
3 stalks celery, chopped
½ teaspoon ground cinnamon
1 teaspoon garam masala
1 cup dried black beans, rinsed and drained
2 bay leaves
½ teaspoon sea salt
¼ teaspoon black pepper
1. In the Instant Pot, heat the oil on Sauté mode.
2. Add the onion and garlic and sauté for 2 minutes until the onion is soft.
3. Add the carrots and sweet potato and sauté for another 3 minutes.
4. Add the tomatoes, celery, cinnamon, and garam masala and stir to coat all the vegetables with the spices.
5. Add the black beans, bay leaves, and vegetable broth. Stir to combine.
6. Secure the lid. Select Manual mode and set cooking time for 24 minutes.
7. When timer beeps, use a natural pressure release for 15 minutes, then release any remaining pressure.
8. Remove the lid, remove the bay leaves, stir in the salt and pepper, and serve.

Apple Wontons

Prep time: 10 minutes | Cook time: 12 minutes | Serves 8

1 (8-ounce / 227-g) can refrigerated crescent rolls
1 large apple, peeled, cored, and cut into 8 wedges
4 tablespoons unsalted butter
2 teaspoons ground cinnamon
¼ teaspoon ground nutmeg
½ cup brown sugar
1 teaspoon vanilla extract
¾ cup orange juice
1. Make the dumplings: Unfold the crescent rolls on a clean work surface, then separate into the 8 triangles. Place 1 apple wedge on each crescent roll triangle and fold the dough around the apple to enclose it. Set aside.
2. Select the Sauté mode of the Instant Pot. Add the butter and heat for 2 minutes until melted.
3. Add the cinnamon, nutmeg, sugar, and vanilla, heating and stirring until melted.
4. Place the dumplings in the Instant Pot and mix in the orange juice.
5. Lock the lid. Select the Manual mode. Set the time for 10 minutes at High Pressure.
6. When cooking is complete, let the pressure release naturally for 5 minutes, then release any remaining pressure. Unlock the lid.
7. Serve immediately.

Apple and Oatmeal Crisps

Prep time: 15 minutes | Cook time: 5 minutes | Serves 4

5 apples, cored and chopped
1 tablespoon honey
2 teaspoons cinnamon powder
½ teaspoon nutmeg powder
1 cup water
¾ cup old fashioned rolled oats
¼ cup all-purpose flour
4 tablespoons unsalted butter, melted
½ teaspoon salt
¼ cup brown sugar
1 cup vanilla ice cream, for topping
1. In the Instant Pot, mix the apples, honey, cinnamon, nutmeg, and water.
2. In a medium bowl, combine the rolled oats, flour, butter, salt, and brown sugar. Drizzle the mixture over the apples.
3. Seal the lid, set to the Manual mode and set the cooking time for 5 minutes on High Pressure.
4. When cooking is complete, allow a natural pressure release for 10 minutes, then release any remaining pressure. Carefully open the lid.
5. Spoon the apple into serving bowls, top with vanilla ice cream and serve immediately.

Apricots Dulce de Leche

Prep time: 15 minutes | Cook time: 25 minutes | Serves 6

5 cups water
2 cups sweetened condensed milk
4 apricots, halved, cored, and sliced
1. Pour the water in the Instant Pot and fit in a trivet. Divide condensed milk into 6 medium jars and close with lids. Place jars on trivet.
2. Seal the lid, set to the Manual mode and set the timer for 25 minutes at High Pressure.
3. When cooking is complete, use a natural pressure release for 10 minutes, then release any remaining pressure. Unlock the lid.
4. Use a fork to whisk until creamy. Serve with sliced apricots.

Brown Rice and Coconut Milk Pudding

Prep time: 15 minutes | Cook time: 22 minutes | Serves 6

1 cup long-grain brown rice, rinsed
2 cups water
1 (15-ounce / 425-g) can full-fat coconut milk
½ teaspoon pure vanilla extract
½ teaspoon ground cinnamon
$^1/_3$ cup maple syrup
Pinch fine sea salt
1. Combine the rice and water in the Instant Pot and secure the lid. Select the Manual mode and set the cooking time for 22 minutes on Low Pressure.
2. When timer beeps, allow the pressure to naturally release for 10 minutes, then release any remaining pressure. Carefully open the lid.
3. Add the coconut milk, vanilla, cinnamon, maple syrup, and salt. Stir well to combine.
4. Use an immersion blender to pulse the pudding until creamy. Serve warm or you can refrigerate the pudding for an hour before serving.

Bourbon and Date Pudding Cake

Prep time: 15 minutes | Cook time: 25 minutes | Serves 4

¾ cup all-purpose flour
¼ teaspoon allspice
½ teaspoon baking soda
¼ teaspoon cloves powder
½ teaspoon cinnamon powder
¼ teaspoon salt
1 teaspoon baking powder
2 tablespoons bourbon
3 tablespoons unsalted butter, melted
6 tablespoons hot water
2 tablespoons whole milk
1 egg, beaten
½ cup chopped dates
1 cup water
½ cup caramel sauce
1. In a bowl, combine the flour, allspice, baking soda, cloves, cinnamon, salt, and baking powder.
2. In another bowl, mix the bourbon, butter, hot water, and milk. Pour the bourbon mixture into the flour mixture and mix until well mixed. Whisk in egg and fold in dates.

3.	Spritz 4 medium ramekins with cooking spray. Divide the mixture among them, and cover with foil.
4.	Pour the water in the Instant Pot, then fit in a trivet and place ramekins on top.
5.	Seal the lid, select the Manual mode and set the cooking time for 25 minutes at High Pressure.
6.	When cooking is complete, perform a natural pressure release for 10 minutes, then release any remaining pressure.
7.	Unlock the lid and carefully remove ramekins, invert onto plates, and drizzle caramel sauce on top. Serve warm.

Caramel Apple Cobbler

Prep time: 30 minutes | Cook time: 2 minutes | Serves 4
5 apples, cored, peeled, and cut into 1-inch cubes, at room temperature
2 tablespoons caramel syrup
½ teaspoon ground nutmeg
2 teaspoons ground cinnamon
2 tablespoons maple syrup
½ cup water
¾ cup old-fashioned oats
¼ cup all-purpose flour
$^1/_3$ cup brown sugar
4 tablespoons salted butter, softened
½ teaspoon sea salt
Vanilla ice cream, for serving
1.	Place the apples in the Instant Pot and top with the caramel syrup, nutmeg, cinnamon, maple syrup, and water. Stir to coat well.
2.	Combine the oats, flour, brown sugar, butter and salt in a large bowl. Mix well and pour over the apple mixture in the pot.
3.	Secure the lid, then select the Manual mode and set the cooking time for 2 minutes on High Pressure.
4.	When cooking is complete, perform a natural pressure release for 20minutes, then release any remaining pressure. Carefully open the lid.
5.	Transfer the cobbler to a plate, then topped with vanilla ice cream and serve.

Creamy Raspberry Cheesecake

Prep time: 3 hours 30 minutes | Cook time: 40 minutes | Serves 4
12 graham crackers, crushed
2 tablespoons melted butter
1 pound (454 g) cream cheese, softened
1 cup granulated sugar
12 large raspberries, plus more for garnish
2 eggs
1 teaspoon vanilla extract
3 tablespoons maple syrup
2 teaspoons cinnamon powder
½ cup heavy cream
1 cup water
1.	Make the crust: Mix the crushed graham crackers with butter. Pour the mixture into a springform pan and press to fit with a spoon. Refrigerate for 15 minutes or until firm.

2.	In a bowl, whisk the cream cheese and sugar until smooth. Add the raspberries, eggs, vanilla, maple syrup, cinnamon, and heavy cream, and mix until well combined.
3.	Remove the cake pan from refrigerator and pour cream cheese mixture on top. Spread evenly and cover pan with foil.
4.	Pour the water in Instant Pot, then fit in a trivet, and place cake pan on top.
5.	Seal the lid, select the Manual mode and set to 40 minutes on High Pressure.
6.	When cooking is complete, allow a natural pressure release for 10 minutes, then release any remaining pressure.
7.	Unlock the lid and carefully remove the pan. Allow cooling for 10 minutes and chill in the fridge for 3 hours. Invert the cake on a plate and garnish with more raspberries. Slice and serve.

Cardamom Yogurt Pudding

Prep time: 20 minutes | Cook time: 15 minutes | Serves 4
1½ cups Greek yogurt
1 teaspoon cocoa powder
2 cups sweetened condensed milk
1 teaspoon cardamom powder
1 cup water
¼ cup mixed nuts, chopped
1.	Spritz 4 medium ramekins with cooking spray. Set aside.
2.	In a bowl, combine the Greek yogurt, cocoa powder, condensed milk, and cardamom powder. Pour mixture into ramekins and cover with foil.
3.	Pour the water into the Instant Pot, then fit in a trivet, and place ramekins on top.
4.	Seal the lid, select the Manual mode and set the cooking time for 15 minutes at High Pressure.
5.	When cooking is complete, perform a natural pressure release for 15 minutes, then release any remaining pressure. Unlock the lid.
6.	Remove the ramekins from the pot, then take off the foil. Top with mixed nuts and serve immediately.

Classic Cheesecake

Prep time: 3 hours 40 minutes | Cook time: 40 minutes | Serves 4
2 cups graham crackers, crushed
3 tablespoons brown sugar
¼ cup butter, melted
2 (8 ounce / 227-g) cream cheese, softened
½ cup granulated sugar
2 tablespoons all-purpose flour
1 teaspoon vanilla extract
3 eggs
1 cup water
1 cup caramel sauce
1.	Make the crust: Mix the crushed crackers with brown sugar and butter. Spread the mixture at the bottom of a springform pan and use a spoon to press to fit. Freeze in refrigerator for 10 minutes.
2.	In a bowl, whisk the cream cheese and sugar until smooth. Mix in the flour and vanilla.

Whisk in the eggs. Remove the pan from refrigerator and pour mixture over crust. Cover the pan with foil.
3.		Pour the water in Instant Pot, then fit in a trivet and place the pan on top.
4.		Seal the lid, select the Manual mode and set the timer for 40 minutes on High Pressure.
5.		When cooking is complete, allow a natural pressure release for 10 minutes, then release any remaining pressure. Open the lid.
6.		Carefully remove the cake pan and take off the foil. Let cool for 10 minutes. Pour the caramel sauce over and refrigerate for 3 hours.
7.		Remove the pan from the refrigerator and invert the cheesecake on a plate. Slice and serve.

Coconut-Potato Pudding

Prep time: 5 minutes | Cook time: 10 minutes | Serves 4
1 cup water
1 large sweet potato (about 1 pound / 454 g), peeled and cut into 1-inch pieces
½ cup canned coconut milk
6 tablespoons pure maple syrup
1 teaspoon grated fresh ginger (about ½-inch knob)
1.		Pour the water into the Instant Pot and fit in a steamer basket.
2.		Place the sweet potato pieces in the steamer basket and secure the lid. Select the Manual mode and set the cooking time for 10 minutes at High Pressure.
3.		When timer beeps, use a quick pressure release. Unlock the lid.
4.		Transfer the cooked potatoes to a large bowl. Add the coconut milk, maple syrup, and ginger. Use an immersion blender to purée the potatoes into a smooth pudding.
5.		Serve the pudding immediately or chill in the refrigerator for an hour before serving.

Classic New York Cheesecake

Prep time: 3 hours 45 minutes | Cook time: 40 minutes | Serves 4
12 graham crackers, crushed
2 tablespoons melted salted butter
1½ tablespoons brown sugar
16 ounces (454 g) cream cheese, softened
1 cup granulated sugar
2 eggs
½ cup sour cream
2 tablespoons cornstarch
1 teaspoon vanilla extract
¼ teaspoon salt
1 cup water
1.		Mix the crushed graham crackers with butter and brown sugar. Pour mixture into a springform pan and use a spoon to press to fit. Freeze for 15 minutes until firm.
2.		In a bowl, beat cream cheese and sugar until smooth. Whisk in the eggs, sour cream, cornstarch, vanilla, and salt.
3.		Remove the pan from refrigerator and pour cream cheese mixture on top. Spread evenly using a spatula and cover the pan with foil.

4.		Pour the water in Instant Pot, then fit in a trivet, and place cake pan on top.
5.		Seal the lid, select the Manual mode and set the cooking time for 40 minutes on High Pressure.
6.		When cooking is complete, do a natural pressure release for 10 minutes, then release any remaining pressure.
7.		Unlock the lid and carefully remove cake pan. Allow cooling for 10 minutes and chill in refrigerator for 3 hours. Remove from refrigerator, then slice and serve.

Chocolate Pudding

Prep time: 15 minutes | Cook time: 5 minutes | Serves 4
4 tablespoons cocoa powder
3 medium eggs, cracked
3¼ cups whole milk
¼ cup collagen
1¼ teaspoons gelatin
1½ tablespoons vanilla extract
¼ cup maple syrup
1 tablespoon coconut oil
1 cup water
1.		In a blender, combine all the ingredients, except for the water. Process until smooth.
2.		Pour the mixture into 4 ramekins and cover with aluminum foil. Pour the water in Instant Pot, fit in a trivet, and place the ramekins on top.
3.		Seal the lid, select the Manual mode and set cooking time to 5 minutes on High Pressure.
4.		When cooking is complete, allow a natural pressure release for 10 minutes, then release any remaining pressure. Unlock the lid.
5.		Refrigerate overnight and serve.

Caramel Glazed Popcorns

Prep time: 5 minutes | Cook time: 7 minutes | Serves 4
4 tablespoons butter
1 cup sweet corn kernels
3 tablespoons brown sugar
¼ cup whole milk
1.		Set the Instant Pot to Sauté mode, melt butter and mix in the corn kernels, heat for 1 minute or until the corn is popping.
2.		Cover the lid, and keep cooking for 3 more minutes or until the corn stops popping. Open the lid and transfer the popcorns to a bowl.
3.		Combine brown sugar and milk in the pot and cook for 3 minutes or until sugar dissolves. Stir constantly.
4.		Drizzle caramel sauce over corns and toss to coat thoroughly. Serve warm.

Creamy Banana Pudding

Prep time: 5 minutes | Cook time: 5 minutes | Serves 4
1 cup whole milk
2 cups half-and-half
¾ cup plus 1 tablespoon granulated sugar, divided
4 egg yolks
3 tablespoon cornstarch

2 tablespoons cold butter, cut into 4 pieces
1 teaspoon vanilla extract
2 medium banana, peeled and sliced
1 cup heavy cream

1. Set the Instant Pot to Sauté mode. Mix the milk, half-and-half, and ½ cup of sugar in the pot.
2. Heat for 3 minutes or until sugar dissolves. Stir constantly.
3. Meanwhile, beat the egg yolks with ¼ cup of sugar in a medium bowl. Add cornstarch and mix well.
4. Scoop ½ cup of milk mixture into egg mixture and whisk until smooth. Pour mixture into Instant Pot.
5. Seal the lid, select the Manual mode and set the cooking time for 2 minutes on High Pressure.
6. When cooking is complete, do a quick pressure release and unlock the lid.
7. Stir in butter and vanilla. Lay banana pieces into 4 bowls and top with pudding.
8. In a bowl, whisk heavy cream with remaining sugar; spoon mixture on top of pudding. Refrigerate for 1 hour before serving.

Chocolate Oreo Cookie Cake

Prep time: 8 hours 35 minutes | Cook time: 35 minutes | Serves 6

12 Oreo cookies, smoothly crushed
2 tablespoons salted butter, melted
16 ounces (454 g) cream cheese, softened
½ cup granulated sugar
2 large eggs
1 tablespoon all-purpose flour
¼ cup heavy cream
2 teaspoons vanilla extract
16 whole Oreo cookies, coarsely crushed
1½ cups water
1 cup whipped cream
2 tablespoons chocolate sauce, for topping

1. Line a springform pan with foil, then spritz with cooking spray.
2. Make the crust: In a bowl, combine smoothly crushed Oreo cookies with butter, then press into bottom of pan. Freeze for 15 minutes.
3. In another bowl, add cream cheese, and beat until smooth. Add sugar to whisk until satiny. Beat in the eggs one by one until mixed. Whisk in flour, heavy cream, and vanilla.
4. Fold in 8 coarsely crushed cookies and pour the mixture onto the crust in the springform pan. Cover pan tightly with foil.
5. Pour the water in the Instant Pot and fit in a trivet. Place the pan on trivet.
6. Seal the lid, set to the Manual mode and set the cooking time for 35 minutes at High Pressure.
7. When cooking is complete, allow a natural pressure release for 10 minutes, then release any remaining pressure. Carefully open the lid.
8. Remove the trivet with cake pan from the pot. Remove foil and transfer to a cooling rack to chill. Refrigerate for 8 hours. Top with whipped cream, remaining cookies, and chocolate sauce. Slice and serve.

Classic Pumpkin Pie

Prep time: 4 hours 20 minutes | Cook time: 35 minutes | Serves 6

½ cup crushed graham crackers (about 7 graham crackers)
2 tablespoons unsalted butter, melted
½ cup brown sugar
1 large egg
1½ cups canned pumpkin purée
1½ teaspoons pumpkin pie spice
½ teaspoon sea salt
½ cup evaporated milk
1 cup water

1. Make the crust: In a small bowl, combine the graham cracker crumbs and butter and mix until well combined. Press the mixture into the bottom and 1 inch up the sides of a springform pan. Set aside.
2. In a large mixing bowl, whisk together the egg, pumpkin purée, pumpkin pie spice, sugar, salt, and milk. Pour the filling into the prepared crust. Cover the pan with aluminum foil.
3. Place a trivet in the Instant Pot and pour in the water. Lower the pan onto the trivet.
4. Lock the lid. Select the Manual mode. Set the time for 35 minutes on High Pressure.
5. When timer beeps, let the pressure release naturally for 10 minutes, then release the remaining pressure.
6. Unlock the lid. Remove the pan from the pot and then remove the foil. Allow the pie to cool. Cover with plastic wrap and refrigerate for at least 4 hours before serving.

Easy Bread Pudding

Prep time: 15 minutes | Cook time: 25 minutes | Serves 8

2 cups milk
5 large eggs
$^1/_3$ cup granulated sugar
1 teaspoon vanilla extract
5 cups (about ½ loaf) bread, slice into 2-inch cubes
2 tablespoons unsalted butter, cut into small pieces

1. In a medium bowl, whisk together the eggs, milk, sugar, and vanilla. Add the bread cubes and stir to coat well. Refrigerate for 1 hour.
2. Spritz the Instant Pot with cooking spray. Pour in the bread mixture. Scatter with the butter pieces.
3. Lock the lid. Select the Manual mode. Set the timer for 25 minutes on High Pressure.
4. When timer beeps, let the pressure release naturally for 10 minutes, then release the remaining pressure. Unlock the lid.
5. Serve the pudding immediately or chill in the refrigerator for an hour before serving.

Easy Orange Cake

Prep time: 5 minutes | Cook time: 30 minutes | Serves 6

1½ cups orange soda
1 (15.25-ounce / 432-g) box orange cake mix
1 cup water
1 tablespoon caster sugar, for garnish

1. Spritz a bundt pan with cooking spray.
2. In a bowl, mix orange soda and orange cake mix until well combined. Pour into bundt pan, cover with a foil.
3. Pour the water in the Instant Pot, then fit in a trivet, and place the pan on top.
4. Seal the lid, select the Manual mode and set the cooking time for 30 minutes at High Pressure.
5. When cooking is complete, do a quick pressure release. Open the lid.
6. Remove the pan from the pot and allow cooling. Turn over onto a platter, sprinkle with caster sugar. Slice and serve.

Easy Pecan Monkey Bread

Prep time: 15 minutes | Cook time: 25 minutes | Serves 6

1½ cinnamon powder
¼ cup brown sugar
¼ cup toasted pecans, chopped
1 pound (454 g) dinner rolls, cut in half lengthwise
½ cup butter, melted
1 cup water
2 teaspoons whole milk
½ cup powdered sugar

1. Spritz a bundt pan with cooking spray.
2. In a shallow plate, mix the cinnamon, brown sugar, and pecans. Coat the dinner rolls in the mixture, then in butter, and then place in bundt pan, making sure to build layers. Cover pan with foil and allow rising overnight.
3. Pour the water into Instant Pot, then fit in a trivet and place bundt pan on top.
4. Seal the lid, select the Manual mode and set the cooking time for 25 minutes at High Pressure.
5. When cooking is complete, allow a natural release for 10 minutes, then release any remaining pressure.
6. Unlock the lid, remove the pan from the pot, take off the foil, and allow to cool completely.
7. In a bowl, whisk milk with sugar until smooth.
8. Invert the bread on a serving platter and drizzle with sweetened milk.
9. Slice and serve.

Flourless Chocolate Brownies

Prep time: 15 minutes | Cook time: 15 minutes | Makes 16 brownies

1 egg
¾ cup almond butter
$^1/_3$ cup raw cacao powder
¾ cup coconut sugar
½ teaspoon baking soda
¼ teaspoon fine sea salt
½ teaspoon pure vanilla extract
½ cup dark chocolate chips
1 cup water

1. Line a springform pan with parchment paper. In a large bowl, whisk together the egg, almond butter, cacao powder, coconut sugar, baking soda, salt, and vanilla and stir well until it has a thick consistency.

2. Transfer the batter to the prepared pan and level the batter with a spatula. Sprinkle with the chocolate chips.
3. Pour 1 cup water into the Instant Pot and fit in a trivet. Place the pan on top of the trivet and cover it with an upside-down plate.
4. Secure the lid. Select the Manual mode and set the cooking time for 15 minutes at High Pressure.
5. When timer beeps, let the pressure naturally release for 10 minutes, then release any remaining pressure. Unlock the lid.
6. Slice into 16 brownies and serve.

Tapioca Pudding

Prep time: 12 mins, Cook Time: 15 mins, Servings: 4

- 1 cup water
- 1¼ cups almond milk
- ¼ cup rinsed and drained seed tapioca pearls
- ½ cup sugar
- ½ tsp. lemon zest

1. Pour the water into the Instant Pot.
2. Add the steamer basket inside the pot.
3. In a heat-proof bowl, mix all the ingredients until the sugar has dissolved.
4. Cover with foil and put the bowl on top of the basket.
5. Lock the lid. Set the Instant Pot to Manual mode, then set the timer for 10 minutes at High Pressure.
6. When the timer goes off, perform a natural release for 5 minutes, then release any remaining pressure. Carefully open the lid.
7. Serve immediately or refrigerate for several hours and serve chilled.

Chocolate Chia Pudding

Prep time: 6 mins, Cook Time: 3 hours, Servings: 4

- 2 tbsps. cacao powder
- ¼ tsp. salt
- ¼ cup chia seeds
- ½ tsp. liquid stevia
- 1 cup freshly squeezed coconut milk

1. Pour all the ingredients in the Instant Pot and stir to mix well.
2. Lock the lid. Set the Instant Pot to Slow Cook mode, then set the timer for 3 hours at High Pressure.
3. When the timer goes off, perform a natural release for 10 minutes, then release any remaining pressure. Carefully open the lid.
4. Serve immediately or refrigerate for several hours and serve chilled.

Coconut Pudding

Prep time: 6 mins, Cook Time: 3 hours, Servings: 2

- 1 tsp. erythritol
- ½ cup coconut milk
- A dash of vanilla extract

- ½ tsp. cinnamon powder
- ¼ cup dried coconut flakes
- Salt, to taste
- ½ cup water
1. Put all ingredients in the Instant Pot.
2. Mix until well combined.
3. Lock the lid. Set the Instant Pot to Slow Cook mode, then set the timer for 3 hours at High Pressure.
4. When the timer goes off, perform a natural release for 10 minutes, then release any remaining pressure. Carefully open the lid.
5. Serve immediately or refrigerate for several hours and serve chilled.

Cream and Cinnamon Puddings
Prep time: 20 mins, Cook Time: 15 mins, Servings: 6

- 2 cups fresh cream
- 1 tsp. cinnamon powder
- Zest of 1 orange
- 5 tbsps. sugar
- 6 egg yolks
- 2 cups water
1. Set the pot on Sauté mode and heat it up.
2. Add cream, cinnamon and orange zest and sauté for a few minutes and leave aside for 20 minutes.
3. Using a bowl, combine the sugar and egg yolks. Pour the egg yolk mixture in the cream mixture, whisk well, strain the mixture, divide it into ramekins and cover them with tin foil.
4. Clean the pot, add the water, add steamer basket, add ramekins.
5. Lock the lid. Set the Instant Pot to Manual mode, then set the timer for 10 minutes at High Pressure.
6. When the timer goes off, perform a natural release for 5 minutes, then release any remaining pressure. Carefully open the lid.
7. Refrigerate the puddings for several hours, then serve chilled.

Lemon and Maple Syrup Pudding
Prep time: 12 mins, Cook Time: 5 mins, Servings: 7

- ½ cup maple syrup
- 3 cups milk
- Lemon zest from 2 grated lemons
- 2 tbsps. gelatin
- Juice of 2 lemons
- 1 cup water
1. In the blender, mix milk with lemon juice, lemon zest, maple syrup and gelatin, pulse really well and divide into ramekins.
2. In the Instant Pot, set in the water, add steamer basket, add ramekins inside.
3. Lock the lid. Set the Instant Pot to Manual mode, then set the timer for 5 minutes on High Pressure.
4. When the timer goes off, perform a natural release. Carefully open the lid.

5. Refrigerate and serve the puddings chilled.

Pineapple Pudding
Prep time: 12 mins, Cook Time: 5 mins, Servings: 8

- 1 cup rice
- 1 tbsp. avocado oil
- 14 oz. milk
- Sugar, to taste
- 8 oz. chopped canned pineapple
1. In the Instant Pot, mix oil, milk and rice, stir.
2. Lock the lid. Set the Instant Pot to Manual mode, then set the timer for 3 minutes at Low Pressure.
3. When the timer goes off, perform a natural release. Carefully open the lid.
4. Add sugar and pineapple, stir.
5. Lock the lid, then set the timer for 2 minutes at Low Pressure.
6. When the timer goes off, perform a natural release. Carefully open the lid.
7. Divide into dessert bowls and serve.

Coconut Cream and Cinnamon Pudding
Prep time: 12 mins, Cook Time: 10 mins, Servings: 6

- Zest of 1 grated lemon
- 2 cups coconut cream
- 5 tbsps. sugar
- 6 tbsps. flour
- 1 tsp. cinnamon powder
- 1 cup water
1. Set the Instant Pot on Sauté mode and add coconut cream, cinnamon and orange zest, then stir.
2. Simmer for 3 minutes then transfer to a bowl and leave aside.
3. Add flour and sugar, stir well and divide this into ramekins.
4. Add the water to the Instant Pot, add steamer basket, add ramekins.
5. Lock the lid. Set the Instant Pot to Manual mode, then set the timer for 10 minutes at Low Pressure.
6. When the timer goes off, perform a natural release for 5 minutes, then release any remaining pressure. Carefully open the lid.
7. Serve cold.

Coconut and Avocado Pudding
Prep time: 2 hours, Cook Time: 2 mins, Servings: 3

- 14 oz. canned coconut milk
- 1 tbsp. cocoa powder
- 1 avocado, pitted, peeled and chopped
- 4 tbsps. sugar
- ½ cup avocado oil
1. In a bowl, mix oil with cocoa powder and half of the sugar, stir well, transfer to a lined container, keep in the fridge for 1 hour and chop into small pieces.

2.	In the Instant Pot, mix coconut milk with avocado and the rest of the sugar, blend using an immersion blender.
3.	Lock the lid. Set the Instant Pot to Manual mode, then set the timer for 2 minutes at High Pressure.
4.	When the timer goes off, perform a natural release. Carefully open the lid.
5.	Add chocolate chips, stir, divide pudding into bowls and keep in the fridge until you serve it.

Cocoa and Milk Pudding

Prep time: 50 mins, Cook Time: 3 mins, Servings: 4

- 2 cups hot coconut milk
- 4 tbsps. sugar
- ½ tsp. cinnamon powder
- 4 tbsps. cocoa powder
- 2 tbsps. gelatin
- 1 cup plus 2 tbsps. water

1.	In a bowl, mix the milk with sugar, cinnamon and cocoa powder and stir well.
2.	In a bowl, mix gelatin with 2 tablespoons of water, stir well, add to cocoa mix, stir and divide into ramekins.
3.	Add 1 cup of water to the Instant Pot, add the steamer basket and ramekins inside.
4.	Lock the lid. Set the Instant Pot to Manual mode, then set the timer for 4 minutes at High Pressure.
5.	When the timer goes off, perform a natural release. Carefully open the lid.
6.	Serve puddings cold.

Cream Cheese Pudding

Prep time: 12 mins, Cook Time: 20 mins, Servings: 2 minutes

- ¼ tsp. vanilla extract
- 1½ tsps. caramel extract
- 2 eggs
- 2 oz. cream cheese
- 1½ tbsps. sugar
- 1 cup water

1.	Mix cream cheese with eggs, caramel extract, vanilla extract and sugar in a blender and pulse well to divide into greased ramekins.
2.	In the Instant Pot, set in the water, add steamer basket and ramekins inside.
3.	Lock the lid. Set the Instant Pot to Manual mode, then set the timer for 20 minutes at High Pressure.
4.	When the timer goes off, perform a natural release for 10 minutes, then release any remaining pressure. Carefully open the lid.
5.	Serve the puddings cold.

Cinnamon Butter Bites

Prep time: 6 mins, Cook Time: 5 hours, Servings: 12

- 5 eggs, beaten
- 1 cup all-purpose flour
- 1 grass-fed unsalted butter stick

- 1 tbsp. cinnamon
- ¼ cup liquid stevia
- ¼ cup olive oil
- Salt, to taste

1.	Mix all ingredients in a mixing bowl, except for the olive oil.
2.	Grease the Instant Pot with olive oil.
3.	Pour in the batter.
4.	Lock the lid. Set the Instant Pot to Slow Cook mode, then set the timer for 5 hours at High Pressure.
5.	When the timer goes off, perform a natural release for 10 minutes, then release any remaining pressure. Carefully open the lid.
6.	Serve immediately.

Keto Almond Bread

Prep time: 12 mins, Cook Time: 5 hours, Servings: 10

- 1½ tsps. baking powder
- 1½ cups erythritol
- 3 eggs, beaten
- 2½ cups all-purpose flour
- ¼ cup olive oil
- Salt, to taste

1.	Mix all ingredients in a mixing bowl.
2.	Once properly mixed, pour the batter in the greased Instant Pot.
3.	Lock the lid. Set the Instant Pot to Slow Cook mode, then set the timer for 5 hours at High Pressure.
4.	When the timer goes off, perform a natural release for 10 minutes, then release any remaining pressure. Carefully open the lid.
5.	Serve immediately.

Apple Bread

Prep time: 12 mins, Cook Time: 1 hour, Servings: 4

- 1 tbsp. baking powder
- 3 eggs
- 1½ cups sweetened condensed milk
- 2½ cups white flour
- 3 apples, peeled, cored and chopped
- 1 tbsp. melted coconut oil
- 1 cup water

1.	In a bowl, mix the baking powder with eggs and whisk well.
2.	Add the milk, flour and apple pieces, whisk well and pour into a loaf pan greased with coconut oil.
3.	In the Instant Pot, add the water. Arrange a trivet in the pot, then place the loaf pan on the trivet.
4.	Lock the lid. Set the Instant Pot to Slow Cook mode, then set the timer for 1 hour at High Pressure.
5.	When the timer goes off, perform a natural release for 10 minutes, then release any remaining pressure. Carefully open the lid.
6.	Leave apple bread to cool down, slice and serve.

Bulletproof Hot Choco

Prep time: 6 mins, Cook Time: 5 mins, Servings: 1

- 2 tbsps. coconut oil, divided
- ½ cup coconut milk
- ½ cup water
- 2 tbsps. unsweetened cocoa powder
- Dash of cinnamon
- 1 tsp. erythritol

1. Place 1 tablespoon of coconut oil and milk in the Instant Pot and pour in the water.
2. Lock the lid. Set the Instant Pot to Manual mode, then set the timer for 5 minutes at High Pressure.
3. When the timer goes off, perform a quick release.
4. Open the lid and press the Sauté button.
5. Add 1 tablespoon of coconut oil, cocoa powder, cinnamon and erythritol. Stir to combine well and the mixture has a thick consistency.
6. Transfer the mixture on a baking sheet, then put the sheet in the refrigerator for several hours. Serve chilled.

Coconut Boosters

Prep time: 2 hours, Cook Time: 5 mins, Servings: 5

- 1 cup coconut oil
- ½ cup chia seeds
- 1 tsp. vanilla extract
- 1 tsp. erythritol
- ¼ cup unsweetened dried coconut flakes

1. Press the Sauté button on the Instant Pot.
2. Heat the coconut oil and add the chia seeds, vanilla extract, erythritol, and coconut flakes and sauté for 5 minutes.
3. Allow to cool and remove the mixture from the pot. Form the mixture into balls and set on a baking sheet.
4. Allow to set in the refrigerator for 2 hours before serving.

Keto Brownies

Prep time: 12 mins, Cook Time: 5 hours, Servings: 9

- 2 tsps. erythritol
- ¼ cup all-purpose flour
- ½ cup coconut oil
- ⅓ cup dark chocolate chips
- 5 beaten eggs
- Salt, to taste
- 2 tbsps. olive oil

1. Place all the ingredients in a mixing bowl, except for the olive oil.
2. Make sure they are well combined.
3. Grese the Instant Pot with olive oil. Pour the mixture into the greased Instant Pot.
4. Lock the lid. Set the Instant Pot to Slow Cook mode, then set the timer for 5 hours at High Pressure.
5. When the timer goes off, perform a natural release for 10 minutes, then release any remaining pressure. Carefully open the lid.
6. Transfer the brownies on a platter and slice to serve.

Chocolate Mug Cake

Prep time: 12 mins, Cook Time: 10 mins, Servings: 1

- 1 cup water
- 6 drops liquid stevia
- 1½ tbsps. cocoa powder
- 1 egg, beaten
- ¼ tsp. baking powder
- ¼ cup almond powder
- Salt, to taste

1. Place a steam rack in the Instant Pot and pour in the water.
2. In a bowl, add all the remaining ingredients.
3. Mix until well combined.
4. Pour into a heat-proof mug.
5. Place the mug on the steam rack.
6. Lock the lid. Set the Instant Pot to Steam mode, then set the timer for 10 minutes at High Pressure.
7. When the timer goes off, perform a quick release. Carefully open the lid.
8. Serve the cake immediately.

Chocolate Cake

Prep time: 12 mins, Cook Time: 6 mins, Servings: 3

- 4 tbsps. self-raising flour
- 1 egg
- 4 tbsps. sugar
- 4 tbsps. milk
- 1 tbsp. cocoa powder
- 1 tbsp. melted coconut oil
- 1 cup water

1. In a bowl, combine the flour, egg, sugar, milk and cocoa powder, stir well and set the mixture to a cake pan greased with coconut oil.
2. Add the water to the Instant Pot, add steamer basket, add cake inside.
3. Lock the lid. Set the Instant Pot to Manual mode, then set the timer for 6 minutes at High Pressure.
4. When the timer goes off, perform a natural release for 5 minutes, then release any remaining pressure. Carefully open the lid.
5. Serve the cake warm.

Dates and Ricotta Cake

Prep time: 30 mins, Cook Time: 20 mins, Servings: 6

- 1 lb. softened ricotta cheese
- 4 eggs
- 4 oz. honey
- 6 oz. dates, soaked and drained
- Juice of 2 oranges
- 1 cup water

1. In a bowl, mix soft ricotta with eggs and whisk well.
2. Add honey, dates, and orange juice, whisk, pour into a cake pan and cover with tin foil.

3.	Add the water to the Instant Pot, add steamer basket, add cake pan.
4.	Lock the lid. Set the Instant Pot to Manual mode, then set the timer for 20 minutes at High Pressure.
5.	When the timer goes off, perform a natural release for 10 minutes, then release any remaining pressure. Carefully open the lid.
6.	Allow cake to cool down, slice and serve.

Simple Banana Cake

Prep time: 12 mins, Cook Time: 1 hour, Servings: 4

- 1 tsp. nutmeg powder
- 2 cups flour
- 1 tsp. cinnamon powder
- ¼ cup sugar
- 4 bananas, peeled and mashed
- 1 cup water

1.	In a bowl, mix sugar with flour, bananas, cinnamon and nutmeg, stir, pour into a greased cake pan and cover with tin foil.
2.	In the Instant Pot, set in the water, add steamer basket, add cake pan.
3.	Lock the lid. Set the Instant Pot to Manual mode, then set the timer for 1 hour at High Pressure.
4.	When the timer goes off, perform a natural release for 10 minutes, then release any remaining pressure. Carefully open the lid.
5.	Slice and divide between plates to serve cold.

Beer Poached Pears

Prep time: 5 minutes | Cook time: 10 minutes | Serves 2

3 peeled (stem on) firm pears
1½ cups (1 bottle) stout beer
½ cup packed brown sugar
1 vanilla bean, split lengthwise and seeds scraped

1.	Slice a thin layer from the bottom of each pear so they can stand upright. Use a melon baller to scoop out the seeds and core from the bottom.
2.	Stir together the beer, brown sugar, and vanilla bean and seeds in the Instant Pot until combined. Place the pears upright in the pot.
3.	Lock the lid. Select the Manual mode and set the cooking time for 9 minutes at High Pressure.
4.	When the timer beeps, perform a quick pressure release. Carefully remove the lid.
5.	Using tongs, carefully remove the pears by their stems and transfer to a plate and set aside.
6.	Set the Instant Pot to Sauté and simmer until the liquid in the Instant Pot is reduced by half.
7.	Strain the liquid into a bowl through a fine-mesh sieve, then pour over the pears.
8.	Serve at room temperature or chilled.

Black Bean and Oat Brownies

Prep time: 5 minutes | Cook time: 25 minutes | Serves 4

1½ cups canned black beans, drained
½ cup steel-cut oats
½ teaspoon salt
3 tablespoons unsweetened cocoa powder
½ cup maple syrup
¼ cup coconut oil
¾ teaspoon baking powder
½ cup chocolate chips
Cooking spray
1½ cups water

1.	Pulse the black beans, oats, salt, cocoa powder, maple syrup, coconut oil, and baking powder in a food processor until very smooth.
2.	Pour the batter into a medium bowl and fold in the chocolate chips.
3.	Spray a 7-inch springform pan with cooking spray and pour in the batter. Cover the pan with aluminum foil.
4.	Pour the water into the Instant Pot and insert a trivet. Place the pan on the trivet.
5.	Lock the lid. Select the Manual mode and set the cooking time for 25 minutes at High Pressure.
6.	When the timer beeps, perform a natural pressure release for 10 minutes, then release any remaining pressure. Carefully remove the lid.
7.	Let cool for 5 minutes, then transfer to the fridge to chill for 1 to 2 hours.
8.	Cut the brownies into squares and serve.

Cardamom Rice Pudding with Pistachios

Prep time: 15 minutes | Cook time: 10 minutes | Makes 4 cups

½ cup long-grain basmati rice
1½ cups water
1 (13.5-ounce / 383-g) can coconut milk
1 small (5¼-ounce / 149-g) can coconut cream
½ cup brown rice syrup or agave nectar
½ teaspoon ground cardamom
¼ teaspoon fine sea salt
¼ cup currants
¼ cup chopped pistachios

1.	Combine the rice and water in the Instant Pot. Secure the lid. Select Manual mode and set the cooking time for 5 minutes at High Pressure.
2.	Meanwhile, in a blender, combine the coconut milk, coconut cream, brown rice syrup, cardamom, and salt. Blend at medium speed for about 30 seconds, until smooth. Set aside.
3.	When timer beeps, let the pressure release naturally for 10 minutes, then release any remaining pressure. Open the pot and use a whisk to break up the cooked rice. Whisking constantly, pour the coconut milk mixture in a thin stream into the rice.
4.	Select the Sauté setting. Cook the pudding for about 5 minutes, whisking constantly, until it is thickened and bubbling.
5.	Sit the pudding until set. Remove the pudding from the pot. Stir in the currants.
6.	Pour the pudding into a glass or ceramic dish or into individual serving bowls. Cover and refrigerate the pudding for at least 4 hours.
7.	Sprinkle the pudding with chopped pistachios. Serve chilled.

Carrot Raisin Halwa

Prep time: 10 minutes | Cook time: 14 minutes | Serves 6
2 tablespoons coconut oil
2 tablespoons raw cashews
2 tablespoons raisins
2 cups shredded carrots
1 cup almond milk
¼ cup sugar
2 tablespoons ground cashews
¼ teaspoon ground cardamom
Chopped pistachios, for garnish
1. Set the Instant Pot to Sauté and melt the coconut oil until it shimmers.
2. Add the cashews and raisins and cook them until the cashews are golden brown, about 4 minutes.
3. Add the carrots, milk, sugar, and ground cashews, and stir to incorporate.
4. Lock the lid. Select the Manual mode and set the cooking time for 10 minutes at High Pressure.
5. When the timer beeps, perform a natural pressure release for 10 minutes, then release any remaining pressure. Carefully remove the lid.
6. Stir well, mashing the carrots together a bit. Set the Instant Pot to Sauté again and cook, stirring, for about 2 to 3 minutes, until thickened.
7. Turn off the Instant Pot. Stir in the cardamom and let the mixture sit for 10 minutes to thicken up.
8. Garnish with the pistachios and serve.

Chocolate Cake with Ganache

Prep time: 10 minutes | Cook time: 30 minutes | Serves 10
1 cup water
1 cup whole wheat pastry flour
½ cup unsweetened cocoa powder
½ cup raw turbinado sugar
1 teaspoon baking soda
½ teaspoon baking powder
½ teaspoon instant coffee
¼ teaspoon salt
¾ cup unsweetened almond milk
1 teaspoon pure vanilla extract
1 tablespoon apple cider vinegar
¼ cup melted coconut oil
¼ cup chopped, toasted hazelnuts, for garnish
1 cup fresh raspberries, for garnish
Fresh mint leaves, for garnish
For the Ganache:
¾ cup chopped dairy-free dark chocolate
¼ canned coconut milk
1. Fit the Instant Pot with a trivet and add the water. Coat a springform pan with cooking spray.
2. In a medium bowl, whisk together the flour, cocoa powder, sugar, baking soda, baking powder, instant coffee, and salt.
3. In another medium bowl, whisk together the almond milk, vanilla, vinegar, and oil. Stir the wet mixture into the dry mixture to form a batter.
4. Transfer the batter into the prepared pan and smooth into an even layer with the back of a spoon.

5. Cover the pan with foil and place on the trivet. Lock the lid. Select Manual mode and set the cook time for 30 minutes on High Pressure.
6. Once the cook time is complete, allow the pressure to release naturally for 10 minutes, then quick release any remaining pressure.
7. Carefully remove the lid and the cake pan. Remove the foil and let the cake cool on a cooling rack.
8. Meanwhile, make the ganache: Place the chocolate in a small glass bowl. Heat the coconut milk in a small saucepan, until it just begins to simmer.
9. Carefully pour the coconut milk over the chocolate and stir until all the chocolate has melted and the mixture is smooth.
10. Pour the ganache over the top of the cooled cake, letting it drip down the sides. Serve with the hazelnuts, berries, and mint on top.

Chocolate Pudding with Raspberry Sauce

Prep time: 20 minutes | Cook time: 15 minutes | Serves 4
Chocolate Pudding:
5 tablespoons flaxseed meal plus 1 cup water
6 tablespoons unsweetened cocoa powder
$^1/_3$ cup cornstarch
Salt, to taste
4½ cups almond milk
4 ounces (113 g) butter
2 teaspoons vanilla extract
Raspberry Sauce:
1 pound (454 g) fresh raspberries
2 tablespoons freshly squeezed lemon juice
¼ cup beet sugar
1 tablespoon water
1. In a bowl, mix the flaxseed meal with the water until evenly combined and allow to sit for 15 minutes to thicken.
2. In a separate bowl, combine the cocoa powder, cornstarch, and salt.
3. Press the Sauté button on the Instant Pot and pour in the almond milk. Let simmer for a few seconds, but not to boil.
4. Fetch a tablespoon of the milk into the cocoa powder mixture and stir. Pour the mix into the milk and stir in the flaxseed mixture (flax egg), butter, and vanilla extract. Allow to simmer for 6 minutes, stirring frequently, and spoon into dessert bowls. Turn the pot off and wash the Instant Pot clean.
5. Select the Sauté mode and add the raspberries, lemon juice, sugar, and water. Allow to simmer for 6 minutes.
6. Drain the sauce through a strainer into a bowl. Allow to cool for 5 minutes and spoon the raspberry sauce over the chocolate pudding. Serve immediately.

Cinnamon Balls

Prep time: 15 minutes | Cook time: 20 minutes | Serves 8
¼ cup whole-wheat flour
½ cup all-purpose flour
½ teaspoon baking powder

3 tablespoons sugar, divided
¼ teaspoon plus ½ tablespoon cinnamon
¼ teaspoon sea salt
2 tablespoons cold butter, cubed
$^1/_3$ cup almond milk
1 cup water
1.	Mix the whole-wheat flour, all-purpose flour, baking powder, 1 tablespoon of sugar, ¼ teaspoon of cinnamon, and salt in a medium bowl.
2.	Add the butter and use a pastry cutter to cut into butter, breaking it into little pieces until resembling cornmeal. Pour in the milk and mix until the dough forms into a ball.
3.	Knead the dough on a flat surface. Divide the dough into 8 pieces and roll each piece into a ball. Put the balls in a greased baking pan with space in between each ball and oil the balls.
4.	Pour the water into the Instant Pot. Put in a trivet and place the pan on top.
5.	Seal the lid, select Manual mode and set the time for 20 minutes on High Pressure.
6.	When timer beeps, perform a natural pressure release for 5 minutes, then release any remaining pressure.
7.	In a mixing bowl, combine the remaining sugar and cinnamon. Toss the dough balls in the cinnamon and sugar mixture to serve.

Cinnamon Glaze Apple Cake

Prep time: 20 minutes | Cook time: 30 minutes | Serves 4
Apple Cake:
2 tablespoons flaxseed meal plus 6 tablespoons water
1½ cups all-purpose flour
½ tablespoon baking powder
½ teaspoon salt
3 cups apples
½ tablespoon cinnamon powder
¾ cup beet sugar
½ cup butter, melted
2 tablespoons orange juice
1 teaspoon vanilla extract
Cooking spray
1 cup water
Cinnamon Glaze:
1 cup beet powdered sugar
½ teaspoon cinnamon powder
1 tablespoon coconut milk
1.	In a bowl, mix the flaxseed meal with the water and set aside. Allow to sit for 15 minutes to thicken.
2.	In a separate bowl, combine the flour, baking powder, and salt.
3.	In a third bowl, mix the apples, cinnamon, and beet sugar.
4.	When the flax egg is ready, whisk in the butter, orange juice, and vanilla. Stir together all three ingredients until well mixed.
5.	Lightly spray a springform pan with cooking spray and pour the batter into the pan.
6.	Add the water to the Instant Pot and insert a trivet. Place the springform pan on the trivet.

7.	Lock the lid. Select the Manual mode and set the cooking time for 30 minutes at High Pressure.
8.	When the timer beeps, perform a natural pressure release for 15 minutes, then release any remaining pressure. Carefully remove the lid.
9.	Remove the cake pan, the trivet and discard the water. Leave the cake cool for 5 to 10 minutes in the pan.
10.	Meanwhile, in a bowl, make the cinnamon glaze by whisking the sugar, cinnamon powder, and coconut milk until mixed.
11.	Remove the cake from the pan and cut into slices. Serve drizzled with the cinnamon glaze.

Citrus Apple Crisps with Oat Topping

Prep time: 10 minutes | Cook time: 9 minutes | Serves 4
1 cup water
For the Filling:
3½ cups peeled and diced apples (1-inch chunks)
1 tablespoon fresh lemon juice
1 tablespoon fresh orange juice
½ teaspoon ground cinnamon
2 teaspoons coconut sugar
For the Topping:
½ cup old-fashioned rolled oats
½ cup almond flour
3 tablespoons almond butter
1 tablespoon pure maple syrup
¼ cup coconut sugar
¼ teaspoon sea salt
1.	To make the filling: In a medium bowl, toss together all the ingredients. Portion the filling into 4 ramekins, filling all the way to the top. Cover the ramekins with foil.
2.	Fit the Instant Pot with a trivet and add the water. Place the ramekins on the trivet.
3.	Lock the lid. Select Manual mode and set the cook time for 9 minutes on High Pressure.
4.	Once the cook time is complete, quick release the pressure.
5.	Meanwhile, make the topping: Place all the ingredients for the topping in the food processor, and pulse to combine. Preheat the oven to 500°F (260°C).
6.	Carefully remove the lid and the ramekins. Remove the foil.
7.	Spoon the topping evenly over the apple mixture. Transfer the ramekins to the oven, and bake until the topping is golden brown, about 4 minutes.
8.	Serve warm.

Creamy Lemon Custard Pie

Prep time: 10 minutes | Cook time: 15 minutes | Serves 6
½ cup coconut oil, melted, plus more for greasing the pan
¾ cup coconut flour
½ cup plus 2 tablespoons unrefined sugar, divided
1 (13.5-ounce / 383-g) can full-fat coconut milk
½ cup freshly squeezed lemon juice (from 4 lemons)
¼ cup cornstarch or arrowroot powder
2 cups water

1.   Grease a 6-inch springform pan or pie dish with melted coconut oil.
2.   Stir together ½ cup of coconut oil, coconut flour, and 2 tablespoons of sugar in a small bowl. Press the crust into the greased pan.
3.   In a medium bowl, whisk together the coconut milk, lemon juice, cornstarch, and remaining ½ cup of sugar until the starch is dissolved. Pour this mixture over the crust. Cover the pan with aluminum foil.
4.   Pour the water into the Instant Pot and insert a trivet. Using a foil sling or silicone helper handles, lower the pan onto the trivet.
5.   Lock the lid. Select the Manual mode and set the cooking time for 15 minutes at High Pressure.
6.   When the timer beeps, perform a quick pressure release. Carefully remove the lid.
7.   Serve at room temperature or chilled.

Crunchy Mini Cinnamon Monkey Breads

Prep time: 10 minutes | Cook time: 20 minutes | Serves 4

1 (1-pound / 454-g) can buttermilk biscuits, cut into 6 pieces
$^1/_3$ cup granulated sugar
Salt, to taste
½ cup crushed cinnamon crunch cereal, divided, plus more for sprinkling
¼ cup melted unsalted butter
1 cup water
1 cup maple syrup
2 tablespoons almond milk

1.   In a bowl, combine the sugar, salt and half of the crushed cereal. Add the cut biscuit pieces to the bowl. Toss to evenly coat.
2.   Place 2 tablespoons of the coated biscuits, along with a spoonful of the cereal mixture, in each well of a silicone egg bite mold. Top each pile of coated dough with melted butter.
3.   Pour the water into the Instant Pot and insert a trivet. Place the filled mold on top of the trivet.
4.   Secure the lid. Press the Manual button and set cooking time for 20 minutes on High Pressure.
5.   When timer beeps, quick release the pressure. Remove the lid and take out the silicone mold. Let the monkey breads cool in the mold.
6.   Meanwhile, in a medium bowl, mix the milk and maple syrup until smooth.
7.   Remove the monkey breads from the mold. Drizzle each monkey bread with milk mixture. Top with a sprinkle of crushed cereal.

Fast Pear and Cranberry Crisps

Prep time: 10 minutes | Cook time: 5 minutes | Serves 6

3 large pears, peeled, cored and diced
1 cup fresh cranberries
1 tablespoon granulated sugar
2 teaspoons ground cinnamon
½ teaspoon ground nutmeg
½ cup water
1 tablespoon pure maple syrup
6 tablespoons almond butter
1 cup old-fashioned rolled oats
$^1/_3$ cup dark brown sugar
¼ cup all-purpose flour
½ teaspoon sea salt
½ cup pecans, toasted

1.   In the Instant Pot, combine the pears and cranberries and sprinkle with the granulated sugar. Let sit for a few minutes, then sprinkle with the cinnamon and nutmeg. Pour the water and maple syrup on top.
2.   In a medium bowl, stir together the almond butter, oats, brown sugar, flour and salt.
3.   Spoon the mixture on the fruit in the Instant Pot.
4.   Secure the lid. Select Manual mode, and set cooking time for 5 minutes on High Pressure.
5.   When timer beeps, use a quick pressure release. Open the lid.
6.   Spoon into bowls. Top with pecans and serve.

Fresh Lemon Mousse

Prep time: 5 minutes | Cook time: 10 minutes | Serves 4

2 tablespoons butter, room temperature
$^1/_3$ cup beet sugar
½ cup plus ¼ cup plus ¼ cup plus ¼ cup coconut cream, whipped
2 lemons, zested and juiced
Pinch of salt
1 cup water
Extra lemon zest, for garnish

1.   Whisk the butter with the beet sugar with a hand mixer in a bowl. Beat in ½ cup of coconut cream, lemon zest and juice, and salt. Cover the bowl with aluminum foil.
2.   Pour the water into the Instant Pot and insert a trivet. Put the bowl on the trivet.
3.   Secure the lid. Select the Manual mode and set the cooking time for 10 minutes at High Pressure.
4.   Once cooking is complete, do a natural pressure release for 10 minutes, then release any remaining pressure. Carefully open the lid.
5.   Take out the bowl and remove the foil. The mixture will be curdy and clumpy, so whisk until smooth, and strain through a fine mesh into a bowl.
6.   Cover the mixture itself with plastic wrap, making sure to press onto the curd. Place in the refrigerator for 2 hours.
7.   When ready, remove the wrap and whisk the cream until stiff peak forms. Gently fold in the second portion (¼ cup) of coconut cream, then the third portion, and the last portion. Spoon the mousse into serving bowls.
8.   Garnish with the extra lemon zest and serve.

Fudgy Chocolate Brownies

Prep time: 10 minutes | Cook time: 5 minutes | Makes 3 brownies

2 cups water
3 ounces (85 g) dairy-free dark chocolate
1 tablespoon coconut oil

½ cup applesauce
2 tablespoons unrefined sugar
$^1/_3$ cup all-purpose flour
½ teaspoon baking powder
Salt, to taste
1. Pour the water into the Instant Pot and insert a trivet. Set the Instant Pot to Sauté.
2. Stir together the chocolate and coconut oil in a large bowl. Place the bowl on the trivet. Stir occasionally until the chocolate is melted, then turn off the Instant Pot.
3. Stir the applesauce and sugar into the chocolate mixture. Add the flour, baking powder, and salt and stir just until combined. Pour the batter into 3 ramekins. Cover each ramekin with aluminum foil. Using a foil sling or silicone helper handles, lower the ramekins onto the trivet.
4. Lock the lid. Select the Manual mode and set the cooking time for 5 minutes at High Pressure.
5. When the timer beeps, perform a quick pressure release. Carefully remove the lid.
6. Cool for 5 to 10 minutes before serving.

Hearty Apricot Cobbler

Prep time: 15 minutes | Cook time: 25 minutes | Serves 4

4 cups sliced apricots
½ cup plus ¼ cup brown sugar, divided
2 tablespoons plus ¾ cup plain flour, divided
½ teaspoon cinnamon powder
¼ teaspoon nutmeg powder
1½ teaspoons salt, divided
1 teaspoon vanilla extract
¼ cup water
½ teaspoon baking powder
½ teaspoon baking soda
3 tablespoons butter, melted
1 cup water
1. In a heatproof bowl, mix the apricots, ½ cup of brown sugar, 2 tablespoons of flour, cinnamon, nutmeg, ½ teaspoon of salt, vanilla, and water; set aside.
2. In another bowl, mix the remaining flour, salt and brown sugar, baking powder and soda, and butter. Spoon mixture over apricot mixture and spread to cover.
3. Pour the water in the pot, fit in a trivet and place heatproof bowl on top.
4. Seal the lid, select Manual mode, and set cooking time for 25 minutes on High Pressure.
5. When timer beeps, allow a natural release for 10 minutes, then release any remaining pressure. Open the lid.
6. Remove bowl and serve.

Hearty Giant Chocolate Cookies

Prep time: 5 minutes | Cook time: 6 minutes | Serves 8

2 cups blanched almond flour
3 tablespoons arrowroot starch
1 teaspoon baking soda
¼ teaspoon sea salt
4 tablespoons melted coconut oil
2 tablespoons pure maple syrup
1 teaspoon pure vanilla extract
$^1/_3$ cup chopped dairy-free dark chocolate
1 cup water
1. In a medium bowl, whisk together the almond flour, arrowroot, baking soda, and salt.
2. Make a well in the middle of the dry ingredients. Pour the coconut oil, maple syrup, and vanilla into the well, and whisk to combine.
3. Stir in the dark chocolate. The mixture may be a little crumbly but should hold together when pressed.
4. Cut out a piece of parchment paper to fit the bottom of a springform pan. Press the dough firmly on top of the parchment. Cover the pan with foil.
5. Fit the Instant Pot with a trivet and add the water. Place the foil-covered springform pan onto the trivet.
6. Lock the lid. Select Manual mode and set the cook time for 6 minutes on High Pressure.
7. Once the cook time is complete, allow the pressure to release naturally for 6 minutes, then quick release any remaining pressure.
8. Preheat the oven broiler.
9. Carefully remove the lid and take the pan out of the Instant Pot. Remove the sides of the springform pan.
10. Transfer the cookie under the broiler for 1 minute, or just until golden on top. Let the cookie cool for 10 minutes, then cut into 8 wedges and serve.

Lemon Blueberry Cheesecake

Prep time: 10 minutes | Cook time: 6 minutes | Serves 6

1 tablespoon coconut oil, melted, for greasing the pan
1¼ cups soft pitted Medjool dates, divided
1 cup gluten-free rolled oats
2 cups cashews
1 cup fresh blueberries
3 tablespoons freshly squeezed lemon juice or lime juice
1¾ cups water
Salt, to taste
1. Grease a 6-inch springform pan or pie dish with melted coconut oil.
2. In a food processor, combine 1 cup of dates and the oats. Processor until they form a sticky mixture. Press this mixture into the prepared pan.
3. In a blender, combine the remaining ¼ cup of dates, cashews, blueberries, lemon juice, ¾ cup of water, and a pinch of salt. Blend on high speed for about 1 minute, until smooth and creamy, stopping a couple of times to scrape down the sides. Pour this mixture over the crust. Cover the pan with aluminum foil.
4. Pour the remaining 1 cup of water into the Instant Pot and insert a trivet. Using a foil sling or silicone helper handles, lower the pan onto the trivet.
5. Lock the lid. Select the Manual mode and set the cooking time for 6 minutes at High Pressure.
6. When the timer beeps, perform a natural pressure release for 10 minutes, then release any remaining pressure. Carefully remove the lid.

7.   Cool for 5 to 10 minutes before slicing and serving.

Raspberry and Oat Crumble

Prep time: 10 minutes | Cook time: 20 minutes | Serves 4

2 tablespoons arrowroot starch
½ cup plus 1 tablespoon water, divided
1 teaspoon lemon juice
5 tablespoons sugar, divided
2 cups raspberries
½ cup flour
¼ cup brown sugar
½ cup rolled oats
1 teaspoon cinnamon powder
¼ cup cold butter, cut into pieces
1.   In a small bowl, combine the arrowroot starch, lemon juice, 1 tablespoon of water, and 3 tablespoons of sugar. Mix in the raspberries, and toss well. Pour the mixture in a baking pan.
2.   In a separate bowl, mix the flour, brown sugar, oats, cinnamon, butter, and remaining sugar, and form crumble. Spread the crumble evenly on the raspberries.
3.   Put a trivet in the pot. Cover the pan with foil and pour half cup of water into the pot. Put the pan on the trivet.
4.   Seal the lid, select Manual mode, and set cooking time for 20 minutes on High Pressure.
5.   When timer beeps, do a quick pressure release. Open the lid.
6.   Remove foil and serve.

Rhubarb and Strawberry Compote

Prep time: 10 minutes | Cook time: 5 minutes | Makes 4 cups

1 pound (454 g) rhubarb (about 4 large stalks), trimmed and cut into 1-inch pieces
1 pound (454 g) strawberries, hulled and quartered lengthwise
½ cup turbinado sugar
½ teaspoon ground cardamom
1.   Combine the rhubarb, strawberries, sugar, and cardamom in the Instant Pot and stir well, making sure to coat the rhubarb and strawberries evenly with the sugar. Let the mixture sit for 15 minutes. Stir.
2.   Secure the lid. Select Manual mode and set the cooking time for 5 minutes at Low Pressure.
3.   When timer beeps, let the pressure release naturally for about 15 minutes, then release any remaining pressure. Open the pot and stir the compote to break down the rhubarb.
4.   Serve the compote warm.

Simple Lemon Squares

Prep time: 20 minutes | Cook time: 30 minutes | Serves 6

Lemon Squares:
2 tablespoons flaxseed meal plus 6 tablespoons water
1¼ cup almond flour
3 tablespoons coconut flour

1 cup beet sugar
1 large lemon, zested and juiced
¼ cup butter, melted
2 cups almond milk
Cooking spray
1 cup water
Topping:
5 tablespoons beet sugar
1 lemon, zested and juiced
1.   In a bowl, mix the flaxseed meal with water and allow to sit for 15 minutes to thicken.
2.   In a separate bowl, combine the almond flour, coconut flour, beet sugar, and lemon zest until mixed. Whisk in lemon juice, butter, milk, and the flax egg.
3.   Grease a springform pan lightly with cooking spray and pour the batter into the pan.
4.   Pour the water into the Instant Pot and insert a trivet. Place the pan on the trivet.
5.   Lock the lid. Select the Manual mode and set the cooking time for 20 minutes at High Pressure.
6.   When the timer beeps, perform a natural pressure release for 10 minutes, then release any remaining pressure. Carefully remove the lid.
7.   Remove the pan and pierce the top of the cake with a skewer.
8.   Make the topping by whisking together the beet sugar, lemon juice, and zest. Sprinkle the mixture on top of the cake and cut into squares to serve.

Vanilla Crème Brûlée

Prep time: 7 minutes | Cook time: 9 minutes | Serves 4

1 cup heavy cream (or full-fat coconut milk for dairy-free)
2 large egg yolks
2 tablespoons Swerve, or more to taste
Seeds scraped from ½ vanilla bean (about 8 inches long), or 1 teaspoon vanilla extract
1 cup cold water
4 teaspoons Swerve, for topping
1.   Heat the cream in a pan over medium-high heat until hot, about 2 minutes.
2.   Place the egg yolks, Swerve, and vanilla seeds in a blender and blend until smooth.
3.   While the blender is running, slowly pour in the hot cream. Taste and adjust the sweetness to your liking.
4.   Scoop the mixture into four ramekins with a spatula. Cover the ramekins with aluminum foil.
5.   Add the water to the Instant Pot and insert a trivet. Place the ramekins on the trivet.
6.   Lock the lid. Select the Manual mode and set the cooking time for 7 minutes at High Pressure.
7.   When the timer beeps, perform a quick pressure release. Carefully remove the lid.
8.   Keep the ramekins covered with the foil and place in the refrigerator for about 2 hours until completely chilled.
9.   Sprinkle 1 teaspoon of Swerve on top of each crème brûlée. Use the oven broiler to melt the sweetener.

10.	Allow the topping to cool in the fridge for 5 minutes before serving.

Lemon and Ricotta Torte

Prep time: 15 minutes | Cook time: 35 minutes | Serves 12
Cooking spray
Torte:
$1^1/_3$ cups Swerve
½ cup (1 stick) unsalted butter, softened
2 teaspoons lemon or vanilla extract
5 large eggs, separated
2½ cups blanched almond flour
1¼ (10-ounce / 284-g) cups whole-milk ricotta cheese
¼ cup lemon juice
1 cup cold water
Lemon Glaze:
½ cup (1 stick) unsalted butter
¼ cup Swerve
2 tablespoons lemon juice
2 ounces (57 g) cream cheese (¼ cup)
Grated lemon zest and lemon slices, for garnish
1.	Line a baking pan with parchment paper and spray with cooking spray. Set aside.
2.	Make the torte: In the bowl of a stand mixer, place the Swerve, butter, and extract and blend for 8 to 10 minutes until well combined. Scrape down the sides of the bowl as needed.
3.	Add the egg yolks and continue to blend until fully combined. Add the almond flour and mix until smooth, then stir in the ricotta and lemon juice.
4.	Whisk the egg whites in a separate medium bowl until stiff peaks form. Add the whites to the batter and stir well. Pour the batter into the prepared pan and smooth the top.
5.	Place a trivet in the bottom of your Instant Pot and pour in the water. Use a foil sling to lower the baking pan onto the trivet. Tuck in the sides of the sling.
6.	Seal the lid, press Pressure Cook or Manual, and set the timer for 30 minutes. Once finished, let the pressure release naturally.
7.	Lock the lid. Select the Manual mode and set the cooking time for 30 minutes at High Pressure.
8.	When the timer beeps, perform a natural pressure release for 10 minutes. Carefully remove the lid.
9.	Use the foil sling to lift the pan out of the Instant Pot. Place the torte in the fridge for 40 minutes to chill before glazing.
10.	Meanwhile, make the glaze: Place the butter in a large pan over high heat and cook for about 5 minutes until brown, stirring occasionally. Remove from the heat. While stirring the browned butter, add the Swerve.
11.	Carefully add the lemon juice and cream cheese to the butter mixture. Allow the glaze to cool for a few minutes, or until it starts to thicken.
12.	Transfer the chilled torte to a serving plate. Pour the glaze over the torte and return it to the fridge to chill for an additional 30 minutes.
13.	Scatter the lemon zest on top of the torte and arrange the lemon slices on the plate around the torte.
14.	Serve.

Easy Chocolate Fondue

Prep time: 5 minutes | Cook time: 2 minutes | Serves 4
2 ounces (57 g) unsweetened baking chocolate, finely chopped, divided
1 cup heavy cream, divided
$^1/_3$ cup Swerve, divided
Fine sea salt
1 cup cold water
Special Equipment:
Set of fondue forks or wooden skewers
1.	Divide the chocolate, cream, and sweetener evenly among four ramekins. Add a pinch of salt to each one and stir well. Cover the ramekins with aluminum foil.
2.	Place a trivet in the bottom of your Instant Pot and pour in the water. Place the ramekins on the trivet.
3.	Lock the lid. Select the Manual mode and set the cooking time for 2 minutes at High Pressure.
4.	When the timer beeps, perform a natural pressure release for 10 minutes. Carefully remove the lid.
5.	Use tongs to remove the ramekins from the pot. Use a fork to stir the fondue until smooth.
6.	Use immediately.

Deconstructed Tiramisu

Prep time: 5 minutes | Cook time: 9 minutes | Serves 4
1 cup heavy cream (or full-fat coconut milk for dairy-free)
2 large egg yolks
2 tablespoons brewed decaf espresso or strong brewed coffee
2 tablespoons Swerve, or more to taste
1 teaspoon rum extract
1 teaspoon unsweetened cocoa powder, or more to taste
Pinch of fine sea salt
1 cup cold water
4 teaspoons Swerve, for topping
1.	Heat the cream in a pan over medium-high heat until hot, about 2 minutes.
2.	Place the egg yolks, coffee, sweetener, rum extract, cocoa powder, and salt in a blender and blend until smooth.
3.	While the blender is running, slowly pour in the hot cream. Taste and adjust the sweetness to your liking. Add more cocoa powder, if desired.
4.	Scoop the mixture into four ramekins with a spatula. Cover the ramekins with aluminum foil.
5.	Place a trivet in the bottom of the Instant Pot and pour in the water. Place the ramekins on the trivet.
6.	Lock the lid. Select the Manual mode and set the cooking time for 7 minutes at High Pressure.

7.	When the timer beeps, use a quick pressure release. Carefully remove the lid.
8.	Keep the ramekins covered with the foil and place in the refrigerator for about 2 hours until completely chilled.
9.	Sprinkle 1 teaspoon of Swerve on top of each tiramisu. Use the oven broiler to melt the sweetener.
10.	Put in the fridge to chill the topping, about 20 minutes.
11.	Serve.

Cinnamon Roll Cheesecake

Prep time: 15 minutes | Cook time: 35 minutes | Serves 12
Crust:
3½ tablespoons unsalted butter or coconut oil
1½ ounces (43 g) unsweetened baking chocolate, chopped
1 large egg, beaten
$^1/_3$ cup Swerve
2 teaspoons ground cinnamon
1 teaspoon vanilla extract
¼ teaspoon fine sea salt
Filling:
4 (8-ounce / 227-g) packages cream cheese, softened
¾ cup Swerve
½ cup unsweetened almond milk (or hemp milk for nut-free)
1 teaspoon vanilla extract
¼ teaspoon almond extract (omit for nut-free)
¼ teaspoon fine sea salt
3 large eggs
Cinnamon Swirl:
6 tablespoons (¾ stick) unsalted butter (or butter flavored coconut oil for dairy-free)
½ cup Swerve
Seeds scraped from ½ vanilla bean (about 8 inches long), or 1 teaspoon vanilla extract
1 tablespoon ground cinnamon
¼ teaspoon fine sea salt
1 cup cold water
1.	Line a baking pan with two layers of aluminum foil.
2.	Make the crust: Melt the butter in a pan over medium-low heat. Slowly add the chocolate and stir until melted. Stir in the egg, sweetener, cinnamon, vanilla extract, and salt.
3.	Transfer the crust mixture to the prepared baking pan, spreading it with your hands to cover the bottom completely.
4.	Make the filling: In the bowl of a stand mixer, add the cream cheese, sweetener, milk, extracts, and salt and mix until well blended. Add the eggs, one at a time, mixing on low speed after each addition just until blended. Then blend until the filling is smooth. Pour half of the filling over the crust.
5.	Make the cinnamon swirl: Heat the butter over high heat in a pan until the butter froths and brown flecks appear, stirring occasionally. Stir in the

sweetener, vanilla seeds, cinnamon, and salt. Remove from the heat and allow to cool slightly.
6.	Spoon half of the cinnamon swirl on top of the cheesecake filling in the baking pan. Use a knife to cut the cinnamon swirl through the filling several times for a marbled effect. Top with the rest of the cheesecake filling and cinnamon swirl. Cut the cinnamon swirl through the cheesecake filling again several times.
7.	Place a trivet in the bottom of the Instant Pot and pour in the water. Use a foil sling to lower the baking pan onto the trivet. Cover the cheesecake with 3 large sheets of paper towel to ensure that condensation doesn't leak onto it. Tuck in the sides of the sling.
8.	Lock the lid. Select the Manual mode and set the cooking time for 26 minutes at High Pressure.
9.	When the timer beeps, use a natural pressure release for 10 minutes. Carefully remove the lid.
10.	Use the foil sling to lift the pan out of the Instant Pot.
11.	Let the cheesecake cool, then place in the refrigerator for 4 hours to chill and set completely before slicing and serving.

Cocoa Custard

Prep time: 5 minutes | Cook time: 7 minutes | Serves 4
2 cups heavy cream (or full-fat coconut milk for dairy-free)
4 large egg yolks
¼ cup Swerve, or more to taste
1 tablespoon plus 1 teaspoon unsweetened cocoa powder, or more to taste
½ teaspoon almond extract
Pinch of fine sea salt
1 cup cold water
1.	Heat the cream in a pan over medium-high heat until hot, about 2 minutes.
2.	Place the remaining ingredients except the water in a blender and blend until smooth.
3.	While the blender is running, slowly pour in the hot cream. Taste and adjust the sweetness to your liking. Add more cocoa powder, if desired.
4.	Scoop the custard mixture into four ramekins with a spatula. Cover the ramekins with aluminum foil.
5.	Place a trivet in the Instant Pot and pour in the water. Place the ramekins on the trivet.
6.	Lock the lid. Select the Manual mode and set the cooking time for 5 minutes at High Pressure.
7.	When the timer beeps, use a quick pressure release. Carefully remove the lid.
8.	Remove the foil and set the foil aside. Let the custard cool for 15 minutes. Cover the ramekins with the foil again and place in the refrigerator to chill completely, about 2 hours.
9.	Serve.

APPENDIX : RECIPES INDEX

Blackberry Egg Cake 20
Black-Eyed Pea and Kale Curry 68
Black-Eyed Peas with Greens 44
Black-Eyed Peas with Swiss Chard 66
Blade Pork with Sauerkraut 146
BLT Chicken Salad 108
Blue Cheese Mushroom Soup 166
Blue Pork 147
Blueberry Baked Oatmeal with Almonds 25
Bo Ssäm 147
Bourbon and Date Pudding Cake 180
Braised Collards with Red Wine 85
Braised Kale with Garlic 50
Braised Lamb Ragout 151
Braised Tri-Tip Steak 134
Bread Pudding 19
Breakfast Burrito with Scrambled Tofu 26
Breakfast Cobbler 21
Breakfast Quinoa Salad 17
Breakfast Rice Pudding 19
Broccoli and Bacon Appetizer Salad 33
Broccoli and Bacon Cheese Soup 166
Broccoli and Egg Casserole 20
Broccoli and Mushrooms 88
Broccoli and Red Feta Soup 166
Broccoli Chicken with Black Beans 107
Broccoli Chicken with Parmesan 106
Brown Rice and Coconut Milk Pudding 180
Bruschetta Chicken 109
Brussels Sprouts and Apples Appetizer 31
Brussels Sprouts and Broccoli Appetizer Salad 34
Brussels Sprouts with Maple Glaze 41
Brussels Sprouts with Sesame Seeds 46
Buffalo Chicken Soup 167
Buffalo Wings 115
Bulletproof Hot Choco 187
Butternut Squash and Cauliflower Soup 175
Butternut Squash and Kale Chili 172
Butternut Squash Arborio Risotto 61
Butter-Parmesan Wings 115

C

Cabbage and Mushroom Pasta 57
Cabbage and Pork Soup 167
Cabbage in Cream Sauce 87
Caesar Salad Dressing 12
Calamari Stew 170
Caramel Apple Cobbler 181
Caramel Glazed Popcorns 182
Caramelized Onions 89
Caramelized Sweet Potatoes 50
Cardamom Rice Pudding with Pistachios 188
Cardamom Yogurt Pudding 181
Carolina-Style Pork Barbecue 141
Carrot and Beet Spread 31
Carrot and Cabbage Beef Stew 161
Carrot and White Bean Dip 15
Carrot Raisin Halwa 188
Carrots with Honey Glaze 40
Cashew Spread 31

Cauliflower and Cashew Sour Cream 15
Cauliflower and Pineapple Rice 54
Cauliflower Mash 91
Cauliflower Mushroom Risotto 89
Cauliflower Rice and Chicken Thigh Soup 167
Cauliflower Spinach Medley 86
Celery and Carrot Broth 14
Celery and Pepper Red Beans 13
Celery Wheat Berry Salad 38
Chanterelle Mushrooms with Cheddar Cheese 84
Cheddar Broccoli Egg Bites 22
Cheddar Chicken Casserole 22
Cheesy and Creamy Delmonico Steak 120
Cheesy Bacon Quiche 18
Cheesy Bacon Stuffed Meatloaf 134
Cheesy Beef Soup 161
Cheesy Breakfast Potato Casserole 17
Cheesy Broccoli Appetizer Salad 34
Cheesy Cauliflower Soup 167
Cheesy Chicken Drumsticks 113
Cheesy Egg and Bacon Muffins 20
Cheesy Fish Bake with Veggies 97
Cheesy Jalapeño Chicken 106
Cheesy Pesto Chicken 110
Cheesy Pork Taco Casserole 147
Cheesy Shrimp and Tomatoes 32
Cheesy Spaghetti Squash and Spinach 81
Cheesy Veggie Orzo Soup 162
Chicken Alfredo with Bacon 111
Chicken and Bacon Ranch Casserole 109
Chicken and Mixed Greens Salad 110
Chicken and Quinoa Stew 170
Chicken and Zoodles Soup 167
Chicken Bone Broth 13
Chicken Cacciatore 114
Chicken Chili Verde Soup 167
Chicken Chipotle Stew 168
Chicken Fajita Bowls 112
Chicken Fillets with Cheese Sauce 115
Chicken Legs with Mayo Sauce 113
Chicken Liver Pâté 116
Chicken Meatballs in Barbecue Sauce 33
Chicken Piccata 110
Chicken Soup with Egg Noodles 162
Chicken Stew with Tomatoes and Spinach 105
Chicken Tacos with Fried Cheese Shells 109
Chicken Thigh and Shrimp Stock 168
Chicken Tomato Stew 170
Chicken Wingettes with Cilantro Sauce 115
Chicken with Artichokes and Bacon 108
Chicken With Cheese Mushroom Sauce 114
Chicken Yogurt Salsa 106
Chickpea and Lamb Soup 162
Chickpea and Tomato Rice 54
Chickpea Tagine with Pickled Raisins 74
Chickpeas with Jackfruit 68
Chile Verde Pulled Pork with Tomatillos 147
Chili Aioli 13
Chili Endives Platter 33

Italian Pork Cutlets 142
Italian Salmon with Lemon Juice 95
Italian Vegetable Medley 87

J

Jackfruit and Tomatillos Tinga 76
Jalapeño Peanuts 30
Jamaican Curry Chicken Drumsticks 113
Jamaican Pork Roast 141
Jamaican Pumpkin and Potato Curry 81
Jollof Rice 55

K

Kale and Carrots Salad 35
Kale and Sweet Potatoes with Tofu 88
Kale and Veal Stew 171
Kale and Wild Rice Appetizer Salad 35
Kashmiri Tofu 77
Keto Almond Bread 186
Keto Brownies 187
Keto Cabbage Hash Browns 23
Keto Chicken Enchilada Bowl 110
Keto Gravy 13
Khichdi Dal 61
Kidney Bean Stew 171
Kidney Bean Vegetarian Étouffée 66
Kidney Beans with Ajwain Sauce 65
Korean Flavor Beef Ribs 123

L

Lamb and Tomato Bhuna 157
Lamb Biryani with Raisins 152
Lamb Chops in Picante Sauce 152
Lamb Curry with Tomatoes 153
Lamb Curry with Zucchini 153
Lamb Kleftiko with Turnip 157
Lamb Kofta Curry 157
Lamb Koobideh 157
Lamb Rostelle 158
Lamb Sirloin Masala 158
Lamb Tagine with Carrots 153
Lamb with Peppers and Tomatoes 153
Leek and Mushroom Risotto 71
Lemon and Maple Syrup Pudding 185
Lemon and Ricotta Torte 194
Lemon Beef Meal 129
Lemon Blueberry Cheesecake 192
Lemon Garlic Chicken 107
Lemon Pepper Salmon 94
Lemon Pepper Salmon 95
Lemon-Dill Salmon 103
Lemongrass Beef and Rice Pot 123
Lemony Asparagus with Gremolata 83
Lemony Black Bean Curry 70
Lemony Bow Tie Pasta 60
Lemony Broccoli 82
Lemony Endives Appetizer 31
Lemony Fennel Chicken 104
Lemony Fish and Asparagus 99
Lemony Mahi-Mahi fillets with Peppers 98
Lemony Peas with Bell Pepper 81
Lemony Potato Cubes 30
Lemony Salmon 93

Lemony Salmon with Avocados 102
Lemony Salmon with Tomatoes 101
Lemony Spinach Pasta 58
Lemony Tilapia Fillets with Arugula 97
Lentil and Beef Slider Patties 30
Lentil Soup with Garam Masala 175
Lentils with Rutabaga and Rice 67
Lentils with Spinach 67
Lettuce Wrapped Chicken Sandwich 23
Little Smokies with Grape Jelly 30

M

Maple Brussels Sprouts with Walnuts 51
Maple Cereal Bowls 26
Maple Mashed Sweet Potato Casserole 48
Maple-Glazed Carrots 40
Maple-Glazed Spareribs 138
Mascarpone-Mushroom Pasta 57
Mediterranean Couscous Salad 63
Mexican Beef Shred 123
Mexican Chili Pork 142
Mexican Pulled Pork 143
Mexican Shredded Chicken 105
Milky Lamb with Potatoes 154
Mini Frittata 18
Mini Tofu and Vegetable Frittatas 76
Minty Kale Salad with Pineapple 35
Minty Paneer Cubes with Cashews 79
Miso Soup with Tofu and Kale 176
Mongolian Arrowroot Glazed Beef 123
Moong Bean with Cabbage 68
Mujadara (Lebanese Lentils and Rice) 64
Mushroom and Beef Meal 129
Mushroom and Cabbage Dumplings 76
Mushroom and Carrot Broth 15
Mushroom Barley Risotto 62
Mushroom Rice Pilaf 49
Mushrooms Farro Risotto 64
Mustard Flavored Artichokes 38
Mustard Pork and Mushrooms 143

N

New York Strip with Heavy Cream 124
Nutty Raisin Oatmeal 25

O

One Pot Black-Eyed Peas with Rice 67

P

Paprika Chicken with Tomatoes 107
Paprika Pork and Brussels Sprouts 141
Paprika Pork Loin Roast 143
Parmesan Baked Eggs 21
Parmesan Drumsticks 113
Parmesan Mushroom-Spinach Pasta 58
Parmesan Risotto 61
Pea and Mint Risotto 62
Pear and Apple Crisp 36
Pear and Pork Butt 143
Pear Oatmeal with Walnuts 25
Penne Pasta with Tomato-Vodka Sauce 56
Penne Pasta with Zucchini 58
Perch Fillets with Red Curry 100
Pesto Lamb Rack 158

Pesto Salmon with Almonds 102
Philly Steak Sub 124
Pine Nut Pork 143
Pineapple Pudding 185
Pinto Bean Dip 30
Polenta and Mushrooms 63
Pork and Quill Egg Cups 23
Pork and Sweet Potato 143
Pork Chops and Peas 144
Pork Chops in Mushroom Sauce 137
Pork Chops with Bell Peppers 137
Pork Chops with Brussels Sprouts 138
Pork Chops with Onions 144
Pork Chops with Sauerkraut 137
Pork Coconut Curry 144
Pork Cutlets with Creamy Mustard Sauce 140
Pork Medallions and Mushrooms 144
Pork Potato Lunch 144
Pork Roast with Sweet Potatoes 140
Pork Shoulder and Celery 140
Pork Tenderloin in Salsa 139
Pork Tenderloin with Celery 145
Pork Tenderloin with Cherry and Rosemary 139
Pork Vindaloo (Curry Pork) 145
Pork with Cherry Sauce 138
Pork with Coconut Meat 145
Pork, Green Beans, and Corn 140
Potatoes and Cauliflower Masala 76
Prosciutto-Wrapped Chicken 112
Pumpkin and Apple Butter 20
Pumpkin Spice Carrot Cake Oatmeal 25

Q

Quick Cozy Spiced Fruit 25
Quick Salmon 95
Quinoa and Spinach 71
Quinoa and Veggies 91
Quinoa Pilaf with Cranberries and Almonds 72
Quinoa Risotto 61
Quinoa Salad with Apples and Pecans 71
Quinoa Vegetable Stew 177

R

Ranch Dip 13
Raspberry and Oat Crumble 193
Red Curry Halibut 97
Red Lentils with Butternut Squash 69
Red Onion-Feta Couscous Pilaf 65
Red Wine Poached Pears 36
Rhubarb and Strawberry Compote 193
Rhubarb Strawberry Tarts 36
Ribeye Steak with Cauliflower Rice 124
Rich Acorn Squash Chili 173
Rich Brown Lentil and Millet Chili 173
Ritzy Bean, Pea, and Lentils Mix 69
Ritzy Beans and Quinoa Chili 173
Ritzy Green Pea and Cauliflower Curry 78
Ritzy Summer Chili 174
Ritzy Winter Chili 174

S

Salmon Fillets and Bok Choy 101

Salmon Head Soup 169
Salmon Steaks with Garlicky Yogurt 101
Salmon Stew 171
Salmon Tandoori 93
Salmon with Basil Pesto 93
Salsa Chicken Legs 114
Salsa Verde Cannellini Bean Chili 174
Satarash with Eggs 85
Satay Sauce 12
Sauce Glazed Lamb Chops 154
Saucy Italian Beef Chuck 124
Saucy Mushroom Lettuce Cups 35
Saucy Short Ribs 125
Sautéed Beef and Green Beans 130
Sautéed Beluga Lentil and Zucchinis 73
Sautéed Brussels Sprouts And Pecans 89
Savory Salmon with Dill 93
Scallion and Mayo Spread 32
Scarlet Runner Bean and Potato Hash 73
Seitan and Rutabaga Stew 178
Sesame Bok Choy 90
Sesame Chicken 105
Sesame Zoodles with Scallions 82
Simple Almond Milk 16
Simple Banana Cake 188
Simple Cauliflower Gnocchi 82
Simple Chicken and Kale Soup 169
Simple Egg Spread 32
Simple Hard-Boiled Eggs 21
Simple Herbed Beef Chuck Roast 125
Simple Lemon Squares 193
Simple Mexican Corn 52
Simple Roast Lamb Leg 158
Simple Shredded Chicken 112
Simple Spiced Russet Potatoes 79
Simple Steamed Salmon Fillets 93
Simple Stone Fruit Compote 26
Simple Tomato Pasta 59
Slow Cooked Beef Pizza Casserole 136
Slow Cooked Beef Steak 136
Slow Cooked Lamb Shanks 154
Slow-Cooked Cabbage and Chuck Roast Stew 171
Smokey Garbanzo Mash 51
Smoky Carrots and Collard Greens 45
Smoky Paprika Chicken 104
Snapper in Spicy Tomato Sauce 100
Sour and Sweet Beets and Kale 51
Soya Granules and Green Pea Tacos 77
Spaghetti Squash Noodles 86
Spaghetti Squash Noodles with Tomatoes 83
Spaghetti Squash With Olives and Tomatoes 42
Spaghetti Squash with Pesto 47
Spaghetti with Veggie Bolognese 56
Special Pancake 20
Special Ranch Spread 32
Spiced Carrots 48
Spiced Chicken Drumsticks 104
Spiced Orange Carrots 40
Spicy Ginger-Garlic Kale 52

Spicy Green Beans 44
Spicy Lamb Shoulder 154
Spicy Lamb with Anchovies 155
Spicy Minced Lamb Meat 155
Spicy Ratatouille 44
Spicy Thousand Island Dressing 12
Spinach and Bacon Quiche 17
Spinach and Tomato Couscous 72
Spinach Mushroom Treat 38
Spinach with Almonds and Olives 86
Sriracha Collard Greens 41
Steak and Bell Pepper Fajitas 125
Steak, Pepper, and Lettuce Salad 125
Steamed Artichoke with Aioli 51
Steamed Asparagus with Mustard Dip 30
Steamed Broccoli with Lemon 40
Steamed Chili-Rubbed Tilapia 96
Steamed Cod and Veggies 92
Steamed Greek Snapper 94
Steamed Herbed Red Snapper 94
Steamed Leeks with Tomato and Orange 42
Steamed Leeks with Tomato Sauce 49
Steamed Lemon Mustard Salmon 94
Steamed Paprika Broccoli 88
Steamed Tomato with Halloumi Cheese 85
Strawberry and Orange Juice Compote 19
Strawberry Quinoa 20
Stuffed Apples with Coconut Muesli 17
Stuffed Chicken with Spinach and Feta 111
Stuffed Eggs 36
Stuffed Sweet Potatoes 87
Summer Squash and Tomatoes 41
Sumptuous Beef and Tomato Biryani 126
Sumptuous Lamb Casserole 155
Sumptuous Navy Beans 70
Sumptuous One-Pot Garden Pasta 59
Sumptuous Spring Veggie Chili 174
Sumptuous Vegetable and Tofu Curry 81
Super Bean and Grain Burgers 66
Super Beef Chili 130
Super Easy Caramel Sauce 14
Super Flageolet Bean and Millet Stew 178
Super West African Chickpea Stew 178
Sweet and Sour Beet Salad 43
Sweet Apricot Beef 130
Sweet Potato and Black Bean Stew 179
Sweet Potato and Kale Egg Bites 26
Sweet Potato Beef 130
Sweet Potato Gratin 47
Sweet Potato Mash with Sage 50
Sweet Roasted Cashews 38
Sweet Turnip Greens 49
Swiss Chard and Leek Soup 168
Szechuan Honey-Glazed Asparagus 47

T

Tapioca Pudding 184
Tequila Short Ribs 126

Tex Mex Tofu Scramble 24
Thai Coconut Beef with Snap Peas 126
Thai Coconut Shrimp Soup 168
Thai Fish Curry 95
Thai Peanut Chicken 104
Thai Tom Saap Pork Ribs Soup 168
Three Bean Salad with Parsley 39
Thyme Carrots 37
Thyme Chicken with Brussels Sprouts 107
Thyme-Sesame Crusted Halibut 97
Tofu and Greens with Fenugreek Sauce 78
Tofu and Mango Curry 79
Tomato and Black Bean Rotini 60
Tomato and Parsley Quinoa Salad 39
Tomato Basil Campanelle Pasta 59
Traditional Lamb Rogan Josh 155
Tropical Fruit Chutney 24
Tuna Fillets with Lemon Butter 97
Tuna Salad with Lettuce 96
Turkey with Ginger and Turmeric Soup 168
Turmeric Chicken Soup 169
Tuscan Sausage and Kale Soup 164

V

Vanilla Crème Brûlée 193
Vanilla Rice Pudding 36
Vanilla-Cinnamon Applesauce 14
Veal and Buckwheat Groat Stew 171
Vegetable and Lentil Soup 169
Vegetable Fried Millet 63
Vegetarian Mac and Cheese 91
Vegetarian Smothered Cajun Greens 89
Vegetarian Thai Pineapple Fried Rice 55
Veggie Quiche 18
Veggie Stew 172
Vinegary Broccoli with Cheese 84
Vinegary Brown Rice Noodles 57
Vinegary Pearl Onion 37
Vinegary Pork Chops with Figs and Pears 137

W

Watercress Appetizer Salad 35
Western Omelet 19
White Bean and Kale Soup 169
White Bean and Swiss Chard Stew 177
White Beans and Greens Soup 176
White Beans with Poblano and Tomatillos 65
Wild Alaskan Cod with Cherry Tomatoes 92
Wild Rice and Basmati Pilaf 55
Winter Beef Roast Pot 126

Z

Za'atar-Spiced Bulgur Wheat Salad 63
Zoodles with Mediterranean Sauce 86
Zucchini and Bell Pepper Stir Fry 90
Zucchini and Chickpea Tagine 43
Zucchini and Daikon Fritters 82
Zucchini and Tomato Melange 89
Zucchini Spread 32